The Library Reference Series

LIBRARIANSHIP AND LIBRARY RESOURCES

The Library Reference Series

Lee Ash
General Editor

BASIC REFERENCE SOURCES

An Introduction to
Materials and Methods

By
LOUIS SHORES
With a Chapter on Science Reference Sources by
HELEN FOCKE

GREGG PRESS
Boston 1972

This is a complete photographic reprint of a work
first published in Chicago by the American Library Association in 1954.
Reproduced from an original copy in the library of Louis Shores.

First Gregg Press edition published in 1972.

Copyright 1954 by the American Library Association
Reprinted with permission.

Printed on permanent/durable acid-free paper in
The United States of America.

Library of Congress Cataloging in Publication Data

Shores, Louis, 1904-
    Basic reference sources.

    (Library reference series)
    Reprint of the 1954 ed.
    1. Reference books--Bibliography. 2. Reference
services (Libraries) I. Title
Z1035.1.S45 1972   028.7   72-8771
ISBN 0-8398-1887-4

BASIC REFERENCE SOURCES

Basic Reference Sources

An introduction to materials and methods

by LOUIS SHORES

Dean, Library School, Florida State University

with a chapter on science reference sources

by HELEN FOCKE

School of Library Science, Western Reserve University

Chicago

AMERICAN LIBRARY ASSOCIATION

1954

Copyright 1954 by the American Library Association

Manufactured in the United States of America

Library of Congress catalog card number 53-7487

PREFACE

This book is based on the author's *Basic Reference Books*. Like its predecessor, *Basic Reference Sources* aims to present the content of a general reference course. It is divided into three parts: (1) an opening chapter which describes reference practice in terms of six fundamental functions, (2) thirteen chapters describing general reference books, and (3) five chapters dealing with reference sources in special subject fields.

Because the emphasis is more on types of reference sources than on specific titles and because the organization and approach have been considerably changed it was the decision of the editors and the author not to call this work the third edition of *Basic Reference Books*. The title and subtitle chosen seemed to represent more nearly the augmented purposes of this book; namely, to include more nonbook materials and to give more attention to reference practice.

Reference Practice. The six functions of reference described in the opening chapter present a synthesis of reference duties listed in such instruments as the American Library Association's classification plans for both public and academic libraries and in various professional books and articles. Under the information function, for example, the principal classes of reference questions have been indicated as they have been identified by research. The discussion of bibliographic form has been liberalized in view of the great number of variations found in the manuals of style followed by learned societies and institutions of higher education. A section at the beginning of each chapter describes and gives examples of the kinds of questions typically answered by the sources discussed in that chapter. Tables of criteria for evaluating various classes of reference sources—notably the one for encyclopedias, the result of analyzing *Subscription Books Bulletin* reviews

PREFACE

from 1930 to 1948—have been included. Other features are the discussion of subscription books in the chapter on encyclopedias and of audio-visual sources and how-to-do tools in separate chapters.

Selection of Sources. The selection of titles was determined for both editions of *Basic Reference Books* by a tabulation of lists checked by reference librarians and teachers of reference in library schools. Although the present selection has been similarly influenced the final list has been modified by the author's own classroom experience, by reviews of reference books in *Subscription Books Bulletin,* "Current Reference Books" in the *Wilson Library Bulletin,* the annual reference roundups in the *Saturday Review,* and by the *Guide to Reference Books.* The seventh edition of the last title did not appear until after the selection had been completed. The selection was also greatly influenced, as was the entire manuscript, by Helen Focke, of Western Reserve University, who not only wrote Chapter 18 but also read and criticized the other chapters.

Inevitably many favorites have been omitted. In some cases the author has replaced a personal choice with a title that was almost universally endorsed by teachers and librarians. More often he has indicated alternatives, since the emphasis throughout is on types rather than titles. A case in point is synonym books: Webster's received the highest vote, but strong support for Roget, its historical place, and its unique organization pleaded for equal consideration.

The number of basic titles has been increased from 172 in the second edition of *Basic Reference Books* to 554 in *Basic Reference Sources.* One hundred and forty-seven types are described in *Basic Reference Sources,* and because of the emphasis on types it is possible to teach intensively only one title of each type and group the remaining titles with the textual references as books for general acquaintance.

General Reference Sources. Distribution of the general reference sources by class and type is shown in this table:

Class	Number of Types	Number of Titles
Dictionaries	14	60
Encyclopedias	6	21
Yearbooks	4	15
Biographical Dictionaries	5	18
Geographical Sources	3	15
Directories of Agencies	5	14
Handbooks	8	20

Preface

Manuals	5	13
Serials	8	17
Indexes	6	16
Bibliographies	9	32
Government Publications	6	20
Audio-Visual Sources	2	9
Total	81	270

These 13 classes or groups of reference sources are basic to general reference practice. Their study constitutes the introductory course in most programs of professional library education. The text is so organized as to fit the academic two-semester hour or three-quarter hour courses. It can be used also in general book selection courses which include reference.

Special Reference Sources. Any classification of subject fields is likely to be arbitrary. In a textbook of this scope only examples from very large units of knowledge can be studied. Such specific small areas as nuclear physics, vocational guidance, and similar topics cannot be analyzed here, though their literature is considerable. The final part of this book therefore follows a broad, functional library classification rather than one based on an academic curriculum. It begins with the special tools for reference in the professional field of librarianship and then in succession presents a selection of reference sources in history and its auxiliary subjects, in the social sciences, in the natural sciences, and in the humanities. The last three broad areas necessarily cover a number of component subjects. Treatment is intended only as an introduction. Reference work in the subject fields will entail more intensive individual study on the job.

This part of the book may be used as a text in advanced reference courses or as a supplementary text in the bibliographic courses in the humanities, social sciences, and natural sciences now offered by many library schools.

Distribution of special reference sources is shown in this table:

Class	*Number of Types*	*Number of Titles*
Librarianship	3	15
History	6	31
Social Sciences	11	55
Natural Sciences	22	84
Humanities	24	99
Total	66	284

PREFACE

Closing Date and Prices. The closing date for listing new works and new editions is December, 1951. Prices as of that date are included when they were readily available, not for their value in purchasing, since price changes are frequent, but because a general indication of cost is helpful in evaluating and choosing reference books.

Acknowledgments. Many have read the various revisions of this manuscript, and to all of them I am grateful. My especial thanks go to Margaret G. Cook, Drexel Institute of Technology; Jack Dalton, University of Virginia; Alice Louise LeFevre, Western Michigan College of Education; Eleanor Plain, Aurora Public Library; Katherine M. Stokes, Western Michigan College of Education; and Florence R. Van Hoesen, Syracuse University. Frances N. Cheney, Peabody College, also read the whole manuscript and made many valuable suggestions. I owe very much to Helen Focke, Western Reserve University, who not only read the manuscript but made many careful corrections, suggested numerous changes, and wrote Chapter 18 on the sciences, which I believe will prove a chapter of essential importance in the teaching of reference. To the staff at A.L.A. Headquarters, and especially to Pauline Love, Samray Smith, and Everett Fontaine, go my grateful thanks for their understanding effort in preparing the manuscript for publication. Whatever faults this work has are the sole responsibility of the author.

Louis Shores

June 20, 1953

CONTENTS

Chapter 1 Introduction: The Practice of Reference — 1

PART I: TYPES OF REFERENCE SOURCES

2 Dictionaries — 23
3 Encyclopedias — 56
4 Yearbooks — 88
5 Biographical Dictionaries — 98
6 Geographical Sources — 111
7 Directories of Agencies — 126
8 Handbooks — 136
9 Manuals — 150
10 Serials — 159
11 Indexes — 173
12 Bibliographies — 190
13 Government Publications — 207
14 Audio-Visual Sources — 226

PART II: REFERENCE SOURCES IN SPECIAL SUBJECTS

15 The Subject Approach; Librarianship — 236
16 History and Auxiliary Studies — 249
17 Social Sciences — 266
18 The Sciences—Pure and Applied — 290
19 The Humanities — 326

Index — 357

chapter 1

INTRODUCTION: THE PRACTICE OF REFERENCE

The place of reference, The supervision function, The information function, The guidance function, The instruction function, The bibliographic function, The appraisal function.

The place of reference

Library organization. Every well-organized library, large or small, public, college, school or special, includes these four major divisions: acquisitions, preparations, circulation, reference.

The acquisitions division selects, orders, purchases or otherwise acquires the books, periodicals, manuscripts, pictures and whatever else goes into the library. Once these materials belong to the library they are passed on to the preparations division which classifies, catalogs and otherwise prepares the acquisitions for use. After the materials have been acquired and prepared they become the responsibility of the two public service divisions, circulation and reference.

The circulation division is generally charged with the dissemination of materials that may leave the library. In most libraries, nearly all books except those marked "reference" and current and bound periodicals are circulated. Some libraries circulate other materials such as pictures, phonograph records, films, pamphlets and even periodicals. Whatever the scope of library materials that may be taken from the building, such items come within the jurisdiction of the circulation division.

Reference is the division that interprets the library's collection to its users. Primarily the reference division is responsible for non-circulating library materials, but in the performance of its interpretative function the whole library collection and indeed resources outside the library may be used.

The meaning of reference. Here are two definitions, each by outstanding reference librarians:

> Reference work is organized effort on the part of libraries in aid of the most expeditious and fruitful use of their libraries.—*William Warner Bishop.*

> Sympathetic and informal personal aid in interpreting library collections for study and research.—*James Ingersoll Wyer.*

And here is the definition chosen by the compilers of the *A.L.A. Glossary:*

> That phase of library work which is directly concerned with assistance to readers in securing information and in using the resources of the library in study and research.

Reference is to library service what intelligence is to the military. In the reference room the library's resources are utilized to meet specific needs. Most frequently the need is for a particular fact to answer a question. Almost as often the request is for the location of certain material. Other demands involve aid to research and instruction or simply counsel on cultural and recreational reading.

In 1942 the American Library Association undertook a series of library job analyses that resulted in setting up suggested classification and pay plans for municipal public[1] and for college and university libraries.[2] An examination of these pay plans reveals six major functions of reference. These six functions, discussed in the following pages, are supervision, information, guidance, instruction, bibliography, and appraisal.

The supervision function

The supervision function consists of maintaining an efficient reference service through (1) the proper organization of facilities, (2) selection of materials, (3) direction of personnel, and (4) study of clientele. This function involves all of the elements of good management. It includes also adequate co-ordination with other departments of the library and close association with the objectives of the community served.

The reference room. There is probably no such thing as a typical reference room. But if there were it would most often be located in a room nearly twice as long as it is wide. Wall shelving would run around the room, there would be two rows of long tables with chairs for readers, a few single study tables with individual shelves, aisles down the center and on both sides. A desk or two near the entrance with a section of shelves behind or beside it would be reserved for the reference staff. Not far away would be a battery of steel vertical files, some card catalog trays, an atlas stand, a dictionary stand, a globe, and possibly some large maps on rollers. Small adjoining rooms for conferences and for audio-visual listening and viewing and a stack room for bound periodicals would be possibilities.

To make our typical reference department as comprehensive as possible, organization both by kinds of materials and by subjects is indicated. Current periodicals and newspapers would be found on special shelves and racks. Back issues, bound or in neat bundles, would be kept in adjacent stacks. Government publications currently received would be in the reference room, and bound volumes nearby.

The library with a single reference room would place there all of the subject departments found in large public and university libraries. Public libraries with multiple reference departments often devote individual reference rooms to science and technology, to business, to art, to music, to education (teachers' room), to genealogy, to local history, to municipal reference. Characteristic area rooms within the university library, either in the central or in departmental libraries around the campus, are those of physical sciences, biological sciences, social sciences, humanities, medicine, law, agriculture, engineering.

Organization of the reference service will depend on the scope and size of the library. In a school library room, reference is centered in a section. The small college or public library may set aside one major room for reference service. Within the larger public or university

---

[1] A.L.A. Board on Salaries, Staff and Tenure, *Classification and Pay Plans for Municipal Public Libraries* (Chicago, A.L.A., 1939), 189p.

[2] A.L.A Board on Salaries, Staff and Tenure, *Classification and Pay Plans for Libraries in Institutions of Higher Education* (Chicago, A.L.A., 1947), 3v.

THE PRACTICE OF REFERENCE

library one or more rooms might be designated for each of these types of reference materials: periodicals, government publications, maps, microfilm, microcard and photostat, manuscripts and rare items, bibliography.

Some of the special units that may be found in a large reference division are (1) an information desk where inquiries and requests are screened and routed to the proper section; (2) a telephone; (3) reproduction equipment, where parts of books and other materials are reproduced by photostat or microfilm; (4) interlibrary loan, where arrangements are made to borrow from other libraries; (5) records, where shelf list, catalog and citation file are maintained; (6) files, including pamphlets, clippings, pictures; and (7) audio-visual facilities, including "listening posts" and rooms for disc, tape and wire recording, and still and motion picture projection.

Reference materials. A wide range of materials is used in reference work. First of all there are the "R" books, usually arranged on the shelves by Dewey Decimal number. These are the heart of a reference collection and the major subject of this textbook. They include dictionaries, encyclopedias, yearbooks, directories, handbooks, manuals, serials, indexes and bibliographies. Some reference collections also contain periodicals, newspapers, clippings, pamphlets, pictures, documents, music scores, films, recordings, and even museum objects. A typical reference collection is therefore as improbable as a typical reference room.

Personnel. The A.L.A. *Descriptive List of Professional and Non-Professional Duties in Libraries,* compiled by the Board on Personnel Administration and published in 1948, describes the various reference positions to be found in libraries. A chief reference librarian is usually responsible for administration of the division, and reference assistants either have general assignments or are especially assigned to the units or departments described above. Increasingly, reference workers with subject specialization are being sought by large college and public libraries and by special libraries.

Perhaps nowhere in library work is an encyclopedic mind more needed than in reference. Again and again a retentive memory will be rewarded. Ability to systematize knowledge as acquired is a distinct advantage, and imagination is essential. Over and above this natural endowment, continuous and wide reading, an alert curiosity, and an awareness of community activities will prove very real assets.

Patrons. Everyone asks questions. Potentially, therefore, all humans from cradle to grave are patrons of reference rooms. Because of the importance of ranges in their age, education, occupation, and place of residence, patrons affect the quality of reference service fully as much as does the librarian or the materials. A good reference librarian may use different reference tools to answer questions on the same subject asked by a fourth grade boy, a housewife, a college professor, or a recently arrived immigrant. Further, such community factors as school or college courses of study or the city's or county's principal industries, resources, recreational facilities and local history significantly affect the nature of reference service to be offered.

The information function

The most common duty of the reference department is to answer questions. There is no logical sequence to these questions. During any hour, in a metropolitan municipal library, the first inquirer may be a man who wants the full story of Pearl Harbor; the second a woman who would like a recipe for hush-puppies; the third a child who needs a full-length picture of Uncle Sam; the fourth a university professor in search of a Rowe edition of Shakespeare; the fifth a businessman looking for ideas on grocery store display. And all day long it goes on: How tall is the Empire State Building? Who holds the strike-out record, Walter Johnson or Bob Feller? What is the air distance from Karachi to Miami? Something about Unesco. Latest on biological warfare. Help on a crossword puzzle. Proper form for a wedding invitation. Best grease remover for clothing. The reference librarian in a public library must be prepared to produce without delay the sources that will answer all of these questions and many more.

In a college or school library it is sometimes possible to anticipate the nature of the reference help that will be sought by consulting syllabi, courses of study, or teachers. Generally, however, there is no sequence, logical or otherwise, to questions as they come into the library. In spite of this random sequence of questions several attempts have been made to classify questions asked in libraries by (1) subject, (2) type, (3) purpose, (4) inquirer, and (5) sources consulted.

Classification of questions by subject. One of the earliest attempts to classify questions by subject was that made by Martha Conner[3] in the Pittsburgh Public Library in 1927. An analysis of

---

[3] For citation of this and the following studies see *Reading list* at end of chapter.

THE PRACTICE OF REFERENCE

24,727 questions asked from September to December in each of the years 1905, 1910, 1915, 1920 and 1925 revealed heavy emphasis in two subject areas—social sciences and science and technology.

These findings were somewhat confirmed more recently by two investigations carried on in the Graduate Library School of the University of Chicago. One of these, by Dorothy E. Cole, examined 1026 questions asked in 13 libraries, including large, medium, and small public libraries, junior and liberal arts colleges, and special libraries in the fields of social sciences, business and technology, and general reference. From 69 per cent to 80 per cent of all the questions asked fell in the subject fields of the social sciences, useful arts and history. The smaller percentage occurred in public and college libraries, the larger in special libraries.

The other study, by Florence Van Hoesen, examined 3596 questions in six public library systems and found that the subjects of dominant interest were those that fall in the Dewey Decimal classes 300 (social sciences), 900 (social sciences—history), 500 (natural sciences), 600 (applied sciences). However, recognizing that other Dewey classes contained subjects of high interest, Miss Van Hoesen compiled these two ranked lists of the ten most popular question subjects:

In main libraries	*In branch libraries*
1. Biography	1. Biography
2. Education	2. Geography
3. Geography	3. United States history
4. Laws	4. History
5. Medical terms and topics	5. Poems, songs, hymns
6. History	6. Medical terms and topics
7. Poems, songs, hymns	7. Literature
8. United States history	8. United States government
9. Art terms and topics	9. Art terms and topics
10. Musical terms and topics	10. Commercial products

Classification of questions by type. Attempts to classify questions by types have been made at various times. For example, Iva I. Swift's classification of questions asked in the Washington, D.C. Public Library resulted in four types: (1) directory questions, concerned with the location of places or materials in the library or in the city; (2) simple fact or material finding involving the use of the *World Almanac* or the *Readers' Guide;* (3) personal choice of best materials; that is, the "best" books for a particular purpose; and (4)

The information function

subject-specialized questions requiring knowledge of the literature and of special reference tools.

The same four types of questions were identified by Helen Darsie in her analysis of questions asked in two Chicago and one New York public library where nearly half of all of the questions asked were in the fact-finding and subject-specialty categories.

The same four types are found also in the analysis of some 100,000 questions examined by an A.L.A. Committee on the Measurement of Reference Service, under the chairmanship of Edith Guerrier. The four types are designated in this study as (1) location of persons and places; (2) fact-finding; (3) readers' advisory; and (4) extended search in aid of research. The first two types accounted for 83 per cent of all the questions.

In Miss Cole's study, which classified questions by type as well as by subject, 93 per cent of the questions were of these four types: (1) fact, 55 per cent; (2) general subject information, 20 per cent; (3) how to do, 10 per cent; (4) supporting evidence, 8 per cent. Her study utilized to some extent a very detailed classification of questions by type developed by Carter Alexander as a result of his experience with graduate students at Teachers College, Columbia University.

Classification of questions by purpose and inquirer. Who are these inquirers and to what use do they put the answers they seek for their questions? Miss Van Hoesen's dissertation shows that there are five classes of purpose: (1) school assignment, including term papers, debates, adult education; (2) vocational, in connection with such jobs as advertising, personnel, architecture, teaching; (3) organization, such as clubs, Girl Scouts, P.T.A., church; (4) independent study or investigation; (5) miscellaneous purposes, such as keeping up with current events, solving crossword puzzles. According to Miss Van Hoesen, more than half of the inquirers are students and professional workers. An additional 10-20 per cent are housewives. The remaining identified classes of inquirers are, in descending order, clerks and stenographers, shopkeepers and salesmen, skilled workers, unskilled workers, and farmers. Miss Cole likewise found that 356 of her 1026 questions were asked by students and 210, the next greatest number, by professional workers.

Classification of questions by sources consulted. In 1935 Helen C. Carpenter analyzed 989 reference questions asked in a New York elementary school library. Of these questions, 510, or more than half, were answered by reference books. Encyclopedias alone answered

290 questions, the *World Almanac* 42, and the unabridged dictionaries 33. Similar reports have been made for high school library reference work. In an analysis of 1000 questions asked in Tennessee high school libraries the author found that more than one third of the answers came from encyclopedias and yearbooks.

Miss Van Hoesen's study of reference questions shows that reference books answered 1136 out of 3596 or roughly one third of the inquiries in the main and branch libraries of six public library systems. However, if to the category of reference books are added the other classes of reference materials such as periodicals, government publications, pamphlets and pictures, it is seen that 2064 or approximately 60 per cent of all the reference questions were answered with reference materials.

When the sources used to answer Miss Cole's sample of questions were classified, it became evident that reference books represented about half of the sources used in answering factual questions, about one third of the sources used for statistical questions, one half of the sources used for historical questions, and three quarters of the sources used to answer biographical questions and questions relating to books and publishing.

Value of classification of reference questions. All of these classifications of reference questions are helpful to the reference librarian in preparation for his work. It is well to know, for example, that most questions asked in general reference service fall within the broad subject areas of the social sciences and science and technology, and that inquirers appear to be most interested in biography and geography. It is of some advantage to realize that a very large portion of the questions will be of the location or directory type, that simple fact-finding will be next most common, with a fair sprinkling of reader advisory and subject investigation questions included in the day's work. Selection of reference materials cannot but be affected by findings indicating that more than half the inquirers in a public library are students or professional workers. Nor can the implications of heavy emphasis on school assignments and job requirements be ignored. But of major importance is identification of the sources consulted to answer these questions. The very heavy reliance on reference materials suggests close attention to the selection, evaluation and study of these tools. The following summary classification of reference questions takes into account all of the classifications described thus far.

The information function

Class of question	Sample types	Representative sources
1. Language	Definition, spelling, abbreviation, symbols, foreign terms, usage	Dictionary
2. Background	"Something about," general information, self-education	Encyclopedia
3. Trend	Current events, past year's developments, recent happenings	Yearbook, serial
4. People	Notables, specialists, socialites, others	Biographical dictionary
5. Places	Locations, descriptions, distances	Gazetteer, atlas
6. Organizations	Addresses, purposes	Directory
7. Facts	Curiosities, statistics, events, formulas, allusions	Handbook
8. Activities	"How to do," "How to make"	Manual
9. Bibliography	Reviews, best books, subject literature	National, trade, subject bibliography
10. Illustrations	Pictures, cartoons, slides, films, recordings	Audio-visual material

Answering reference questions. The principal purpose of classification of questions is to arrive at a proper answer source and so perform adequately the information function. Practice varies in details but reveals fairly consistent principles of procedure.

Question analysis. A good reference librarian listens carefully to the inquirer's question, encouraging him to amplify. No question is ever met immediately by a flat "No," nor is the inquirer made to feel that his inquiry is insignificant, unjustified or obvious. Instead every effort is made to draw him out by tactful questions or by indicating what is understood. If the reference worker doesn't understand the question he will inquire further until he can at least place it in its broad subject area.

Source approach. Reference books are the natural starting point in the majority of questions. In general any representative source will provide an adequate beginning. If, for example, the inquirer's question involves a definition of a term, any standard dictionary is eligible. Similarly a general information question beginning "I want to find out something about"—for instance, the Red Cross, or coal mining, or old age—calls for reference to a modern, reasonably up-to-date encyclopedia.

Follow through. Some reference librarians believe the sources should be delivered to the reader and that he should then be left to make his own appraisals. Others insist on assuming much more responsibility not only for the appraisal of the sources but actually for the reading, abstracting and even discovering of facts. At the one extreme, a sharp distinction is made between the research worker who is the scholar in the inquiry or investigation and the librarian who is merely the aide or assistant. At the other, the librarian may well be the inquirer's peer, capable of critical evaluation not only of the source but of the subject itself. Somewhere between these extremes is a philosophy of reference service which provides a flexible adjustment to the requirements of the individual inquiry. This working principle might be stated, "Give the inquirer as much assistance as he requires and let the margin of error be on the side of more rather than less."

Devices. It is well to place something in the inquirer's hands as soon as possible, so that he may be occupied while the librarian is seeking further. Whatever is given him must, of course, help the patron in his search. The librarian is also well advised to be modest in presenting his materials and information, rather than to create the impression of a "walking encyclopedia." If the sources first suggested fail to meet the inquirer's need, the librarian will examine the whole body of literature on the subject. As a final resource, he will consult a specialist.

The guidance function

In some libraries, readers' advisory service is a function of the reference department. Much of this advice is vocational, involving recommendation of good books about medicine, engineering, carpentry, dietetics, acting, writing or possibilities in other careers.

A great deal more guidance is concerned with general self-education. On an individual basis the reference librarian undertakes to guide a particular reader progressively from the place on the educational ladder where he now is to the rung he seeks for himself. This involves a knowledge both of the reader's capabilities and of the books which might be recommended to him.

Still a third type of reading guidance has found expression in what is now known as bibliotherapy. It involves the prescription of reading as a treatment for certain mental and physical ills. A phase of this art has been practiced by hospital and special librarians with hospitalized servicemen.

In the subject-subdivided or special library the guidance, information and circulation functions may be combined. The reference librarian in such a situation is either himself a specialist or has devoted considerable study to the subject covered in addition to his professional preparation. Such double education on the part of the librarian enables him to provide an advanced type of guidance which may lead to such expert activities as abstracting, compiling bibliographies, writing, and teaching in the subject field.

The instruction function

Informal library teaching. The good reference librarian is teaching all of the time. Every time a reader is being helped he is being taught to use the library better. Direction of a reader to the card catalog, to an index or to any specific reference book should involve an unobtrusive assurance that the reader knows how to handle the tool involved.

Most school and college libraries offer an orientation period in the library. All types of libraries issue manuals describing the use of library facilities. Any of these instructional efforts may be the responsibility of the reference librarian.

Formal library teaching. Courses of study for elementary and secondary schools often prescribe programs of formal library instruction. Instruction given commonly includes arrangement of books by Decimal Classification and use of the card catalog, the periodical indexes and the essential reference books such as dictionaries and encyclopedias. Colleges may offer a unit on library use as part of the Freshman English course or require a separate course dealing with the use of the library. Very often these teaching assignments go to the reference librarian.

The bibliographic function

Bibliographies are compiled for different purposes—for the vertical file; for the library's own use; for promotion of reading, as in reading lists; for student term papers; for club projects; for research aid in connection with scholars' investigations. A bibliography is a list of written, printed or otherwise produced records of civilization. Distinctions are sometimes made among the following types: *list,* a brief bibliography, generally with no annotations; *enumerative bibliography,* usually a complete or nearly complete list on a limited subject or aspect of a subject; *descriptive bibliography,* usually an annotated list; *critical bibliography,* an evaluative list; *bio-bibliography,* a list of works by and about an author.

Good bibliographic work involves accuracy, consistency and discrimination. Misspelled names, misquoted titles, mistaken pages, wrong dates may cause hours of needless search. Unless the bibliography aims to be exhaustive, items for inclusion will need to be selected with judgment, and the basis for selection, if not obvious, must be clearly stated.

Establishing bibliographic form. There is no single generally accepted bibliographic form; the following techniques and procedures are only suggestions. A great many learned societies follow the University of Chicago *Manual of Style.* Whatever form is adopted, it should be followed consistently.

Entry form. Each item in a bibliography is called an entry. This entry for a book is an example:

Eastman, Max. *Enjoyment of Poetry.* N.Y., Scribner, 1934. 254p.

There are four basic elements in this as in all bibliographic entries for books. They are:

1. AUTHOR: Eastman, Max
2. TITLE: *Enjoyment of Poetry*
3. IMPRINT, consisting of place, publisher, date: N.Y., Scribner, 1934
4. COLLATION, which in addition to pagination as in the example may include number of volumes, illustrations, and size

These four elements are present in most bibliographic entries. Other secondary elements, such as series, price, location of copies of the publication, and annotation, may be included as required.

Variations in bibliographic form arise from different prescriptions as to—(1) sequence of these elements (e.g., in some bibliographies the title is given first); (2) capitalization (e.g., only the initial letter of the first word is capitalized in some bibliographies); (3) punctuation (e.g., a colon, rather than a comma, often separates place of publication from publisher). Other variations in the elements themselves are necessitated by the variety of publications. These elements

The bibliographic function

(and some variations) will now be considered, first for books and then for other kinds of publications.

Author element. Since arrangement on the shelf or in a list is either primarily or secondarily alphabetical by author, the author's name is the key element in a bibliographic entry. When the book is by one person, the surname is given first, followed by a comma and the forename, as in the above example, or as in the following:

>Cross, Tom Peete
>Wood, Charles Erskine Scott
>Fisher, Mrs. Lettice (Ilbert)

A common variation is the use of initials where there is more than one forename: (Cross, T. P.); but single forenames and a woman's forename are usually spelled out. A married woman's maiden name is placed in parentheses as in the Fisher entry.

If the book is by more than one person, it is customary to give the names of two—or in some cases three—joint authors. If there are more authors, the practice is to name the first, followed by the words *and others* (or *et al.*).

>Hill, Helen, and Maxwell, Violet
>Reavis, W. C., *and others*

If an organization is responsible for authorship, the name of the organization is entered as the author element. The organization is then called a corporate author, and the entry is a corporate entry.

>U.S. Office of Education
>Chicago. University
>General Motors Corporation

Anonymous works, collections for which no one contributor has most responsibility, serials, and certain reference works are entered under title.

>*Encyclopaedia Britannica*
>*Publishers' Weekly*

Title element. The title is entered as it appears on the title page or at the head of a periodical article. The subtitle may be omitted. Omissions from the title are indicated by ellipses (...), and additions are enclosed in brackets.

Other elements. The imprint, found at the bottom of the title page, is generally entered in a sequence of place, publisher, and date.

If no date is given on the title page, the last copyright date, found on the verso of the title page, is used. Collation may consist of the total number of pages, inclusive pages when part of a book is being cited, the number of volumes of a set, or a combination of volume number and page numbers.

Non-book variations. The author and title of a periodical article are given in the usual form, but the imprint varies. The following is a commonly used form:

> Larrick, Nancy. "Design in Children's Books," *Library Journal,* October 15, 1950, v.75, p.1776-81.

Publications of governments and learned societies generally follow the form for books. Since these publications are often entered under corporate names, a good rule to follow is to choose a personal author whenever possible, including the name of the government agency or learned society in the series note if it is not the publisher.

Arrangement of bibliography. After all entries are completed on cards, they may be kept in their alphabetical order or sorted into one of the following arrangements:

> 1. Title. An arrangement frequently followed in reading lists.
> 2. Alphabetical subject. Especially useful in a long bibliography which covers numerous important topics. Under each subject, items are usually arranged alphabetically by author.
> 3. Classified subject. An arrangement favored over the alphabetical by scholars who know the field. In this arrangement, items under each subject are usually entered alphabetically by author.
> 4. Dictionary. Authors, titles and subjects in one alphabet.

There are many other arrangements and combinations of arrangements; booksellers' lists, for example, are frequently arranged by publisher.

Citations. It is good reference practice to record answers to reference questions asked repeatedly for which considerable search is entailed. For example, each year in the early summer along the shores of the Great Lakes, thousands of insects known as "Canadian Soldiers" (or in Canada as "Yankee Sailors") hatch out. These terms are not to be found in the usual reference works on insects. A citation file entry under "Canadian Soldiers" with cross reference to "Mayflies" (another name for the same insect) and a list of references to sources of information will save unnecessary repetition of search. Usually the citation file is kept on three by five inch cards and arranged alphabeti-

The bibliographic function

cally by subject or "catch" subject; that is, the significant word in the title.

Citation form. In making references for a citation file, one should take care to include all information necessary to locate the book or article and to give this information in generally accepted bibliographic form. This is important not only to enable the searcher to locate the material again without loss of time, but also to help any other person in search of the same material. Citation form is similar to bibliographic form but is often somewhat shortened, as follows: (1) *author,* last name only, if distinctive; (2) *title,* short title, or identifying title; (3) *imprint,* last copyright date only; (4) *page numbers* on which the information is found. Series note is usually omitted, unless necessary for identification. The sample citation card illustrates the form suggested.

SAMPLE CITATION CARD INDICATING SOURCES FOR INFORMATION
ABOUT FLAGS

```
                           FLAGS


   Funk & Wagnalls New Stand. Dict.    c.1940    p.934
   Lincoln Library.   c.1949.   p.2065
   Kane.    Famous First Facts.    1933.    p.251
   Shankle.    State Names.    1934.    522p.
   Boy Scouts.    Handbook.    1948.    p.59-78
```

Footnotes. Footnotes are used (1) to provide exact sources of evidence, (2) to acknowledge indebtedness to those sources, (3) to refer to other parts of the manuscript, and (4) to amplify the discussion in the text.

There is no universally accepted footnote form although, as with bibliographic form, a great many journals of learned societies follow the University of Chicago *Manual of Style.* Essentially, a footnote is a simplified bibliographic entry in which most often the imprint is reduced to date only and the collation is only the specific page or pages of citation. The most striking common variation is the reversal of author style for bibliography by giving first name first. Other variations include the use of Roman numerals for volumes, quotation marks instead of italics for titles of articles, and italics for the names of periodicals.

Footnote abbreviations. Certain abbreviations and Latin words are customarily used in footnotes. Some of these are:

cf. (abbreviation for *confer,* "compare")
cf. ante (*confer ante,* "compare above")
cf. post (*confer post,* "compare after")
et al. (*et alii,* "and others")
et passim ("and here and there")
ibid. (*ibidem,* "in the same place")—used in repeating reference to the work last cited
loc. cit. (*loco citato,* "in the place cited")—used when several footnotes intervene between two citations not only to the same work, but also to the same place in that work
op. cit. (*opera citato,* "in the work cited")—used when several footnotes intervene between two citations to the same work, in the same chapter
supra ("above") and *infra* ("below")—used to refer to other parts of the book itself
vid. (*vide,* "see")
viz. (*videlicet,* "namely")

Style manuals. The selected list of style manuals which follows includes specifications for the bibliographic forms most frequently used in the world of scholarship.[4]

American Library Association. *A.L.A. Cataloging Rules for Author and Title Entries.* Chicago, A.L.A., 1949. 265p.

Anderson, J. E., and Valentine, W. L. "The Preparation of Articles for Publication in the Journals of the American Psychological Association," *Psychological Bulletin,* June, 1944, v.41, p.345-76.

Appel, Livia. *Bibliographical Citation in the Social Sciences; a Handbook of Style.* 2d rev. ed. Madison, Univ. of Wisconsin Pr., 1946. 30p.

Chicago. University. *A Manual of Style.* 11th ed. Chicago, Univ. of Chicago Pr., 1949. 497p.

Hook, Lucyle, and Gaver, Mary V. *The Research Paper.* N.Y., Prentice-Hall, 1948. 64p.

Hubbell, G. S. *Writing Documented Papers.* N.Y., Barnes & Noble, 1941. 164p.

Hurt, Peyton. *Bibliography and Footnotes: A Style Manual for*

The appraisal function

College and University Students; rev. and enl. by Mary L. Hurt Richmond. Berkeley, Univ. of Calif. Pr., 1949. 167p.

Joughlin, G. L. *Basic Reference Forms; a Guide to Established Practice in Bibliography, Quotations, Footnotes, and Thesis Format.* N.Y., Crofts, 1941. 94p.

Taube, Mortimer, and Conover, Helen F. *Manual for Bibliographers in the Library of Congress.* Washington, Govt. Print. Off., 1944. 28p.

Turabian, Kate L. *A Manual for Writers of Dissertations.* Chicago, Univ. of Chicago Pr., 1937. 61p.

U.S. Government Printing Office. *Style Manual.* Rev. ed. Washington, Govt. Print. Off., 1945. 435p.

The appraisal function

Reference materials. The success of any reference department depends upon two factors: (1) possession of the right materials and (2) knowledge of how to get the most out of those materials.

At the outset let it be understood that any medium is a potential reference source. Not only the whole world of print but also audio-visual materials and the natural and man-made resources of any locality may well provide answers to people's questions. The resourceful reference librarian uses every possible medium to fulfill his mission.

But the reference librarian should also realize that there are in the world thousands of printed sources created specifically to answer questions. Because they contain such a large proportion of the answers to the questions asked by library patrons, the use of these reference works is worthy of separate consideration.

Reference book defined. One does not usually read a dictionary through from cover to cover. The reason is fairly obvious. Dictionaries do not present related material in a sequence intended to invite continuous reading; they contain separate facts conveniently arranged for intermittent consultation. Conversely, a novel is not frequently referred to for specific facts; it is written to be read through. In general, reference books are distinguished from other books because they are meant to be *referred* to for specific information. A reference book may

---

[4] [This is an example of a footnote.] For a comparison of bibliographic and footnote form found in the publications of ten selected learned societies consult Mary Lee Winston, *Bibliographies and Footnotes in the Publications of Selected American Learned Societies* (Master's paper; Tallahassee, Florida State Univ., 1950). William R. Parker's "The MLA Style Sheet," *PMLA*, v.66, no. 3, p.3-31, also has valuable comparative material, as does the pamphlet by Appel cited in the style manuals.

THE PRACTICE OF REFERENCE

therefore be defined as any book which is chiefly consulted for specific information. The *A.L.A. Glossary* gives these two definitions of a reference book.

> 1. A book designed by its arrangement and treatment to be consulted for definite items of information rather than to be read consecutively.
> 2. A book whose use is restricted to the library building.

Kinds of reference books. Reference books may be classified by subject and by type. Among reference books which cover many subjects several types are commonly recognized: dictionaries, encyclopedias, yearbooks, biographical dictionaries, atlases and gazetteers, directories, handbooks, manuals, indexes, bibliographies. There are also two special classes of materials, namely government publications and audio-visual sources, that have distinctive reference qualities as groups. They include examples of several types of reference books and cover many subjects. For that reason they are treated in this book as general reference sources.

Study and evaluation of reference books. Because reference books are different in purpose from other books they require special study and evaluation. For convenience in examining and appraising reference books the following checkpoints are suggested:

I. Authority
  1. Authorship. What are the qualifications in experience and education of the author, authors, contributors, and editors by reputation and as revealed in previous works? To what extent are the authors responsible for the materials attributed to them?
  2. Auspices. What is the reputation of the publisher or the sponsoring agency?
  3. Genealogy. Is the work new? If it is based on a previous publication, what is the extent of the revision?

II. Scope
  4. Purpose. To what extent is the statement of purpose in the preface fulfilled in the text?
  5. Coverage. What is the range of subject matter and what are the limitations? How does this work relate to and compare with other works of similar scope?
  6. Recency. How up to date is the material? Are all of the articles and bibliographies as recent as the last copyright date?

The appraisal function

      7. Bibliographies. To what extent do the bibliographies indicate scholarship and send the user on to additional information?
III. Treatment
      8. Accuracy. How thorough, reliable and complete are the facts?
      9. Objectivity. Is there any bias in controversial issues? How balanced is the space given one subject as compared with others of equal importance?
      10. Style. Is the level of writing for layman or scholar, adult or child? How readable is the work?
IV. Arrangement
      11. Sequence. Does the sequence of content follow classified, chronologic, geographic, tabular or alphabetic order? If alphabetic, are the topics large or small? How are they alphabeted?
      12. Indexing. Is the main text arrangement adequately complemented by indexes and cross references?
V. Format
      13. Physical make-up. Do binding, paper, type and layout meet minimum specifications?
      14. Illustrations. Are the illustrations of good quality, are they of real significance, and are they directly related to the text?
VI. Special features
      15. Distinction. What features distinguish this reference book from all others?

The literature of reference. Sources for the evaluation of reference books fall into three groups: (1) retrospective, for the evaluation of old reference books, (2) current, for the evaluation of new or revised reference books, and (3) manuals dealing with methods and criteria for evaluation.

Retrospective sources. The fullest list of reference books among retrospective sources is Winchell's *Guide to Reference Books,* a worthy successor to the six previous editions, two of which (1902, 1908) were prepared under the editorship of Alice Bertha Kroeger of Drexel Institute, and four (1917, 1923, 1929, 1936) under the editorship of Isadore Gilbert Mudge of Columbia University. Supplements were published at varying intervals for each of these editions. The present seventh edition includes some 5500 entries arranged broadly by Decimal Classification, representing all subjects and both English and foreign languages. A detailed index emphasizes the subject approach and the annotations for individual titles are both evaluative and critical.

A more selective list is Hirshberg's *Subject Guide,* which differs in plan from Winchell, being arranged alphabetically by subjects about which questions are most frequently asked in public libraries. The subjects range from Abbreviations through Zoology and the arrangement involves frequent repetition of titles. An author index including some title entries complements the subject arrangement. Still more selective is the Barton list, intended primarily for the library user rather than for the library worker, but helpful to both.

The British counterpart of Winchell is Minto, now considerably out of date. A more selective list related to instruction in the School of Librarianship and Archives of the University of London is that included in A. D. Roberts' textbook.

❧ RETROSPECTIVE SOURCES

Winchell, Constance M. Guide to Reference Books. 7th ed. Chicago, A.L.A., 1951. 645p.

Hirshberg, H. S. Subject Guide to Reference Books. Chicago, A.L.A., 1942. 259p.

Barton, Mary N., comp. Reference Books; a Brief Guide for Students and Other Users of the Library. Baltimore, Enoch Pratt Free Library, 1951. 99p.

Minto, John. Reference Books. London, Library Assn., 1929. 356p. Supplement, 1931.

Roberts, A. D. Introduction to Reference Books. 2d ed. London, Library Assn., 1951. 214p.

❧ CURRENT SOURCES

Subscription Books Bulletin, 1930-   (quarterly). Chicago, A.L.A.

❧ REFERENCE MANUALS

Hutchins, Margaret. Introduction to Reference Work. Chicago, A.L.A., 1944. 214p.

Wyer, J. I. Reference Work. Chicago, A.L.A., 1930. 315p.

Butler, Pierce, ed. The Reference Function of the Library. Chicago, Univ. of Chicago Pr., 1943. 366p.

Cowley, J. D. The Use of Reference Material; an Introductory Manual for Librarianship Students and Assistants. London, Grafton, 1937. 158p.

Bagley, W. A. Facts and How To Find Them; a Guide to Sources of Information and to the Method of Systematic Research. 4th ed. London, Pitman, 1950. 135p.

The appraisal function

Current sources. The best current review of reference books is the quarterly *Subscription Books Bulletin* edited by a committee of the American Library Association. Long, critical reviews of reference books feature courageous closing statements—"recommended" or "not recommended."

Other current review sources are the section on reference books in the *United States Quarterly Book Review,* prepared by the Library of Congress and described in the chapter on bibliography; *Current Reference Books,* a column which appears monthly in the *Wilson Library Bulletin,* discussed in Chapter 15; annotations which appear in issues of the *A.L.A. Booklist* and in the *Library Journal;* the annual special issue of *Publishers' Weekly* featuring reference books, and the annual roundup of reference books in a special issue of the *Saturday Review,* which is discussed in the chapter on serials. Supplements to the *Guide to Reference Books* should provide an especially comprehensive current source for reference book appraisal.

Reference manuals. In the books on reference method there is much guidance for the study and evaluation of reference books. Hutchins' *Introduction to Reference Work* is a thoughtful and provocative survey. Chapters on reference questions, on organization of materials and service, on the evaluation and reporting of reference and on sources for biography and geography are particularly significant. Wyer's *Reference Work,* although twenty years old, has excellent appraisals of classes of reference books in relation to questions asked.

Several other books are useful to the reference librarian concerned with studying his job and evaluating his tools. Butler's *Reference Function of the Library,* a collection of papers presented before the University of Chicago Library Institute, covers a variety of aspects of method and materials. Cowley's *Use of Reference Materials,* although intended for British students, has much to contribute to American practice. Another British book, Bagley's *Facts and How To Find Them,* is intended primarily for writers and teachers but is helpful in presenting library consumers' problems to librarians.

Chapters on reference service in school, college and public libraries are included in the textbooks for these areas of librarianship.

Reading list

Alexander, Carter. "Technique of Library Searching," *Special Libraries,* September, 1936, v.27, p.23-28.

Asheim, Lester. "Publicity for a University Library's Reference Department," *Library Journal,* March, 1941, v.66, p.206-07.

Carpenter, Helen C. "What Is Back of Efficient Reference Work in an Elementary School Library?" *Wilson Library Bulletin,* September, 1935, v.10, p.15-19.

Cole, Dorothy E. "Some Characteristics of Reference Work," *College and Research Libraries,* January, 1946, v.7, p.45-51.

Conner, Martha. "What a Reference Librarian Should Know," *Library Journal,* April 15, 1927, v.52, p.415-18.

Darsie, Helen. "Measuring the Results of Reference Service," *A.L.A. Bulletin,* September, 1935, v.19, p.604-05.

Guerrier, Edith. "Measurement of Reference Service," *Library Journal,* July, 1936, v.61, p.529-31.

Swift, Iva I. "Classifying Readers' Questions," *Wilson Library Bulletin,* January, 1934, v.8, p.274-75.

Van Hoesen, Florence R. *Analysis of Adult Reference Work in Public Libraries As an Approach to the Content of a Reference Course.* Doctoral dissertation, University of Chicago, 1948. 219p.

part one | *chapter 2*

DICTIONARIES

Introduction, Unabridged dictionaries, Abridged dictionaries,

Supplementary English language sources,

Foreign language dictionaries.

Introduction

Language questions. Frequently the first step in answering a question is defining terms. Dictionaries and language books are the key sources for meanings, spelling, pronunciation, usage and synonyms. Among the types of questions that can be answered by language reference sources are those involving—

1. Definition. Meanings of words, phrases, and expressions such as *protocol, frame of reference, pork barrel, nuclear fission.*
2. Spelling. Does *Cincinnati* have one *n* before and two *t*'s after the *a*? How are such catchy words as *believe, camouflage,* and *mnemonic* spelled?
3. Pronunciation. What do the authorities say about such words as *either, tomato, creek?*
4. Usage. What is the proper use of such words as *lay* and *lie?* What is a split infinitive?
5. Synonyms, antonyms and homonyms. How many alternative expressions can be found for "This book is interesting"? The writer who wants to vary the expression of an idea by using many equivalent words can find help in general dictionaries and supplementary synonym books.

DICTIONARIES

6. Abbreviations, signs and symbols. In a single day the reference librarian may be asked to identify *CWT*, #, *, *j.n.d.*, and may be asked to supply the symbols representing English pounds, coefficient of correlation, 3.14159. These may be found in dictionaries and in special abbreviation books.

7. Slang. What is the slang meaning of *violin case, squeeze play, pulling a fast one, taking a powder?*

8. New words, and new meanings for old words. *Jet, radar,* and *television* are examples of new words. Radar has given a new meaning to the word *scope*.

9. Dialect. Identification of various regionalisms and national idioms is made easier by the use of special dialect dictionaries.

10. Foreign terms used in English writing. *Sine qua non, voilà, gestalt* require translation by readers.

For all of the above types of questions and for many similar ones, dictionaries and supplementary language books are indispensable.

Language sources. A dictionary is a book containing the words of a language, or the terms of a subject, arranged in some definite order, usually alphabetic, with explanation of their meanings and use.

In this chapter, three large classes of dictionaries are considered: (1) English language; (2) supplementary English language; (3) foreign language. Subject dictionaries, a fourth class, are described under their respective subjects.

English language dictionaries include every kind of common dictionary from the large, unabridged volume or set to the simple picture dictionary.

The terms *supplementary English language book* or *wordbook* are used to cover titles which deal with special phases of English language use such as grammar, synonyms, abbreviations, slang, dialect, rhyme, and foreign terms.

Foreign language dictionaries may be all in one language—French or Spanish or Russian—in two languages, such as English and French, or in many languages—like *Duden's Pictorial Encyclopedia,* which undertakes to give word equivalents in English, French, Spanish, Italian, and German.

The subject dictionary supplements the unabridged dictionary with the specialized terms of one subject or of several related subjects. Examples are Warren's *Dictionary of Psychology* and Crowell's *Dictionary of Business and Finance*.

There are other types of dictionaries. The glossary, for example, is a partial list of dialectal, antiquated, or technical terms in a special field accompanied by explanations or glosses. A *gradus* is a dictionary designed to aid in the writing of poetry. *Lexicon* is a term frequently used for a dictionary of some foreign language. Some specially arranged collections of words use the term *thesaurus* (*verborum*) which means literally a treasury (of words). The vocabulary in the back of a foreign language reader, and the wordbook, a collection of words, have had a variety of educational uses. But it is easily seen that all of these terms are comprehended in the four large classes of dictionaries.

History of English dictionaries. Today's unabridged English language dictionary is the result of an evolution through various degrees of abridgment. The first English dictionary, for example, Robert Cawdrey's *A Table Alphabeticall,* published in 1604, was little more than an interlinear glossary to Latin and French texts. It, like all the previous interlinear glosses, was limited to difficult words on the assumption that other words need no explanation. This principle of selection or abridgment was also true of the next famous example. *New Worlds of English Words,* produced by John Milton's nephew, Edward Phillips, in 1658, was described as "containing the interpretation of such hard words as are derived from other languages."

It was not until sixty-three years later that a long step toward the unabridged dictionary was taken. Nathan Bailey collected and defined in his *Universal Etymological Dictionary* the easy as well as the hard words. But this collection by no means included all of the words then in use by the English people. Rather, the Bailey dictionary aimed to present only the words in good standing.

To understand the philosophy of this type of abridgment it is necessary to look at contemporary lexicography in the Latin-European countries. In France, Italy, and Spain the national academies had undertaken to codify, so to speak, in a scholarly dictionary, the acceptable language for each country. There being no comparable academy in England, the task of creating a national dictionary was assumed informally by the literary men of the period, who unanimously agreed that the editorship should go to Samuel Johnson.

Dr. Johnson's complete confidence in his ability to undertake this tremendous project alone is illustrated by an excerpt from Boswell's *Journal* of a conversation in which Johnson was asked, "But sir, how can you do this in three years? The French Academy which consists of forty members took forty years to complete their dictionary." To this Dr. Johnson is quoted as having replied, "I have

DICTIONARIES

no doubt I can do it in three years. . . . As three to 1600; so is the proportion of an Englishman to a Frenchman." Actually the plan or prospectus, addressed to Philip Dormer, Earl of Chesterfield, was published in 1747 and the dictionary itself in 1755.

The work represented an almost unbelievable accomplishment for one man. It introduced quotations as a means of illustrating definition and included a larger number of words than Bailey. But the Johnson *Dictionary of the English Language* is not an unabridged dictionary in the modern sense and many of its definitions are distorted by bias, complexity or lack of clearness. Some often quoted examples are the following:

> NETWORK—anything reticulated or decussated at equal distances, with interstices between the intersections.
>
> PENSION—pay given to a state hireling for treason against his country.

Johnson's contempt for the Scotch often referred to by Boswell finds expression in the definition of

> OATS—a grain which in England is generally given to horses, but in Scotland supports the people.

To which last, it is said, a Scotch wit replied: "England is known for its horses and Scotland for its people."

Samuel Johnson's own definition of a lexicographer, and consequently a characterization of himself, was modest enough:

> LEXICOGRAPHER—a writer of dictionaries; a harmless drudge.

Notwithstanding some weaknesses, Johnson's *Dictionary of the English Language* remained the final word authority for over a century.

The first great American dictionary was born early in the nineteenth century. Noah Webster, as American as Johnson was British, set out to build a dictionary for his new country that would rank with the national lexicographical masterpieces of England, France, Italy and Spain. With this in mind, he spent many years abroad studying etymologies, and when he returned he applied his knowledge by assembling various Americanisms representing the English spoken in the new world. In 1828 there appeared *An American Dictionary of the English Language* containing 70,000 entries, 12,000 more than Johnson's. Despite this increased vocabulary Webster's dictionary was not unabridged in the modern sense. Its dominant note remained the

Introduction

critical one expressed by the national projects of the Latin-European countries, and by Samuel Johnson, in which the lexicographers set themselves up as censors to determine what words were proper for the people to use.

The big change came to English lexicography in 1857, when Dean Trench read before the London Philological Society his protest, *Some Deficiencies in Existing English Dictionaries*. Fortunately, Samuel Johnson did not live long enough to hear Dean Trench take issue with the academician and sound the keynote of modern lexicography. A dictionary, declared Dean Trench, "is an inventory of the language. It is no task of the [dictionary] maker to select the good words of the language. . . . He is an historian not a critic."

Although this idea had never been expressed so forcefully before in English, it had actually been realized in Germany. Early in the century the Grimm brothers, now widely known for their fairy tales, set out to discover the language of the people and to record it. The result was a great German dictionary, the *Deutsches Wörterbuch*, the first volume of which appeared in 1854. Therefore when Dean Trench's paper stimulated the idea for a great English dictionary in 1857 there was already a German precedent. With the help of the Oxford University Press it was decided to undertake a grand inventory of all the English words from the time they came into our language until the present, or until they passed out of it. To accomplish this, some 1300 scholars of the English-speaking world went to work on all of the written and spoken language and assembled some 5,000,000 quotations from over 5000 writers. The task took seventy years and resulted in the great *Oxford English Dictionary*.

Dictionary evaluation. Today's dictionaries of the English language are many and varied. They have elements in common but differ in detail. In the United States they are produced both by publishers whose main business is dictionary-making and by general, trade and textbook publishers. In evaluating dictionaries, reference librarians have come to consider five basic criteria: (1) scope, (2) authority, (3) format, (4) word treatment or arrangement, and (5) special features.

Scope. Vocabulary size is an indication of dictionary scope. In this chapter, six classes of English language dictionaries ranging in vocabulary from hundreds of thousands to only hundreds of words are described. The unabridged is commonly known as the "big" dictionary. It represents the inventory concept of dictionary-making de-

DICTIONARIES

scribed by Dean Trench, and has resulted in compilations of well over 400,000 entries. Included are obsolete and little-used words as well as the common ones. Major attention is given to definition, etymology, citation, and history of the word.

The largest abridged dictionaries include all of the words except the obsolete and little used. With over 200,000 entries, this type of dictionary will meet all but the exceptional and highly specialized needs. Most other classes of dictionaries are school-graded, vocabulary selection being based on the users' needs. Particularly for the school-graded dictionaries, scientific studies have produced frequency lists which insure vocabulary selection of the words most used in English reading, speaking, and writing.

Language like the humans who use it is a living and growing phenomenon. Some old words die or become obsolete. New words are born and develop into common parts of our daily communication. Numerous reference sources record these changes. Revisions of the basic dictionaries increasingly tend to keep abreast of language developments. The G. and C. Merriam Company, publishers of Webster dictionaries, issue periodically a new word supplement. Daily newspapers, magazines, radio programs and Hollywood movies contribute new words and new meanings to our developing language, and records of these developments appear in popular periodicals and language journals. But the up-to-date dictionary through continuous revision must give evidence of growing with the changing language of the people.

Aside from vocabulary size, the following are considered in measuring a dictionary's coverage: supplementary lists of places, persons, rhymes, new and special terms, and added features like tables of weights and measures, colored plates, and other encyclopedic material. To evaluate the scope of a dictionary, therefore, some of the criteria to consider are the size of the vocabulary, the basis for word selection, up-to-dateness, and supplementary materials.

Authority. Publisher and editor are the two main considerations in determining the authority of a dictionary, and therefore its reliability.

In the United States, the G. and C. Merriam Company of Springfield, Massachusetts, Funk and Wagnalls Company of New York, John C. Winston Company of Philadelphia, and Appleton-Century-Crofts of New York have long established reputations as dictionary publishers. But general trade and textbook publishers, too, have served

Introduction

the dictionary user well. The American Book Company, a textbook publisher, has provided American schools with good, graded versions of Merriam-Webster dictionaries. Scott, Foresman, another textbook publisher, has performed a similar service with Century dictionaries; and Row, Peterson, with Funk and Wagnalls dictionaries. General trade publishers, like Macmillan and Random House, have contributed notable new abridged dictionaries. It is reasonable to expect authority from dictionaries bearing the imprint of any of these publishers.

As for editors, there are a great many names of importance in lexicography. Usually a linguist or a philologist heads a dictionary project. He is assisted by experts in etymology, pronunciation, spelling, and in the various subject fields that contribute terms to the language. Identification of these experts by their education and by their scholarly contributions, usually through writings, is a basis for evaluation.

Format. Some of the unabridged dictionaries appear in single, jumbo, heavy volumes, or in two- or three-volume editions; others are multivolume sets.

There is much to be said for the single volume: convenience of having the entire alphabetic sequence between two covers, economy in binding cost and necessary compact organization. There are also these disadvantages: curling front pages, heavy weight, fine print, uninviting page make-up and the impossibility of use by more than one person at a time.

In evaluating format of a dictionary, opaque though thin paper, well-leaded though small type, adequate inside and outside margins, narrow columns, and plenty of aids and devices such as running heads, thumb indexes and guide keys are features to look for.

Word treatment. Eight items are included in word treatment: spelling, pronunciation, syllabication, etymology, definition, quotation, synonym, syntax.

Spelling (orthography) in a dictionary turns on two issues—British or American, conservative or simplified. The former choice can be checked by looking up words like *labour,* the latter by words like *thru* and *bot.*

Pronunciation (orthoepy) varies with English-speaking country and American region. American *clerk* and British *clark,* New England and Midwest pronunciations of *class* are examples of contrasts. Several devices are used to indicate pronunciation. Most common are the diacritical markings: ă, ā, ĕ, ē, etc. More scientific are the so-called amplified or phonetic alphabets, in which to the 26 regular letters are added enough symbols to provide a different representation for each sound. When a word is spelled phonetically, each letter or symbol of the phonetic alphabet always represents the same sound.

Syllabication is usually indicated by spaces between parts of words, or by centered periods, or by hyphens. To denote stress, an underline, double hyphen or accent mark is used. These differences in syllable markings are probably much more important to the publisher's blurb writer than to the user.

Etymology is indicated in some dictionaries by roots in Greek or Hebrew symbols; in others the symbols are transliterated. Variations range from detailed, chronological listings of derivations to complete omission of any etymology.

Definitions are given in one of two sequences. *Webster's* and *Oxford English* dictionaries follow historical order, giving the oldest meaning of a word first and the newest meaning last. *Funk and Wagnalls,* on the other hand, gives the commonest meaning first. Aside from sequence, clarity and simplicity of definition are paramount.

Often the use of a word in a sentence tells more about it than a definition. Every unabridged English dictionary since Johnson's has made much of quotations. Authoritative, numerous, and applicable examples are desirable. Authority and often understanding are aided by reference to the context of the quotation. Such reference is hindered by omission of a full citation to the source. A quotation from Shakespeare is more useful if it includes an exact reference to the play, act, scene. Like quotations, illustrations are used effectively by many dictionaries to extend the verbal definitions.

Synonyms and antonyms are included in most dictionaries. Their placement is important in evaluation. Some dictionaries have separate lists; others include synonyms and antonyms in the word entry to clinch definitions.

Part of speech is usually indicated by an abbreviation—"n." for noun, "v." for verb. While the ordinary dictionary does not contain the type of discussion about word use that is found in a supplementary language book on usage, it will give such things as past tenses of irregular verbs, variations in spelling of plurals, compounding or phrase forming with the word.

Special features. Dictionary purists tend to look with disfavor upon the trend to crowd the dictionary with encyclopedic material.[1] But whether for sales purposes or out of consideration for the home that can afford only one reference book, certain special features that are not strictly a part of the dictionary as defined in this chapter are becoming dictionary fixtures. Among them are lists of personal names, giving enough information to qualify as short biographical sketches of notables; place names, identifying geographic and historical points of interest; census figures; maps; tables of weights and measures; colored plates of flags, birds, flowers, cathedrals, automobiles; black-and-white illustrations with words, and a host of other items. The biographical and geographical names are entered sometimes in the main dictionary alphabet, sometimes separately. Other special features are more dictionary-like: rhymes; terms in special subject fields like business; lists of abbreviations, signs, symbols; and comparative tables of pronunciation.

Evaluation sources. Dictionaries are reviewed in many publications. Book review periodicals like the *Saturday Review* and the modern language and English journals can be counted on to give attention to new titles and editions. All of the reference lists, current as well as retrospective, described in the first chapter, conscientiously consider new dictionaries. Special attention is called to issues of *Subscription Books Bulletin* like that of October, 1934, which dealt with basic principles of dictionary evaluation.

Unabridged dictionaries

Four unabridged English dictionaries are found in many American library reference rooms. Two American publications, *Webster's New International* and *Funk and Wagnalls New Standard,* are almost universal. A third American dictionary, the *Century,* a multivolume set, is out of print but is still found in a number of libraries. The fourth dictionary is the scholarly British *Oxford English,* frequently referred to as the *O.E.D.* Complementary to the last is the *Dictionary of American English.*

Webster's New International Dictionary. *Webster's,* the oldest and most famous American dictionary, although now listed in its "second" edition, has appeared in at least five previous editions. Not counting Noah Webster's *A Compendious Dictionary* of 1806, which

---

[1] For the pure dictionary point of view, see page 47 of Bessie Graham, *Bookman's Manual* (N.Y., Bowker, 1948); in favor of cyclopedic information, see the article by F. Sturgis Allen in Paul Monroe, *Cyclopedia of Education* (N.Y., Macmillan, 1911-13), v.2, p.324-27.

DICTIONARIES

included only about 38,000 words, the following notable "Websters" have appeared:

1828 *An American Dictionary of the English Language,* prepared by Noah Webster and containing 70,000 words, in two volumes. As early as 1783, Webster had published his *American Spelling Book,* destined to become the "blue book" best seller. In a sense there was a part of the American Revolution in all of Noah Webster's work—a successful rebellion against British English and the dictates of Dr. Samuel Johnson.

1847 Same title, but under the Merriam imprint for the first time. Webster had issued an enlarged edition in 1840, which was acquired, upon his death in 1843, by the present publishers. Webster's son-in-law, Professor Chauncey A. Goodrich of Yale College, edited the new edition, which now appeared in one volume. A reissue in 1859 introduced two innovations: pictorial illustrations and synonyms.

1864 Same title, but popularly referred to as the "Unabridged," revised by Noah Porter, who later became president of Yale. Two distinguished assistants aided in the revision—William Dwight Whitney, who later edited the *Century Dictionary,* and Daniel Coit Gilman, who later became president of Johns Hopkins. The etymologies were modernized by C. A. F. Mahn of Berlin, and the vocabulary was increased to 114,000 words.

1890 *Webster's International Dictionary,* edited by Noah Porter, with the assistance of Loomis J. Campbell as head of the office staff and F. Sturges Allen as general editor. The vo-

---

❦ UNABRIDGED DICTIONARIES

Webster's New International Dictionary of the English Language. 2d ed., unabridged. Springfield, Mass., Merriam, 1950. 3214p.

Funk and Wagnalls New Standard Dictionary of the English Language. N.Y., Funk & Wagnalls, 1950. 2895p.

Oxford English Dictionary; Being a Corrected Reissue, with an Introduction, Supplement and Bibliography, of A New English Dictionary on Historical Principles. Oxford, Clarendon Pr., 1933. 12v. and Supplement.

Craigie, Sir William, and Hulbert, J. R. A Dictionary of American English on Historical Principles. Chicago, Univ. of Chicago Pr., 1936-44. 4v.

Century Dictionary and Cyclopedia. N.Y., Century, 1911. 12v.

Unabridged dictionaries

cabulary was increased to about 175,000 words. An edition containing a supplement of 25,000 additional words appeared in 1900.

1909 *Webster's New International Dictionary of the English Language,* edited by William T. Harris and F. Sturges Allen. The vocabulary totaled more than 400,000 words. Much of the supplement and appendixes to the previous edition was embodied in the main vocabulary.

1934 The present edition is the second of the *New International* title. There have been many reissues since, but these reissues must not be confused with editions. In the former, partial changes and some additions are made. In the latter the type is completely reset. The publishers say this edition cost $1,300,000. Obviously, such an investment cannot be made more often than once in twenty-five years. The description which follows is based on the 1950 issue of the second edition.

Scope. Publishers' statistics claim 600,000 entries, including 13,000 biographical and 35,000 geographical names in separate lists. Some 12,000 terms are illustrated in black and white and in color.

Primarily, the editors emphasize, *Webster's* is a "citations dictionary." That is, terms have been selected and defined after examining a very large part of English literature and collecting hundreds of thousands of quotations. About one third of the terms belong to the "literary vocabulary"; the rest are a part of special subjects—engineering, medicine, psychology, religion, science, social science, the trades, professions, business. Considerable attention has been paid to newer specialties—to aeronautics, radio, motion pictures. But the old specialties—obsolete words, lowland Scottish, scripture names—have not been neglected. As one scans the photographs of the special editors in the introduction one notes the dictionary's attention to such popular interests as archery, brewing, card games, golf, heraldry, philately, tapestries and wine. From the above random list it is evident that the vocabulary scope is comprehensive, varied and representative of many walks of American life.

Authority. The century-old publishing house of G. and C. Merriam in Springfield has assembled a staff of distinguished editors to match its own reputation. Starting at the top, the late William A. Neilson, Harvard Shakespeare scholar, President of Smith College, and co-editor of the *Five-Foot Shelf,* continues the fine tradition of editors, ably assisted by General Editor Thomas A. Knott, former University of Iowa English professor and army intelligence officer.

Continuity with the previous edition is provided by the managing editor, Paul W. Carhart, an authority on pronunciation, and by A. G. Baker, the Merriam president.

The specialists, all authorities on terminology in their respective fields, number 207. At random, here are some well-known names: Clark Wissler (Anthropology); Roscoe Pound (Law); W. W. Atwood (Geography); George Lyman Kittredge (Synonyms).

Format. Available in either one large or two or three medium-sized volumes, the physical make-up is as good as can be expected of a volume of this abnormal size. Even considering the use to which it is put in the average library the binding does remarkably well. But something should be done to reinforce the pages in the first signature which curl, crease and tear early in the book's life. The divided page is a less marked feature in this edition than in the previous one, although virtually every page of the vocabulary has a miniature lower section of six columns for obsolete words and cross references for many irregular verbs treated only in the present tense in the main alphabet. The upper section of three columns is devoted to the living language. Reasonable margins, small but clear type, fairly opaque paper, and narrow columns contribute to readability. Thumb index along the side, first and last word on top, and pronunciation key at the bottom of each page are ready-reference features.

Word treatment. Attention is called to certain features of word treatment in *Webster's* that occur with variations in other dictionaries.[2]

    1. Syllabication. Indicated with centered period; heavy and light accent marks are used for major and minor stress.

    2. Pronunciation. Webster diacritical marks are used for respelling, that is, "āle, ădd," etc.

    3. Part of speech. Abbreviated; "n." for noun, etc.

    4. Inflectional forms. When irregular, these are in small caps.

    5. Etymologies. In the spelling of foreign words etymologies tend "to an increased use of the Latin alphabet." Hence in the latest edition, "Greek is transliterated in the etymologies."

    6. Definitions. In historical order. This is important to the reader who inclines to stop at the end of the first definition, giving a meaning which may have been common in Chaucer's day but is virtually unknown now.

    7. Labels. Labels are used to indicate subject (Law, anat.), usage (obsolete, slang), geography (U.S., Brit.).

    8. Synonyms and antonyms. Frequently given.

    9. Spelling. Most of the simplified spellings recommended by

the American Philological Association and the Simplified Spelling Board have been included but not necessarily given preferential placement.

10. Quotations. The 29,000 included have been selected from a collection of 1,655,000. Citations are bibliographically incomplete, providing the reader with no more of a clue, generally, than "Shak."

Special features. A few special features are commented on here; many more await discovery during firsthand examination. In the introduction, Kittredge's revision of Hadley's *Brief History of the English Language* is monumental. It is solid rather than easy reading. The synopsis of words differently pronounced by different pronunciation experts is entertaining. For instance, although Hollywood has converted all of its starlets to the "eyether" pronunciation, it is not supported by any of the four great unabridged dictionaries. *Webster's, Funk and Wagnalls, Oxford,* and *Century* all prefer "eether."

In the appendix, there are lists of abbreviations, of signs and symbols, forms of address, persons, and places, including population figures. But other reference books are better for these classes of information.

Scattered through the text are plates and full-page illustrations of flags, seals, coats of arms, aircraft, alphabets, architecture, automobiles, bridges, gems, trees, wild flowers, and many other subjects. Some of these illustrations come within a dictionary's scope; others are encyclopedic. Many terms are illustrated by black-and-white drawings.

Summary. Webster's New International Dictionary is still the best dictionary value on the market and must continue to head the first purchase list for all types of libraries. Its strong points are excellent definitions, a long tradition of careful editing, the largest number of word entries, and a conservative and reliable policy with regard to innovations that only too often prove to be unnecessary frills and fads. Its list of contributors includes some of the most distinguished scholars in nearly every field of human activity. For most Americans, Merriam-Webster has become synonymous with the word *dictionary.*

Funk and Wagnalls New Standard Dictionary. In 1893, *A Standard Dictionary of the English Language,* containing 304,000 terms and edited by Dr. Isaac Funk, was published by the Funk and Wagnalls Company. A supplement to a later issue added 13,000

---

[2] The publishers have included an explanatory chart which analyzes the typical Webster entry. Copies of this chart are also available separately.

terms. The present edition was created in 1913. There have been regular, partial revisions since. The following analysis is based on the 1950 issue of the edition bearing a 1949 copyright date.

Scope. The publisher's statistics indicate 455,000 entries plus additional entries in the 34-page supplement in the front of the volume. Variations in defining an entry and continuous additions and subtractions render statistical comparison with *Webster's* difficult, but probably the scope is generally the same. Emphasis in *Funk and Wagnalls* is placed on selection and modernity: "The vocabulary should, first of all, embrace *all the live words* of the English language as used in the standard speech and literature of the day." New words and the language of science, commerce and industry find generous recognition.

Authority. Among the 380 editors and contributors to *Funk and Wagnalls* are to be found names that are prominent in most of the important fields of human endeavor, among them, Robert Edward Peary (arctic explorer), Jacob Ruppert (brewer), Emanuel Lasker (chess), William J. Henderson (music critic). But many of the authorities listed are now dead.

Format. Funk and Wagnalls New Standard is available in either one large or two medium-sized volumes. In physical appearance the *New Standard* seems to have a slight advantage over its chief competitor. The type seems blacker and clearer, the page make-up simpler, and the paper more nearly opaque. Thumb index and margins are the same. Pronunciation keys are at the top of the page but, with all due respect to the psychologist who proved it to be sight-saving, the advantage of that location is debatable. A single alphabet includes all terms, modern and obsolete, and persons, places, and abbreviations —each of which has a separate list in *Webster's New International.*

Word treatment. Certain differences in word treatment distinguish the *New Standard* from the *New International.*

    1. Definitions. The commonest meaning is given first. This often makes the *New Standard* especially desirable at the telephone desk in the reference room for prompt answers to telephone queries.

    2. Spelling. Liberal preferences for simplification are indicated: This dictionary generally prefers the simpler form when two ways of spelling the same word are used by acknowledged authorities."

    3. Pronunciation. Two keys are used: (1) the Revised Scientific or National Education Association and (2) the "Text-book key," which is the Funk and Wagnalls way of referring to the diacritical marks used by Merriam-Webster.

Unabridged dictionaries

4. Quotations. There are more quotations in the *New Standard* and the citations are fuller than in *New International.*

Special features. Statistically speaking the *New Standard* can add 30,000 place names and 16,000 personal names to its vocabulary of 450,000 terms. Some 7000 illustrations including about 10,000 separate items enhance the definitions. The pictures appear to be better than those in the *New International* in detail and in color.

Introductory materials of more than passing interest are the section on spelling and pronunciation, with its information about scientific alphabets, and the foreign language chart of equivalents, giving exceedingly interesting language comparisons. Among the appendixes, disputed pronunciations, simplified spelling rules, and the glossary of foreign words and phrases are notable.

Summary. The *New Standard* is a worthy competitor of *Webster's New International.* In reference class debates, where members have undertaken to act as sales representatives of the two American dictionaries and the rest of the class has agreed to assume the roles of prospective purchasers, *Webster's* has not always outsold *Funk and Wagnalls.* Here are two good dictionaries, both desirable library purchases, with *Funk and Wagnalls New Standard* in the role of first alternate to *Webster's New International* when selecting an unabridged English language dictionary.

Oxford English Dictionary. The *Oxford English Dictionary,* which originally consisted of ten volumes in twenty parts, is variously cited as *Oxford Dictionary, Murray's,* the *New English Dictionary, N.E.D.,* or *O.E.D.* Since the publication in 1933 of the $125 edition, the official title of this work is *Oxford English Dictionary.* The title page reads: *"A New English Dictionary on Historical Principles; Founded Mainly on the Materials Collected by the Philological Society . . . Edited by James A. H. Murray . . . with the Assistance of Many Scholars and Men of Science."* The work is "dutifully" dedicated "To the Queen's most Excellent Majesty" by the University of Oxford.

Scope. "To furnish an adequate account of the meaning, origin and history of English words now in general use, or known to have been in use at any time during the last seven hundred years," is the stated purpose. The statement is amplified as follows:

1. To trace the historical development of every word from the time it became English through its various changes in meanings to its present signification

37

2. To illustrate this development by a series of chronologically arranged quotations

3. To treat each word etymologically on the basis of historical fact and with the method of philological science

Further elaborating on the dictionary's scope the preface offers a distinction between a dictionary and an encyclopedia:

> In connexion with this, it has to be borne in mind, that a dictionary of the English Language is not a Cyclopedia: the Cyclopedia *describes things;* the Dictionary explains words and deals with the description of things only so far as is necessary in order to fix the exact significations and use of words. ... A Cyclopedia consists mostly of nouns ... an English Dictionary consists of words belonging to all the parts of speech. ...

The *Oxford English Dictionary,* adhering strictly to word definition, contains some 414,825 words, plus 26,000 in the supplement. Of these, 240,165 are main words, 67,105 are subordinate words, 47,800 are special combinations, and 59,755 are obvious combinations. A total of 1,827,306 of the five million quotations assembled by the compilers have been used to illustrate these words.

To indicate the expanded scope of the *Oxford English Dictionary* by comparison with some of its illustrious multivolume predecessors, the following statistics are notable:

Dictionary	Number of words found between letters Ti and Z	Number of quotations found within letters O and P
Johnson	4,888	12,111
Cassell	21,661	9,642
Century	28,457	20,340
Oxford	61,055	175,130

The full story of the *Oxford English Dictionary's* scope, however, is not told in statistics. Overwhelming superiority over other dictionaries in number of quotations is incidental to the fact that in the *Oxford English Dictionary* alone can be found the complete biography of every word in the language, from the time it first became English to the date of publication of the dictionary or to its obsolescence. Only words which had become obsolete by 1150 and some slang are excluded. All others are here as revealed by the most searching examination of the literature of the English language.

Unabridged dictionaries

Authority. It would be difficult to assemble a corps of lexicographers, philologists and other scholars more distinguished than the 1300 who built the *Oxford English Dictionary*. Dean Trench, Sir James A. H. Murray, Dr. Henry Bradley, Sir William A. Craigie, and Mr. Charles T. Onions, together and successively provided incomparable leadership over seven decades. To that must be added the prestige of a famous university press.

Format. As originally published, the set consisted of ten volumes bound in twenty parts and priced at $400. A reprint in 12 volumes and supplement released at a price of $125 has become the more common library purchase. Both sets are printed on good paper, and the over-all impression of format is clear, conservative, and readable. There are no illustrations or cyclopedic features.

Word treatment. Because of its unique aim and scope among English dictionaries, care must be exercised in using the *Oxford English Dictionary*. All words and phrases are classed as main words, subordinate words, or combinations. Main words represent the living language and are entered in bold type; subordinate words are variant and obsolete forms of the main words, are entered under the main words which form their first elements, and usually conclude the article. In the alphabetical place where the subordinate word would normally appear a reference is made to the main word under which it is entered; e.g., "Abaundon, *see* Abandon."

The treatment of a word, which for much-used words often extends to several three-column pages, covers identification, morphology, sematology (definition) and quotation. Under identification, the *Oxford English Dictionary* usually provides in succession the main form of the word, pronunciation by means of the scientific, amplified alphabet, part of speech, and specification—that is, the subject to which the word is most closely related. In addition, information on the present status of the word, whether obsolete, colloquial or dialectal, is given. This is followed by the spelling, history, and inflection of the word. Under morphology, form history is presented (within heavy square brackets) by means of etymology, subsequent change and miscellaneous historical facts. Definitions are the third part of the entry. Quotations, the fourth part, are all fully cited.

Special features. The *Introduction, Supplement and Bibliography,* which appeared in 1933, contains approximately 26,000 additional entries. Besides new words which have appeared since 1884, there are many additions to the meanings of old words, an excellent history of the whole work, a list of spurious words, and a list of books quoted. Because of the large number of quotations, the *Oxford English Dictionary* has a distinct added reference use as a quotation book. To find suitable quotations or to identify them, one may search under any of several key words with reasonable expectation of success.

Summary. No library can be considered scholarly without possessing the *Oxford English Dictionary,* which serves other fields than English language and literature. To the student of any subject in which the history of word usage is important, this dictionary is basic.

Dictionary of American English. In 1924, while Sir William Craigie was reading proof on the *Oxford English Dictionary,* it occurred to him that it would be desirable to trace the history of English words in America from the seventeenth century to the present. He at once communicated with Professor John M. Manley of the University of Chicago, who interested his institution in the project. Under the editorship of Sir William Craigie, the dictionary first appeared in paper-bound parts. It is now complete in four volumes. Its purpose is "to obtain and present all that is really significant in the history of the language in the area now covered by the United States." Words and phrases clearly or apparently of American origin, or of greater currency here than elsewhere, or related to the development of this country and the history of its people, through the end of the nineteenth century, are included. To complete the history of a word that originated in the British Isles it is necessary to consult both this work and the *Oxford English Dictionary.* But for words of American origin, indicated by a plus sign, the *Dictionary of American English* is complete in itself, tracing the history of the word through quotation, after the pattern of the older work.

Century Dictionary. Still found on library shelves, though long out of print, is the old *Century Dictionary and Cyclopedia.* The format best known is a 12-volume set, ten devoted to words, one to names, and one to an atlas. In the opinion of many this was the greatest of American dictionaries. Its aim was to provide a general dictionary for every literary and practical use with special emphasis on technical terms in science, art and trades. Its authority was excellent, its illustrations were especially good, and its early attention to simplified spelling, antonyms and accurate references—though not complete citations—heralded many subsequent dictionary innovations. Although the vocabulary is now behind the times, the old *Century* remains a useful tool.

Abridged dictionaries

Largest abridged dictionaries. Two dictionaries, one American and one British, are worthy of consideration as an addition to relieve the wear on the unabridged works. They are the *New Century* and the *Shorter Oxford*. Both are only slightly abridged, containing well over 200,000 words.

The *New Century* is based on the fine, old, 12-volume *Century*. The publishers state that it is an "abridged, condensed and popular rendering of the original *Century*."[3] It has retained much of the scholarly lexicography of its predecessor and something of its superiority of format. Good paper, dark legible type, attractive make-up, and significant illustrations, from the standpoint of both selection and reproduction, commend the *New Century* for reference use. In addition to the regular vocabulary, the dictionary contains these special lists: (1) synonyms, antonyms and discriminations; (2) abbreviations in common use; (3) business terms; (4) foreign words and phrases; (5) personal names; (6) place names; and (7) table of measures and weights. The business terms, alone, earn their reference cost in public library service.

The *Shorter Oxford* is an officially authorized abridgment of the *Oxford English Dictionary* first issued in 1933, revised in 1936 and again in 1944, and reprinted with corrections in 1947. In the words of Editor Onions, "For those who possess the great Oxford dictionary the 'Shorter' will serve as a key to its treasures, for those who do not it will form the only possible substitute."

The 15,500 pages in the great dictionary have been reduced to 2500, but actually the abridgment contains more than two thirds of the vocabulary of the large work. The greatest cut is in the number of quotations and of obsolete and subordinate words. However, even so, the *Shorter Oxford* probably has more quotations than either the *New International* or the *New Standard* unabridged dictionaries. In spite

---

❦ LARGEST ABRIDGED DICTIONARIES

New Century Dictionary of the English Language; Based on Matter Selected from the Original Century Dictionary. N.Y., Appleton-Century-Crofts, 1948. 2v.

The Shorter Oxford English Dictionary on Historical Principles; 3d ed., rev., with addenda. Oxford, Clarendon Pr., 1947. 2v.

---

[3] A subscription edition is sold by P. F. Collier and Sons.

of its general excellence, the *Shorter Oxford* falls short of being classed with the unabridged dictionaries because of the reduced number of entries and the complete absence of compensating encyclopedic matter.

College abridged dictionaries. There are five American abridged dictionaries with a vocabulary range of over 100,000 words available at a price under ten dollars. These dictionaries are the ones most frequently found in homes, in professional and business offices and on the desks of teachers. In these dictionaries will be located nearly all of the words used by most adults.

The *American College Dictionary* has 132,000 entries selected from the *New Century Dictionary,* the *Dictionary of American English* and the Thorndike-Lorge *Teacher's Wordbook of 30,000 Words.* The Lorge-Thorndike Semantic Count, which measures the occurrences of various meanings, was used to assure inclusion on a scientific basis of the meanings most important to the modern reader. In addition, a large number of authorities and specialists were enlisted to make sure that basic current terms were included and that the facts about them, including their definitions, were accurate.

The editor of the *American College Dictionary* had previously edited the Thorndike-Century series of elementary and secondary school dictionaries described later in this chapter and the *Dictionary of U.S. Army Terms.* His advisory committee includes Leonard Bloomfield, Yale's Sterling professor of linguistics, Charles C. Fries, W. Cabell Greet, Irving Lorge, and Kemp Malone. Special consultants represent every field of human study and activity from accounting to zoology. A textbook edition is issued by Harpers in addition to the Random House trade edition.

☞ COLLEGE ABRIDGED DICTIONARIES

The American College Dictionary, ed. by Clarence L. Barnhart with the assistance of 355 authorities and specialists. N.Y., Random House, 1947. 1432p.

Webster's New Collegiate Dictionary . . . Based on Webster's New International Dictionary, 2d ed. Springfield, Mass., Merriam, 1951. 1230p.

Funk and Wagnalls New College Standard Dictionary; ed. by Charles Earle Funk. N.Y., Funk & Wagnalls, 1950. 1404p.

Macmillan Modern Dictionary; ed. by Bruce Overton. Rev. school ed. N.Y., Macmillan, 1951. 1509p.

Winston Dictionary. College ed. Philadelphia, Winston, 1947. 1276p.

Abridged dictionaries

The format of the *American College Dictionary* is appealing throughout. The paper has high opacity and the buckram binding appears to be sturdy. About 1600 illustrations and spot maps supplement text information at various places. The spot maps in black and white serve to identify places; for example, in Alaska the Alaska Highway, Alaska Peninsula and Alaska Range.

Word treatment in the *American College Dictionary* includes spelling, syllabication, pronunciation, part of speech, inflected forms, definitions numbered consecutively, illustrations of use, usage label, etymology, synonyms and antonyms. The 43 pronunciation symbols include the common diacritical marks plus one symbol borrowed from the International Phonetic Alphabet.

Some of the special features of note in the *American College Dictionary* are the inclusion of proper nouns in the main alphabet, the pictures of animals giving scale of reduction in each case, a list of colleges and universities in the United States, and the authoritative prefatory statement on pronunciation, etymologies, synonyms and antonyms, British and American usage and other subjects. There is a handbook section on punctuation, letter writing, manuscript and proof, signs and symbols and other useful information.

The first edition of *Webster's Collegiate Dictionary* appeared in 1898. Successive revisions followed in 1910, 1916, 1931, and 1936, so that in reality *Webster's New Collegiate* is the sixth edition of an abridged college dictionary produced by Merriam. Principal changes from earlier editions are improved format, including wider pages and columns, enlarged vocabulary, and greater emphasis on technical and scientific terms.

The publisher claims over 125,000 entries, 2300 pictorial illustrations. There are 10,000 geographical and 5000 biographical names in the special vocabularies. Information prepared for the *New International* by 207 consulting editors has been drawn upon for the *New Collegiate,* and some of the consultants did special work for this abridgment. Dr. Lucius H. Holt served as managing editor for the *New Collegiate,* assisted by several associates and consultants. The general editor was John P. Bethel.

Unlike the *American College Dictionary,* persons and places are listed in separate vocabularies, there is a special rhyming dictionary, and the list of colleges and universities is arranged in one alphabet rather than by states.

Webster's New Collegiate is an old stand-by and its solid, conservative editorship is bound to be preferred by a significant portion of dictionary owners. Other dictionaries in this class include the "Emphatype" *Funk and Wagnalls New College Standard,* which uses type emphasis to indicate pronunciation, a new edition of *Macmillan's Modern,* and the college edition of the *Winston Dictionary.* The first, with more than 145,000 entries, appears to have the largest vocabulary of any dictionary in this class.

There are still other college or popular adult dictionaries on the market. One of the lowest priced is *Words,*[4] published by Grosset and Dunlap, which contains only 70,000 entries but is available at a list price of only $2.50. Another is the *Thorndike-Barnhart Comprehensive Desk Dictionary* (Doubleday) available for $2.95. Pocket and so-called vest pocket dictionaries range in price to as low as 35c.

High school abridged dictionaries. The dictionaries in this group are all textbook publications. Standard dictionary publishers like Merriam and Century have collaborated with textbook publishers like American Book Company and Scott, Foresman to produce abridged versions ranging from 45,000 to 75,000 entries selected especially with secondary school needs in mind. These needs have been met scientifically through frequency counts on words appearing in the reading suitable for the grades concerned.

There are 63,370 entries and 1975 illustrations in the *Thorndike-Century Senior Dictionary.* The words were selected in accordance with the Thorndike frequency principle, namely, those words most frequently found in American popular literature. A numeral indicates whether a word is among the first thousand words most frequently used, the second, the third, etc. Definitions are simple, supplemented by pictures wherever possible, and illustrated by the use of the word in

---

☞ HIGH SCHOOL ABRIDGED DICTIONARIES

Thorndike-Century Senior Dictionary; ed. by E. L. Thorndike. Chicago, Scott, Foresman, 1941. 1065p.

Webster's Students' Dictionary. Cincinnati, American Book Co., 1945. 1001p.

Funk and Wagnalls Standard High School Dictionary; ed. by Frank H. Vizettelly and Charles Earle Funk. N.Y., Funk & Wagnalls, 1950. 1008p.

New Winston Dictionary for Young People. Philadelphia, Winston, 1948. 974p.

Abridged dictionaries

short sentences. Special features include suffixes and parts of speech. A great many secondary schools in the United States have officially adopted the *Thorndike-Century Senior* for grades seven through twelve. The publishers announce new editions of all three of their school dictionaries to be known hereafter as the Thorndike-Barnhart dictionaries.

Webster's Students' Dictionary is the Merriam competitor of the *Thorndike-Century Senior,* serving the junior and senior high school reading range. Its 57,000 entries are also based on a word count frequency, but the selection is on the basis of their occurrence in textbooks and other books of the upper school levels rather than in popular reading. Among its unique features are a list of books of the Bible, a geological table, over 1200 black-and-white illustrations and eight full-color plates.

Other dictionaries in this class are *Funk and Wagnalls Standard High School Dictionary* and the *New Winston Dictionary for Young People.* Macmillan has also issued a high school edition of its *Modern Dictionary* reduced in vocabulary to 60,000 words.

Intermediate abridged dictionaries. In 1935 Dr. E. L. Thorndike, noted psychologist, made educational and book review headlines in *Time* and *The Saturday Review* by creating what the publishers claimed was "the first dictionary ever made from scratch for use and understanding by children." This was the *Thorndike-Century Junior Dictionary,* incorporating (1) scientific vocabulary selection based on children's actual needs and capabilities; (2) simplification of definitions rather than condensation from an adult dictionary. Intended for grades five to eight, the 1942 edition includes 32,294 words, 50,252 meanings, 23,110 illustrative sentences and phrases, and

---

❦ INTERMEDIATE ABRIDGED DICTIONARIES

Thorndike-Century Junior Dictionary; ed. by E. L. Thorndike. Chicago, Scott, Foresman, 1942. 940p.

Webster's Elementary Dictionary; a Dictionary for Boys and Girls. Cincinnati, American Book Co., 1948. 739p.

Funk and Wagnalls Standard Junior Dictionary. N.Y., Funk & Wagnalls, 1950. 752p.

Winston Dictionary for Children. Philadelphia, Winston, 1948. 644p.

---

4 *Words: The New Dictionary,* ed. by Charles P. Chadsey (N.Y., Grosset & Dunlap, 1947), 704p.

2305 pictures. *Thorndike-Century Beginning Dictionary* is intended for grades four to five, has only 14,085 words, 30,577 meanings, 14,949 sentences, 1419 pictures. Definitions are simple, striking, clear. Easy words like *the, if, and,* are not defined; they are used in a sentence. Attractive illustrations and make-up contribute to realizing the Thorndike dictionary objective. A figure following the entry indicates, as in the case of the *Thorndike-Century Senior Dictionary,* in which thousand frequency the word occurs. Animal illustrations are supplemented with a statement on size.

Other dictionaries in the intermediate abridged class include *Webster's Elementary Dictionary* with 38,500 vocabulary entries, "selected on the basis of their occurrence in printed matter which is actually studied and read by boys and girls," *Funk and Wagnalls Standard Junior Dictionary,* with 43,000 entries and 150 illustrations, and the *Winston Dictionary for Children.*

Primary abridged dictionaries. The picture dictionary for the very young child made its appearance even before the Second World War. In a sense, of course, the ABC book (A is for apple) was the first primary dictionary. Watters-Courtis, *The Picture Dictionary for Children* and Staats-Frasier's *The Right Word,*[5] were the immediate predecessors of the current examples.

Of the postwar dictionaries, two have had outstanding success. The format of both *The Rainbow Dictionary* and *The Golden Dictionary* feature color—color for pictures and color for text. Alphabeting is deliberately and attractively brought into the child's experience as a basis for all future dictionary use. Wherever possible, pictures define;

❧ PRIMARY ABRIDGED DICTIONARIES

The Picture Dictionary for Children; Words by Garnette Watters and Stuart A. Courtis; Pictures by Doris and Marion Henderson and Barry Bart. N.Y., Grosset & Dunlap, 1948. 383p.

The Rainbow Dictionary; Words by Wendell W. Wright, Pictures by Joseph Low. Cleveland, World Pub., 1947. 433p.

The Golden Dictionary; Words by Ellen W. Walpole; Pictures by Gertrude Elliott. N.Y., Simon & Schuster, 1947. 94p.

Courtis-Watters Illustrated Golden Dictionary for Young Readers. N.Y., Simon & Schuster, 1951.

My First Dictionary; the Beginner's Picture Word Book; by Laura Oftedahl and Nina Jacobs; illus. by Pelagie Doane. N.Y., Grosset & Dunlap, 1948. 140p.

Supplementary English language sources

where not, the word is used in an easy sentence. There are 2300 entries and 1100 illustrations in *The Rainbow Dictionary;* 1030 entries and 1500 illustrations in *The Golden Dictionary.* The *Rainbow Dictionary* is the product of Indiana University educators; *The Golden Dictionary* is the work of a Teachers College, Columbia University, author.

The elementary school librarian who has long felt a need for reference tools specifically for young children can set these titles down to begin her list of basic reference books.

Supplementary English language sources

For most purposes the unabridged dictionary will answer questions on etymology, synonyms, slang and dialect. It is certain that no smaller work can hope to do more for etymology than the *Oxford English Dictionary.* But occasionally there are questions relating to colloquialisms of a locality too special for a work as broad as an unabridged dictionary. Then, too, many libraries cannot afford the *Oxford English Dictionary.* Also, there are certain advantages in separate wordbooks of synonyms, antonyms, and rhymes, which make it possible to divert readers from the overworked dictionary. Finally, separate collections of such terms are an inducement to their study. For these reasons a few selected supplementary wordbooks are here described. These wordbooks are grouped by their specialties as follows: (1) usage; (2) synonyms; (3) abbreviations; (4) slang and dialect; (5) pronunciation; (6) rhyme; (7) foreign terms and comparative language.

For each type of language book there are many good examples. To discuss all of them here would be impossible; therefore, the first of each type is most fully discussed. The additional titles listed are more desirable for some libraries than for others.

Usage books. Five examples are listed; there are many more. All of them have this in common: they include rules and directions for correct English expression. Porter G. Perrin, professor of English at the University of Washington, has in his *Writer's Guide and Index to English*—the third edition of the book originally titled *Index to English* (1939)—achieved completeness and compactness, as has Clarence Stratton in his *Effective English.* Both are outstanding examples

---

[5] Pauline G. Staats and Clark M. Frasier, *The Right Word* (Boston, Allyn & Bacon, 1937), 371p.

of usage books, of which the number is legion. Perrin is selected for description because it illustrates the usage book at its best. Part one is the basis for a college course in English, including such standard topics as punctuation, spelling, paragraphs and problems of English grammar; but it is part two, "Index to English," which is the real reference tool. It contains an amazing amount of information readably presented, with good cross references to the first part. It is particularly helpful because of its American and modern approach to language.

Especially for young people is the *Handbook of English for Boys and Girls,* prepared by a Committee of the National Conference on Research in English under the chairmanship of C. C. Certain, founder and editor of the *Elementary English Review.* It does on a more elementary level what Perrin and Stratton do at the college level. Two British sources, *A Dictionary of Modern English Usage* by Fowler, an authority of long standing on such moot questions of proper usage as the split infinitive, *shall* and *will, lie* and *lay,* and *A Dictionary of Modern American Usage* by Horwill, a colorful view of American English through an Englishman's eyes, are standard in public and college reference rooms. Both are arranged alphabetically. Horwill has included nine different classes of words whose use in England varies in some way from their use in the United States.

Synonyms. Because of the number of synonyms and the fine discriminations it makes between them, *Webster's Dictionary of Synonyms* is the favorite among many reference librarians. There are about 1950 discriminating articles in this work; the preface contains a history of synonym books; other features include cross-indexing aids

---

❦ USAGE BOOKS

Perrin, P. G. Writer's Guide and Index to English. Chicago, Scott, Foresman, 1950. 833p.

Stratton, Clarence. Effective English. N.Y., McGraw-Hill, 1951. 324p.

Certain, C. C., ed. Handbook of English for Boys and Girls; Prepared by a Committee of the National Conference on Research in English. Chicago, Scott, Foresman, 1939. 128p.

Fowler, H. W. A Dictionary of Modern English Usage. N.Y., Oxford Univ. Pr., 1937. 742p.

Horwill, C. P. A Dictionary of Modern American Usage. N.Y., Oxford Univ. Pr., 1944. 360p.

for quick location of equivalents, antonyms, and extended lists of contrasts.

Peter Roget (ro-*zhā*) (1779-1869), a London physician and secretary of the British Royal Society, had a conviction that words arranged "not in alphabetical order as they are in a dictionary, but according to the ideas which they express, would be more useful" than a dictionary. Accordingly he worked for nearly fifty years in the preparation of this standard and indispensable reference tool for writers and speakers.

The Roget classification scheme for words somewhat resembles the classification schemes for plants and animals. There are six broad categories dealing with abstract relations, space, matter, intellect, volition and affections, each class with numerous subdivisions under which words and their opposites are listed in parallel columns. An alphabetic index at the end aids in locating not only each particular word but also its synonyms and antonyms.

In general, the practiced writer tends to favor the *Thesaurus* over alphabetic arrangements of synonyms and antonyms chiefly because the comprehensive and thought-provoking content of the former more than compensates for the facility of reference of the latter. Nevertheless, Mawson, who has edited the latest edition of the *Thesaurus* and added to it American spelling, idioms, and obsolete words, has also edited a dictionary arrangement of Roget.

Abbreviations. Full as the lists of abbreviations are in all of the unabridged and many of the abridged dictionaries, there is still a need for a special source to cope with the increasing number of abbre-

---

❦ SYNONYMS

Webster's Dictionary of Synonyms. 1st ed. Springfield, Mass., Merriam, 1942. 907p.

Roget's International Thesaurus. New ed., rev. N.Y., Crowell, 1946. 1194p.

Mawson, C. O. S. Thesaurus of the English Language in Dictionary Form. Garden City, N.Y., Garden City, 1934. 600p.

❦ ABBREVIATIONS

Shankle, G. E. Current Abbreviations. N.Y., Wilson, 1945.

Stephenson, H. J. Abbrevs (Dictionary of Abbreviations). N.Y., Macmillan, 1943. 126p.

Allen, E. F. Dictionary of Abbreviations and Symbols. N.Y., Coward-McCann, 1946. 189p.

DICTIONARIES

viations found in every medium of communication. Shankle's *Current Abbreviations* is the most general, but each of the other two listed will prove of supplementary use. Examples of types of abbreviations in Shankle are names of government bureaus, administrative agencies, civil, political and religious organizations, Greek letter fraternities and sororities, college degrees, common musical and other well-known terms. Stephenson's *Abbrevs* is arranged topically: general, Bible, Shakespeare, legal, Christian names, geography, months and days, American railroads, chemical elements, foreign monetary units, federal agencies. Allen's *Dictionary of Abbreviations and Symbols* lists "over 6000 abbreviations and symbols commonly used in literature, science, art, education, business, politics, religion." The abbreviations are alphabetically arranged, but the symbols at the end are grouped under proofreading, mathematics, commerce, medicine, music, reference, religion, astronomy, meteorology, botany, pharmacy, and Roman numerals.

Slang, colloquialisms and dialect. Separate collections of slang and colloquialism range in scope from daily press and radio vocabulary to obscene terms prohibited for dissemination through the mail. Here national and regional collections are of importance.

The "unprintable" words are in Partridge's *Dictionary of Slang and Unconventional English.* They are not segregated, however, and the curious will have to hunt for them! The author commented thus on the content:

> I have given them all. (My rule, in the matter of unpleasant terms, has been to deal with them as briefly, as astringently, as aseptically as

---

☞ SLANG, COLLOQUIALISMS AND DIALECT

Partridge, Eric. A Dictionary of Slang and Unconventional English; Colloquialisms and Catch-Phrases, Solecisms and Catachreses, Nicknames, Vulgarisms and Such Americanisms As Have Been Naturalized. 3d ed., rev. and much enl. London, Routledge, 1949. 1230p.

Berrey, L. V., and Van den Bark, Melvin. American Thesaurus of Slang; a Complete Reference Book of Colloquial Speech. N.Y., Crowell, 1947. 1174p. $7.50.

Wentworth, Harold. American Dialect Dictionary. N.Y., Crowell, 1944. 747p. $6.

A Dictionary of Americanisms on Historical Principles; ed. by M. M. Mathews. Chicago, Univ. of Chicago Pr., 1951. 2v.

Supplementary English language sources

was consistent with clarity and adequacy; in a few instances, I had to force myself to overcome an instinctive repugnance; for these I ask the indulgence of my readers.)

Some 85 per cent of the vocabulary is devoted to slang, cant, colloquialism. Only ½ per cent represents vulgarisms. There are, besides, nicknames, catch phrases, solecisms. The arrangement is alphabetical, with a separate alphabet for the supplement of words added after the vocabulary was completed.

Berrey and Van den Bark's *American Thesaurus of Slang* is a classified vocabulary arranged by ideas for which a series of colloquialisms, slang, and vulgarisms are given. A good index complements the idea arrangement.

Sectional language variations in the United States are most strikingly revealed in the pronunciation of certain words by people from the South, from New England, from New York City, and from the Middle West. But there are also other differences among the regions in the use of expressions and words. These differences are described in Wentworth's *American Dialect Dictionary*, "primarily concerned with variations—vocabular, phrasal, semantic, philological and morphological—in the English language as spoken and written by natives of North America, and especially with those variations that are due to or coincident with geographical location." In all, some 15,000 terms and 60,000 quotations are included. Standard pronunciation is followed by variations in regions and states. Words like *creek* and *house* illustrate United States sectional pronunciation differences.

A Dictionary of Americanisms appeared in 1951. As used in this work "Americanism means a word or expression that originated in the United States," such as *appendicitis, hydrant, adobe, faculty*. The 50,000 entries, illustrated by quotations and drawings, aim to cover the history of the American language from the Jamestown settlement to publication date. Both words that originated in the United States and others that developed a special meaning in this country are included.

Pronunciation. Pronunciations provided in dictionaries often lag behind the influx of new and frequently imported words. To meet current needs special pronunciation tools that can be revised more frequently than unabridged dictionaries are available. Of the four representative titles listed, Greet's *World Words* and Bender's *NBC Handbook of Pronunciation* were produced for radio networks and were intended to aid broadcasters and listeners. Colby's *American Pro-*

DICTIONARIES

nouncing Dictionary and Kenyon's *Pronouncing Dictionary of American English* are broader in scope and purpose.

Rhymes. In a rhyming dictionary, alphabeting is by sound. Reference has already been made to the separate vocabulary of rhymes in *Webster's New Collegiate Dictionary*. There are also complete books devoted to rhymes for the assistance of the verse writer. The oldest of these is Walker's *Rhyming Dictionary,* first published in 1775 and reissued many times since. Words are "grouped not phonetically, but strictly alphabetically in accordance with the reversed spelling of the word." Somewhat different is the arrangement of Wood's *Complete Rhyming Dictionary,* which is based first on vowel sound, and is then alphabeted under the terminal sound of the word.

Foreign terms and comparative language. English speech and writing include many foreign words and phrases. Some of these can be found in standard English dictionaries. A great many other terms are included only in collections of international and foreign words. To

---

❦ PRONUNCIATION

Colby, F. O. American Pronouncing Dictionary of Troublesome Words. N.Y., Crowell, 1950. 379p.

Kenyon, J. S., and Knott, T. A. Pronouncing Dictionary of American English. Springfield, Mass., Merriam, 1944. 484p.

Greet, W. C. World Words; Recommended Pronunciations. 2d ed., rev. and enl. N.Y., Columbia Univ. Pr., 1948. 608p. $6.75.

Bender, J. F. NBC Handbook of Pronunciation. 2d ed. N.Y., Crowell, 1951. 372p.

❦ RHYMES

Walker, John. Rhyming Dictionary of the English Language . . . with an Index of Allowable Rhymes; rev. and enl. by Lawrence H. Dobson. N.Y., McKay, 1950. 549p.

Wood, Clement. Complete Rhyming Dictionary and Poet's Craft Book. Garden City, Halcyon House, 1947. $1.98.

❦ FOREIGN TERMS AND COMPARATIVE LANGUAGE

Duden Pictorial Encyclopedia; in Five Languages . . . Containing 30,000 Words Explained by Pictures. N.Y., Ungar, 1943. 2588p.

Mawson, C. O. S. Dictionary of Foreign Terms Found in English and American Writings of Yesterday and Today. N.Y., Crowell, 1934. 389p.

the traditional vocabulary of scholarship, World War II added a great many words acquired from nations where American troops were stationed. Sources for the foreign terms of scholarship, for words made popular by World War II, and for equivalents in the most frequently used occidental languages are many. For the first two purposes the American unabridged and largest abridged dictionaries will be supplemented by such special vocabularies as are included in such books as *Duden Pictorial Encyclopedia* and Mawson's *Dictionary of Foreign Terms*.

The *Duden Pictorial Encyclopedia* is really a polylingual dictionary of homonyms and synonyms in five languages—English, French, German, Italian, Spanish—which "represents pictorially more than 10,250 different expressions... taken from the vocabularies of various callings and from the language of every day life." In all some 30,000 words are explained by pictures. The work is based on the Duden picture vocabularies originally produced in Germany toward the end of the 1930's, and includes a picture along with the equivalent words and phrases in the five languages. Every item is keyed by number to its picture. High schools have found Duden especially valuable.

Mawson is bilingual and is keyed to give English equivalents only.

Foreign language dictionaries

Three types of foreign language dictionaries are most useful in American reference work: the standard dictionary, in the original language, most wanted by the scholar or the foreign-born reader; the bilingual dictionary, which gives the English equivalent for a foreign word or vice versa; the polylingual dictionary, which gives equivalents in three or more languages.

Based on class enrollments in American colleges and high schools the trend now seems to be toward a foreign language preference in the United States in approximately this order: (1) Spanish; (2) French; (3) Latin; (4) German; (5) Italian; (6) Russian; (7) Greek (classical); (8) Brazilian Portuguese. Many graduate schools, however, still adhere to a French and German doctoral requirement. The growing interest in Russian and the importance of the U.S.S.R. in international relations may result in placing that language much higher in the ranking. This rank factor as well as the presence of nationality groups in a community should influence foreign language dictionary selection for a reference room.

🕮 FOREIGN LANGUAGE DICTIONARIES

SPANISH

* Cuyas, Arturo. Appleton's New English-Spanish Spanish-English Dictionary. Rev. and enl. N.Y., Appleton-Century, 1940. 1135p. $7.
* Velázques de la Cadena, Mariano. A Dictionary of the Spanish and English Languages. Abridged ed. N.Y., Appleton-Century, 1943. 665p.

Academia Española. Diccionario de la lengua española. 16. ed. Madrid, Espasa-Calpe, 1939. 1334p.

FRENCH

* Mansion, J. E. Mansion's Shorter French and English Dictionary. Boston, Heath, 1947. 685 + 940p. $4.50.

Académie Française. Dictionnaire de l'Académie Française. 8. éd. Paris, Hachette, 1931-35. 2v.

LATIN

* Harper's Latin Dictionary; rev., enl., and in great part rewritten by Charlton Lewis and Charles Short. N.Y., American Book Co., 1907. 2019p.

GERMAN

* Breul, Karl. Heath's New German-English, English-German Dictionary; rev. and enl. by J. Heron Lepper and Rudolph Kottenhahn. Boston, Heath, 1936. 2v. $4.75.

Grimm, Joseph, and Grimm, Wilhelm. Deutsches Wörterbuch. Leipzig, Hirzel, 1845-1938. v.1-16 (in progress).

ITALIAN

* Hoare, Alfred. Short Italian Dictionary. N.Y., Macmillan, 1947. 421p.

RUSSIAN

* Segal, Louis. New Complete Russian-English Dictionary. N.Y., Hafner, 1948. 1016p.

GREEK

* Liddell, H. G., and Scott, Robert. Greek-English Lexicon. New ed., rev. and augmented throughout by Henry Stuart Jones. Oxford, Clarendon Pr., 1940. 10 parts. $35.

PORTUGUESE

* Richardson, E. L., and Sa Pereira, M. Modern Portuguese-English, English-Portuguese Dictionary. Philadelphia, McKay, 1943. 347p. $3.

Foreign language dictionaries

A selected list of foreign language dictionaries arranged by language is given on page 54. Bilingual dictionaries are starred. Additional titles can be found in the Library of Congress list in the Reading list below.[6]

Reading list

Eakin, M. K., and Brooks, A. R. "Picture Dictionaries," *Elementary School Journal,* January, 1949, v.49, p.260-61.

McMillan, J. B. "Five College Dictionaries," *College English,* January, 1949, v.10, p.214-21.

Starnes, D. T., and Noyes, Gertrude E. *The English Dictionary from Cawdrey to Johnson.* Chapel Hill, Univ. of North Carolina Pr., 1946. 299p.

Thorndike, E. L. "Improving Ability to Read," *Teachers College Record,* 1934, v.36, p.1-19, 123-44, 229-41.

U.S. Library of Congress. *Foreign Language–English Dictionaries; a Selected List,* comp. by Grace Hadley Fuller. Washington, 1942. 132p. Supplement, 1944.

G. and C. Merriam Company, Springfield, Massachusetts, supply libraries and library schools with helpful publications. Examples are the periodical *Word Study,* edited by Max J. Herzberg, which devotes articles to new words and changing language, and during early 1951 treated such subjects as "Today's Collegiate English," "Origin of the Term G.I.," and "English Books and Colonial Readers." The company also issues pamphlets, such as *The War and Language; a Symposium on the Possible Effects of World War II* and *Interesting Origins of English Words.*

Subscription Books Bulletin reviews of dictionaries and discussions of criteria for evaluating them are excellent readings. The October, 1934, issue deals with fundamental principles in dictionary evaluation.

---

[6] Also helpful is C. H. Handschin, "French, German, Spanish and Italian Service Dictionaries for Students and Teachers," *Modern Language Journal,* May, 1939, v.23, p.602-07.

chapter 3

ENCYCLOPEDIAS

Introduction, Comprehensive adult encyclopedias,

Popular encyclopedias, One-volume encyclopedias,

School encyclopedias, Foreign encyclopedias.

Introduction

Background questions. Studies examined in Chapter 1 indicated an extraordinary reliance on encyclopedias in reference rooms for answering questions. In elementary school libraries, Helen Carpenter found that of 510 questions answered by reference materials no less than 290 were satisfied by encyclopedias. The Chait, Cole, and Van Hoesen studies[1] indicated a comparable heavy referral to encyclopedias of public library inquiries. Reference librarians in undergraduate college reference rooms will attest that students frequently begin with encyclopedias when embarking on term papers and reports. All of which points to the universality in general reference rooms of the so-called background question.

The background question is usually phrased by the inquirer in one of the following ways: "I want something on, or something about, or general information on, or all about. . . ." Subjects like these are typical: communism in China; Carrie Nation; television; how shoes are made; United States housing; socialized medicine; status of children in Elizabethan England; heavy water; flood control; Pestalozzi's

Introduction

influence on American education. Background questions are also illustrated by some of these actual inquiries made in American libraries in recent years: "I need material for a paper on the great depression." "Can you help me find out something about real estate deeds?" "Do you have anything that will help me contrast David Livingstone's and Cecil Rhodes' motives and treatment of natives in Africa?" "I want to trace the history of taxation from the pre-Christian period to the present."

All of these questions have two elements in common: they require background information basically and separate facts only incidentally; and they suggest a summary source prepared for the layman. Although other tools will yield results, and perhaps ultimately more satisfying answers, none is so suited for a beginning as the basic background source—the encyclopedia.

Background sources. An encyclopedia may be defined as a systematic summary of all the information significant to mankind. The *A.L.A. Glossary of Library Terms* offers this definition: "A work containing informational articles on subjects in every field of knowledge, usually arranged in alphabetical order, or a similar work limited to a special field or subject." Sometimes the latter is called a cyclopedia.

In this chapter, encyclopedias are considered in five groups: (1) comprehensive adult, (2) popular adult, (3) adult one-volume, (4) school—alphabetical and classified, and (5) foreign. Subject cyclopedias are treated in later chapters.

Despite the fact that nearly everyone has used encyclopedias at one time or another, these reference books are not as fully understood as efficient use requires. Misunderstandings arise partly from failure to distinguish between the two basic methods of encyclopedia construction. One type is organized into long articles, and the smaller topics within these general subjects must be located by using an index; the other type contains many more articles under smaller topics, and uses cross references to guide the reader to related subjects. Statistically this principle can be illustrated through the *Encyclopaedia Britannica*, a long article work. That encyclopedia has only 40,000 separate articles in the alphabetic sequence that makes up its first 23 volumes. But the index in its 24th volume reveals treatment of some 500,000 subjects. The chances, therefore, of locating a small subject in the *Britannica* without consulting the index are no better than 2 in 25!

---

[1] See *Reading list*, Chapter 1.

ENCYCLOPEDIAS

Other qualities about encyclopedias are important to reference librarians, and these will be considered against the background of the evolution of modern encyclopedias.

Encyclopedia history. Today's encyclopedia has a long and distinguished past. Since the beginning of writing, one of man's stronger impulses seems to have been to record everything he knew for the information of his contemporaries and for posterity.

The earliest records taken together form a kind of encyclopedia, the "circle of knowledge" of the ancients. In the complete works of Plato or Aristotle there is such a systematic summary, concerned as both of them were with the epistemological question, "What do we know?" But it is important to remember that these early encyclopedias were intended for only the select few, the scholars, the peers of Aristotle and Plato. This was also true of Pliny's *Natural History,* often cited as the first encyclopedia because of its method of compilation. Although not a naturalist himself, Pliny meticulously analyzed some 2000 ancient books by a hundred different authors and compiled a classified encyclopedia in 37 books consisting of 2493 chapters. The 20,000 claimed facts were grouped under such broad headings as cosmography, astronomy and meteorology, geography, zoology, botany, medicine, magic, and fine arts.

The Middle Ages produced several encyclopedic works of note, for the most part systematic summaries of man's knowledge for scholars. There was the work of the Dominican Friar, Vincent of Beauvais, about 1260 A.D., which resulted in an encyclopedia arranged topically under three heads—history, natural and physical sciences, moral sciences. There was the poetry of the African Capella that became an allegorical encyclopedia bounded by the then Seven Liberal Arts. The first English encyclopedia is supposed to have been Caxton's translation of *Image du monde,* about 1460. In 1541 *Night Studies, or the Most Complete Circle of Education* was produced by Ringelberg of Basel. It was supposed to have been the first to use the term *encyclopedia* and contained in its title a suggestion of the self-education function.

Three seventeenth century encyclopedists of note were Johann Heinrich Alsted, Pierre Bayle and Louis Moreri. Alsted's *Encyclopaedia septem tomis distincta* (1630) was probably the first to give major attention to arrangement. The material was classified under seven heads and treated topically in 35 books. Bayle and Moreri engaged in a curious rivalry. When Moreri issued in 1674 *Le Grande*

Introduction

dictionnaire historique Bayle followed with his *Dictionnaire historique et critique* (1697) designed to be a dictionary correcting the errors and omissions in Moreri; to this Moreri responded by incorporating Bayle's corrections and additions in his revision.

But it was the eighteenth century that saw the encyclopedia come into its own. Beginning in 1701, Vincenzo Maria Coronelli, a Franciscan friar, issued in Italian what is supposed to have been the first alphabetical encyclopedia, *Biblioteca universale sacraprofana.* Only seven volumes (A-Caque) were published. In that century also Voltaire's *Philosophical Dictionary,* alphabetically arranged and by no means restricted to pure philosophy, appeared. There one will find in the "B's" an astute observation on the place of books in life, and under "D" two reviews of contemporary dictionaries, one a scathing denunciation of an inferior work and the other some reflections of an academician on the French Academy's dictionary.

Of more significance to encyclopedia history, however, were two English ventures of the eighteenth century. In 1704 a London clergyman named John Harris published what was probably the first English alphabetical encyclopedia. He called it *Lexicon technicum, or an Universal English Dictionary of Arts and Sciences.* A quarter of a century later, Ephraim Chambers, probably the first great English encyclopedist, published in two volumes his *Cyclopaedia* (1728), with the alternate title, "An universal dictionary of arts and sciences, containing an explication of the terms and an account of the things signified thereby in the several arts, liberal and mechanical, and the several sciences, human and divine." He endeavored to connect the scattered articles relating to one subject by a system of cross references and to consider "the several matters not only in themselves, but relatively or as they respect each other; both to treat them as so many wholes and as so many parts of some greater whole."

The French Encyclopédie. It was this Chambers' *Cyclopaedia,* translated into French by John Mills, an English resident in France, that led to the great French *Encyclopédie.* When the French publishers in a subsequent issue of Chambers' demanded more changes than the translator would agree to, the editorship was turned over first to Jean Paul de Gua de Malves and then to Denis Diderot.

Between 1751 and 1772 Diderot and his staff of 21 contributors, which included such luminaries as Voltaire, Rousseau, Condillac, D'Alembert, Montesquieu, Turgot, D'Anville, D'Holbach, Marmontel and Euler, prepared 28 volumes of a completely new encyclopedia.

This set was followed by a five-volume supplement in 1776-77 and a two-volume analytical index in 1780.

The stormy three decades of the Encyclopedists' efforts illustrate some of the major problems of encyclopedia making today. Multiple authorship troubled editor Diderot almost from the start. In his first burst of enthusiasm he had called for all of the contributions to be ready in three months. Only Rousseau's article on music made that deadline. Moreover, the articles were uneven in quality.

Almost from the beginning the Encyclopedists became involved in controversial issues. Diderot himself was thrown into jail. In these pre-Revolutionary times all publications were suspected of political implications. Upon the appearance of the first two volumes the work was suppressed as injurious to the King's authority and religion. The Jesuits then tried to continue the work, but on the completion of eight volumes, in 1757, objection to the *Encyclopédie* became so insistent that it was again suspended. Weary of this spasmodic censorship D'Alembert retired in 1759. The following year Diderot was warned that the authorities intended to search his quarters and seize his manuscripts. A compromise was finally effected under which no part of the set would be distributed before the whole was completed.

By 1765, nearly 10,000 pages of text were done and 4250 persons had subscribed. Finished volumes were then distributed secretly in Paris and Versailles, with the inevitable consequence—discovery by the authorities, imprisonment of the printer in the Bastille and confiscation of the distributed sets. A story that Madame de Pompadour rescued the set from oblivion is probably inaccurate. Rescued it was, however, but not produced without one last incident.

The printer, having spent eight uncomfortable days in the Bastille, took it upon himself to edit out of the corrected proof such passages as he thought might offend the authorities. When Diderot discovered these changes he was furious and insisted that his own copy in St. Petersburg be brought to Paris. In this way the great French *Encyclopédie,* with its propaganda, uneven articles, and remarkable list of contributors was completed.

To Chambers and Diderot must be added the name of Zedler whose 64-volume *Universal Lexicon* appeared serially from 1732 to 1750. A staff of nine editors, each responsible for a group of subjects, shared editorial responsibility. In these three encyclopedias are found two of the major features of modern encyclopedia making: distribution of editorial responsibility and attention to arrangement.

Introduction

Modern encyclopedias. The first edition of the *Encyclopaedia Britannica* appeared serially, 1768-71. Here for the first time history and biography, omitted from the French *Encyclopédie,* were systematically treated. Subsequent editions through the fourteenth contributed significantly to the evolution of the modern encyclopedia.

In the United States, two adult sets of nineteenth century origin markedly influenced encyclopedia editing. One of these, the *Encyclopedia Americana,* was first published in Philadelphia in 1829 in 16 volumes. It brought American interests into the circle of knowledge early in our separate national history. The other, the *New International Encyclopaedia,* partly based on the English *Cyclopaedia* of Chambers, ushered in with its appearance in 1884 the era of journalistic style in encyclopedia writing. For the first time it was recognized that a scholarly article by an authority could be made more readable if rewritten by one talented in communicating with the lay mind.

School encyclopedias. What was probably the first American school encyclopedia was published in 1893 under the title *Student's Cyclopedia.* In England John Newbery and his successors had previously issued *The Circle of the Sciences* in seven volumes (1745-70), "a compendious library, whereby each branch of polite learning is rendered extremely easy and instructive." Several other sets, including the English serial *Book of Knowledge,* were issued before 1893, but none of these quite approached the modern conception of an encyclopedia. After the First World War the school encyclopedias, notably *Compton's* and *World Book,* undertook some advanced experimentation in terms of readers' needs. A clear break was made with the principle that an encyclopedia should contain the body of knowledge necessary to the learning of the medieval scholar. Instead, taking a cue from educational research, systematic and scientific investigation of reader interest was begun and space allotted accordingly. In every way encyclopedia material was humanized and related to the profound postwar social changes. The *New International's* innovation of combining authority and readability was developed to an unusual extent in the school encyclopedias and considerable attention was devoted to making material more available through improved format and mechanical arrangement. So far-reaching has been the influence of the school encyclopedia that certain criteria for evaluating all encyclopedias have had to be restudied in the light of their innovations.

Subscription book publishing. In the quarter of a century between the two world wars encyclopedia making in the United States has definitely associated itself with what is known as subscription book publishing, which is not to be confused with trade or textbook publishing. The greatest volume of trade book publications is sold through the trade, which means the bookstores. By far the greatest volume of textbooks is sold through state and local school adoptions. The greatest volume of subscription books is sold by the publisher's representative direct to the home. Although a few encyclopedias are sold through bookstores or school adoptions, it is safe to say that over 90 per cent of all encyclopedias sold in the United States are sold direct from the publisher to the consumer.

This direct method of distribution is an important fact for an understanding of today's encyclopedia. Out of this fact have developed many of the innovations found in our new encyclopedias. From this fact alone stems the whole series of distribution problems peculiar to house-to-house sales. Because of this fact the reference librarian needs a background of understanding somewhat different from that which he has gained in preparation for the selection of trade books.

By the end of the first decade after the First World War the *American Book Trade Directory* listed no fewer than 162 subscription book publishers. All of these publishers had representatives in the little towns and big cities offering sets of books, mostly encyclopedias, to the householders of America. Many of these sets had reference value and represented good book quality. But many others were spurious, antiquated, highly overpriced. In the hands of adroit salesmen, even the poorest products took on an irresistible glamor in the eyes of the uninitiated. It was not long, therefore, until community librarians were appealed to by an ever increasing number of disillusioned purchasers for protection from misrepresentation.

From the start librarians had the support of some subscription book publishers in their efforts to protect the consumer. In 1924, four years before the librarians took any national action, 31 subscription book publishers met with John F. Nugent of the Federal Trade Commission in Washington to draw up 14 resolutions condemning unfair trade practices in subscription book selling. In Massachusetts, the state library association, and in the northwestern United States, the regional library association, began publishing subscription book review periodicals. Two years later the American Library Association appointed a committee to study the problem of subscription book appraisal and out of this committee's recommendations, made in 1928, were born the Subscription Books Committee and the *Subscription*

Introduction

Books Bulletin, the first issue of which appeared in January, 1930.

In 1931 a joint meeting of librarians and publishers was held in New Haven under the sponsorship of the Subscription Book Publishers of the National Association of Book Publishers. The stated purpose of the meeting was to formulate a code of practice for the publication and sale of subscription books. That purpose was only partially fulfilled. Thirteen of 25 articles of faith originally proposed were agreed on; 12 were held in abeyance. Two years later another code with 18 headings was agreed on. When the New Deal's NRA came along, the 18 principles were codified into 24 rules of trade practice, which lasted barely a year, until the NRA itself was invalidated by the Supreme Court.

Not discouraged, the Federal Trade Commission and the subscription book publishers tried again in 1940. After a preliminary conference in New York and a subsequent hearing in Washington, a set of 21 trade practice rules for the subscription and mail order book publishing industry was produced as the Code of Fair Trade Practices. Every reference librarian should have an understanding of what some of the unfair trade practices are and how they are likely to affect citizens in his community. Sooner or later the library will be appealed to for guidance. Such guidance should be positive. Subscription book publishing is an ancient and honorable profession and the representative of the legitimate publisher is entitled to a fair hearing in the community. The American Library Association by council resolution in 1951 went on record as supporting such community consideration of subscription book publishers. Their contribution to reading in the home has been considerable and through proper library co-operation can be a force for good. Proper library co-operation means informing the public of the good reference sets as well as cautioning them against the inferior ones.

By keeping up with the *Subscription Books Bulletin* and other review sources, and by using and examining the sets themselves, the reference librarian will be in a better position to offer sound professional advice to the community. Sets are changed constantly. If they are not, time changes them for the worse. A set which was formerly inferior may be sufficiently revised and improved to warrant favorable consideration. Another set which formerly ranked high may deteriorate. There can be no question about the librarian's responsibility to keep abreast of developments in the contents of reference sets.

There is some disagreement, however, on whether the librarian should consider trade practices at all. Some publishers believe that sales methods have nothing to do with the quality of the product. These same publishers believe sales methods are outside librarians' competence and should be appraised by a qualified agency like the Federal Trade Commission or the subscription book publishers themselves.

With that point of view few librarians will agree. Librarians are, for the most part, public servants. Their professional ethics require them to inform the book consumer, not alone about book preparation but about book distribution as well.

In the librarian's thinking there is a difference between good salesmanship, which earns a hearing for a good product, and objectionable sales practices, which include misrepresentation. Some examples of trade practices which are generally considered unfair to consumer and competitor are—

"Marked up" contracts. This takes one of several forms—a "give-away" plan, where the supposedly reduced price is offered in return for an indorsement; an exaggerated price for annuals, supplements, consultations or other services, which more than compensates for the reduced price on the set. (This should not be confused with a combination offer which is considered legitimate if each of the items in the combination has a standard price and a reduction is offered if all or several of the items are purchased.)

Falsifying a competitor.

Exaggerated revision claims. Declaring a work is new, or completely or largely revised, when this is not true.

Name confusion. Using a term such as "University," "Foundation" or something similar in a firm's name to suggest a non-profit organization.

Limited period offer. Threatening that price will go up after a certain time when such is not the case.

School prescribed. Misrepresentation to parents that a publication is "prescribed by a school as a textbook."

Bribery. Payment to a school official for use of his influence.

Fifteen for one plan. Promising a free set to a school if fifteen sets are purchased in the community.

After the Second World War, six subscription book publishers organized as the Reference Division of the American Institute of Textbook Publishers. They were: Encyclopaedia Britannica, Chicago; P. F.

Introduction

Collier and Sons, New York; F. E. Compton and Company, Chicago; Grolier Society, New York; W. F. Quarrie and Company (now Field Enterprises), Chicago; and United Educators, Chicago. Other subscription book publishers and trade book publishers of reference books have joined the Institute. At A.L.A. midwinter and annual meetings members of this group and other subscription book publishers have met with the Subscription Books Committee in a series of programs aimed to develop mutual understanding in the field of subscription book publishing.

Evaluation of encyclopedias. At one of the meetings the author of this book presented a set of criteria for evaluating encyclopedias based upon an analysis of encyclopedia reviews in the *Subscription Books Bulletin* from 1930 to 1948. With the help of encyclopedia editors and librarians the following evaluation checklist for encyclopedias was compiled:

I. Authority
   1. Publisher. Reputation; other publications; resources; distributors
   2. Editors. Reputation; experience; education; other works; known point of view
   3. Contributors. Reputation; experience; education; other works; known point of view
   4. Genealogy. If based on previous work, titles and history; reset or printed from old plates
   5. Reviews. Criticism by experts
II. Scope
   6. Purpose. Preface vs. content
   7. Plan. Evenness of articles; extent of editorial supervision
   8. Range. Completeness of coverage; limitations by subject, class of readers; emphasis on fact-finding or reading for self-improvement
   9. Selection. Scholar's "circle of knowledge" vs. popular or school interests
   10. Balance. Ancient vs. modern; science vs. humanities; American vs. British; other
   11. Comparative. Relation to works in various subject fields
III. Arrangement
   12. Organization. Alphabetic large subject; alphabetic small topic; classified; other
   13. Index. Analytical alphabetic; fact; classified; other
   14. Study guide. Classified; alphabetic subject

15. Cross references. See; see also
16. Alphabeting. Consistency
17. Devices. Whole-letter volume; running heads; other

IV. Treatment
18. Style. Scholarly; popular (check unknown subject for readability)
19. Objectivity. On controversial subjects (check Reformation, Civil War, New Deal)
20. Accuracy. Statistics; facts; names; places (check home town or known subject)

V. Format
21. Binding. Fabrikoid; buckram; leather; other
22. Paper. Opaque; calendered; machine-coated; other
23. Type. Size; style; legibility
24. Page make-up. Margin width; general attractiveness
25. Illustrations. Kinds (line, halftone, color); quality; relation to text
26. Maps. Kinds; quality; location; adequacy; indexing

VI. Special features
27. Bibliographies. Relation to text; accessibility of titles; citation form
28. Revision. Continuous or periodical; yearbook; loose-leaf insertion; supplementary service; other
29. Reader service. Questions answered
30. Other. Teacher aids; periodical service

Of first importance in evaluating an encyclopedia is authority. Five checks are suggested in the preceding list. These include investigations of the reputations of publishers, editors, and contributors, and attention to genealogy and reviews. Spurious sets have a habit of changing names. Trade practices now require that previous copyrights be indicated. Some reviews are more helpful than others; those in *Subscription Books Bulletin* are usually most informative.

Equally important is scope. Comparison of the prefatory statement of purpose with actual content reveals the degree to which the publishers have realized their aims. Examination of the articles themselves indicates the extent of editorial supervision. Most encyclopedias try to serve both quick, fact-finding needs and slower, self-education requirements. Sometimes failure is evident in one or the other aim. The conflict between the scholar's "circle of knowledge" and the layman's or child's popular interests has been indicated. Balance as between

Introduction

modern and ancient, science and humanities, American and British subjects may be determined by use of checkpoints six to nine in the preceding list.

There are two basic encyclopedia arrangements—alphabetic and classified. In the former arrangement two patterns are evident.[2] Some encyclopedias present a great many short articles covering small topics. In these encyclopedias many cross references and sometimes classified indexes or readers' guides serve to relate and synthesize parts into whole subjects. Other encyclopedias favor longer articles which make their own syntheses of smaller topics. In such cases an analytic index is a necessity.

In evaluating treatment, three checks are suggested. The first is reading an article on an unfamiliar subject. If the encyclopedia gives some understanding and a clearer concept of the subject, then it has passed a readability test. Second is the reading of an article on a controversial subject—the Reformation, the United States Civil War, the New Deal. Does the article fairly present both sides? If it does, then the encyclopedia has passed an objectivity test. Third is the reading of an article on a familiar subject—a favorite sport, one's home town. If the facts are as accurate as one's knowledge indicates they should be, then the encyclopedia has passed an accuracy test.

Encyclopedia format is increasingly replacing somberness with color. The school encyclopedias have been in the vanguard, but more recently adult sets have appeared with colorful bindings and illustrations reproduced on text pages by the newer methods. This is possible only by the use of a calendered or other specially prepared stock throughout, and the paper of any set which includes illustrations on the text page should be carefully examined for absence of glare as well as for opacity.

Maps may be placed all together to form an atlas, as in the *Encyclopaedia Britannica,* or may be scattered through the text. The former plan, especially if it calls for sharing a volume with the general index, makes both index and maps less accessible, since the volume can be used by only one patron at a time. The latter plan calls for duplication of maps. For example, Rumania will appear on a map with the article on that country, on the Balkans, on Europe, and in part on maps relating to articles on contiguous countries and component or historically connected regions like Moldavia, Wallachia, Bessarabia. These

---

[2] *See also* page 57.

duplicate maps, which may be line drawings, are an asset because of their proximity to the discussion.

In brief, six quick checks on format can be made by the reference librarian. First, is the binding attractive and durable? Has it been treated for insect resistance? Second, is the paper opaque enough to prevent type from showing through to the other side of the page and is it able to carry halftone photographs as well as line drawings and text? Third, is the type large and clear enough to be easy to read? Fourth, does the page invite or discourage reading, and are the margins wide enough to permit rebinding? Fifth, are the illustrations real support for the text both because of placement and because of choice and quality? Sixth, are the maps clear, related to the text, indexed, and up to date?

Among special features, bibliographies top the list. They should be keyed to the encyclopedia material, should pick up the reader at the point where the articles leave off, and carry him forward progressively. Titles listed should be accessible, if not in a bookstore at least through America's public library system.

The process of keeping an encyclopedia up to date is a problem which librarians and publishers have never satisfactorily solved. A million-dollar set is printed today; tomorrow a discovery or invention renders a considerable part of the text antiquated. To cope with this problem encyclopedia editors have adopted one or more of the following devices:

1. *The supplement,* usually a quarterly pamphlet service, has proved unsatisfactory because of the number of alphabets one soon has to consult (of these, *World Topics Quarterly* issued by United Educators is distinctive, and easily the best).

2. *The loose-leaf insertion,* used by medical and legal reference tools, and by *Nelson's Encyclopedia,* is expensive because of the binders, and impractical because of the procrastination of the user, who delays removing the old pages until there is a great accumulation of new ones.

3. *The yearbook* is favored by several reputable American encyclopedias. Of the major American sets, *Americana, Britannica, Collier's* and *World Book* all issue annual supplements. These are described in Chapter 4.

In addition to the above supplementary devices, provision is also made for the encyclopedia itself to undergo revision editorially according to one of two plans:

Comprehensive adult encyclopedias

1. Periodical revision. Under this plan, plates are completely scrapped and the entire encyclopedia reset. Because of the expense no publisher can afford to do this oftener than once every ten to twenty-five years.

2. Continuous revision. Under this plan some changes are made in each successive printing. Generally, encyclopedia publishers issue a new printing every year. A permanent editorial staff systematically revises the changing content in articles which cover continents, countries, cities and states, science, technology, and numerous other subjects. In addition, the school encyclopedia's continuous revision must take into account frequent school curriculum revisions.

Among services offered by some encyclopedia publishers is a readers' reference bureau which undertakes to answer questions not found in the encyclopedia. Teachers' aids and self-improvement syllabi are other special services.

Comprehensive adult encyclopedias

Encyclopaedia Britannica. The oldest of the modern English language encyclopedias, the *Encyclopaedia Britannica,* was first printed in Edinburgh, Scotland, by "A Society of Gentlemen" consisting of three printers, one of whom, William Smellie, was a scholar of note and a fellow of the Royal Society. The first of one hundred weekly "numbers" that eventually comprised the first edition was released in 1768, and the entire three-volume first edition was completed in 1771. Succeeding numbered editions were issued through the eighteenth and nineteenth centuries by British companies. Since 1902 the *Britannica* has been American-owned and American-published, although there continues to be a British subsidiary company and an auxiliary editorial office in London.

The *Britannica* was purchased in 1920 by Sears, Roebuck and Company, then headed by the philanthropist, Julius Rosenwald. Under Sears sponsorship, the 29-volume eleventh edition of 1911 was combined with supplementary volumes and issued as the twelfth and thirteenth editions. Then in 1927 Rosenwald suggested that, should the University of Chicago become the American publisher of a new edition, he would advance one million dollars to be expended in making a new fourteenth edition. The trustees of the university at first declined to accept the responsibility of publishing the work and the fourteenth edition (a complete revision) was published under a financial arrangement with Sears, Roebuck. In 1943 William Benton, then a vice-president of the University of Chicago, again brought up the matter of *Britannica's* affiliation with that institution. General Robert E. Wood of Sears offered the *Britannica* to the university, but once more the trustees were reluctant to use university funds for the venture. Benton accordingly advanced personal funds, in an amount said to be $100,000, under an arrangement giving him ownership of the common stock and the titles of publisher and chairman of the board of Encyclopaedia Britannica, Incorporated. The University of Chicago retains the preferred stock. According to Robert M. Hutchins, chairman of *Britannica's* board of editors and formerly chancellor of the University of Chicago, the university has received about one million dollars from this arrangement.

The fourteenth is the last edition to be published under the plan of periodical revision. In 1932 it was announced that the *Britannica* would be kept up to date by continuous revision, a plan which has resulted in 18 new printings of the *Britannica* in the last ten years. The publishers claim that from 1936 through 1947 the continuous revision policy has entailed the handling of 39,181 articles, all either revised or completely new. During the same period 3072 new pictures were added to the set. For the 1948 printing alone, the publishers say, more than 2,300,000 words were changed, affecting a total of 2151 articles, and 300 pictures were added. From 1946 to 1950, 434 new articles were added and 15,233 revised. To explain how these revisions are planned the following publisher's statement is quoted.

> All articles in the Encyclopaedia Britannica are divided into 30 major classifications (e.g., history, engineering, biography, industry) and while any article in any classification is subject to revision at any time, all 30 major classifications, and every article in each classification, are carefully scrutinized, revised or completely rewritten in accordance with a definite time table. Each article in the set, under this plan, is considered for revision at least twice every ten years.

☛ COMPREHENSIVE ADULT ENCYCLOPEDIAS

Encyclopaedia Britannica; a New Survey of Universal Knowledge. Chicago, Encyclopaedia Britannica, 1948. 24v.

Encyclopedia Americana. N.Y., Americana, 1948. 30v.

Collier's Encyclopedia. N.Y., Collier, 1949-50. 20v.

New International Encyclopedia. 2d ed. N.Y., Dodd, Mead, 1930. 25v.

Comprehensive adult encyclopedias

The *Encyclopaedia Britannica* is published with the editorial advice of the faculties of the University of Chicago, and there are also "additional consultants and advisers" including notables such as John Dewey, Roscoe Pound, Deems Taylor, and Julian Huxley. The *Britannica's* list of contributors numbers over 4000, including some 30 Nobel Prize winners. A tribute to the lasting quality of some of the older contributions is the fact that they have required little or no revision even though their authors are now dead. Examples are Sigmund Freud's article on psychoanalysis; Henry Ford's on mass production; Trotsky's biography of Lenin; Chesterton's life of Dickens; Charles Evans Hughes' article on the Monroe Doctrine. Other notable contributions are: Harold C. Urey—heavy hydrogen; William Rose Bénet—Dreiser, Edgar Lee Masters; Vannevar Bush—harmonic analysis; H. L. Mencken—slang; Raymond Massey—acting; Orville Wright—biography of Wilbur Wright; T. E. Lawrence—guerrilla; Baron Robert Baden-Powell—Boy Scouts; Arthur H. Compton—Compton effect; James H. Breasted—Tutenkhamon; Edouard Herriot—Danton; Julian Huxley—evolution; Albert Einstein—space-time; Sir James Jeans—relativity; Christopher Morley—O. Henry; Gen. John J. Pershing—United States (in part); Max Reinhardt—theater.

From the first edition, when it was advertised as a "compendium of human knowledge," to the present, *Britannica* has tended to favor rather lengthy and discursive articles. Thus, the reader will not find a separate entry on Milton's *Samson Agonistes* nor on Quebracho, the wood whose extract is used in tanning. But if he will turn to the index first he will find references to the articles on English literature and on John Milton under *Samson Agonistes.* Similarly, he will find two references to Quebracho in the article on Argentina. One further example to illustrate the importance of the index: The article on Nietzsche is less than two pages in length, but the index reveals no less than 10,000 words on him in various places in the encyclopedia.

Encyclopaedia Britannica's main index contains 400,000 references to words and concepts treated in the text. A separate index contains 100,000 references to topographical and geographical place names treated in the atlas which shares volume 24 with the two indexes. In addition to the 224 pages of political and physical maps, all in full color, in volume 24, there are hundreds of smaller maps scattered throughout the other 23 volumes, accompanying the articles they illustrate.

Owners and users of the *Encyclopaedia Britannica* may be kept up to date on new information by two principal devices: the annual *Britannica Book of the Year* and the Library Research Service. The latter provides any purchaser of a new set of the *Britannica* with fifty coupons, each of which is valid for a research report on any reasonable question. The *Britannica Book of the Year* is an annual synopsis of the preceding year's principal events. It is about 1,000,000 words in length, compiled in an alphabeted, topical arrangement suggesting major topics in the *Britannica* itself. This annual volume is available for ten successive years to new owners of the *Encyclopaedia Britannica* at about one fourth of the price to nonowners.

Also intended to make the set more useful to owners are 28 reading guides available at the time of purchase. These cover topics as broad as "Interior Decorating," "American History," "Mathematics," and list all the entries pertinent to each topic.

Encyclopaedia Britannica's style is scholarly and at times ponderous. Lucy O'Brien in her newspaper column, "Woman's World," has observed that the average American reader would find the article on Easter difficult to understand. A considerable number of other articles would be somewhat advanced for the ambitious adult who undertakes to educate himself; the college-educated user, however, might find these same articles challenging.

Britannica meets most format requirements exceedingly well. Page make-up is conservative when compared with that of the *Britannica Book of the Year*. Halftone and color illustrations are handled as inserts, but the selection and variety are good. As mentioned earlier, the maps are in the last volume. In the 1950 edition, Rand McNally *Cosmopolitan World Atlas* maps have replaced the Hammond maps except for those of the United States and Canada.

The general excellence of the *Britannica* is apparent. Unchallenged authority, comprehensive scope, a tremendous index, objectivity to a high degree, and a policy of careful and continuous editing combine to give the *Britannica* that eminence it has so well deserved for longer than any other encyclopedia set. Not without reason, *Britannica* and *encyclopedia* have come to be synonymous in the minds of the English-speaking people.

Encyclopedia Americana. The *Americana* was first published in Philadelphia in 1829. Its 16 volumes were edited by Francis Lieber, a scholar and writer, who enlisted the assistance and enthusiasm of such contributors as Edward Wigglesworth of the Boston Athenaeum, descendant of the famous Michael Wigglesworth, Puritan pastor,

Comprehensive adult encyclopedias

physician and poet; Robert Walsh of Maryland, who wrote the American biographies; and Thomas Gamaliel Bradford, an assistant editor, considered the best American geographer of the time. A reprint appeared in 1837, and in 1848 a supplementary volume was added. Other reprints followed after 1848; the exact number is not definitely known.

The first *Americana* published in the twentieth century was the 16-volume 1903-04 edition, edited by Frederick Converse Beach, then editor of the *Scientific American,* and George Edwin Rines. The editorial relationship with the *Scientific American* no doubt influenced its special excellence in the field of science. From 1918 to 1920 the entire work was revised, reset, and published in 30 volumes with Rines as editor. Since that time a program of continuous revision has been followed, and the publishers claim that since 1938, when an accelerated editorial program was adopted, more than two thirds of the entire set has been revised and reset. According to the publisher the 1950 printing added to the previous issue 1525 new articles, 2757 new pages, not including those in the revised index volumes, and 650 new illustrations. This is evidence of the scope of the continuous revision program which the *Americana* has followed.

The sets distributed to schools and libraries are bound in good quality binder's board, and in red and blue library buckram. The text paper has high opacity and is free from fatiguing glare. Illustrations are printed on coated stock. Type is set in narrow columns designed for easy reading. Volumes are marked by whole words stamped on the backstrips.

In 1943 the *Americana,* despite the fact that it tends to be a short-topic encyclopedia, introduced a dictionary index. Its specially trained staff of 40 indexers, directed by a staff of six regular editors, worked for two years to develop 250,000 entries in a 700-page volume which is revised continuously along with the text.

Among the *Americana's* special features the following are notable: (1) biography, especially of many contemporaries; (2) a unique method of giving the complete history of a century under the name of the century (e.g., Sixth or Seventeenth); (3) outlines at the beginning of articles on the larger countries; (4) digests of the great operas, masterpieces of world literature, and lists of literary allusions and personalities; (5) pictures of flags and seals in the 48 articles on the states. To these must be added an outstanding article on the Union of Soviet Socialist Republics subsequently issued as a separate volume by the Cornell University Press, and articles of comparable quality on other nations of the world, notably France, Great Britain, Italy, Argentina, Indonesia and Bolivia.

Without sacrifice of scholarship, the *Americana* has succeeded in developing a high degree of readability. Frequent subheads aid the fact-finder as well as the self-study reader.

Mr. H. L. Mencken considers the *Americana* "the most useful encyclopedia in English on the market." Whether the reader agrees with Mr. Mencken or not, he comes to feel after long use that the *Americana* is especially well balanced from the standpoint of the American people's needs.

Collier's Encyclopedia. In 1946 the Crowell-Collier Publishing Company, publishers of the three mass media, *Collier's, Woman's Home Companion* and *American Magazine,* launched a major encyclopedia project. Under the editorial direction of a board of editors that included a library consultant[3] and some 80 subject specialists, nearly 2000 scholars were enlisted to write some 14 million words. By November, 1951, the twentieth and last volume was on the press.

As the volumes began to appear it was evident that several innovations had been introduced into adult encyclopedia making. First of these was the concept of scope. Deliberately, the editors sought to determine a new balance of subjects—one based not on the scholar's "circle of knowledge" but rather upon the layman's everyday subject interests.

The second innovation was the visual emphasis. In order to place half tones and color as well as line drawings near the related text a special paper was used throughout. Among adult encyclopedias, *Collier's* most nearly approaches the school encyclopedia in quantity and quality of illustrations.

Third was the special attention to maps. With Rand McNally, the Collier editorial staff developed a series of maps that would adequately represent the air age and the strategic regions and points displayed to the world by war and postwar developments. Out of this collaboration came such specifics as a single map for the whole of the U.S.S.R., regional maps for the top of the world, the Persian Gulf, and the Pacific, and inclusion of individual places in all of the continents made famous for the first time by the millions who served in the armed forces of the United Nations.

Fourth was the construction of a graded bibliography, placed all together in the last volume, keyed to the encyclopedia articles and intended to be a self-education aid. Titles were selected by a staff of library readers' advisers under the direction of Robert Kingery of the New York Public Library. Readability, accessibility in bookstores and libraries as well as authority guided the bibliographers in their choice of titles.

According to the publisher, the cost of producing the encyclopedia exceeded two and a half million dollars. The format features distinctive black binding, red trim and gold letters, machine-coated paper, brilliant color illustrations, good black-and-white illustrations, and effective maps placed near related text. An index of 400,000 entries analyzes text, illustrations and bibliographies.

Collier's Encyclopedia is especially strong in modern subjects. There are nearly one hundred pages on various phases of aeronautics in the first volume alone. The article on ballet exemplifies the high degree of co-ordination between text and pictures. Individual articles on political parties, extra-sensory perception, atomic energy, and adult education illustrate its modernity. American libraries have been quick to accept the new *Collier's Encyclopedia* as one of the major reference sets.

New International Encyclopedia. The *New International Encyclopedia,* formerly the third choice among American comprehensive encyclopedias, is out of date. Once published by Dodd, Mead and more recently by Funk and Wagnalls, the *New International's* genealogy can be traced through the first edition of the *International Cyclopedia,* 1886, which had acquired the American edition of Chambers' *Cyclopaedia* by the purchase of Alden's *Library of Universal Knowledge.* The first edition of the *New International,* in 17 volumes, appeared in 1902-1904, was partially revised and expanded to 20 volumes in 1907, and reissued in 1912 with the 1910 census figures. A complete revision was undertaken and the second (which is the present) edition appeared in 1914-1916. This second edition contained 80,000 articles fifteen years before the *Britannica* broke up its monographs into 45,000 subjects, illustrating the pioneering of the *New International* in arrangement principles. The changes made in the 1922 issue of the second edition were only of a supplementary nature, such as to add 1920 census figures and some new pages for recent events. Two supplementary volumes were also published in

---

[3] The author of this book served as library consultant and advisory editor to *Collier's Encyclopedia* beginning in June, 1946.

1925 in two editions: one edition, to supplement the 1914-1916 encyclopedia, contained the additional information in the 1922 printing besides later supplementary material, and was numbered volumes 1 and 2; the same material was edited to supplement the 1922 printing and was numbered volumes 24 and 25. In the same year, the publisher issued a cheaper edition by binding the 23-volume encyclopedia and the two-volume supplement into 13 volumes. A supplementary, unnumbered volume for both editions contains courses of reading for study.

Associated with the building of the *New International* were such illustrious names as Daniel Coit Gilman, Harry Thurston Peck, Lyman Abbott, Isaiah Bowman and Melvil Dewey. The *New International* contributed most significantly to lightening the ponderous tone of earlier encyclopedias. In its preface it declared rebelliously: "There exists a kind of writing which has become so stereotyped ... which might be fittingly described as the encyclopedia style. It is in literature what a monotone is in music—utterly devoid of individuality, of variety, of interest." The *New International* introduced the style of the modern newspaper into encyclopedia writing.

At this writing, the *New International* is out of print. In a letter dated October 7, 1948, and signed by Victor E. Campbell, General Manager, Trade Department, the publishers state, "At present, plans are underfoot to issue the *New International Encyclopedia* in one volume. This will be a huge book and certainly will not be in readiness for another couple of years or so."

Popular encyclopedias

There is need for a popular American encyclopedia, less comprehensive and expensive than the *Americana, Britannica,* or *Collier's,* but more adult in appeal than the school encyclopedias. Numerous attempts to meet this need have been made. Most of these sets are priced at under one hundred dollars and all of them are aimed to meet the whole range of family needs in the American home.

POPULAR ENCYCLOPEDIAS

The American Peoples Encyclopedia. Chicago, Spencer Pr., 1948. 20v.

Grolier Encyclopedia. N.Y., Grolier Soc., 1950. 10v.

One-volume encyclopedias

The American Peoples Encyclopedia, distributed by the publishers and also by Sears, Roebuck through its catalog, seems to have gained more favorable acceptance by librarians than any other encyclopedia in this group. The publishers say it is a "new encyclopedia developed with *Nelson's Encyclopedia* as a background." Percentages are difficult to compile since many of the articles that are the same as in *Nelson's* need no changes and others have had some revision. The *Nelson* three-column page has been retained. Offset printing has enabled the publishers to include relatively fine screen half tones on dull finish paper. The articles are generally of the fact-finding variety and the coverage is good.

Grolier Encyclopedia, based originally on *Harmsworth's Universal Encyclopedia* and the later *Doubleday's Encyclopedia,* was acquired by the Grolier Society in 1941 and renamed in 1944. It contains over 28,000 articles of the short, fact-finding type and 9000 illustrations. A policy of continuous revision is making the set increasingly useful.

One-volume encyclopedias

Like the original edition of 1935, the second edition of the *Columbia Encyclopedia* aims to provide "first aid and essential facts" in some 70,000 articles and 75,000 cross references. Articles are of necessity very short and in most cases are little more than identifications. The arrangement is alphabetical, and cross references are indicated ingeniously by printing in small capitals in the text of the articles words which are used as subjects of other articles. There are no maps or illustrations. Although the encyclopedia is in no sense an official or an unofficial publication of Columbia University, "it is deeply indebted to members of its teaching staff." Articles are unsigned. Because of its wide coverage of both current and retrospective topics, its compactness and alphabetic arrangement, *Columbia Encyclopedia* is one of the two one-volume encyclopedias found near the reference librarian's desk.

❦ ONE-VOLUME ENCYCLOPEDIAS

Columbia Encyclopedia, in One Volume; ed. by William Bridgewater and Elizabeth J. Sherwood. 2d ed. N.Y., Columbia Univ. Pr., 1950. 2203p.
Lincoln Library of Essential Information. Buffalo, N.Y., Frontier Pr., 1949. 2175p.

The other one-volume encyclopedia so favored generally is the *Lincoln Library*. Unlike the alphabetic arrangement of the *Columbia Encyclopedia*, the material in the *Lincoln Library* is classified into 12 divisions: (1) English language, (2) literature, (3) history, (4) geography, (5) science, (6) mathematics, (7) economics and useful arts, (8) government and politics, (9) fine arts, (10) education, (11) biography, (12) miscellany. The very full index at the end, which reference librarians use and find productive of results in many instances, compensates for the inconvenience of the classification. *See* references, to a limited extent, are used in the text, and there are bibliographies at the end of every section. The thumb index and the index references to quarters of a page facilitate rapid use.

Comparison between samplings of the *Lincoln Library*'s index entries and the *Columbia Encyclopedia*'s articles and cross references in "A—Abbott," "L—LaBruyère," and "Tolstoy, L. N.—Tonga tally" reveals 24 entries in *Lincoln Library* not found in *Columbia Encyclopedia* and 111 entries in *Columbia Encyclopedia* not found in *Lincoln Library*. The significance of this statistical comparison must be tempered by the consideration that omitted entries may have little reference value.

The *Lincoln Library*, unlike *Columbia Encyclopedia*, does include illustrations and maps. Among its other reference assets are definitions of terms for various subject areas, biographies of notables and subject specialists, and chronological tables.

School encyclopedias

Differences in scope, treatment, and format distinguish the school from the adult encyclopedias. Even in the popular adult encyclopedias the scholarly concept of the "circle of knowledge" dominates the scope and the allocation of space to each subject. Aristotle may still top Franklin D. Roosevelt in number of lines, and the philosophic debate

---

❦ SCHOOL ENCYCLOPEDIAS
Compton's Pictured Encyclopedia. Chicago, Compton, 1950. 15v.
World Book Encyclopedia. Chicago, Field Enterprises, 1950. 19v.
Britannica Junior. Chicago, Encyclopaedia Britannica, 1950. 15v.
American Educator Encyclopedia. Chicago, United Educators, 1946. 10v.
Golden Encyclopedia. N.Y., Simon & Schuster, 1946. 125p.

School encyclopedias

on monism absorb more type than a comparison of Diesel and steam locomotives. Not so in the school encyclopedia. An attempt has been made to study the interests of young people today, both in school as reflected by courses of study and out of school as evidenced in activities, all for the purpose of encyclopedia space allotment. Amateur radio, aviation, home making, fashions, photography, philately, sports, courtship, all high in interest, receive considerable attention. There is a strong emphasis on "how to do" and "how to make." The seven liberal arts may earn some space, but hardly in proportion to their medieval importance. Other subjects suitable for adults may be entirely omitted. School encyclopedia scope is therefore at times based on a philosophy of selection almost directly opposed to that of the adult encyclopedia. Subjects are chosen and space assigned largely on the basis of current interest among those for whom the set is intended.

In treatment, the difference is not in writing down to the level of the young people. That was an early mistake both in children's literature and in the so-called "juvenile" sets, a term wholly inappropriate for the modern school encyclopedia. Today, treatment in a good school encyclopedia is characterized by a high degree of readability—by simple, straightforward writing that is as challenging to the adult as to the child. A further characteristic is the pictorial character of both verbal and graphic materials. Text and picture alike seem to strive to reduce to simplest terms the significant knowledge passed on by the older generation to the new.

As to format, the school encyclopedia was on the market even before *Life* magazine and its competitors with pictures—pictures in black and white and in colors—(colors so brilliant and varied that the child opened his eyes wide and read and learned). Of course the idea was not new. Without going back as far as Confucius one can cite Comenius' *Orbis pictus* (1658, translated into English as *The Visible World* in 1659) for precedent. But in our own times, the good school encyclopedia did it first and did it exceedingly well.

Compton's Pictured Encyclopedia. Although *Compton's Pictured Encyclopedia* was first published in 1922, its publishers were associated with what was probably the first school encyclopedia printed in the United States. In 1894 Mr. F. E. Compton entered the firm of Chandler B. Beach who had the year before published the *Student's Cyclopedia,* and in 1907 he purchased the business. In the meantime the encyclopedia had twice changed its name, first to *Student's Reference Work* and then to *New Student's Reference Work,* under which title Compton issued nine editions between 1912 and 1921. When *Compton's Pictured Encyclopedia* appeared, the copyright to the *New Student's Reference Work* was sold to S. L. Weedon, who issued one more edition under a 1923 copyright.

Since 1922 *Compton's* has through many printings introduced significant innovations. Among these, the heavy emphasis on illustration is notable. Approximately a third of the space in the encyclopedia is devoted to photographs, drawings, diagrams, maps. *Compton's* was probably the first encyclopedia to include reproductions of direct color photographs, and was the first to put all entries beginning with the same letter in the same volume. Likewise, it was the first to discard the then prevailing method of periodic revision in favor of a program of continuous revision. But perhaps the great innovation in *Compton's Pictured Encyclopedia* was the inclusion of a Fact Index, which not only indexed all information in the encyclopedia, including pictures, but carried in the same alphabetical arrangement thumbnail articles on thousands of subjects too unimportant for separate treatment in the main text. Because of this feature, *Compton's* is a handy source of information about small towns and rivers, rare plants, and living people. All difficult words are marked for pronunciation.

Soon after World War II, *Compton's* appeared in a new dress with newly designed covers, pages, and endpapers. A greater number of its illustrations are now in color; direct color photographs are used in preference to paintings whenever the subject lends itself to such illustration. Photographs reproduced in sepia through the sheet-fed gravure process have replaced half-tones in many places. This process is especially effective in the articles on sculpture and fine arts.

The political maps in *Compton's* are by the C. S. Hammond Company. Since separate physical maps are provided, many of which are in color, the political maps are free from the heavy color often used to show physical features, thus increasing the legibility of boundaries and place names. Many special purpose maps are also included, such as those devoted to river basins of the United States, products and population.

Continuous revision, scheduled on an annual basis, includes a considerable amount of new, revised and rewritten text and new illustrations. The Fact Index is kept up to date. Editions of the encyclopedia from 1946 through 1951, according to the publishers, show an expansion of 1374 pages.

School encyclopedias

The fourfold purpose of *Compton's* is indicated by the editors as:

(1) accuracy and breadth of view; (2) interesting treatment, obtained by focusing the attention on the most striking, salient, and picturesque aspects of each topic discussed; (3) simplicity, clearness and directness of language, without insulting the reader's intelligence by trying to "write down" to him; (4) an abundance of illustrations which visualize and dramatize the text.

Since many elementary school pupils read high school material and vice versa, any good school encyclopedia should appeal to readers from fourth grade to junior college. *Compton's* is effective in that range to a high degree and belongs as a basic reference book in libraries serving school, public, and junior college communities.

World Book Encyclopedia. First copyrighted in 1917 as an eight-volume set, the *World Book* has been continuously revised and enlarged. In 1918 it was expanded to ten volumes, which were re-edited and reset in 1929. In 1933 it was still further expanded to 18 volumes, with a "Reading and Study Guide" added.

For the guidance of *World Book* editors in determining what topics should be included and how their contents should be organized in the postwar edition, an Editorial Advisory Board, composed of seven distinguished members, analyzed hundreds of elementary and high school courses of study and summarized the results. Consultants in special fields also worked with editors and artists, and at the conclusion of this preparatory work an extensive revision of the encyclopedia was undertaken. This postwar *World Book,* containing more than 10,000 pages and more than 15,000 articles, has been reset in new type and printed from new plates. Readers will find it completely re-edited and brought up to date, with many new articles and illustrations added. All the colored maps have been remade and 22 pages of new colored maps have been added. Of more than 18,000 illustrations approximately 1500 are in color with special attention given to "America the Beautiful" (in the article on the United States), dress, animals, paintings, and Indians.

All articles beginning with the same letter of the alphabet are found in one volume. In addition there are more than 13,000 cross references which enable the user to locate information readily, without resorting to an index. Following major articles are questions for review, outlines, and lists of related subjects. Graded bibliographies accompany broad topic articles and serve as a selective buying list for school libraries. Vocational guidance information is given in connection with articles on various occupations.

Product maps of states, provinces, countries, and continents, and display pages of memorable events in states and provinces and of leading events in presidential administrations are some of the special features. Among drawings, graphs or pictographs especially worthy of note are those in the articles on jet propulsion, exploration, immigration, and ancient civilization.

The Reading and Study Guide, volume 19, organizes the contents of the *World Book* into major divisions of knowledge around main topics of importance. In a sense, this serves as a synthetic index, drawing together the many articles that relate to large subjects. The *World Book* is revised under a continuous revision policy. An annual supplement, described in the next chapter, is published.

The *World Book* presents its information in simple, direct, and clear language. Its treatment of a topic is comparable to that of a good adult encyclopedia, except that the language is simpler and the contents suited to the needs of young people.

World Book is in the category of those encyclopedias which favor a single alphabet, with many short topics and an abundance of cross references. As has been pointed out, there is no unanimity of opinion among librarians on the relative merits of the cross-reference and index schemes and, until studies of the comparative ready reference value of the two kinds of arrangements have been completed, preferences must continue to be purely subjective.

The *World Book* has, however, outdistanced the adult encyclopedias which use the cross-reference arrangement scheme by providing synthesizing devices. First, many long articles on major subjects have been included. Second, the reading and study guide volume enables the user to relate articles and parts of articles to the subject wanted. Third, lists of related topics follow the articles themselves, performing some of the functions of an index.

Many special features in the *World Book* are of particular significance to reference librarians who serve both young people and adults with limited formal schooling. There is first of all a high degree of balance between popular and academic subjects. Unusually full coverage of subjects provides answers to queries that range from elementary school through junior college interests. The encyclopedia is written in a compact, factual style. This readable language is considerably enhanced by a rich array of visual aids adjoining the text. The paper used

School encyclopedias

is adequate for halftone illustrations. There is a great deal of emphasis on graphs, diagrams, tables, black-and-white maps, artists' drawings, flow charts, and pictographs which present statistics, comparisons, and contrasts dramatically.

Annotated bibliographies following the general articles are graded and keyed to the quantity of information provided by the encyclopedia. Treatment of vocational guidance in *World Book* is especially worthy of note. A virtual key to job opportunities is provided. The article on vocational guidance surveys the principles of self-analysis and describes the major vocational areas. A list of references to articles on individual occupations is followed by bibliographic references to other sources.

The Reading and Study Guide, volume 19, classifies all of the encyclopedia information into 44 major areas, arranged alphabetically from Agriculture to Transportation. Each of these classified sections has important implications for reference service. Of special significance are the list of masterpieces at the end of the section on painting, the list of agencies with their addresses in the area on organizations, and the biography guide where notables are classified by the field in which they made their greatest contribution. For the reference librarian who wants an outline of a subject about which he knows little, these study guides furnish excellent beginnings.

Because of all these features, the *World Book Encyclopedia* is valuable as a reference set in the whole school range—from elementary school through junior college.

Other alphabetic school encyclopedias. Based originally on *Weedon's Encyclopedia,* which the *Encyclopaedia Britannica* purchased in 1933, *Britannica Junior* is intended for use by grade school and junior high school children. The 1947 edition, completely reset and revised (called the "M" printing by the publishers), comprised some significant changes. An increase in number of volumes, from 12 to 15, the creation of a separate atlas volume (volume 15), and the addition of many new articles and illustrations have considerably enhanced the value of this school set. Volume one, a ready-reference index, resembles the *Compton* Fact Index, except that the entire index is together in one volume. The new type face used in this edition is said by the publisher to have been selected for legibility by children of the University of Chicago Laboratory School and is certainly attractive.

The question is often asked, is *Britannica Junior* a simplified rewrite of the *Encyclopaedia Britannica?* The answer is no. *Britannica*

Junior is "prepared under the supervision of the Editors of the *Encyclopaedia Britannica*" and Walter Yust is editor-in-chief of both. The original *Weedon's Encyclopedia,* which the *Britannica* purchased, consisted of eight volumes, which were expanded to ten volumes of text, one volume of ready reference and a twelfth volume of miscellaneous material and study guides. Both periodical and continuous revisions have been employed. The present edition, though it still uses many Weedon headings, has been completely rewritten, and provides a good additional encyclopedia for the elementary grades.

American Educator Encyclopedia was originally made by the same company and by the same group of editors as the *World Book.* Consequently the patterns are somewhat alike although the scope of the *World Book* is broader and the articles longer. An interesting comparison of the two sets is included in the April, 1938, issue of the *Subscription Books Bulletin.*

Continuous revision by a competent editorial staff has made the *American Educator* into a good value at the low quoted price. The present edition provides a good additional encyclopedia for the intermediate and secondary levels. The publishers issue a quarterly supplement called *World Topics,* printed in offset with colored illustrations in the same medium, which provides the users of *American Educator* with a readable periodical at low cost (see also Chapter 4).

The inexpensive one-volume *Golden Encyclopedia* presents very simply in color a relatively few subjects of interest to children in the primary grades.

Classified school encyclopedias. There is a place in school and public library reference for the classified encyclopedia. It is especially useful for the readers' advisory and self-education type of service, since the logical sequence and long articles provide a continuity and relationship that the alphabetical arrangement sometimes interrupts. This type of encyclopedia should have special appeal in elementary classroom reference.

Perhaps the best known of the school classified encyclopedias is

---

❦ CLASSIFIED SCHOOL ENCYCLOPEDIAS

Book of Knowledge; the Children's Encyclopedia. N.Y., Grolier Soc., 1950. 20v.

Oxford Junior Encyclopedia. London, Oxford Univ. Pr., 1948-   .
To be complete in 12v. and Index.

the *Book of Knowledge,* first published in the United States in 1910 and revised on a continuous basis in recent years. Material in the set is arranged by such major classifications as science, plant life, animal life, literature, familiar things (industry), the arts, and men and women. There are also stories, poems, things to make and to do. The index volume contains general, poetry, and fine arts indexes. A new treatment of classics, planned by Hilda Grieder of the Columbia University Library School and Margaret Grant of the New York Public Library, provides a thoughtful introduction to selected good books.

The new *Oxford Junior Encyclopedia* is to be a cross between the classified and alphabetic arrangements. According to the announced plan each volume deals with a broad area and has a separate alphabetic sequence of articles. The volumes are entitled: (1) Mankind, (2) Natural History, (3) The Universe, (4) Communications, (5) Great Lives, (6) Farming and Fisheries, (7) Industry and Commerce, (8) Engineering, (9) Recreations, (10) Law and Order, (11) The Home, (12) The Arts. There is to be a general index volume.

Foreign encyclopedias

The first foreign encyclopedia to be recommended might well be the English *Chambers's Encyclopaedia,* a revision of the famous old set. Articles are brief and generally of the fact type, but despite this pattern there is also an index and an atlas. Its use in America will probably be limited to supplementing American sets on English subjects, since its scope is more traditional than that of the United States

---

✌ FOREIGN ENCYCLOPEDIAS

Chambers's Encyclopaedia. N.Y., Oxford Univ. Pr., 1950. 15v.

Enciclopedia universal ilustrada Europeo-Americana. Barcelona, Espasa, 1907-33. 80v. in 81 (including Apendice in 10v.)

Larousse du XXe siècle. Paris, Larousse, 1928-33. 6v.

Brockhaus' Konversations-Lexikon; der Grosse Brockhaus. Leipzig, Brockhaus, 1928-35. 20v.

Enciclopedia italiana di scienze, lettere, ed arti. Roma, Instit. della Encic. Ital., fondata da Giovanni Treccani, 1929-37. 35v. and Indici (v.36), 1939; Appendici I, 1938; Appendici II, 1938-1948.

Bol'shaīa sovetskaīa entsiklopediīa. Moskva, 1927-47. 65v.

encyclopedias with their increasing emphasis on subjects of popular interest.

Following the language frequency indicated under foreign language dictionaries in Chapter 2, the Spanish *Enciclopedia universal ilustrada Europeo-Americana,* generally known as *Espasa,* will be next most frequently consulted among foreign encyclopedias in American libraries. The set is especially useful for Latin American biographies. Its numerous and excellent illustrations and maps aid the slow Spanish reader.

In addition to *Larousse du XXe siècle* two older works, *La Grande encyclopédie* (Lamirault, 1886-1902, 31v.) and Larousse, *Grand dictionnaire universel du XIXe siècle français* (1866-90, 17v.), are found in many American libraries. The twentieth century Larousse is more popular in style than its nineteenth century predecessor, has briefer articles, but compensates for its brevity with modernity and profuse illustrations.

The German *Brockhaus* is an excellent example of the short article type of encyclopedia and has many illustrations. In format, it resembles earlier editions of the *World Book Encyclopedia.* One of the best of the foreign encyclopedias, judged by American standards, is the Italian *Enciclopedia.* Its striking illustrations, especially of art and travel subjects, its excellent maps, its authoritative bibliographies, and its numerous biographies of living as well as dead notables earn for it an important place in American reference. Increasingly, the Russian *Entsiklopediia* should find its niche in information services.

Reading list

Compton, F. E. *Subscription Books* (R. R. Bowker Memorial Lectures, no.4). N.Y., New York Public Library, 1939. 54p. Reprints obtainable from F. E. Compton Company free. The F. E. Compton Company also issues free educational materials of value in encyclopedia study, such as the booklet, *Continuous Revision.*

"Encyclopaedia," in *Encyclopaedia Britannica,* 14th ed. v.8, p.424-31.

Malclès, L. N. *Les sources du travail bibliographique.* Genève, Librairie E. Droz, 1950. v.1, p.332, and scattered pages list and describe foreign encyclopedias.

Morley, John. *Diderot and the Encyclopedists.* 1886. 2v.

Shores, Louis. "The Ideal Encyclopedia," *Wilson Bulletin,* June, 1937, v.11, p.68-81.

Foreign encyclopedias

—————"Subscription Books and Library Reviewers," *A.L.A. Bulletin,* December, 1948, v.42, p.606-08.

U.S. Federal Trade Commission. "Trade Practice Rules for the Subscription and Mail Order Book Publishing Industry, as Promulgated September 3, 1940." Washington, Federal Trade Commission, 1940.

Wells, H. G. "The Role of an Encyclopedia in a Progressive Civilization." In his *Wealth, Work and Happiness of Mankind.* N.Y., Doubleday, 1931. v.2, p.840-54.

On subscription books, evaluation of reference books, and fair trade practices, the files of *Subscription Books Bulletin* are basic. Note particularly v.3, p.49 for discussion of short-topic vs. long-subject encyclopedias; v.17, p.9-11 and v.20, p.33-35 for other phases of encyclopedia evaluation.

chapter 4

YEARBOOKS

Introduction, Encyclopedia supplements,

Almanacs, Subject records of progress.

Introduction

Trends questions. Questions involving trends and current developments in specific areas of human activity or study comprise a significant portion of the day's reference work. The following questions illustrate the forms taken by these inquiries: What were the trends in women's fashions during the past year? What were the outstanding movies of the past year? Where can I find a summary of recent boundary disputes and settlements? Of all scientific developments in the last year, which contributed most to peace? Are price-income relations becoming more or less favorable to the low-income customer? What were the dates of certain significant events during the past year? All of these questions have in common the element of recency and suggest that encyclopedias may not cover current developments and trends. For that reason a smaller summary work more frequently produced and limited to recent information is needed to supplement background reference sources. Such reference works comprise the class of tools called yearbooks or annuals.

Trends sources. According to the *A.L.A. Glossary of Library Terms* an *annual* is a "yearly publication that reviews events or developments during a year," and a *yearbook* is "an annual volume of current information in descriptive and/or statistical form."

Introduction

As far back as 1923 H. G. T. Cannons compiled *A Classified Guide to 1700 Annuals, Directories, Calendars and Yearbooks.* If all the yearly publications now issued by learned societies, trade and professional organizations, educational, scientific, social and other agencies were to be listed the number would far exceed the total in the Cannons list. The purpose of this chapter is not to examine any great number of these sources, but to identify three groups of annual publications— (1) encyclopedia supplements, (2) almanacs, and (3) subject records of progress—and to illustrate these groups by means of brief reviews of selected titles. Each group can be defined as follows:

Encyclopedia supplements are annual or periodic publications issued by an encyclopedia publisher for the purpose of supplementing encyclopedic information with more recent developments.

According to the *A.L.A. Glossary* an *almanac* is "(1) An annual publication containing a calendar, frequently accompanied by astronomical data and other information. (2) An annual yearbook of statistics and other information sometimes in a particular field." In justification of what may appear to be tautology in the last sentence of the A.L.A. definition it should be pointed out that some publications called yearbooks do not appear annually.

Subject records of progress are annual summaries of significant developments in one or several areas of human activity or study.

Yearbook evaluation. The encyclopedia evaluation checklist of the previous chapter can be applied to yearbook study with only slight modifications. Date or period covered becomes at once an important criterion. Generally, yearbooks tend to use a title date one year in advance of the actual twelve months covered. The 1951 *World Almanac,* for example, covers the year 1950. Occasionally a yearbook carries in its title not the imprint date but the year covered by the content. This is the case in the *New International Yearbook.* Unique among yearbooks is the *American Ephemeris,* which because it must provide data on the location of stars for use in navigation includes information several years in advance of its imprint date. Other criteria—authority, scope, arrangement, treatment and format—can be applied to yearbooks as well as to encyclopedias.

Special features to note are frequency of publication, format—whether loose-leaf or permanent—and the presence or absence of cumulative indexes that cover previous years. With regard to scope it is important to remember that in the case of encyclopedia supplements not all of the yearbook material is necessarily incorporated in revised editions of supplemented encyclopedias. Consequently, the maintenance and use of a file of yearbooks may provide retrospective material not included in the encyclopedia. Moreover, a succession of yearbook articles will often enable the inquirer to find answers to trends questions for himself.

Encyclopedia supplements

Adult encyclopedia supplements. All of the major adult encyclopedias issue annual supplements. Although the *New International Yearbook* can no longer be said to supplement the *New International Encyclopedia* it is the longest continuous series of any adult encyclopedia supplement found currently on American reference shelves. Special features are its useful glossaries, its tables of universities and colleges, and its brief descriptions of organizations and agencies. Its format is the dullest of any of the encyclopedia supplements. Its treatment of subjects tends to be factual but not colorful.

Next in length of continuous publication is the *Americana Annual*. Its distinguishing features include a chronological index in front. Other notable aids are the list of important dates, necrology, list of prizes and awards, and tabulations of colleges, universities, societies, and organizations, with considerable data on each agency. The section on sports brings records and scores together.

The *Britannica Book of the Year* surpasses other yearbooks in number of entries and attractiveness of format. Its striking use of typography and its dramatic layout immediately appeal to the average

---

❦ ADULT ENCYCLOPEDIA SUPPLEMENTS

The New International Year Book; a Compendium of the World's Progress, 1907-   . N.Y., Dodd, Mead, 1908-31; Funk & Wagnalls, 1932-   .

The Americana Annual; an Encyclopedia of Current Events, 1923- N.Y., Americana Corporation.

Britannica Book of the Year; a Record of the March of Events, 1938-   . Chicago, Encyclopaedia Britannica.

Collier's Yearbook, 1939-   Covering the Events of the Year. N.Y., Collier.

The Story of Our Time; Encyclopedia Yearbook, 1947-   . N.Y., Grolier Soc.

Encyclopedia supplements

yearbook user. Coverage is consistently superior year after year for almost all fields, and the statistics and bibliographies are so well selected that reference librarians regularly turn to the *Britannica Book of the Year* first. Of the many special features the calendar of events, with outstanding events noted in red, the comprehensive obituaries, the articles on individual sports, the survey articles of "the present and its roots in the past" which summarize cultural, scientific, economic and political events of the year, and the cumulative index are significant.

In *Ten Eventful Years*,[1] the *Britannica* editors gave perspective and relationship to the records of a decade (1937-1946) that encompassed mankind's greatest war. There is enough difference in the alphabetically arranged material of *Ten Eventful Years* to warrant consulting it in addition to the annual supplements.

Collier's Yearbook, which antedates and which at this writing has not yet been fully related to the new *Collier's Encyclopedia,* is a well-written and well-organized annual. Because subjects are treated under broad headings, the number of entries does not adequately reflect *Collier's Yearbook's* coverage. Special features include a supplementary almanac including such material as time zones, election results, chronology, and necrology. The detailed article on sports is outstanding.

Story of Our Time is intended as a supplement for the *Grolier Encyclopedia.* It does not follow the pattern of the other encyclopedia supplements but it provides a good deal of popular information in a very readable style.

School encyclopedia supplements. All school encyclopedias

☞ SCHOOL ENCYCLOPEDIA SUPPLEMENTS

The World Book Encyclopedia Annual Supplement; Reviewing Important Events and Developments, 1922-   . Chicago, Field Enterprises.

The Book of Knowledge Annual, 1940-   . N.Y., Grolier Soc.

World Topics Quarterly, 1931-   . Chicago, United Educators.

---

[1] *Ten Eventful Years; a Record of Events Preceding, Including and Following World War II, 1937 through 1946* (Chicago, Encyclopaedia Britannica, 1947), 4v. For a comparison of this work with the *Britannica Book of the Year* see *Subscription Books Bulletin,* January, 1948, v.19, p.10.

91

now issue annual supplements. Presumably *Britannica Junior* readers can use the *Britannica Book of the Year*. *Compton's Pictured Encyclopedia* does not issue a yearbook.

The *World Book Encyclopedia Annual Supplement* is paperbound and punched for insertion in a binder supplied to encyclopedia purchasers. About 350 articles are included in each supplement covering subjects selected because of their interest to young people. Statistics are simplified and used sparingly. A number of articles conclude with a list of "books of the year."

The *Book of Knowledge Annual* presents about 80 very broad subjects chosen for interest to children. A section on things to make and do, a lengthy article on sports, and a chronology are special features. This yearbook was formerly known as *Children's Book of the Year*.

World Topics, already mentioned in Chapter 3, is a quarterly, paper-bound supplement to the *American Educator*, punched for a loose-leaf binder. Each issue contains 96 two-column pages, printed in black and one color to provide an interesting appearance. Topics are arranged alphabetically under large subjects. Once each year an alphabetic index to the four issues is provided.

Almanacs

The almanac, originally related to the calendar, has evolved into an annual compend of statistics and facts, some retrospective and others current. Newspaper publishers have produced almanacs as by-products of the requirements of daily news reporting. In a sense the newspaper almanac is a systematic selection, from the newspaper's morgue, of facts and figures of interest to the public.

Because these yearbooks are not associated with encyclopedias, some retrospective as well as current information is furnished. The best of them are as indispensable for reference as the dictionary and encyclopedia. In the better almanacs one will find a record of the

---

ALMANACS

Information Please Almanac, 1947- . John Kieran, ed.; planned and supervised by Dan Golenpaul Associates. N.Y., Farrar, Strauss.

The World Almanac and Book of Facts, 1868- . N.Y., World Telegram and Sun.

Whitaker, Joseph. Almanack, 1869- . London, Whitaker.

year's events in chronological order, or classified by the divisions of human endeavor. One will be further impressed by the economy practiced in conveying this information. Journalistic style, presence of statistical tables, and absence of illustrations generally characterize the format and content of almanacs.

Information Please Almanac. Born in 1947, this radio-inspired source of almost unlimited information went to the top of the almanac best seller list with its second issue. It is planned and supervised by the Dan Golenpaul Associates; its editor is the encyclopedia-minded John Kieran.

The fifth annual issue with its 896 pages presents information under 18 divisions: news record of the year, the United States, United States mileage maps, crossword puzzle guide, American economy, who's who, associations and societies, astronomy and calendars, other nations, world maps, science, religion, chronology, aviation, United Nations, awards, sports, and index.

The news record runs from December through November and includes in addition to a day-by-day chronology a pungent, short narrative of the month. Thus January, 1951, is introduced with a statement that two new crazes were sweeping the country—canasta and nylon shirts.

Special features of the *Information Please Almanac* especially to be noted are the black-and-white maps of cities, continents, and territorial expansion of the United States. The crossword puzzle guide provides such first-aid features as lists of words with two, three, four, five and six or more letters and a list of mythological names. The detailed index at the end is compiled by Robert E. Grayson, a director of the Special Libraries Association.

World Almanac. Ever since 1868 the *World Almanac* has been the standard reference almanac. In that year it was first published by Joseph Pulitzer's famous newspaper, the *New York World*. When the *World* papers were taken over by the Scripps-Howard syndicate, the *Almanac* was continued by the *World-Telegram* and *Sun*. Though formerly handicapped by the presence of objectionable advertising it is now published without such material.

The 66th issue of the *World Almanac* has one advantage for quick reference over its younger competitor—the index is in the beginning of the book, following the table of contents. Without this index, fact location would be considerably delayed. Following the index, texts and tables provide data on such subjects of current interest as Korea, major events of the year, census, government, the United States, New York State and City, the states, Washington, D.C., the United Nations, science, labor, medicine, aviation, sports, literature, education, agriculture, and people. In format the *World Almanac* is less attractive than the *Information Please Almanac* but, as can be seen, the two are comparable in content. Most libraries will need both if for no other reason than the necessity of duplicating such popular information in reference service.

Whitaker's Almanack. The index of the 82d annual volume of Whitaker's *Almanack* for 1950 contains, according to the statement on the title page, some 30,000 references. Placed in front and immediately following the table of contents, the index provides an excellent quick approach to miscellaneous current facts. The sequence of data following the 83-page index is miscellany, calendar, the world, Great Britain, British Commonwealth of Nations, and, in the "complete" and "library" editions, the individual nations of the commonwealth, India, Eire, the United States, and then the other countries of the world, alphabetically arranged, followed by data on science and inventions, literature of the year, sports, and other activities.

As might be expected Whitaker's *Almanack* is stronger in British Commonwealth data than are the two American almanacs. It is especially useful for information about royalty, the peerage, baronetage and knightage, and English universities and other institutions, societies and agencies.

There are other almanacs. Some are free and are issued by manufacturers of patent medicines and products. Others, like the *Dallas News Almanac,* place greater emphasis on other parts of the United States than New York. An almanac of historical interest is Thomas' *Old Farmer's Almanack* which in 1948 had issued its "156th continuous edition" and which contains world calendars, astronomical calculations, weather predictions, tide schedules, time of eclipses, time of sunrise and sunset, digests of fish and game laws, tables for planting, growing and harvesting, and other information of particular value to the farmer. Included also are recipes, puzzles, charades, and anecdotes, as well as advertisements.

Subject records of progress

Annual subject records of progress, sometimes on a single subject and sponsored by a single learned society, sometimes sponsored by

Subject records of progress

several agencies co-operatively and covering many areas of human activity, are rich reference sources for answers to trends questions. This type of yearbook is generally highly authoritative and is becoming better organized for ready reference. Four examples, outstanding for their world-wide coverage and authority, are here briefly described. Other subject annuals will be treated in the chapters on subject reference sources.

The American Yearbook. The 36th issue of the *American Yearbook* aims not only to cover the salient events of the year but also to evaluate "their trends and portents." As in the past the work has been done with the assistance of an advisory council consisting of representatives of 45 learned and professional societies and associations. Over 150 contributors, all authorities in their fields, have written the summaries, which include developments in all major human activities and studies.

The seven parts are designated political, American government, government functions, economics and business, social conditions and aims, science, and humanities. There are 27 divisions under these seven parts including arts, sciences, social sciences and their applications—each unit summarizing events and trends during the year. A special feature is the bibliography of periodical publications and the list "Cognate Societies and Research Associations" at the end of the discussion. A necrology and an index complete the contents.

The Statesman's Year-Book. The 88th annual issue of the *Statesman's Year-Book* follows the now familiar pattern: After a section of comparative tables of statistics and folded maps on boundary adjustments, the four parts of the book deal successively with (1) international organizations, (2) British Commonwealth and Empire, (3) United States of America, and (4) other countries, alphabetically arranged.

For each country and political unit compact information is provided about government, area and population, religion, education, justice and crime, social welfare, finance, defense, production and industry, commerce, communications, banking, money and weights. A list of diplomatic representatives and a bibliography is included. Information on British and United States units is more detailed than that on other countries. The international section provides information about the United Nations, Unesco, the Arab League, and other organizations and movements affecting more than one nation. There is a full index.

YEARBOOKS

The Annual Register. In its 192d year of publication the *Annual Register* followed its traditional pattern as an annual summary of world history. Following a brief preface and a roster of the British government there are six chapters on the history of the United Kingdom during the year, five on the British Commonwealth of Nations, nine on foreign countries (including the United States), a chronicle of events, and a 130-page review of literature, art, science, finance, trade, industry, and law. Of special reference value is the reproduction of significant documents of the year. There is also a chronological necrology and an index. Since 1948 a board selected by five of the organizations concerned with the subjects covered by the *Annual Register* has advised the editors. A distinguished list of contributors is named in the preliminary pages. Despite its British emphasis the *Annual Register* is one of the most effective annual summaries in American reference departments.

Yearbook of the United Nations. Three volumes of the *Yearbook of the United Nations* have been issued. The first covered the period from the inception of the United Nations to July 1, 1947. The second brought the record up to September 21, 1948. The third volume describes the organization's activities through December 31, 1949. Since no further volumes had appeared before 1952, it was not possible to predict whether or not this publication is to continue as a yearbook for each calendar year. Despite the irregularity of its publication the *Yearbook of the United Nations* is a basic reference book. The third *Yearbook* reviews briefly the origin and evolution of the United Nations to September, 1948, and then in greater detail covers the activities for the period until December, 1949, under the following broad headings: functions and organization; political and security

---

☞ SUBJECT RECORDS OF PROGRESS

The American Yearbook; a Record of Events and Progress, 1925-   ; editor, S. Michaelis. N.Y., Nelson.

The Statesman's Year-Book; Statistical and Historical Annual of the States of the World, 1864-   ; ed. by S. H. Steinberg. London, Macmillan.

The Annual Register; a Review of Public Events at Home and Abroad, 1758-   ; ed. by Ivison S. Macadam. London, Longmans, Green.

Yearbook of the United Nations, 1947-   . Lake Success, N.Y., United Nations Dept. of Public Information.

questions; economic questions; social, humanitarian, and cultural; coordination, consultation and implementation in economic and social matters; non-self-governing territories; trusteeship; budgetary and financial; administrative; legal; the headquarters of the United Nations. The specialized agencies, such as Unesco, WHO (World Health Organization), and the Universal Postal Union, are dealt with in a second part. Appendixes give the roster of the United Nations and the members of the specialized agencies. Charts describing the structure of the organization, texts of documents, and the folded color map of the member nations are features frequently sought in general reference.

Besides the international records of progress there are comparable national and regional yearbooks and handbooks. A comprehensive list of these yearbooks will be found in Winchell's *Guide to Reference Books*.

Reading list

Hutchins, Margaret. *Introduction to Reference Work*. Chicago, A.L.A., 1944. p.69-74.

Subscription Books Bulletin reviews yearbooks periodically. The January, 1950, issue, "Encyclopedia Supplements," is basic reading for this chapter.

chapter 5

BIOGRAPHICAL DICTIONARIES

Introduction, Universal biographical dictionaries,

Retrospective biographical dictionaries,

Current biographical dictionaries.

Introduction

Questions about persons. Almost all analyses of reference questions by frequency show that questions on biography are at or near the top of the frequency list. People are interested in people. Facts about great people's lives, their vocational and avocational interests, religion, philosophy, reading, recreation, courtship, family life, education, and adventures, are sought avidly by young and old. In addition, there are the prosaic queries—about dates of birth and death, colleges attended, degrees earned, names of wife and children, present address.

Even a detailed classification of biographical questions is likely to fall short of comprehensiveness. The following classification has the virtue of suggesting applicable groups of reference sources. Biographical inquiries can be said to cluster about:

    1. Notables: living and dead, including statesmen, soldiers, explorers, scientist-inventors, athletes, artists, philosophers, religious leaders

    2. Specialists: in the sciences, social sciences, humanities; in the professions of law, medicine, teaching, engineering; in the trades, business and industry

Introduction

3. Socialites: including royalty, nobility, first families, social club members

4. "We, the People": in all walks of life, in telephone and city directories, on store signs, in news notices

The variety of purposes that impel inquirers to libraries for information about persons is sometimes a clue to the kinds of sources that should be stocked as well as to the manner in which the queries should be treated. For example, a very common biographical interest is expressed by students in connection with papers and talks. A comparable interest is that indicated by chairmen and hosts responsible for the introduction of speakers and guests. Employers frequently seek information about prospective employees. Research workers sometimes attempt to establish authority of authors and specialists by means of biographical data. Libraries have assisted government agents in loyalty, espionage and criminal investigations. Finally, many inquiries that appear to be dictionary or encyclopedia questions can frequently be better answered through the biographical approach. Because of this variety of purposes and interests in people the number of biographical sources available probably exceeds the number of titles found in any other class of reference tool except bibliographies, and there is perhaps no phase of reference work that will challenge the ingenuity of a reference worker more than biographical inquiries.

Types of biographical sources. In this chapter biographical sources are discussed in three groups: (1) universal, which include notable persons of all times and all places; (2) retrospective, which are limited to notable persons now dead; and (3) current, which must answer the wide range of questions on living persons. All of these sources are usually called biographical dictionaries. The phrase *biographical dictionary,* universally used in reference work, is nowhere defined in the literature of librarianship. It is essentially a directory of notable persons, usually arranged alphabetically by surnames, with biographical identifications that range from brief outline to extended narrative.

Of these three groups, current biographical sources fall into the widest variety of types. One kind of current biographical dictionary is the directory of notables, listing persons whose contribution in any one field has made them figures of public interest. A second variety of current biographical dictionary is the directory of specialists, a list of names of persons identified with a specialty—such as a profession, trade or field of knowledge—usually arranged alphabetically by surname. Biographical identification in outline or narrative form may accompany the listings in both these types of current biographical dictionaries. A third type of current biographical source is the index, which usually provides no biographical information itself but cites literature in which such information can be found. The familiar general directory, another type, is a list of names of persons residing in one locality, associated in some relationship, or subscribing to a common service. Social registers are here grouped with genealogies, which vary from the directory form in giving an account, or history, of the descent of a person, family, or group from common ancestors. The term *genealogy* is used to designate both a branch of literature and a type of reference source.

Besides these specific groups of biographical reference sources almost every type of reference book, as is pointed out in Chapter 16, provides direct and indirect information about people. Dictionaries, as already indicated, have either separate biographical lists or incorporate names of persons in the main vocabulary. Encyclopedias and yearbooks devote a major portion of their space to biography. Indirectly, information about persons may be obtained through a study of the subject, place or activity with which the individual has been associated.

Evaluation of biographical sources. The general criteria for evaluation of reference books are applicable to the study of biographical sources. Authority is peculiarly important, since certain unscrupulous publishers, to exploit individual vanity, produce a class of biographical publication often referred to as "vanity" books. Such biographical enterprises not only secure subscriptions at exorbitant prices in advance of publication but frequently extort payment for inclusion. A more despicable variation is exploitation of the grief of survivors to sell memorialization in a questionable biographical work. The reputation of publishers, editors, and sponsors is, therefore, of extreme importance in evaluating biographical sources.

Time, place and subject are important elements in the scope of a reference work. Since dead and living notables of all countries and in all significant areas of human activity are included, universal sources are limited by none of these factors.

Treatment varies from the stereotyped outline adopted by most "who's who" sources to scholarly narratives such as are found in the *Dictionary of American Biography*. Some dictionaries feature portraits and may thus provide a specific answer to requests for likenesses.

Material is generally arranged alphabetically by surname but may also be classified by subject or arranged chronologically by period, birth dates, or events. The presence or absence of bibliographies is related to the authority of the work. Documented biographies, besides offering some assurance of accuracy, provide suggestions for additional sources of information.

Universal biographical dictionaries

"A dictionary of names of noteworthy persons, with pronunciations and concise biographies," is the official description of *Webster's Biographical Dictionary,* produced under the authoritative editorship of William Allen Neilson. The editor's and publisher's stated aim is "to provide in a single handy volume a work of biographical reference not restricted in its selection of names by considerations of historical period, nationality, race, religion or occupation. . . ." American and British celebrities receive some preference in selection and treatment but other nationalities are generously represented. In all there are over 40,000 brief biographies, including some of living persons. Pronunciation is indicated for forenames as well as for last names, and also for place names. Useful lists of United States officials, diplomatic agents from other countries, heads of foreign states, and popes are given in tabular form. Their usefulness is increased by an index. *Webster's Biographical Dictionary* is a basic reference book for every type of library.

Thomas' *Universal Pronouncing Dictionary of Biography and Mythology,* known to older librarians simply as *Lippincott's,* is still useful despite its lack of recent revision. Its scope is comprehensive. It includes not only the famous names in the history of all peoples and

---

✻ UNIVERSAL BIOGRAPHICAL DICTIONARIES

Webster's Biographical Dictionary. 2d ed. Springfield, Mass., Merriam, 1943. 1736p.

Thomas, Joseph. Universal Pronouncing Dictionary of Biography and Mythology. Philadelphia, Lippincott, 1930. 2550p.

Chambers's Biographical Dictionary: The Great of All Nations and All Times; ed. by William Geddie and J. Piddell Geddie. N.Y., Macmillan, 1949. 1010p.

DeFord, Miriam A. Who Was When? N.Y., Wilson, 1951. [162p.]

periods, but mythological characters as well. The articles are principally of the identifying variety, brief and factual. Two appendixes provide a vocabulary of Christian (first) names with foreign language equivalents and pronunciations, and a list of disputed pronunciations.

The 1949 edition of *Chambers's Biographical Dictionary* is the latest revision of another standard work.

DeFord's *Who Was When? A Dictionary of Contemporaries* indicates in comparative tables who were the contemporaries of any celebrated person from 500 B.C. to the present. Under 22 headings, such as government and law, military, industry, music, and education, celebrities are arranged chronologically by dates of birth and death. An alphabetic index of names gives birth and death dates, and each celebrity appears twice in the tables, under the date of his birth and of his death.

The eleventh volume of the old *Century Dictionary*, it will be remembered from Chapter 2, is a "cyclopedia of names." Along with the two other unabridged dictionaries—*Webster's,* which provides a separate list of biographies, and *Funk and Wagnalls,* which includes proper nouns in the regular dictionary vocabulary—it provides an example of a general language dictionary which can serve as a universal biographical source.

Retrospective biographical dictionaries

For the most part, the great national biographical sets of the world are biographical dictionaries devoted to notables now dead. There is

---

❦ RETROSPECTIVE BIOGRAPHICAL DICTIONARIES

Dictionary of American Biography. N.Y., Scribner, 1928-44. 20v. and Index.

National Cyclopaedia of American Biography. N.Y., White, 1892-1949. v.1-35 (in progress).

Dictionary of National Biography; ed. by Leslie Stephen and Sidney Lee. London, Smith, Elder, 1885-1901. 63v. Reissued by Oxford Univ. Pr., 1922, in 22v. Supplements cover 1912-21, 1922-30, 1931-40.

———— Concise Dictionary from the Beginnings to 1921; Being an Epitome of the Main Work and Its Supplement. London, Oxford Univ. Pr., 1930. 1456 + 142p.

Retrospective biographical dictionaries

at least one such great work for nearly every nation. As examples, the two great English language sets—one American and one British—are described. An additional American set which provides current as well as retrospective biographies is also considered.

Dictionary of American Biography. Lack of a national biographical dictionary comparable to the British *Dictionary of National Biography* led the American Council of Learned Societies in 1922 to appoint a committee to consider the possibility of such a project. The committee reported the undertaking would require a half-million dollars. Various plans to defray the expenses were then considered and dismissed one by one. Finally, the committee submitted the plan to the late Adolph S. Ochs, publisher of *The New York Times,* who generously agreed to supply the required sum. An agreement between the American Council of Learned Societies and *The New York Times* was then effected which placed the entire project in the hands of a committee of management composed of four members appointed by the Council, two appointed by the *Times,* and an editor-in-chief elected by the six.

The title-page verso of each volume bears the following statement:

> Prompted solely by a desire for public service the New York Times Company and its President, Mr. Adolph S. Ochs, have made possible the preparation of the manuscript of the Dictionary of American Biography through a subvention of more than $500,000 and with the understanding that the entire responsibility for the contents of the Volumes rests with the American Council of Learned Societies.

The selection of names for inclusion was begun by examining earlier works of reference, lists of occupations, trades and professions, necrologies, and a tentative roll for volume one was developed and circulated three months prior to publication. In general, only those "who had made some significant contribution to American life in its manifold aspects" were included. Three general restrictions on inclusion were imposed: (1) no living persons; (2) no persons who had not lived in the territory now known as the United States; (3) no British officer serving in America after the Colonies had declared their independence.

Contributors were urged to write fresh sketches based on source materials wherever possible. Ancestry, parentage, childhood experiences, educational advantages, physical and social environment were stressed in the articles. Altogether the American Council succeeded in preparing a work which compares favorably with its British counterpart. At present the *D.A.B.* (as it is cited) is available in 22 volumes: the original 20, the index volume, and supplement I, which includes "biographies of persons whose deaths occurred [no] later than December 31, 1935." Index is both to names and to subjects.

National Cyclopaedia of American Biography. Combining the features of a retrospective and a current biographical dictionary, the *National Cyclopaedia of American Biography* provides the most comprehensive list of American notables, living and dead, available in any one source. The work was founded a half-century ago by James Terry White in whose memory an award for distinguished library service has been established. It differs from the *Dictionary of American Biography* in that it emphasizes information rather than interpretation. Librarians have failed to use it as much as they might because of the complexity of its organization. The *National Cyclopaedia* consists of these parts:

1. Dead notables, arranged somewhat chronologically.
2. Living notables, also arranged somewhat chronologically.
3. Index in three parts: (1) to volumes 1-30; (2) to subsequent volumes; and (3) to current volumes covering living persons only. Indexing includes subjects, institutions, events, as well as biographies.

A distinctive feature of this work is the amount of private correspondence examined as a basis for the biographical sketches. Of great reference value is the subject index by means of which the history of an industry or movement can be traced.

Dictionary of National Biography. The *Dictionary of National Biography* (cited as *D.N.B.*) was begun in 1882 by George M. Smith of the publishing firm of Smith, Elder, and Company. Leslie Stephen was appointed editor and Sidney Lee assistant editor the following year. Lists of names were compiled letter by letter throughout the alphabet, and writers qualified to write about them were sought. The first volume appeared in 1885 and succeeding volumes quarterly thereafter until the 66 volumes covering the alphabet were completed in 1900.

The whole work contains biographies of 29,120 individuals "of British or Irish race who have achieved any reasonable measure of

Retrospective biographical dictionaries

distinction in any walk of life; every endeavour has been made to accord admission to every statesman, lawyer, divine, painter, author, inventor, actor, physician, surgeon, man of science, traveller, musician, soldier, sailor, bibliographer, book collector, and printer whose career presents any feature which justified its preservation from oblivion." Early settlers in America have also been included on the same basis.

Commenting on the problem of selecting names for inclusion, Sir Sidney Lee wrote:

> Actions, however beneficent or honourable, which are accomplished or are capable of accomplishment by many thousands of persons are actions of mediocrity, and lack the dimension which justifies the biographer's notice. The fact that a man is a devoted husband and father, an efficient school master, an exemplary parish priest, gives him in itself no claim to biographical commemoration.

Statistics concerning the distribution of biographies contribute many interesting facts. For example, the sixteenth century appears to have had more great men in proportion to the total population than any other, although, as would be expected, the nineteenth century contributes the greatest number of names. The longest single article in the *Dictionary of National Biography* is that on Shakespeare, which covers 49 pages. Other long articles are those on the Duke of Wellington, 34 pages; Francis Bacon, 32 pages; Oliver Cromwell, 32 pages; and Queen Elizabeth, 28 pages.

As previously indicated, the original edition of the *Dictionary of National Biography* comprised 66 volumes. Later the whole work was reissued in 22 volumes, the 22d volume being the supplement published in 1901 of persons who had been omitted in the first selection either because they were still alive at that time or because their importance had been originally underestimated. The second supplement in three volumes added 1660 articles about individuals who had died up to January 1, 1912; the third supplement covered the period between 1912 and 1921; the fourth, 1922-1930; and the fifth, 1931-1940. The *Concise Dictionary from the Beginnings to 1921*, an epitome volume listing all the persons included in the basic work and its supplements, but with the articles reduced to one fourteenth of the original length, is useful for small libraries and for quick reference, providing a one-volume biographical dictionary. It is often cited as *Index and Epitome*.

BIOGRAPHICAL DICTIONARIES

Current biographical dictionaries

Sources of information about current notables, prominent in the news, often present biographies in outline form, much like an application blank, and usually arranged alphabetically. These reference tools are based on questionnaires which request information about birth, date and place, education, experience, honors, creations, etc., of each individual. Most of the "who's who" tools—so called because of the frequency of this phrase in their titles—are issued either annually or biannually. Some are issued less frequently. Supplementing these sources are services issued more frequently which feature names in the news. There is also the "who was who" type of book which includes notables whose death has eliminated them from contemporary sources before revisions of the retrospective tools have had time to include them.

Who's Who in America is, as its subtitle indicates, a biographical dictionary of notable living men and women. The 1948-49 biennial issue commemorated the fiftieth anniversary of this basic reference book. Included are the names of the "best known men and women in all lines of useful and reputable achievement," selected on one of two bases: (1) special prominence in a creditable line of effort, or (2) official position. One out of every 33,000 Americans made the 1948-49 edition. Besides Americans, certain foreigners who have identified themselves with American life or interest are included: Winston Churchill, Joseph Stalin, Fritz Kreisler, Eve Curie. A geographic index has been an added feature. This is the basic current biographical reference book in the United States.

 CURRENT BIOGRAPHICAL DICTIONARIES

Who's Who in America, 1899-   (biennial). Chicago, Marquis.
Who's Who in America . . . Current Biographical Reference Service, 1939-   (monthly). Chicago, Marquis.
Who's Who, 1849-   (annual). London, Black.
World Biography. 4th ed. N.Y., Institute for Research in Biography, 1948. 2v.
International Who's Who. 15th ed. London, Europa Publications, 1951. 1000p.
Current Biography, 1940-   (monthly except August). N.Y., Wilson.

Current biographical dictionaries

Two supplementary publications are issued by the A. N. Marquis Company, publishers of *Who's Who in America*. These are *Who's Who in America Monthly Supplement . . . Current Biographical Reference Service,* which is indexed cumulatively, and *Who Was Who in America,*[1] listing notables removed by death from *Who's Who in America*. Since the *Monthly Supplement* contains biographies not included in the biennial volumes, it is desirable to retain the supplements. A series of regional "who's who's" is under way by the same publisher, beginning with one for New England and one for the South and Southwest.

Who's Who, the British publication, with over a century of issues, does for British notables what *Who's Who in America* does for Americans. It is published annually and includes foreigners of international note. The royal family precedes the alphabetically arranged biographies, which are followed by obituaries and the lists of initials standing for degrees, honors and awards.

World Biography, issued by the Institute for Research in Biography, consists of a fundamental collection (fourth edition, 1948) and a monthly supplement. The former is a two-volume set of over 5000 pages including "who's who" types of biographies of notables in all fields of endeavor and in all countries. The monthly supplements include additional biographies to be incorporated in subsequent editions of the fundamental volumes. Cumulative indexes are included in the monthly issues.

International Who's Who aims at the same coverage, including outline biographies of the "world's most eminent living personalities." Since the form of questionnaire supplied lacks the specificity used by other reference books, the individual biographies are uneven. There are fewer names in the fourteenth edition than in *World Biography,* but form and print are better.

Current Biography, issued monthly except August, presents readable biographical sketches of people in the news. All fields of human endeavor are represented and the information is drawn from newspapers, magazines, books and from the biographees themselves. For each name pronunciation is given, if unusual, as well as date of birth, occupation and address. Sources are cited at the end of the article. For

---

[1] *Who Was Who in America; a Companion Volume to Who's Who in America.* v.1, *1897-1942. Biographies of the Non-Living with Dates of Deaths Appended* (Chicago, A. N. Marquis Co., 1942-50), 2v.

persons whose biographies have previously appeared in *Current Biography,* brief obituary notices with a reference to *The New York Times* obituary are given. Cumulative yearbooks include all the biographies from the monthly issues in one alphabet, revised and brought up to date. The yearbook includes also an index by profession and a necrology.

Directories of specialists. In a world of increasing complexity and specialization the demand for information about specialists is accelerating in all walks of life. World War II dramatized the term "know-how" and the necessity for locating experts.

Stimulated by the emergency and by an editorial in the *Saturday Review,* the A. N. Marquis Company created a new biographical tool, called *Who Knows—and What.* It lists 16,000 knowers of some 35,000 subjects. The book is arranged in two parts. The first is a locator-index, listing topics with page and entry references to authorities. The second or authorities part is arranged alphabetically by last name, and each authority is numbered from 10 upwards, solely "to obtain regularity in spacing." Data provided for each authority include subject, year of birth, education, statement of conversance background, authorship, career, memberships, address. Thirty-two broad areas like architecture, business, chemistry, engineering, fine arts, international relations, psychology, religion, and sociology are represented. But certain specialties covered by subject directories—such as medicine, law, and certain literary, journalistic, industrial and commercial vocations —are here omitted. Examples of specialists' directories in these excepted fields and in others are such tools as *American Men of Science, Leaders in Education, Directory of Medical Specialists,* and *Martindale-Hubbell Law Directory,* which are discussed later in relation to these specialties.

Biographical indexes. The biographical index, although essentially a bibliographic tool intended to point out sources of information, frequently contains some ready references within its own covers, such as the full name of the biographee, his dates, and publications by and about him. Numerous bio-bibliographies and special subject indexes are discussed under their respective subjects; for instance, such special

---

❦ DIRECTORIES OF SPECIALISTS

Who Knows—and What, among Authorities, Experts, and the Specially Informed. Chicago, Marquis, 1950. 796p.

Current biographical dictionaries

tools as Mallett's *Index of Artists* are considered in Chapter 19. Other special indexes are examined in connection with general reference books in succeeding chapters.[2] And indexes to the encyclopedias and yearbooks should not be overlooked as productive locaters.

By all measures of general reference service *Biography Index* is basic. It includes biographical material in the periodicals indexed by Wilson indexes plus certain other selected professional journals; current books of biography in the English language, including fiction, drama, poetry, and juvenile literature; incidental material like prefaces currently indexed by the *Standard Catalog* series, *Essay and General Literature Index* and *Vertical File Service;* obituaries in periodicals and *The New York Times;* portraits, when they occur in indexed materials; and other material about living and dead individuals. *Biography Index* consists of a name alphabet, which is the main part, and an occupations index. The name alphabet provides as far as possible for each entry birth and death dates, nationality, and occupation. Publication is quarterly with periodic cumulations resulting in annual and triennial volumes.

Retrospective index functions are performed by Logasa's *Biography in Collections* and Hefling's *Index to Contemporary Biography and Criticism*. These and the periodical indexes listed in Chapter 11 can be used to supplement *Biography Index* for the years preceding 1946.

General directories. Nearly every person is listed somewhere. The most common sources of names and addresses are city and telephone directories. Most public libraries maintain a collection of such

---

❦ BIOGRAPHICAL INDEXES

Biography Index; a Cumulative Index to Biographical Material in Books and Magazines, 1946- (quarterly). N.Y., Wilson.

Logasa, Hannah. Biography in Collections. 3d ed., rev. and enl. N.Y., Wilson, 1940. 152p.

Hefling, Helen, and Richards, Eva. Index to Contemporary Biography and Criticism. New. ed., rev. and enl. by Helen Hefling and J. N. Dyde. Boston, Faxon, 1934. 229p.

---

[2] Attention is especially called to the profile sketches in the *New Yorker* magazine and to Shaw's *Index to Profile Sketches in the New Yorker Magazine*, both discussed in Chapter 10.

directories for representative cities.The average city directory aims to list all residents, but the telephone directory is, of course, restricted to subscribers. In addition to the alphabetic name list there is usually also a classified section of businesses and agencies. Directories of socially prominent people, known as social registers or "blue books," are published in many localities. Other directory sources for individuals not sufficiently distinguished to be included in biographical dictionaries and specialists' directories are rosters of various lodges, clubs, alumni associations, trade unions, professional organizations, and church memberships. Some clue as to the individual's interests may put the puzzled reference librarian on the right track. The large number of obituaries in *The New York Times* should not be overlooked. A number of libraries have found it profitable to make a regular practice of clipping death notices from daily local papers, mounting them on cards and filing them alphabetically, thus creating their own necrology file. Only one notice for each name is kept but it should be the one with the fullest information. Such a file grows in value with the years. Occasionally the location of a missing heir or a long lost daughter through such a file causes a moment of real drama in a reference room.

Reading list

Hutchins, Margaret. *Introduction to Reference Work*. Chicago, A.L.A., 1944. p.56-63 presents the best discussion of biographical reference questions to be found in library literature.

Subscription Books Bulletin issues reviews of biographical reference sources periodically. Note particularly "Questionable Practices in Biographical Works," April, 1942, v.13, p.9-11.

chapter 6

GEOGRAPHICAL SOURCES

Introduction, Gazetteers, Guidebooks,

Atlases, Maps, Globes.

Introduction

Questions about places. Location and descriptions of places and determination of distances between them comprise a rather large class of reference questions. The Second World War with its far-flung battle fronts and its global concept of operations so stimulated curiosity about cities, islands, mountains, streams, lakes, and other natural and man-made points that geographical questions have increased markedly in the postwar years. Part of the interest can be attributed to the 12 million G.I.'s and their families who want to know about all of the places in which American forces served. Another part of it is no doubt due to the news, which shifts its headlines rapidly and regularly. Finally, the growth of world-wide commercial aviation has had its effect in fixing hitherto little-known centers in the minds of the public.

The type of question stimulated by the above causes may not always be answered by conventional reference sources. For example, the Airways and Air Communications Service of the armed forces maintained during the war over 1000 airways stations all over the world. Some of these stations were located in geographically significant cities in each of the major countries—cities like Miami, London,

Paris, Cairo, Calcutta, Kunming, Sydney. But many more were located at points previously unknown. International air routes have made them strategically significant. This author's book, *Highways in the Sky* (Barnes & Noble, 1947), revealed airways centers like Borinquen, Natal, Accra, Maiduguri, Chabua, Presque Isle, Goose Bay, Keflavik, Gander, and other points previously omitted from geographies but now made important in trans-world aviation. This suggests that war and aeronautical history sources will be required to supplement the basic geographic tools until revised works incorporate these newer places.

Types of geographical sources. Sources for locating places can be divided into three groups:

    1. Gazetteers, for identification (and sometimes brief description)

    2. Guidebooks, for longer descriptions, from the travel point of view

    3. Atlases, maps and globes, for visual location and identification

Although atlases, maps and globes are sometimes classified with audio-visual materials, they are reviewed here in relation to the types of questions they are used to answer, rather than in the audio-visual chapter.

The *A.L.A. Glossary of Library Terms* defines *gazetteer* as "a geographical dictionary." It defines *guidebook* as "a handbook for travelers that gives information about a city, region or country, or a similar handbook about a building, museum, etc." Its definition for *atlas* is "a volume of maps, plates, engravings, tables, etc., with or without descriptive letterpress. It may be an independent publication or it may have been issued to accompany one or more volumes."

Evaluation of geographical sources. Special criteria are involved in evaluating maps, atlases and globes. As a background, a good general article on maps and map making such as is found in one of the adult or school encyclopedias, in the introduction to Goode's *School Atlas,* in the article by Espenshade or in the book by Raisz cited at the end of this chapter should be read.

Of the various kinds of maps, some of the most common found in atlases are political, physiographical, topographical, and geological. Political maps are chiefly concerned with identifying the principal places and boundaries of political units; the other three deal with various aspects of the physical features of the land—above, on, and be-

Introduction

low the surface of the earth. Representations of astronomical, hydrographical, nautical and statistical data range from maps to charts and are featured by some atlases.

The points to be considered in the evaluation of maps naturally differ from those important in book evaluation. Scale indicates the extent of the area to be represented and is usually indicated by a ratio—e.g., 1:30,000,000 where the area is large. Projection is the process of representing a sphere on a plane surface. The Mercator projection, recognizable at once on maps which give a disproportionate size to Greenland as compared with the United States, shows lines of longitude as parallel lines. Other projections which maintain true area relationships among the different land surfaces curve the lines of longitude. Topographical representation is the method of indicating differences of elevation and natural features such as rivers and plains. Elevation is usually indicated by contour lines (often printed in brown on a topographic map) drawn to connect the points on a land surface which have an equal elevation; or by a graded system of color layers showing heights above and depths below sea level; or by means of hachures—short, conventionalized lines used to indicate direction and steepness of slopes. Other points to be noted are the method of reproduction—engraving, photo-engraving or photo-lithograph—and details and date of the culture information, i.e., railroads, highways, streets, cities and towns.

These criteria can be used in checking the maps in an atlas, as well as in checking individual maps. Other criteria to be used in the evaluation of atlases are conveniently arranged in the following checklist:

I. Authority
   1. Publisher's reputation
   2. Editorial staff's experience and education
   3. Cartographer's reputation and previous works
   4. Nation in which atlas is produced
   5. Bibliography and acknowledged sources of information
II. Scope
   6. Region covered—world, continent, country, state, city, or other unit
   7. Kinds of maps—political, physical, etc.
   8. Supplementary materials—gazetteer, population figures, pictorial illustration, narrative descriptions, commercial, ethnographic, transportation, astronomical, and other information

GEOGRAPHICAL SOURCES

III. Date
   9. Imprint, copyright, and revision dates for atlas as a whole
   10. Individual map dates
   11. Text dates for population figures, place names, boundaries
   12. Revision plan—loose-leaf or continuous
IV. Maps
   13. Scale
   14. Location key—letter-figure, latitude, longitude, other
   15. Topography—contour, color layer, hachures
   16. Coloring—variety and quality, relation to lettering
   17. Name forms—vernacular, translated, up to date
   18. Size of actual page
V. Arrangement
   19. Map sequence
   20. Indexing—for each map, or for all maps in one place

Of these 20 check points many are comparable to those established for encyclopedias. A number of points, however, need special emphasis in the evaluation of maps and atlases.

Authority. The authority of several American and foreign cartographers and publishers of atlases is established. Some of their publications, however, are uneven in quality. In the United States the firms of Rand McNally and of Hammond are probably best known for atlases, as is Oxford University Press in the United Kingdom. It is generally said that the workmanship of the best foreign atlases is better than that found in American publications. This means that the reference librarian must frequently choose between foreign atlases with superior maps and domestic atlases with a desirable emphasis on America.

Scope. The practice of determining purpose from the preface, as suggested for encyclopedias, is again urged here. An atlas devoted to a particular region should not be criticized for inadequate representation of other regions. Likewise, a world atlas cannot be expected to emphasize details about a particular locality. The kinds of maps included should be noted. Historical maps indicate boundary lines of the past; political maps, boundary lines of the present. Physical maps are concerned with topography; economic maps with natural resources, industries, transportation, etc. The amount of supplementary material —gazetteer of place names, population statistics, information about government, industry, transportation—determines the scope of the atlas as measured by the kind of information it offers.

Introduction

Date. Justin Winsor, eminent historian and reference librarian, commenting on sixteenth and seventeenth century atlases and charts, said what might well be said of some atlases today:

> Dates were sedulously erased with a deceitful purpose from plates thus made to do service for many years and united with other dated maps, to convey an impression of a like period of production.[1]

How important the date on each individual map in an atlas is can be learned by considering information with regard to population, boundary lines, changing place names. Imprint, copyright, revision and individual map dates should be compared, when they can be found. The problem of keeping his work up to date is of as much concern to the atlas maker as to the encyclopedia publisher. Two methods which have been employed are a loose-leaf service and an annual revision of the entire atlas. Use of decals has also been suggested.

Maps. The points already enumerated for individual maps need to be considered also in collections of maps. In addition, it is important to see whether or not in order to vary color among political units and at the same time employ color layers for topography the publisher has employed tints so dark that the lettering has become obscured. Foreign names of places may be anglicized or given in the native form; e.g., "Rome" or "Roma" may be used. The actual page size of the map is an important part of the collation of an atlas.

Arrangement. Provided the indexes are adequate, the order of maps is of secondary importance. As a rule, atlases follow the pedagogical principle of nearest things first and farthest things last. Most reference librarians prefer to see at least the states of the United States in alphabetical order. Some atlases depend upon one general index to all maps; others furnish an index for each map in addition to a general index. Some, unfortunately, index only separate maps. Indexes frequently give factual information about population, history, and size of the geographical units named. Other points to note about the index or indexes are their location, the amount of information included, and the method of referring to maps.

Three methods of referring to maps are now employed: (1) Marginal letters and figures familiar to all users of state road maps. (2) Indexing frame or grid, as employed in the *Times Survey Atlas.* This

---

[1] *Narrative and Critical History of America* (Boston, Houghton, Mifflin, 1884-89), v.4, p.369.

consists of a transparent sheet covering half of each map and divided into a series of rectangles numbered from 1 to 100. When the index refers to R71 for example, the grid is applied to the right half of the map and the place is located in the 71st rectangle. Libraries find the transparent sheet a nuisance because it is likely to be lost.[2] (3) Latitude and longitude; for example, 41 degrees North and 15 degrees East. This is the most accurate method.

Gazetteers

Gazetteers are alphabetic lists of place names including such information for each place as pronunciation, location, description and statistics. They are issued both separately and as a part of other reference books—notably unabridged dictionaries, encyclopedias and atlases.

Webster's Geographical Dictionary. The best known and most frequently cited separate gazetteer is *Webster's Geographical Dictionary*, with more than 40,000 places in every part of the world listed, marked for pronunciation, located and identified. All incorporated communities in the United States and Canada with a population of 1500 or more are included. Localities in the British Isles, Australia, and New Zealand whose population equals at least 5000, in South Africa 3000, in Latin America 5000 to 10,000, in West and Central Europe 10,000, in the U.S.S.R. 25,000, and in other places 20,000 to 25,000 are also included. Islands, mountains, rivers, lakes, counties, and other geographical units comprise the other entries.

 GAZETTEERS

Webster's Geographical Dictionary; a Dictionary of Names of Places with Geographical and Historical Information and Pronunciations. Springfield, Mass., Merriam, 1949. 1348p.

Complete Pronouncing Gazetteer or Geographical Dictionary of the World; ed. by Angelo and Louis Heilprin. Philadelphia, Lippincott, 1931. 2106p.

U.S. Post Office Dept. United States Official Postal Guide, 1874- Washington, Govt. Print. Off.

Official Guide of the Railways and Steam Navigation Lines of the United States, Porto Rico, Canada, Mexico and Cuba, 1869- (monthly). N.Y., National Railway Pub.

Gazetteers

Some of the items of information included in each entry, in addition to pronunciation, identification, and location, are statistics on area and population, geographical and physical features, economic data, and historical facts. For states of the United States the date of admission to the Union, population rank, name of capital, names of counties and county seats, nickname, state flower, motto, chief cities, rivers, mountains, industries, and history, as well as a full-page map, are given. The 177 maps, of which 24 are in color, are a decided advantage in location. They include a map of every state of the United States and of every foreign country as well as of many of the world's important cities. The historical maps in color present Bible lands, the Roman Empire, territorial growth of the United States, European folk migrations and conquests, and other subjects.

Other gazetteer sources. Although it bears a 1931 imprint date, Lippincott's *Pronouncing Gazetteer* has not been completely revised since 1905. Much of the information on countries, cities, towns, resorts, islands, rivers, mountains, seas, lakes, etc., is still useful. It is alphabetically arranged and includes a conspectus of the 1930 census. A major revision was completed in 1951. Although not a gazetteer in purpose, Greet's *World Words* (see Chapter 2) is particularly good in locating briefly the newer places.

The *United States Official Postal Guide* consists of two parts, (1) domestic, and (2) international postal service. Quarterly supplements record changes in regulations and post offices. The place directory is largely in part one, and consists of a list by states of post offices, branch post offices and stations, followed by alphabetical and county lists. Preceding these directories is a friendly and detailed description of the postal services. Part two treats nation by nation the international postal regulations. Although not a gazetteer by definition, the *United States Official Postal Guide* is especially helpful in locating small places.

The same is true of the *Official Guide of the Railways and Steam Navigation Lines,* usually called the *Official Railroad Guide.* It also includes air lines. Issued monthly since 1869, the *Guide* is, incidentally, a gazetteer of places and an atlas of black-and-white maps. Separate time tables can be secured from each of the railroads, air lines and steamship companies. They provide not only transportation

---

[2] For a better application of this principle see the description of *Advanced Atlas of Modern Geography,* p.121.

guides but gazetteers to places with transportation facilities. Reading of time tables in the *Guide* is sometimes not simple. To locate schedules of trains from Tallahassee to New Orleans, for instance, the names of both cities must be looked up in the index and a table common to both selected. A simpler plan would be to place numbers on the railroad map that would correspond to table numbers, following somewhat the scheme used on American Automobile Association road maps, where the highway number on the map serves to index the mileage table which covers distances between points.

Guidebooks

Intended primarily for the traveler, the guidebook often describes places not found in the more formal gazetteers and atlases. Most guidebooks are arranged by routes or itineraries, but many are organized by countries, states or even localities. Distinctive attention is given to sights such as museums, public buildings, monuments, parks, and amusement places and to accommodations for lodging and food.

Among guidebooks no name is more famous than Baedeker, a Leipzig publisher who, since 1839, has issued individual volumes describing the most important regions, countries, and cities visited by travelers. The fifth generation Karl Baedeker is now preparing new editions of these guidebooks of which two have appeared—one on London and the other on Munich and its environs. Because it will be some time before the new series can replace the old editions, it will

---

❦ GUIDEBOOKS

Baedeker Guide Books. Leipzig, Baedeker, 1839- .

American Guide Series; written by members of the Federal Writers Project, Works Progress Administration. Various publishers, 1937-50.

Guide to America. Washington, Public Affairs Pr., 1948. 705p.

Official Hotel Red Book and Directory, 1886- (annual). N.Y., American Hotel Assn. Directory Corp.

The Sunday Times Travel and Holiday Guide to the Continent of Europe and to the British Isles. London, The Sunday Times, 1951. 2v.

Hanson, E. H., ed. The New World Guide to the Latin American Republics. 3d ed. N.Y., Duell, 1950. 3v.

Guidebooks

be useful to recall that a list of the latest editions can be found in Wright's *Aids to Geographical Research,* discussed in Chapter 16.

Produced by the Federal Writers Project during the W.P.A. Community Service Project days, the American Guide Series includes over one hundred volumes. Many have been revised and reissued recently in new editions. Five types of publications are discernible: (1) state guides, including illustrations and folded maps; (2) city guides, such as those for New Orleans and Washington; (3) regional-local guides, such as that for Dutchess County, New York; (4) tour books, such as *U.S. Number 1,* describing the two thousand mile highway from Maine to Florida; and (5) literary miscellany, such as the anthology *American Stuff,* not considered here. The typical state guide in this series emphasizes the historical significance of the sights described. Selected titles, beginning with the guide to the home state, will be basic in all libraries; all of the titles are desirable in most libraries.

Guide to America is edited by the national travel director of the American Automobile Association. After describing each state in general terms it undertakes to describe the principal points of interest within each state. There is a considerable quantity of information about American places as well as a bibliography. State maps, which border on illegibility in some cases, are included. Comparable information is obtainable in the various tour books, maps and so-called "trip-tiks" furnished by the Association to its members. The *Official Hotel Red Book* is a similar guidebook. Essentially it is a list of hotels arranged alphabetically by state, then by city, then by hotel. Other guides to lodgings and food, to resorts and sights, many of them obtainable free of charge from travel agencies, chambers of commerce, or the places themselves, are useful supplements to the guidebooks.

The two *Sunday Times Travel and Holiday Guides*—one for the Continent of Europe and the other for the British Isles—are entrenched in the affection of travelers. The 1951 guide to the Continent, for example, begins on the end papers and preliminary pages with a dozen good color maps. Compact general information follows on rail and air fares, flying time, passport formalities, rates of exchange, and customs—subjects of absorbing interest to travelers. Information on motoring abroad, coach tours, cruising, and useful phrases in the principal European languages is also included. After these preliminaries the countries are presented to the prospective traveler, beginning with France and ending with East Africa. As an example of the detail given on each country, the section on Spain is outlined. An introduction gives an overview of travel in that country. Then follow descriptions of four districts—their cities, sights, climate, activities. Next come sections dealing successively with disadvantages, communications, food and drink, cigarettes and cigars, hotels, restaurants and bars, and bull fights. The only weakness of these otherwise incomparable guidebooks is the lack of a good index.

Hanson's *New World Guide to the Latin American Republics* includes condensed information about the South and Central American countries.

Atlases

An atlas is a collection of maps or plates or other exhibits bound together in one volume. The word is presumed to come from the picture which adorned the cover of an early collection showing the giant Atlas holding the world on his shoulders. Five modern atlases are selected as representative.

The 114 pages of colored maps in the *Rand McNally Cosmopolitan World Atlas* introduce several new features. Foreign areas are mapped on the so-called "regional basis," meaning that areas surrounding the map's main subject are shown in exactly the same detail. A marginal outline is also provided locating the area covered in each colored regional map.

Following the maps of continents the various parts of each continent are represented on either the same scale or on multiples of the

---

ATLASES

Rand McNally Cosmopolitan World Atlas. Chicago, Rand McNally, 1949. 335p. (9 x 12)

Hammond's Complete World Atlas. N.Y., Hammond, 1950. 375p. (6¾ x 9¾)

Bartholomew, John W. Advanced Atlas of Modern Geography. N.Y., McGraw-Hill, 1950. 108 maps, plus 47p. (10 x 15)

Rand McNally Commercial Atlas. 81st ed. Chicago, Rand McNally, 1950. 500p. (21 x 15¾)

Goode, John Paul. Goode's School Atlas. Chicago, Rand McNally, 1946. 286p., 173 maps. (9½ x 11¼)

Atlases

same scale. Scale is indicated on each map in four different ways—in miles, kilometers, ratio, and miles to the inch. The maps are 9 by 12 inches in size.

Almost all maps depict topography, which is shown in two ways—by hachuring and by the land form method. Up-to-dateness is indicated by the very detailed attention to places brought into prominence by World War II and by world airways. There is a map showing the U.S.S.R. as one nation. The 173-page index lists in one alphabet all the names on all the maps, including administrative divisions of major countries. Most of the *Cosmopolitan Atlas* maps were developed in connection with the new *Collier's Encyclopedia* which includes nearly the same collection except for some changes in color. Special features include tables and lists of data relating to politics, economics, climate, population, etc.

Hammond's Complete World Atlas will fit on ordinary bookshelves, which commends it for quick reference use near the inquiry desk. It has virtually the same information as the larger *Hammond's Library World Atlas,* but the maps are smaller. Included in the contents are a glossary of geographical terms, maps of the earth and solar system, tables of the oceans, seas, lakes, rivers, canals, and mountains, black-and-white maps of climate, vegetation, religions, races, languages, accessibility, occupations, political associations, and resources. There is, of course, a full collection of maps of the various countries of the world. Other special features are the two gazetteers—one of the United States and one of the world—a series of maps showing the high points of World War II, and an index to cities and towns.

There is no more distinguished name among cartographers than John W. Bartholomew. The *Advanced Atlas of Modern Geography* is the latest example of this famous British map-maker's work. Among its new features are so-called "oblique" projections—showing distances as from a fixed point and as they would be seen from high above the earth's surface—which fit the newer concepts of world strategy and travel exceedingly well, population maps to replace the more conventional political maps of continents, place names as they are spelled locally, new layer coloring, and a locater system that more nearly represents the grid graph scheme previously described except that in this scheme the grid consists of squares created by the crossing of lines of latitude and longitude. The collection of maps is admirable. A separate section illustrates the types of map projection. Special maps of world airways, astronomical geography, and world exploration are excellent, and the series of world maps dealing with geology, structures, regions, temperature, oceanography, vegetation, soil, races, commerce routes, and polar regions are excellent and in some respects unique. The whole concept of cutting across national boundaries to present regions like the Great Lakes and the Gulf of St. Lawrence, showing both the American and Canadian sides, and within the United States a map which shows the South, is refreshing. But this atlas confronts the reader with the dilemma previously indicated—good maps and American emphasis or superior maps and British emphasis. The decision should, of course, be "both."

The very large *Rand McNally Commercial Atlas* is revised annually and must be returned each year to the publisher. It is especially detailed for the United States and territories, and its continuous revision program assures a high degree of up-to-dateness.

Goode's School Atlas is adequate for many reference questions. Some of its special features are an excellent introduction to the subject of map reading and making with examples of projection, maps of principal cities and their environs, ocean currents, vegetation, climate, population density, communication, transportation, economic products, and a pronouncing index of 30,000 names.

It should be recalled that the standard encyclopedias provide the equivalent of atlases in their map collections. The 24th volume of the *Encyclopaedia Britannica* is an atlas and the maps of *Collier's Encyclopedia* are practically the same as those in the *Rand McNally Cosmopolitan World Atlas*. Particularly noteworthy are the maps in the school encyclopedias, and special note should be taken of the *Compton Fact-Index,* which includes tables of islands, lakes, rivers, and other geographic features.

Excellent atlases are produced abroad. Bartholomew, the author of the *Advanced Atlas of Modern Geography,* offers also a full range of atlases from the large *Citizens Atlas of the World* to the small *Pocket Atlas of the World.* Oxford University Press also offers a full line of atlases. Its *Oxford Advanced Atlas* has been replaced by a new *American Oxford Atlas* edited by Brigadier Sir Clinton Lewis and Colonel J. D. Campbell. The old *London Times Survey Atlas of the World* is still highly useful for locating small out-of-the-way places in foreign countries.

Good atlases are also produced on the Continent. The Touring Club Italiano *Atlante internazionale,* though out of date, is excellent. From the U.S.S.R. comes *Bol'shoĭ Sovetskiĭ Atlas Mira.*[3]

Maps

There are many sources for maps. A great number are available from United States government agencies like the Army Map Service, the Geological Survey, Department of State, and other divisions.[4] State and local governments, too, provide maps, often free on application. Other sources for maps are the geographical societies. In the United States these are the National Geographic Society of Washington, D.C., and the American Geographical Society of New York. The former publishes indexes for almost all its separate maps. These maps are listed in the *National Geographic Magazine* and with their indexes will prove useful in reference departments. The latter has produced, for example, a map of the world, 57 by 35 inches, equatorial scale 1:30,000,000, and a five-sheet political-relief map of the Americas in color, each sheet 46 x 55 inches, equatorial scale 1:5,000,000, all reasonably priced from $2.50 to $4 per map.

Two of the commercial map-makers have already been introduced as atlas producers. The six major American educational map publishers are:

G. F. Cram & Co., 730 E. Washington St., Indianapolis 7, Ind.
Denoyer-Geppert, 5235 Ravenswood Ave., Chicago 40, Ill.
C. S. Hammond & Co., 80 Lexington Ave., New York 16, N.Y.
A. J. Nystrom and Company, 3333 Elston Ave., Chicago, Ill.
Rand McNally & Co., 536 South Clark St., Chicago, Ill.
Weber-Costello Company, Chicago Heights, Ill.

Some representative wall maps from these firms can be illustrated by the following:

Cram publishes a series (designated as CMS) of political maps of the world (Mercator projection), of the hemispheres, continents, the United States, Canada, and Mexico. Fifty-one inches wide and individually mounted, these are priced from $8 to $14 each, the price depending upon the mounting.

Denoyer-Geppert offers in the series which they designate as J-RP approximately the same subjects in a group of maps 44 by 58 inches, scale 75 miles to one inch, at $10.75 to $12.75 each.

Hammond's *Comparative Wall Atlas* contains 15 maps of the

---

[3] Other foreign atlases are listed in W. W. Ristow, "A Survey of World Atlases," *Library Journal*, 1945, v.70, p.54-57, 100-103.
[4] Walter Thiele, *Official Map Publications* (Chicago, A.L.A., 1938), 356p.

world and the continents, each 29 by 43 inches. Separate physical and political maps are included. The whole set is available for $17.95.

Rand McNally's catalog includes material on selection and evaluation of maps, in addition to description of maps. The Cosmopolitan Map of the World (52 by 34⅝ inches) at $3, plus $7.75 for the cloth mounting on wood rods, is a good purchase. Continental maps on similar mountings (56 by 40 inches) can be purchased for $12 each.

Other sources for acquiring maps include chambers of commerce, travel agencies, periodicals, newspapers, and the American Automobile Association. Among all of these possibilities libraries will be guided in their selection by the specific needs of the community.

Problems of classifying and cataloging maps and of storing them are being solved in various ways. The American Geographical Society has developed a manual, cited in the Reading list at the end of this chapter, that will prove helpful in preparing maps for library service.

Globes

At least one 16-inch globe is basic for adequate reference service. The cradle type of mounting is most flexible because it allows the globe to be completely removed, carried about, and measured. Manufacturers of globes are developing several innovations. Physical features, for example, are indicated on some globes by raised surfaces. The physical-political globe is the one to be chosen if only one is to be provided. Considerable use of a celestial globe can also be made. All of the map and atlas publishers produce globes. Some good ones are:

Publisher	Title	Scope	Mounting	Price
Cram	New Air Age	Physical-Political	Clear view	$27.50
Denoyer	Liberty	Physical-Political	Cradle	$30.00
Nystrom	Parkins	Physical-Political	Cradle	$29.00
Rand	New Horizon	Physical-Political	Cradle	$31.50

For protection, the globe should be covered with a good lacquer finish so that it will withstand rubbing by damp cleaning cloths.

Reading list

American Geographical Society of New York. *Manual for the Classification and Cataloging of Maps in the Society's Collection.* 1947. 43p.

Boggs, S. W., and Lewis, D. C. *Classification and Cataloging of Maps and Atlases.* N.Y., Special Libraries Assn., 1945. 175p.

Espenshade, E. B. "Guide to Map Sources for Use in Building a College Map Library," *College and Research Libraries,* January, 1948, v.9, p.45-53.

───── "Problems in Map Editing," *Scientific Monthly,* September, 1947, v.65, p.217-26.

Raisz, Erwin. *General Cartography.* 2d ed. N.Y., McGraw-Hill, 1948. 354p.

Ristow, W. W. "Maps in Libraries; a Bibliographical Summary," *Library Journal,* September, 1946, v.71, p.1101-07.

Subscription Books Bulletin reviews atlases and maps. The issues of January, 1942 (v.13, p.1-4) and October, 1945 (v.16, p.45-62) are basic.

chapter 7

DIRECTORIES OF AGENCIES

Introduction, International agencies,

United States agencies,

Directories of directories.

Introduction

Agency questions. Organization of man's efforts by agencies is increasing in our civilization. The number of agencies—international, national, state, local, and special—must run into hundreds of thousands. The reference worker is constantly confronted by the need for names, addresses, rosters of officers and members, purposes, publications, qualifications for membership, and a host of other data about organizations. In view of the interest in agencies and organizations the reference books are still too few. But a great many of the reference titles already considered and a great many to be considered include lists of agencies.

The term *agency* is used in this chapter to cover a great many varieties of organizations, including: (1) learned societies, devoted to research and investigation; (2) professional and trade associations, concerned with the study and promotion of practice; (3) institutions

Introduction

—educational, welfare, artistic—including colleges, universities, libraries, museums, observatories; (4) firms, commercial and industrial; (5) clubs, lodges, fraternities, sororities, social organizations—including benevolent and secret societies—women's clubs, sporting, recreational, and youth organizations; and (6) political groups, including political parties, and associations for the advancement of causes.

Typical questions on agencies are: When was the American Philosophical Society founded? Who is the executive secretary of the National Education Association? What is the address of the headquarters of the American Federation of Institutions? What nations are members of Unesco? Where can I get advice on treatment of spastics? Who is the superintendent of schools in Dade County, Florida? The type of reference books best suited to answer these questions is the directory.

Agency sources. A directory, according to the *A.L.A. Glossary of Library Terms,* is "a list of persons or organizations, systematically arranged, usually in alphabetic or classed order, giving addresses, affiliations, etc., for individuals, and address, officers, functions and similar data for organizations."

In this chapter directories of international agencies and of United States agencies are described. Before examining these directories, it is important to review the potential for answering agency questions in the basic reference books considered thus far. Of first importance are the yearbooks. Addresses, personnel, and purpose of agencies are included in the almanacs under the kind of agency—notably international organizations, learned societies, professional and trade associations, colleges and universities, libraries and museums, and some clubs, social organizations and political groups. Especially important for learned societies is the *American Yearbook,* which gives addresses of cognate societies for each subject annually summarized, and the *Yearbook of the United Nations.* The encyclopedias and their supplements, too, identify various agencies. Atlases, gazetteers and guidebooks are especially useful for information about museums, art galleries, and libraries, many of which are often described more fully in those books than in directories. It is also important to recall that biographical and geographical sources are basically directories of persons and places and as such can contribute to answering many agency questions. For example, city and telephone directories identify business and industrial firms, and the *Official guide of the Railways* and the *Official Hotel Red Book* identify types of agencies as well as places.

127

DIRECTORIES OF AGENCIES

Directories in a single subject field are described in the chapters on those subjects.

International agencies

Postwar impetus to international co-operation has been given by the United Nations and related international agencies like Unesco. The *Yearbook of International Organizations* is probably the fundamental directory for world-wide agencies. It is a directory in French and English of diplomatic, scientific, cultural and other international agencies compiled by the Union of International Associations and the Yearbook of International Organizations, and copyrighted by Editions de l'Annuaire des Organizations Internationales of Geneva. Previous annual editions, both of which contained information not included in the 1950 edition, appeared in 1948 and 1949.

The sequence of sections is (1) structure of the organization for European economic co-operation; (2) Council of Europe; (3) Brussels Treaty Organization; (4) Organization of American states; (5) United Nations; (6) specialized agencies; (7) governmental and non-governmental organizations; and (8) miscellany, including forthcoming meetings, lists of diplomatic missions, chambers of commerce, principal abbreviations, calendar of events, alphabetic index of organizations, advertisers' index, and separate French and English indexes to organizations. Some sections are in parallel French and English. Others are in English only, in French only, or partly in one and

---

☞ INTERNATIONAL AGENCIES

Yearbook of International Organizations, 1950. 3d ed. N.Y., Hafner, 1950. 902p.

Unesco. Directory of International Scientific Organizations. Paris, 1950. 227p.

Unesco. Handbook on the International Exchange of Publications. Paris, Unesco, 1951. 224p.

Carnegie Endowment for International Peace. Handbook of International Organizations in the Americas; prepared by Ruth D. Masters and others. Washington, The Endowment, 1945. 543p.

Scientific and Learned Societies of Great Britain; a Handbook Compiled from Official Sources. London, Allen & Unwin, 1951. 227p.

The World of Learning, 1950. 3d ed. London, Europa Pub., 1950. 881p.

International agencies

partly in the other. This irregularity makes use by a monolinguist difficult but not impossible. Approximately 700 organizations are listed in section seven—the largest part of the book—arranged under broad subjects like agriculture, culture, economy, law, peace, social development, and sports. Data provided for each council, agency, or organization include Universal Decimal Classification number for the subject covered, address of central office, history, purpose, membership, governing body, officers, finances, activities, publications. Forthcoming meetings extend to 1953, although the majority are for 1950. The French and English indexes to section seven are arranged alphabetically by catchword entries.

Unesco is responsible for at least two important directories of international agencies. One of these is the *Directory of International Scientific Organizations* which resulted from a resolution passed at the Unesco general conference at Beirut in 1948 to "consider the possibility of publishing a Handbook of international organizations active in the fields of education, science and culture. This directory gives information on international organizations whose activities deal with the various branches of science." Organizations are grouped under basic sciences, applied sciences (subdivided into sections on agricultural, engineering and medical sciences), and miscellaneous, which includes international organizations in a variety of areas. For each organization the following data are given: name, address, aims, officers and membership, member states, their national agencies and their members of Unesco, committees, library and laboratory facilities, finances, meetings, voting procedure, publications, relations to other agencies, history, and other information of interest. There is a subject index.

The other Unesco directory is *Handbook on the International Exchange of Publications*. Essentially, it contains "a list of organizations and their publications offered for exchange"; and it should be useful to "publishers and booksellers wishing to obtain up-to-date addresses of institutions with specific fields of activity." Other items included are lists of bibliographies of official publications and of exchange centers throughout the world and general information on the international exchange of publications. Institutions are grouped according to the subject area in which they publish.

Masters' *Handbook of International Organizations in the Americas* includes information on 109 agencies with headquarters in the Western hemisphere. Arrangement is alphabetic. Another new world directory limited to the Latin American nations is Henry O. Severance, *Handbook of the Learned and Scientific Societies and Institutions of Latin America* (Washington, 1940).

Still useful for retrospective information about international organizations is Gregory's *International Congresses and Conferences, 1840-1937; a Union List of Their Publications Available in Libraries of the United States and Canada* (Wilson, 1938).

Many of the foreign nations have directories of learned societies. Of especial interest to American libraries is the British *Scientific and Learned Societies of Great Britain* which derives from the *Yearbook of Scientific and Learned Societies* published almost continuously for over fifty years until the outbreak of war in 1939 caused its suspension. One of the features of the 1951 issue of the new publication is a section dealing with the organization of scientific research in Great Britain. The agencies themselves are classified under such broad headings as general science, chemistry, anthropology and sociology, and literature and fine arts. There is an index by agencies.

The World of Learning is a directory of educational, scientific and cultural agencies of the world. Organization is in three main divisions: international, national, and index. Under international agencies are included (1) Unesco, (2) International Council of Scientific Unions, and (3) other international agencies arranged alphabetically by subject. Following the international division, the main part of the book is arranged alphabetically by country with subdivisions for learned societies, research institutions, libraries, museums, and institutions of higher education. A rather full list of officers of each institution is included. United States institutions are well represented although many important ones are omitted. The index of institutions and organizations does not include personal names.

United States agencies

The variety and number of learned societies, professional and trade associations, institutions, business firms, and various other organizations in the United States almost precludes the possibility of a single directory for all agencies. Instead, information on addresses, memberships, aims, and publications will have to be found in certain classes of directories if the information is not available in such general sources as almanacs. Directories of United States agencies are discussed in the following groups: (1) learned societies, (2) educational

United States agencies

and cultural institutions, and (3) trade and professional associations. Social welfare agencies, business and industrial firms, and government agencies are reserved for future chapters.

Learned societies. A learned society is an association of scholars organized to promote study and research in a subject field. There is no one directory that can be said to cover as thoroughly the facts about learned societies in all subject fields in the United States as do the directories for international organizations. Most comparable are the handbooks and other publications of the three great councils of learned societies—the National Research Council, the American Council of Learned Societies, and the Social Science Research Council.

National Research Council. At the request of the President of the United States, a federation of governmental, educational, privately endowed, and industrial research agencies was organized in 1916. This organization was founded on the charter of the National Academy of Sciences, established in 1864. On May 11, 1918, the Council was perpetuated by an Executive Order requesting that it undertake: (1) to stimulate research in the mathematical, physical and biological sciences, and in the application of these sciences to agriculture, engineering, medicine, and other useful arts; (2) to survey the larger possibilities of science, formulate comprehensive programs of research and develop effective means of utilizing the scientific and technical resources of the country; (3) to promote co-operation in research at home and abroad; and (4) to engage in other work collateral to these objects.

The National Research Council issues the *Handbook of the Scientific and Technical Societies and Institutions of the United States and Canada.* In all, over 1400 scientific agencies are listed. Data given for each include address, history, objects, membership, library, research funds, medals and awards, and serial publications. There is a companion volume, *Industrial Research Laboratories of the United States,* the eighth edition of which was published in 1946.

American Council of Learned Societies. At the organization of the International Union of Academies in Paris, May, 1919, the United States was represented by the American Academy of Arts and Sciences and by the American Historical Association, there being no national academy devoted to the humanities at that time. To consider the need for such an academy, a meeting of ten learned societies was held in Boston in September of the same year at which it was decided to establish a central body consisting of two representatives from each society. The American Council of Learned Societies Devoted to Humanistic Studies was formally organized on February 14, 1920, with the following constituent societies (foundation dates are given in parentheses): American Philosophical Society (1727), American Academy of Arts and Sciences (1780), American Antiquarian Society (1812), American Oriental Society (1842), American Philological Association (1869), Archaeological Institute of America (1879), Modern Language Association of America (1883), American Historical Association (1884), American Economic Association (1885), American Political Science Association (1906), and American Sociological Society (1905). Additional societies, including the Bibliographical Society of America, have been added. Although the Council arose out of the need for international representation, its chief function has become the promotion of scholarship in the humanities and social sciences.

Information about the constituent societies of the Council comes chiefly from two publications. One is the Bowker *List of American Learned Journals Devoted to Humanistic and Social Studies.* The other is the *A.C.L.S. Newsletter* issued periodically since May, 1949, which describes functions of individual constituent societies and from time to time (as in May, 1951) lists the delegates and secretaries of the constituent societies.

Social Science Research Council. This organization was effected in 1923 for the purpose of furthering closer co-operation between students of politics and of other social sciences. At present, the Council is composed of three representatives of each of seven learned societies, five of which—political science, economics, sociological, historical, anthropological—are also represented in the American Council of Learned Societies. The other two, the American Psychological Association and American Statistical Association, are represented in the

---

☙ LEARNED SOCIETIES

National Research Council. Handbook of Scientific and Technical Societies and Institutions of the United States and Canada. 5th ed. Washington, National Research Council, 1948. 371p.

Bowker, J. W., jr., comp. A List of American Learned Journals Devoted to Humanistic and Social Studies. Washington, American Council of Learned Societies.

United States agencies

National Research Council. Information about these seven societies is therefore provided in the publications of the other two councils.

Educational and cultural institutions. From descriptions of sources already listed it is evident that information about American educational and cultural institutions such as colleges and universities, libraries, museums, and art galleries can be found in a number of international and national directories. Fuller information is available, however, in other sources which are limited to American institutions of a specific type. Only a few examples are noted here; other titles are to be found in Chapter 17.

The United States Office of Education has issued the *Educational Directory* annually since 1912. Prior to that time and as far back as 1895 the directory data had been incorporated in the annual report of the Commissioner of Education. As now issued the directory consists of four parts: (1) state and county school systems; (2) city school systems; (3) higher education institutions; and (4) associations and directories.

From 1904 to 1949 *Patterson's American Educational Directory* was published by Homer L. Patterson. The 1951 issue, the second bearing the imprint of Field Enterprises, publishers of the *World Book Encyclopedia*, introduced a new format featuring increased volume and page size. The content of *Patterson's* includes the following main divisions: school systems, diocesan superintendents, schools classified, school announcements (advertising), schools indexed, public libraries, educational associations and societies, instructional materials and equipment, trade index and buyers' guide. The section on school systems makes up more than half the volume. Arranged alphabetically by state and then by counties and towns, it provides names of officials and location of public, private, and endowed schools and colleges. "Schools Classified" is an alphabetic listing by specialty of colleges and universities and of special and private schools. "Schools Indexed" is an alphabetic finding list by names of individual institutions. Under "Public Libraries," lists of public libraries, state libraries, extension, school and children's library agencies, and of officers and associations are given. These and other lists are helpful and supplement other directories, but *Patterson's* contains a number of inaccuracies and omissions.[1]

American Universities and Colleges, issued by the American

---

[1] Field Enterprises has announced the sale of *Patterson's* to another publisher.

DIRECTORIES OF AGENCIES

Council on Education and revised about every four years, is a basic directory of American higher education. It includes, besides the listing of institutions, many important articles on aspects of higher education in the United States, including information on professional education, foreign students, and accreditation. The main part of the book "supplies pertinent information about 820 accredited institutions supplied by the officers of the respective institutions." For each institution the data included are type of institution, history, requirements, fees, departments and staffs (statistical), degrees granted, enrollment, library, publications, finance, buildings and grounds, and names of administrative officers.

Trade and professional associations. Most of the professions and trades issue their own directories. Basic for all trades and professions is the United States Commerce Department's *National Associations of the United States,* which is both "a directory and a review of the services and accomplishments of trade associations, professional societies, labor unions, farm cooperatives, chambers of commerce, better business bureaus, and other organizations which play a prominent part in American life." Examples of directories of the individual professions are the *American Medical Directory,* the Martindale-

---

❦ EDUCATIONAL AND CULTURAL INSTITUTIONS

U.S. Office of Education. Educational Directory, 1912-   (annual). Washington, Govt. Print. Off.

Patterson's American Educational Directory. Chicago, Field Enterprises, 1951. 814p.

American Council on Education. American Universities and Colleges; ed. by J. A. Brumbough. 5th ed. Washington, American Council on Education, 1948. 1054p.

❦ TRADE AND PROFESSIONAL ASSOCIATIONS

U.S. Commerce Dept. National Associations of the United States, by Jay Judkins. Washington, Commerce Dept., 1949. 634p. $3.50.

❦ DIRECTORIES OF DIRECTORIES

Manley, Marian C. Business Directories; a Key to Their Use. Newark, N.J., Newark Free Public Library, 1934. 63p.

The Directory of Directories, Annuals and Reference Books. London, Business Publications, 1950. 256p.

Directories of directories

Hubbell *Law Directory*, National Education Association *Handbooks*, and American Library Association *Handbooks*. Directories of trade unions such as the Peterson *Handbook of Labor Unions* are guides to labor organizations in this country.

Directories of directories

Although Marian Manley's *Business Directories* is also listed in Chapter 17 it is introduced here because it covers a wide range of subjects and gives so much help in a general understanding of the directory as a reference source. The British *Directory of Directories* is a new publication and indicates the variety of directories issued not only in the United Kingdom but also in Canada and the other Commonwealths.

Reading list

Hirshberg, H. S. *Subject Guide to Reference Books*. Chicago, A.L.A., 1942. Under Associations, Societies, Organizations and Foundations, p.14-19, the author discusses one type of directory; under Business and Trade Directories, p.56-59, there is another major discussion. Discussions occur also under subjects such as Education.

Roberts, A. D. *Introduction to Reference Books*. London, Library Assn., 1948. Chapters 5 and 8 deal with directories of business and of societies and institutions.

chapter 8

HANDBOOKS

*Introduction, Curiosity handbooks,
Literary and historical handbooks, Statistical handbooks,
Documentary handbooks, Parliamentary law and debates,
Fact sources in specific subjects.*

Introduction

Fact questions. All of the classifications of questions asked in libraries show a preponderance of the so-called "fact-finding" type. This type is characterized by the specific answer it requires—the population of a city, exact wording of a rule, content of a law, reproduction of a document, location of a quotation or its author, determination of the yardage of the longest football punt, the melting point of a metallic alloy, details about the first airplane.

The miscellaneous nature of these facts makes classification difficult. Considering, however, all the factors—sources available, inquirers who seek facts, and the use to which these facts are put—the following classification of the more general types is offered:

    1. Curiosities—about customs, traditions, events, superstitions, science, the arts. These questions abound in newspaper columns, on

Introduction

radio quiz programs, in "believe it or not" features, and inevitably find their way into the library.

2. Literary—allusions, identification of plots, characters, incidents, quotations.

3. Statistics—mostly in the social sciences, with heavy emphasis on population, finance, education, business and industry.

4. Documentary—exact wording of rules, regulations, laws, decisions, and documents. Facsimiles or originals come under this category.

5. Parliamentary and debate—questions about conducting meetings, supporting arguments, participating in debates.

6. Specific subject—facts relating to subject areas like government, education, history, geography, sport, science and technology.

Answers to fact questions are elusive. The stray quotation, the odd superstition, the obscure statistic may entail endless search. Because they need a precise answer, discussions of a general nature will not do. The librarian will frequently find it necessary to ask the inquirer to return later, or offer to telephone when the material is found. In searching for quotations and allusions it is helpful to ask co-workers and others for suggestions before too much time is spent in searching. A natural gift for remembering this type of information is a real asset to a librarian. The librarian with talents as a literary sleuth will be in demand in any reference room.

Handbooks as fact sources. There is a type of reference book that includes an assembly of information on one or more subjects brought together in response to popular interest. Such a collection of facts and figures is often called a handbook. The *A.L.A. Glossary of Library Terms* defines *handbook* as "a small reference book; a manual." A differentiation is made in this chapter, however, between a manual, which includes instructions on how to do or make things, or how to perform, and a handbook, which includes information not of a manual nature. This distinction is largely an arbitrary one. Many books whose use would make them conform to this idea of a handbook are called encyclopedias, cyclopedias, dictionaries, guides, or manuals. However, enough examples exist to justify the distinction by type. A handbook, therefore, is defined in this chapter as a reference book of miscellaneous facts and figures on one or many subjects assembled for ready use, in response to popular interest or to a specific need for concise, handy information.

Handbook evaluation. To the general criteria for evaluation of reference books must be added these special criteria for handbooks: (1) source of the data (unfortunately this is often not given); (2)

accuracy of information (inaccuracies occur often in statistics, sometimes due to typographical errors); (3) accessibility of information (how easy are the data to find, and, once found, to interpret?); and (4) recency (this is not essential in some fact books, but is in others).

Curiosity handbooks

Two types of handbooks are considered here, one a collection of miscellaneous facts, the other a collection of answers to actual questions by readers of newspapers, listeners to radio programs, and owners of encyclopedias. In such miscellaneous collections of information are found many of the elusive answers to questions that reference workers call "fugitives," and that frequently involve several hours of search.

Somewhat aroused by these elusive queries, the author of this book started in 1938 in connection with his department, Current Reference Books in the *Wilson Library Bulletin,* a co-operative service known as "Fugitives" through which reference librarians helped each other on unanswered questions. In April, 1941, Walter Pilkington and B. Alterslund launched the monthly periodical *American Notes and Queries,* a "journal for the curious" which also served as a clearing house for answers to elusive questions. The publication was fashioned on the model of the one-hundred-year-old English weekly, *Notes and Queries,* which is a gold mine of curiosities on history, antiquities, local customs, folklore, quotations, proverbs, and other subjects. Cumulative and volume indexes aid in locating answers to questions that have appeared in back issues of *Notes and Queries.* Other sources for answers to fugitive questions are *The New York Times,* certain radio programs—the most famous of which was undoubtedly "Information, Please!" which led to a collection of answers and questions in book form under that title, as well as to the *Information Please*

☞ CURIOSITY HANDBOOKS

Kane, J. N. Famous First Facts; a Record of First Happenings, Discoveries and Inventions in the United States. Rev. and enl. ed. N.Y., Wilson, 1950. 888p.

Tavenner, Blair. Brief Facts. N.Y., Putnam, 1936. 354p.

Stimpson, S. W. Information Roundup. N.Y., Harper, 1948. 587p.

Haskins, F. J. 5,000 New Answers to Questions. N.Y., Grosset & Dunlap, 1933. 502p.

Curiosity handbooks

Almanac—and the standard encyclopedias, most of which maintain a reference service for their subscribers to answer questions not answered by the encyclopedias.

Of all the curiosity handbooks, none is more satisfying for the curious than Kane's *Famous First Facts*. According to Kane, the first year a "first" happened in the United States was 1007 A.D. In that year, the first child of European parents was born on American soil. Other firsts are presented in alphabetic order. There are the date and manufacturer of the first automobile, the year, terms and author of the first baseball game, the name of the first city to employ a city manager, and so on. A geographical index showing the cities in which the events occurred, two chronological indexes—one by year and the other by days of the month—and a biographical index provide additional keys to locating first facts. *Famous First Facts* first appeared in 1933 and was followed by *More First Facts* (1935); the contents of both these volumes plus additional facts are contained in the 1950 edition.

Tavenner's *Brief Facts,* though out of date, nevertheless includes a great many retrospective items in categories of frequent reference demand—"abbreviations, animals, art masterpieces, athletic records, battles, Bible characters, books of first rank"—largely presented in tabular form.

Somewhat different from these books are the compilations of questions frequently asked. There are a great many of these collections. The two chosen for description are intended only to be representative of the type.

Stimpson's *Information Roundup* is the third in a series, including also *A Book about a Thousand Things* (Harper, 1946) and *A Book about the Bible* (Harper, 1945), which attempts to answer "questions that pop up unexpectedly in conversation, at the family dinner table, among a group of friends...at a party...in the barber shop or beauty parlor...on the farm, at the work bench...[as] they are presented to editors, radio commentators, teachers, clergymen"—and, we might add, librarians. Since questions are not presented in subject order, location is made through the index. Sample questions are these: Does hot water crack a thin glass easier than a thick one? What is the legend of the Blarney Stone? How did salt get into the ocean? What is the difference between beer and ale? What causes the holes in Swiss cheese? Although authority is not often given in Stimpson's books, they are tools to resort to when curious bits of information fail to appear in other sources.

Comparable are the various collections of Frederick J. Haskin and of his bureau since his death. These are actual questions, mostly by readers of the newspapers which carry the Haskin service. *5,000 New Answers to Questions* answers questions grouped under 75 subjects listed in the table of contents. There is no index. The Haskin collections have the advantage over Stimpson's of being actual recorded questions in a reference service devoted to answering the American public's specific inquiries.

Literary and historical handbooks

Allusions, quotations, holidays, and events comprise another popular segment of reference inquiries. Questions falling into these types can, of course, be answered by encyclopedias and almanacs, but there are special handbooks for each type that are particularly effective.

Numerous titles are of aid in tracing down allusions. The one selected for illustration, Benét's *Reader's Encyclopedia,* is derived in part from *Crowell's Handbook for Readers and Writers,* by Henrietta Gerwig, published in 1935 and still much used in reference departments; and Gerwig in turn was derived in part from two earlier allusion books—Brewer's *Reader's Handbook* and *Dictionary of Phrase and Fable,*[1] also still found on reference shelves. Here, therefore, are three generations of a basic reference book, Brewer to Gerwig to Benét, all still very much in reference use.

Benét's *Reader's Encyclopedia,* published in 1948, covers briefly authors, figures in literature, movements, terms in aesthetics, science, philosophy, economics, politics, art, and music, and highlights in history, mythology, and other subjects important to readers of books. The arrangement is alphabetical and the notes, though compact, are sufficient to give the reader a clue to the allusion.

❦ LITERARY AND HISTORICAL HANDBOOKS

Benét, W. R. Reader's Encyclopedia. N.Y., Crowell, 1948. 1242p. $6.

Hart, J. D. Oxford Companion to American Literature. 2d ed., rev. and enl. London, Oxford Univ. Pr., 1948. 890p. $5.

Harvey, Sir Paul. Oxford Companion to English Literature. 3d ed. Oxford, Clarendon Pr., 1946. 931p. $10.

——— Oxford Companion to Classical Literature. Oxford, Clarendon Pr., 1937. 468p. $4.

Literary and historical handbooks

Other literary allusion books of note are the three *Oxford Companions*. The *Oxford Companion to American Literature* includes in alphabetic arrangement "short biographies and bibliographies of American authors... nearly nine hundred summaries and descriptions of the important American novels, stories, essays, poems, and plays; definitions and historical outlines of literary schools and movements; and information on literary societies, magazines, anthologies, cooperative publications, literary awards, book collectors, printers and other matters relating to writing in America." A chronological index of literary history is an added feature. The *Oxford Companion to English Literature* includes "a list of English authors, literary works and literary societies, which have historical or present importance [and] the explanation of allusions commonly met with, or likely to be met with, in English literature"—a good definition, by the way, of the allusion book. The *Oxford Companion to Classical Literature* gives information about Greek and Roman institutions, religions, authors, and other subjects necessary for an understanding of classical literature.

Other titles should be cited because they have for so long been a part of the reference librarian's vocabulary. There are three old-timers by William A. Wheeler: *Dictionary of the Noted Names of Fiction, Familiar Allusions,* and *Who Wrote It?*[2] A two volume work by William S. Walsh, *Heroes and Heroines of Fiction* (Lippincott, 1914-15), covers in one volume modern prose and poetry and in the other classical, medieval, and legendary fiction.

The librarian or student who cannot remember these titles specifically will recall that, when a certain reference cannot be located in the basic *Reader's Encyclopedia,* there are many other allusion books to be consulted, if available; or help may be sought through such exchanges as *American Notes and Queries.*

Certain special phases of literary allusion are contained in other works. For example, Helen Rex Keller's *Reader's Digest of Books* (Macmillan, 1929), hidden from high school students in some libraries, tells briefly, in a paragraph or two, what each of some 1500

---

[1] Ebenezer C. Brewer, *Reader's Handbook of Famous Names in Fiction* (Philadelphia, Lippincott, 1898); *Dictionary of Phrase and Fable* (Philadelphia, Lippincott, 1923).

[2] William A. Wheeler, *Explanatory and Pronouncing Dictionary of the Noted Names of Fiction* (22d ed.; Boston, Houghton, Mifflin, 1893); *Familiar Allusions* (5th ed.; Boston, Houghton, Mifflin, 1890); *Who Wrote It?* ed. by C. G. Wheeler (Boston, Lee, 1887).

great books is about. The digests are arranged alphabetically by the title of the book, and there is an author index. The more recent Haydn and Fuller *Thesaurus of Book Digests*[3] digests 2000 books and indexes them by author and character.

Quotation books. Locating stray quotations and finding appropriate ones for special occasions or designated subjects is more than an indoor sport for reference librarians; it frequently involves many hours of search. Quotations can be found in sources other than quotation books. The *Oxford English Dictionary* with its nearly two million quotations is a gold mine. *Notes and Queries* and its American counterpart should not be overlooked. To locate stray quotations the author's name, subject of the quotation, key words in the quotation, date or title of the quotation, and finally the librarian's memory may all be used. But, from the beginning, quotation books will be the primary sources to consult.

Quotation books may be arranged alphabetically by subject, chronologically by author, or alphabetically by author; indexes generally follow the arrangements not chosen as the basic one. Bartlett is arranged chronologically by author, listing famous sayings or writings of English and American authors from Caedmon to the present and including Biblical, anonymous, and translated quotations. A remarkable index of over 500 pages, three columns to a page, reveals

---

❦ QUOTATION BOOKS

Bartlett, John. Familiar Quotations. 12th ed., rev. and enl. by Christopher Morley and L. D. Everett. Boston, Little, Brown, 1948. 1831p.

Hoyt, J. K. New Encyclopedia of Practical Quotations. N.Y., Funk & Wagnalls, 1940. 1343p.

Stevenson, B. E. Home Book of Quotations, Classical and Modern. 6th ed., rev. N.Y., Dodd, Mead, 1949. 2812p.

❦ CALENDAR HANDBOOKS

Douglas, G. W. The American Book of Days. 2d ed., rev. by Helen Douglas Compton. N.Y., Wilson, 1948. 697p.

❦ HISTORICAL FACTS

Langer, W. L. An Encyclopedia of World History. Rev. ed. Boston, Houghton, Mifflin, 1948. 1270p.

Literary and historical handbooks

elusive quotations even when only a word or two is recalled. The *Oxford Dictionary of Quotations* (Oxford Univ. Pr., 1941), is also arranged alphabetically by author. Hoyt's *New Encyclopedia of Practical Quotations* and Stevenson's *Home Book of Quotations,* the other two of the three best known books of quotations, are arranged by subject. The former has the largest collection of quotations, and its index is comparable to that of Bartlett's *Familiar Quotations* in thoroughness. Stevenson is most up to date and includes extracts from authors of all ages and countries. Mencken's *New Dictionary of Quotations* (Knopf, 1942) is also arranged by subject and includes many obscure items, but it is not indexed.

There are variations of the quotation book devoted to proverbs, anecdotes, slogans, and mottoes. Examples of the first are Champion's *Racial Proverbs,*[4] the *Oxford Dictionary of English Proverbs,*[5] and Stevenson's *Home Book of Proverbs;*[6] of the second, Fuller's *Thesaurus of Anecdotes;*[7] and of the third and fourth, Shankle's *American Mottoes and Slogans.*[8]

Calendar handbooks. Half literary and half historical are the calendar books providing information about holidays, anniversaries, and festivals. Two standard reference books in the field are Mary E. Hazeltine's *Anniversaries and Holidays; a Calendar of Days and How To Observe Them* (A.L.A., 1944) and Douglas' *American Book of Days.* The latter includes not only religious and historical holidays but birthdays of famous Americans, local holidays, and anniversaries of events. There is a topical index; location is also possible through the calendar.

Historical facts. History handbooks are of two kinds—alphabetically arranged allusion books and chronologically arranged date books. The Reverend E. Cobham Brewer, who through his *Reader's Handbook* fathered Gerwig and Benét, compiled also a *Historic Notebook* (Lippincott, 1896), an alphabetically arranged collection of historical allusions. His prefaces are always worth reading and the

---

[3] Hiram Haydn and Edmund Fuller, *Thesaurus of Book Digests* (N.Y., Crown, 1949), 831p.

[4] Selwyn G. Champion, *Racial Proverbs* (London, Routledge, 1938), 767p.

[5] W. G. Smith, *Oxford Dictionary of English Proverbs* (2d ed.; Oxford, Clarendon Pr., 1948), 740p., $13.50.

[6] Burton E. Stevenson, *Home Book of Proverbs, Maxims and Familiar Phrases* (N.Y., Macmillan, 1948), 2957p.

[7] Edmund Fuller, *Thesaurus of Anecdotes* (N.Y., Crown, 1942), 489p., $1.98.

[8] George E. Shankle, *American Mottoes and Slogans* (N.Y., Wilson, 1941), 183p.

temptation to quote this quaint postscript to the *Notebook*'s prefatory statement cannot be resisted:

> If I might make the suggestion without being impertinent, I think the book would be admirably adapted to the upper forms of Ladies' Schools, and to those in private life who seek to extend their general knowledge, after having laid aside their elementary books. Of course, these historic notes are mainly designed and were especially written for the general public, and this, their educational use, is a mere afterthought.

Each allusion is entered under the first noun or adjective of a phrase, rather than under the most important word. The list of allusions is followed by an alphabetic list of the chief battles of the world.

Langer's *Encyclopedia of World History* is based on an older work, Ploetz's *Epitome of History*, first translated into English in 1883 and later edited by Harry Elmer Barnes. Under six broad periods—prehistoric, ancient, Middle Ages, early modern, nineteenth century, two world wars and the inter-war period—Langer's handbook presents history chronologically under each major and minor political unit, region by region. A good general index, black-and-white maps, and appendixes of Roman and Byzantine emperors, caliphs, Roman popes, Holy Roman emperors, British, French, and Italian heads of state are other features. The genealogical tables of ruling houses are useful.

Helen R. Keller's *Dictionary of Dates,* more fully described in Chapter 16, emphasizes region in its arrangement. "This history of the world by dates is a record from earliest times through the year 1930 arranged under countries, giving a digest of information contained in many books." Part one, The Old World, is based on Haydn's *Dictionary of Dates* (Putnam, 1911). Under each nation there is a chronological, brief record of events. Part two, The New World, is compiled from standard histories.

Statistical handbooks

Adequate handling of reference questions involving numerical data is frequently aided by some background in statistics. A general encyclopedia article on the subject or an elementary textbook will assist the reference librarian in understanding the principles of average dispersion and other statistical measurements.[9] Also important is a realization of the variety of statistic-gathering organizations and of the problem of proper analysis of figures. One should be sure of the origin

Statistical handbooks

of statistical information, and librarians quoting statistics to patrons should make clear the source quoted. In this connection the United States Census Bureau pamphlet, *Statistical Services of the United States Government,* published by the Bureau of the Budget in 1947 is most useful.

The *Statistical Abstract of the United States,* which might be regarded either as a yearbook or a handbook, "presents in a single volume important summary statistics on the industrial, social, political, and economic organization of the United States and includes a representative selection from most of the important statistical publications." Its twofold purpose is to provide a quantitative summary and to send the seeker for details to authoritative sources which are carefully cited. Significant statistics are given under broad headings like area and population, vital statistics, crime, immigration, education, climate. Some 37 non-governmental statistics-gathering agencies as well as a great many governmental sources are quoted, making it the best general clearing house for statistics on the United States.

Three supplements presenting greater details on cities, counties, and historical statistics have been published. The earliest and briefest of these was the *Cities Supplement* (1944), which "provides 79 different items of information concerning the population, education, housing, labor force, building establishments, government, finance and climate of each of the 397 cities of the United States with 25,000 or more inhabitants in 1940." The second of these useful supplements is the *County Data Book* (1947), which "presents in compact form some of the more important social and economic facts about each county in the United States." It also summarizes data for 138 metropolitan areas made up of whole counties. The third supplement is *Historical Statistics of the United States 1789-1945* (1949), an invaluable source for retrospective statistical reference work. Some fourteen subject areas—wealth, population, labor, agriculture, housing, prices, government, etc.—are represented in this abstract of significant statistics in the history of the United States. There are two indexes, time-period and alphabetic subject.

U.S.A.: Measure of a Nation is a comparable statistical history presented largely in pictographs. It is based on the 812-page 1947 volume, *America's Needs and Resources,* by J. Frederic Dewhurst and

---

[9] A discussion of the differences in meaning of *mean, median* and *mode,* important in the use of some data, will be found in the *Municipal Yearbook,* 1948, p.10-11.

associates. The present simplified version undertakes to present an inventory of our nation's resources, production and potential. Pictographs and text trace the statistics of American achievement from 1800 to 1950 and the possibilities to 1960. Under such heads as eating, drinking, and smoking, dress and adornment, and a roof over our heads, pictorial statistics on our development, our present state and our possible future are presented.

The United Nations *Statistical Yearbook* promises to provide an ever-widening collection of current international statistics.

Once every ten years the Bureau of the Census issues the decennial census. The organization of these decennial censuses has varied since 1790. In each census there is a tendency to feature statistics relating to one great national problem. In 1930 it was unemployment, because of the great depression. In 1940 it was housing, because of the great shortage; other subjects included were population, agriculture, mineral industries, manufactures, and business. These reports cover many volumes. Although they cannot be called handbooks, they are used in a similar manner and for like purposes. The basic reports are numbered—e.g., Population, Volumes I-IV (1940)—the rest are considered to be special reports supplementing the basic subject series.

The *Abstract of the Census,* a decennial government publication, digests some of the most-sought statistics from the full census reports. A letter from Morris H. Hansen, Statistical Assistant to the Director, Bureau of the Census contains a concise comparison in the scope of the *Statistical Abstract of the United States* and of the *Abstract of the Census*:

> The *Statistical Abstract of the United States* and the *Abstract of the Census* are entirely distinct publications. The *Statistical Abstract,* published annually since 1878, is the official statistical year book of the United States. As such, it includes statistics in many broad subject fields contributed by many statistical agencies and organizations, both public and private.

STATISTICAL HANDBOOKS

U.S. Bureau of the Census. Statistical Abstract of the United States, 1878-   (annual). Washington, Govt. Print. Off.

Carskadon, T. R., and Modley, Rudolf. U.S.A.: Measure of a Nation. N.Y., Macmillan, 1949. 101p.

United Nations. Statistical Office. Statistical Yearbook (Annuaire statistique), 1948-   . Lake Success, N.Y.

Documentary handbooks

The *Abstract of the Census,* in contrast, is a statistical summary of a given census and is basically restricted to data published in the detailed reports of that census. An Abstract or Compendium volume has been a part of the publication program since 1840, with few exceptions. Also, in a few instances, an Abstract restricted to a particular subject census has been issued, such as the *Abstract of the Census of Manufactures, 1914.*

An *Abstract of the Sixteenth Census* (1940) was planned but preparation was abandoned because of priority of work relating to the war effort. An abstract volume was included in the preliminary planning of the Seventeenth Census.

The *Federal Statistical Directory* issued by the Bureau of the Budget is as informative for its list of agencies doing statistical work as it is for the names of the personnel in these agencies.

Although the federal government is a major source for statistics, it is by no means the only one. State and local governments also compile statistics, as do large industrial and commercial firms, research agencies connected with learned societies, philanthropic foundations, professional and trade associations, and educational institutions. Most useful are the yearbooks already considered, especially the almanacs. Periodicals and newspapers provide more recent statistics which can be located through the indexes described in Chapter 11.

For older world statistics the encyclopedias can be supplemented by Mulhall's *Dictionary of Statistics*[10] and its complement, Webb's *New Dictionary of Statistics.*[11] Mulhall "comprehends all statistics from the earliest times." Arrangement is alphabetic by subject. Population, for example, begins with that for the Roman Empire at the death of Augustus, 14 B.C. and follows with censuses for the ninth decade of every century from the fifteenth to the present for each of the major European powers.

Documentary handbooks

Many of the more familiar documents of American history like the Declaration of Independence are available in the general encyclopedias. Certain others can be found in the yearbooks. Nevertheless, a great many of the historical documents of United States history in

---

[10] Michael G. Mulhall, *Dictionary of Statistics* (4th ed.; London, Routledge, 1899), 853p.

[11] A. D. Webb, *New Dictionary of Statistics* (London, Routledge, 1911), 682p.

HANDBOOKS

less demand than the Constitution but still not so obscure as to require source materials can be found in documentary handbooks. There are a great many such collections of historic texts and documents. Two examples will serve to describe the type.

Commager's *Documents of American History* is one of the best documentary handbooks available. It includes not only the organic law but also acts such as the Stamp Act, numerous proclamations, state charters, and similar texts in frequent reference demand.

Somewhat comparable is Monaghan's *Heritage of Freedom; the History and Significance of the Basic Documents of American Liberty*, a handbook of the postwar Freedom Train. One hundred thirty-two documents—including text, commentary and facsimile—are presented in chronological order. The first is Columbus' description of his first voyage to the new world and the last a collection of eleven bonds issued by the United States Treasury Department from 1779 to 1947. Facsimiles of the German and Japanese surrender documents, General Wainwright's last message from Corregidor, Roosevelt's message to Stalin that Operation Overlord had been placed under Eisenhower's command, and the formulation of the United Nations Charter are some of the materials in the book relating to the Second World War. Other documents of interest are the title page of the first book printed in the North American Colonies; Tom Paine's rallying message; Washington's memoranda; and an annotated copy of the Constitution.

Parliamentary law and debates

Considerable reference activity in school, public, and college libraries centers on student debates and club activity. Parliamentary and debate handbooks provide answers to questions about conducting

---

❦ DOCUMENTARY HANDBOOKS

Commager, H. S. Documents of American History. 5th ed. N.Y., Appleton-Century-Crofts, 1949. 759p.

Monaghan, Frank. Heritage of Freedom. Princeton, N.J., Princeton Univ. Pr., 1947. 150p.

❦ PARLIAMENTARY LAW AND DEBATES

Robert, H. M. Rules of Order. Chicago, Scott, Foresman, 1943. 323p.

Reference Shelf. N.Y., Wilson, 1922-   .

a meeting and subjects for debate. Perhaps the two most useful reference sources in this connection are Robert's *Rules of Order* and the *Reference Shelf*.

First issued in 1876, Robert's *Rules of Order* reached the best seller class in the first 39 years of its life with a sale of over a half-million copies. Based on the rules and practices of the United States Congress, the object of the *Rules* is "to assist an assembly to accomplish in the best possible manner the work for which it was designed." The two preliminary tables, one ranking motions and the other tabulating rules relating to motions, have quick-reference value. It is a pity that Robert's format is so unattractive.

There are other manuals, each with ingenious devices for instructing in parliamentary procedure. Three suggested for comparison with Robert's are Cruzan, *Practical Parliamentary Procedure* (McKnight, 1946); Cushing, *Manual of Parliamentary Practice* (Winston, 1928); and Reeves, *Parliamentary Procedure* (Heath, 1931).

The *Reference Shelf* is a series of books each of which discusses one debate subject frequently chosen in high school and college competitions. For each subject selected bibliographies and briefs for both sides are presented. Samples of subjects included are: American Capitalism vs. Russian Communism; Free Medical Care; U.N. or World Government; Economic Aid to Europe—the Marshall Plan; Dilemma of Postwar Germany; Should We Have More T.V.A.'s Today? There are a number of similar series.

Fact sources in specific subjects

More than in any other field, the handbook of facts is essential for workers in the fields of science and technology. Guides for nature study, compilations of physical and chemical facts and tables, and brief summaries of present-day knowledge in fields as varied as electrical engineering, metallurgy, and medicine are essential for good reference work. A number of them are studied in later chapters.

Reading list
Morley, Linda H. "Statistical Reference Works," *Special Libraries*, 1936, v.27, p.35-38, 72-75.
U.S. Bureau of the Census. *Annual Report*, 1947/48. Contains information about plans for 1950 census.

chapter 9

MANUALS

Introduction, Cookbooks, Home maintenance, Health and first aid, Etiquette and correspondence, Recreation, handicrafts and hobbies.

Introduction

Activities questions. Answers to "how-to" questions—"how to do," "how to make," "how to perform"—often measure the adequacy of reference service in the eyes of the American public. These questions revolve about domestic matters: food and cooking, home maintenance and repair, first aid, etiquette, correspondence, gardening, home industry, recreation, hobbies, and collecting. These ten activities of daily living provide a convenient outline for grouping a miscellaneous collection of tools extracted from their special subject chapters because of their general, popular interest.

Examples of "how-to" questions are: What is the recipe for hushpuppies? How can I repair a leaking faucet? I've cut my finger—how do I stop the bleeding? How is a woman introduced to a man and wife? What is the form for acknowledging an R.S.V.P. invitation? Can camellias be grown in New Jersey? I want to make my own brass polish. Where can I get instructions on airplane model making? How can I begin a stamp collection?

Cookbooks

Activities sources. The class of reference book best suited to answer the foregoing questions is the manual. From the *A.L.A. Glossary of Library Terms* a manual is defined as: "1. A compact book that treats concisely the essentials of a subject; a handbook. 2. A book of rules for guidance." This chapter seeks further to refine the difference between a handbook and a manual even though the distinction made here is not consistently observed in the titles of reference books. Handbooks are here considered to be primarily sources that contain facts for knowing. Manuals are sources that contain instructions for doing.

Evaluation of manuals. To the general criteria for evaluating all reference books certain special points must be added for manuals. Clarity of instruction, whether verbal or pictorial, is of paramount importance. The significance of the former is well illustrated by the prefatory story in Phyllis Krafft Newill's *Good Food and How To Cook It* in which a cook who has read that a cup of sugar should be placed in a pot of boiling water places both cup and sugar in the boiling water.

Illustrations can add to the effectiveness of instructions but like words should be selected and placed to clarify the directions. Whether text and picture are more or less effective than motion pictures and other audio-visual media in answering "how-to" questions is still a subject for pedagogical investigation. It is certain, however, that books have proved increasingly effective aids in improving manual activities as they have paid greater attention to language and illustration.

Cookbooks

The perennial best seller among reference books is the cookbook. Nearly every home has one, and no library can avoid the responsibility for a collection of them. The arrangement pattern for a cookbook usually consists of a general section dealing with buying and selecting foods, table setting, cooking hints, tables of calories, weights and measures, and other miscellaneous items, followed by recipes, usually grouped under main classes of foods; that is, meats, fish, fowl, vegetables, appetizers, soups, desserts, beverages, etc. Within this pattern there is the variation that results from the individual creativeness of the compilers, the national and regional emphasis on dishes, and the amount and scope of the introductory material. Individual recipes usually include tabulations of required ingredients followed by directions for preparing the dish.

MANUALS

Selection is nowhere more difficult than in the cookbook field. Habit, personal food preferences, and accessibility of information influence kitchen-shelf selections in the average home. The three representative cookbooks cited in this section are not better in all respects than a half-dozen others.[1]

Meta Given's *Modern Encyclopedia of Cooking* is one of the most comprehensive collections of recipes in all cookbook literature. The consumer education introduction is superior, including excellent discussions of diet, planning, menus, and well-organized definitions and tables of measurements. Recipes are numerous and representative of all nations and sections. Instructions are clear and the text is complemented by good illustrations, both black and white and color. The index provides ready reference.

Perhaps the most famous of cookbooks is Fannie Farmer's *Boston Cooking-School Cook-Book* which appeared in a new edition in 1951. In fifty-five years of continuous service over 2,600,000 copies had been sold. Its 3000 recipes include all of the tried and trusted American ones and hundreds of specialties. The *Woman's Home Companion Cook Book,* developed as part of that magazine's service to its readers, features over 2600 recipes tested and developed in the *Woman's Home Companion* kitchen laboratory.

Other cookbooks of note are Kander's *Settlement Cook Book,*[2] which specializes in foreign dishes, the *New York Herald-Tribune Home Institute Cook Book,*[3] Phyllis Krafft Newill's *Good Food and How To Cook It,*[4] the Emily Post *Cook Book,*[5] *Better Homes and Gardens Cook Book,*[6] which claims a sale of over 3,800,000 copies, and *Betty Crocker's Picture Cook Book,*[7] which boosts General Mills products, including Gold Medal Flour and Wheaties, and devotes only 28 out of 449 pages to meat and fish.

❦ COOKBOOKS

Given, Meta. Modern Encyclopedia of Cooking. Chicago, J. G. Ferguson Associates, 1949. 2v.

Farmer, Fannie M. Boston Cooking-School Cook-Book. 9th ed., completely rev. by Wilma L. Perkins. Boston, Little, Brown, 1951. 878p.

Woman's Home Companion Cook Book; ed. by Dorothy Kirk. N.Y., Collier, 1951. 987p.

Home maintenance

Manuals dealing with the last two of the trilogy of subsistence—food, clothing, and shelter—are grouped under the heading of home maintenance manuals. The number and variety of this type of "how-to" reference tool are increasing steadily. Manuals dealing with each of the following problems relating to home maintenance—repairs and decorations, formulas, sewing and gardening—are selected to illustrate the types.

The *Woman's Home Companion Household Book* deals with such maintenance problems as papering, painting, plumbing, pest control, heating, electricity, moving day, room arrangement, interior decoration, slip covers, upholstering, table linens, sewing, spots and stains, and money management. Numerous pictures, diagrams, and designs add materially to the usefulness of the book, which is also supplied with a full index.

In addition to repairing the old home the householder once or twice in a lifetime has the opportunity to plan a new home. There are numerous good collections of house plans available on the news stands and a number of good books on principles of design. The collections of plans revised from time to time by periodicals like *Better Homes and Gardens* are examples of house-plan sources. *Homes of America* (Crowell, 1951) by Ernest Pickering presents in 235 half tones and 39 plans and drawings the homes of America as they have expressed the lives of the people for three centuries.

Closely related to repairs and design is the household problem of cleaning, polishing, and stain removing, covered partly by the *Woman's Home Companion Household Book* but detailed by *Henley's Twentieth Century Book of Formulas* with its directions for mak-

---

[1] A list of cookbooks is included in the article by Ripperger cited at the end of this chapter.

[2] Lizzie Kander, *Settlement Cook Book* (29th ed., enl. and rev.; Milwaukee, Settlement Cook Book Co., 1948), 623p.

[3] New York Herald-Tribune Home Institute, *Home Institute Cook Book* (new ed.; N.Y., Scribner, 1947), 1107p.

[4] Phyllis Krafft Newill, *Good Food and How To Cook It* (N.Y., Appleton-Century, 1939), 555p.

[5] Emily Post, *Cook Book* (N.Y., Funk & Wagnalls, 1951), 384p.

[6] *Better Homes and Gardens Cook Book* (rev. ed.; Des Moines, Iowa, Meredith Publishing Co., 1947), loose-leaf.

[7] General Mills, *Betty Crocker's Picture Cook Book* (2d ed.; N.Y., McGraw-Hill, 1950), 463p.

MANUALS

ing brass polishes, ink stain removers, and other needed household articles. In all, some "10,000 formulas, processes, trade secrets for the laboratory, workshop, factory and home" are included. The range is from adhesives to wood, and the diversity is illustrated by such items as the making of beverages, ceramics, cheese, chewing gum, cigars, disinfectants, embalming fluids, hair preparations, insecticides, lipsticks, plastics, pyrotechnics, soaps, and waterproofing. Although many of the recipes are of the "rule of thumb" variety, they are probably more nearly the kind which the layman can follow than if they were more exact.

Clothing manuals exist, but because of frequent style changes they are too perishable to be listed as basic reference books. Pattern books and sewing manuals are reference sources for those who make their own clothing. Reference libraries with limited funds would be wise to use materials available in the women's magazines. Some manuals of value are Mary Brooks Picken's two books, *Sewing for Everyone* (World, 1944) and *Sewing for the Home* (Harper, 1946). A more recent manual is Marian Corey's *McCall's Complete Book of Dressmaking* (Greystone, 1951).

Gardens as an adjunct to good home maintenance call for a different type of reference book from that associated with botany. Of the many practical aids on the market Seymour's *New Garden Encyclopedia* is selected for its convenient alphabetic arrangement, its coverage, and its simple directions. In all there are some 10,000 articles and 1500 "how-to-do-it" pictures. Better in format and in bibliography is John C. Wister's *Woman's Home Companion Garden Book* (Doubleday, 1947) with particularly outstanding color pictures, but the information is less accessible than in Seymour's book. Other favorites are *Better Homes and Gardens Garden Book* (Meredith, 1951) and Louise and James Bush-Brown's *America's Garden Book* (Scribner, 1939).

☞ HOME MAINTENANCE

Woman's Home Companion Household Book; ed. by Henry Humphrey. N.Y., Collier; Doubleday, 1948. 929p.

Hiscox, G. D., ed. Henley's Twentieth Century Book of Formulas, Processes and Trade Secrets. N.Y., Henley, 1945. 867 + 24p.

Seymour, E. L. D. New Garden Encyclopedia: a Complete, Practical and Convenient Guide. N.Y., Wise, 1946. 1380p.

Home maintenance

A final aspect of home maintenance and management includes the very important subject of buying. One of the hopeful movements in the direction of intelligent household purchasing is the considerable amount of consumer education under way. *Subscription Books Bulletin* is an example from the library field of an attempt to educate the book-buying public on reference books. The Department of Agriculture and the National Bureau of Standards have long been active in informing the public of values in commodities; for example, the Department of Agriculture published *Consumers' Guide* from 1933 to 1947.

Perhaps the most unusual attempt in the direction of educating the homemaker who manages the family budgets of America is that known as Consumers' Research, Incorporated, begun in 1929 under the direction of F. J. Schlink. It issues a general monthly *Bulletin,* available to libraries, schools, corporations, and other institutions as well as to individuals, and an annual confidential cumulative bulletin, available to individuals only for their private use. Products are evaluated and rated in terms of the value per dollar. Included is almost every commodity used by the American consumer—food, clothing, shelter, automobiles, refrigerators, cosmetics, movies, radios, and even books. Although these ratings are based as far as possible on objective criteria there is room for disagreement based on personal differences in taste. The annual automobile ratings elicit the widest interest and debate among subscribers.

Consumers Union of the United States was organized in 1936 by striking employees of Consumers' Research. The newer organization, of which Arthur Kallet is director, carries on a program comparable to that of Consumers' Research, but with the difference that labor conditions under which goods are produced are indicated. The purpose of Consumers Union, as stated in its charter, is "to obtain and provide for consumers information and counsel on consumer goods and services ... to give information and assistance on all matters relating to the expenditure of earnings and the family income ... to initiate and to cooperate with individual and group efforts seeking to create and maintain decent living standards." Ratings of consumer goods, classified by kind and indexed alphabetically, are included in the *Consumers Union Buying Guide,* a handy volume of data taken from the monthly publication *Consumer Reports* and published as the December issue. For each class of goods, products are grouped under such headings as "Best Buys," "Acceptable," "Not Acceptable." Manufacturer, price, and evaluations are given individually. A weekly publication called *Bread and Butter* is also issued.

Health and first aid

Requests for first aid information may involve "hurry" reference service. The *World Almanac* quickly furnishes suggestions for treatment in case of certain accidents, drowning, and poisoning. Antidotes are listed under each poison in *Funk and Wagnalls New Standard Dictionary*. The American Red Cross *First Aid Textbook,* whose directions were practiced by many as a home defense contribution during the Second World War, is a basic source. Most chemical handbooks contain first aid information as introductory material, and pamphlets are available from many reliable drug supply houses.

The Family Physician by Pomeranz and Koll aims "to provide a reliable and up-to-date answer to every question of health, hygiene and medical care that is likely to arise in the average household." Among the subjects covered are first aid and what to do until the doctor comes. This is followed by a discussion of what medical treatment can be expected when the doctor comes. Other subjects covered are new approaches to cancer, tumor, heart disease, allergies, change of life, arthritis, menstrual troubles, sterility, constipation, hygiene of the eye, ear, nose and throat, and pregnancy. There is a good section on the new "miracle" drugs and considerable attention to child health and care. The dictionary of common medical terms should aid in quick reference. A modern note is the section on protection against an atom bomb attack. There are good illustrations, both half tones and drawings, showing such things as first aid, blood circulation, the heart, and child care. The predecessor of this book was originally prepared for the *Review of Reviews.*

One of the best sellers of all times is the United States government

---

❦ HEALTH AND FIRST AID

American Red Cross. First Aid Textbook. American National Red Cross, 1945. 254p.

Pomeranz, Herman, and Koll, I. S. The Family Physician. N.Y., Greystone, 1951. 588p.

U.S. Children's Bureau. Infant Care. Washington, Govt. Print. Off., 1951. 145p.

pamphlet, *Infant Care,* which has been sold to over five million people. It provides an inexpensive supplement to *The Family Physician* on a health subject of concern to many households.

Etiquette and correspondence

"Formalities or usages required by the customs of polite society" is the definition given for *etiquette* in the *Funk and Wagnalls New Standard Dictionary.* Synonymous with the word in America is the name Emily Post. The 52 chapters in her *Etiquette* present instructions on a variety of matters relating to social customs, manners, and human relations—such as introductions, greetings, conversations, restaurant etiquette, invitations, teas, balls, dances, debutantes, college popularity, modern man and girl, engagements, weddings, funerals, the well-appointed house, entertaining, correspondence, travel, and motoring. Some users have found much of the information applicable only to people with large incomes. The index has not always proved adequate.

Other etiquette books are growing in popularity. One of these is Margery Wilson's *The New Etiquette* (Lippincott, 1940) which tries "to take the threat out of etiquette and to give you its release and pleasure instead." There are also etiquette books for young people and children. Edith Heal's *The Teen Age Manual* (Simon & Schuster, 1948) and Munro Leaf's *Manners Can Be Fun* (Lippincott, 1936) are examples for two age groups.

Closely related to etiquette and actually a part of most etiquette books is correspondence. Taintor and Monro's *Secretary's Handbook* has long been a standard work on business and formal social correspondence. Its rival, covering about the same ground and preferred by some, is Lois Hutchinson's *Standard Handbook for Secretaries* (McGraw-Hill, 1947). Taintor and Monro's companion volume *Handbook of Social Correspondence* (Macmillan, 1936) covers formal and informal notes and letters relating to invitations, announcements, acknowledgments, courtesies, etc.

ETIQUETTE AND CORRESPONDENCE

Post, Emily. Etiquette; the Blue Book of Social Usage. N.Y., Funk & Wagnalls, 1945. 654p.

Taintor, Sarah A., and Monro, Kate M. The Secretary's Handbook; a Manual of Correct Usage. 7th ed., rev. N.Y., Macmillan, 1949. 573p.

MANUALS

Recreation, handicrafts and hobbies

It is not the purpose of this chapter to list any portion of the large number of manuals which provide instructions in various recreational activities. Suffice it to say that there are "how-to" books for woodworking and ceramics, for model making and painting, for dancing and photographing, for playing various games indoors and out. In this section two general guides to the sources of information about how to do, make, or behave are described.

The first of these is Robert Kingery's *How To Do It Books,* which lists 2350 books about 346 hobbies. From the index in the beginning of the book one can select hobbies such as acrobatics, acting, airplane model making, alcoholic beverages, animal pets, authorship, babies, barbecue, chess, and at the other end of the alphabet, sports, stamp collecting, tango dancing, ulcers, and wrestling. Following the index of topics, books are listed alphabetically from Afghans to Yachts under broader subjects. Brief annotations are included. The book was originally planned as a supplement to the *Bookman's Manual* (see Chapter 12), a guide to books in most areas except that of "how-to" books.

Lovell and Hall's *Index to Handicrafts* is a key to books and magazines most useful for directions on how to make things like furniture, toys, and many other items.

Reading list

Henne, Frances E., and Cole, Dorothy E. *Course Outline: Reference and Bibliography.* Chicago, Graduate Library School, Univ. of Chicago, 1945. p.51-56.

Hirshberg, H. S. *Subject Guide to Reference Books.* Chicago, A.L.A., 1942. p.73-75, 91, 95-96, 131-32.

Ripperger, Helmut. "A Sport Without a Season," *Publishers' Weekly,* August 11, 1951, v.160, p.548-54. A good discussion of cookbooks.

❦ RECREATION, HANDICRAFTS AND HOBBIES

Kingery, Robert. How To Do It Books; a Selected Guide. N.Y., Bowker, 1951. 319p.

Lovell, Eleanor C., and Hall, R. M. Index to Handicrafts, Model Making, and Useful Projects. Boston, Faxon, 1936. First Supplement, 1943; Second Supplement, 1950.

chapter 10

SERIALS

Introduction, Lists of serials,

Union catalogs of serials, Daily newspapers,

News summaries.

Introduction

Contemporary questions. Inquiries that can be answered only by sources contemporary with the event are classed here as contemporary questions. Such questions may involve current or retrospective information. The former include information so recent that it has been impossible to incorporate it in a book. The latter may require the use of newspapers and periodicals published contemporary with the events either because the inquirer is doing original research, because the information never found its way into a book, or because the article is briefer, historically significant in itself or for other reasons more suitable than current sources. In such cases the reference librarian is called upon to locate and perhaps interpret old issues of serial publications.

Examples of contemporary questions asked in libraries are these: (1) Current in 1951—What are the principal differences between the Korean policies advocated by President Truman and General MacArthur? What was the date predicted by *Collier's* for the beginning of World War III? Which college football teams were selected to rank in the first ten in the pre-season predictions? (2) Retrospective— How did the people accept the results of the Hayes-Tilden presidential election? What most interested the people of the United States twenty years ago? How were Karl Marx's writings received by contemporary reviewers? Can you find an eye-witness account of the first world's heavyweight championship fight?

Contemporary sources. Serials are especially useful sources for answering contemporary questions, current or retrospective. According to the *A.L.A. Glossary of Library Terms* a serial is: "A publication issued in successive parts, usually at regular intervals, and, as a rule, intended to be continued indefinitely. Serials include periodicals, annuals (reports, yearbooks, etc.), and memoirs, proceedings, and transactions of societies." A newspaper is defined by the *Glossary* as "a publication issued at stated and frequent intervals, usually daily, weekly, or semi-weekly, which reports events and discusses topics of current interest." The same authority defines a periodical as: "A publication with a distinctive title intended to appear in successive (usually unbound) numbers or parts as stated at regular intervals and, as a rule, for an indefinite time. Each part generally contains articles by several contributors." The definition makes these discriminations: "Newspapers, whose chief function is to disseminate news, and the memoirs, proceedings, journals, etc., of societies are not considered periodicals under the rules for cataloging."

In this chapter the term *serial* is used to cover all of the publications cited in the *A.L.A. Glossary* definition of the word except annuals, already treated in the chapter on yearbooks. Annuals belong in the class known as *continuations,* often defined as a publication issued in parts not more frequently than once a year. In library acquisition departments a continuation is a standing order for a publication that is issued every year, or every two, three or four years.

Value of serials. Serials have certain advantages over books as sources of information on contemporary questions. In the first place, serials can be more up to date than books. For certain fields like medicine and other sciences, serials tend to become the only reference sources, since subsequent books are frequently only summaries of the serial literature and since the contents of some articles never do appear in books. This criterion of up-to-dateness, although most important in science, is also important in the social sciences.

In the second place, serials tend to contain the major source materials for research. Original researches are often first reported in the journals of learned societies. News about them, too, appears first in newspapers, news magazines, and other serials long before any account appears in books. Even the second-hand interpretative descriptions of

Introduction

new developments are likely to appear in magazines long before a text or popular book can be published. For these reasons source materials for scholars and laymen are more likely to be contained in serial than in book literature.

In the third place, serial articles have the reference advantage of brevity. The popular enquiry can be answered better and in less time through a short article or digest, such as appears in a periodical, than through a whole book. For the scholar, a serial is more likely to have the condensed treatment he seeks.

Finally, serials are steadily becoming more accessible because of increased attention to indexing. The cumulative indexes of the H. W. Wilson Company, for example, reveal the contents of over 1000 different periodicals. Other indexes to groups of periodicals as well as the increasing number of annual and cumulated indexes to individual periodicals are contributing to the accessibility of serial literature.

Selection of periodicals for reference use is influenced by a number of factors. The most useful periodicals are those indexed by the H. W. Wilson services, led off by the *Readers' Guide*. The natural and social sciences, where latest information is most important, should be emphasized when titles are being chosen. In fields where the library's book stock is weak, periodicals can often compensate. For the special fields the library hopes to develop, periodical literature will be indispensable.

One of the obstacles to reference use of periodicals in the past has been the inadequate attention of publishers to bibliographic detail. Periodicals have been known to change their scope, purpose, size, volume, number, and paging within the same volume, to the confusion of librarians and readers alike. The American Standards Association has developed a code (Z39.1-1943) which establishes a well-defined set of specifications for periodical issues.

Other obstacles to reference use of periodicals stem from the library's own limitations. An incomplete file of a certain title often prevents what would otherwise be a sure-fire answer to a question. In such instances the resourceful librarian may be able to draw on other sources or refer the inquirer to nearby libraries for the wanted volume. In certain cases interlibrary loan can be accomplished or arrangements may be made for reproduction of desired articles through photostat or microtext.

Care and handling of serials is treated in a number of professional books. Gable's *Manual of Serials Work* (A.L.A., 1937) is still basic for all phases from acquisition through interpretation. Notes on births and deaths of periodicals are contained in the *Bulletin of Bibliography,* in the H. W. Wilson indexes, in *Public Affairs Information Service,* and in *College and Research Libraries.*

In the present chapter the following types of serial sources are considered: (1) lists; (2) union catalogs; (3) representative newspapers, news summaries and periodicals. Serial indexes are reviewed in the following chapter.

Lists of serials

In 1950 it was estimated by Unesco[1] that 11,861 daily and weekly newspapers and 6893 periodicals were issued in the United States. If to these totals are added the statistics for the rest of the world the selection problem confronting libraries is at once apparent. Fortunately, aid is available in the form of numerous lists of periodicals selected for various purposes and by several techniques. Perhaps the most common method of developing a list is for an authority to exercise his judgment from the standpoint of long experience and submit his selection to other competent individuals for criticism. A second method for serial selection is that of pooled judgments, under which plan a number of authorities collaborate in the selection of a list.

In 1927, P. L. K. and E. M. Gross of Pomona College devised a technique for selecting periodicals in chemistry[2] that has since been imitated for other subjects. Briefly the Gross technique consists in selecting chemical journals on the basis of the frequency of their citation in the *Journal of the American Chemical Society.* The tabulation revealed that next to the *Journal* itself the *Berichte der Deutschen chemische gessellschaft* and the *Journal of the Chemical Society* (London) lead a list of 26 chemical journals so frequently cited that their presence in a library serving chemistry research was considered essential. The technique has been adopted for developing lists of serials

---

❦ LISTS OF SERIALS

Ayer, firm, Philadelphia. N. W. Ayer and Son's Directory of Newspapers and Periodicals, 1880- (annual). Philadelphia, Ayer.

Ulrich's Periodicals Directory; a Classified Guide to a Selective List of Current Periodicals, Foreign and Domestic. 6th ed., by Eileen C. Graves; Caroline F. Ulrich, consulting editor. N.Y., Bowker, 1951. 517p.

in agriculture, engineering, mathematics, and even librarianship. There are, of course, obvious weaknesses as well as strengths in this technique. Selection of the basic journal for the count is critical. A significant journal in a highly specialized and important area may be omitted in the final list because of more frequent references to less significant research in popular phases of a subject.

A final method of selection is based on library holdings. Union catalogs of library resources have had a beneficial influence on serial selection by indicating ways for library co-operation within a region. If a union list reveals heavy duplication of certain serials in special fields and comparative neglect of other publications, serial selection can be influenced to the benefit of library users generally by co-operative selection.

The most comprehensive list of newspapers and periodicals published currently in America is *Ayer's Directory,* which lists 20,000 titles. The major arrangement is geographical. States are arranged alphabetically; under the name of each state, cities and towns with a publication of any kind are listed alphabetically; and under each locality the publications are given in alphabetic order. Basic data about such matters as titles, publisher, editor, political affiliation, frequency, format, price, and circulation are given. Alphabetic and classified indexes assist in quick location. Besides the publication data there are maps of the states, lists of counties, and brief descriptions of localities that make *Ayer's Directory* a favored source for quick information about small American communities.

The sixth edition of *Ulrich's Periodicals Directory* lists 10,000 foreign and domestic periodicals under more than 140 subject headings. Its advantages over *Ayer's Directory* are the inclusion of foreign publications and the careful attention to bibliographic form. Information given for each entry is: title, subtitle, founding date, frequency, price, publisher, address, and special features such as illustration, cumulative indexing, and the indexes and abstracts in which the periodical is analyzed. It is, however, too long a list for selection guidance in small libraries. For such help the reference librarian will have to turn

---

[1] Unesco, *World Communications: Press, Radio, Film* (Paris, Unesco, 1950), p. 167. This publication gives tables of statistics country by country.

[2] "College Libraries and Chemical Education," *Science,* 1927, v.66, p.385-89. One of the more recent references relating to the Gross technique is M. J. Voigt, "Scientific Periodicals As a Basic Requirement for Engineering and Agriculture Research," *College and Research Libraries,* 1947, v.8, p.354-59.

to three special lists. They are Martin's *Magazines for School Libraries*,[3] A.L.A. *Periodicals for Small and Medium-Sized Libraries*,[4] and Lyle's *Classified List of Periodicals for the College Library*.[5] Another indirect aid to periodical selection are the lists of periodicals indexed in the *Readers' Guide* and the other Wilson indexes, since these lists represent the pooled judgments of librarians.

Union catalogs of serials

Sources that reveal library holdings of back files of periodicals and newspapers are exceedingly useful in locating nearest centers for borrowing or for reproducing desired articles on photostat or microtext. To supplement the national union catalogs there are now numerous regional and local union catalogs that reveal holdings within an area.

The basic union catalog is the *Union List of Serials* which includes between 115,000 and 120,000 titles in more than 600 libraries. Each library is designated by a symbol and under each title the libraries and their holdings are listed. Companion to the *Union List of Serials* is *American Newspapers*, which aims to locate all existing files for the dates indicated.[6]

Daily newspapers

Newspapers appeared on the continent of Europe early in the seventeenth century. Not counting the *Acta Diurna* of the Roman Empire, which was copied by scribes and posted on bulletin boards, the first newspaper is supposed to have been issued in Germany in 1609. The first English newspaper appeared in London in May, 1622, and was called *The Weekly Newes from Italy, Germany, etc.* On

---

❦ UNION CATALOGS OF SERIALS

Union List of Serials in Libraries of the United States and Canada. 2d ed. N.Y., Wilson, 1943. Supplement (1941-43), 1945.

American Newspapers, 1821-1936; a Union List. N.Y., Wilson, 1937. 791p.

❦ DAILY NEWSPAPERS

New York Times, 1851-   (daily). N.Y., New York Times Company.

Christian Science Monitor, 1908-   (daily except Sunday). Boston, The Christian Science Publishing Society.

Daily newspapers

November 16, 1665, the first number of the biweekly *Oxford Gazette* was issued. The following year its name was changed to *London Gazette*, and it is still being issued by His Majesty's Stationery Office every Tuesday and Friday. Other historically famous periodicals in England which can be included in the genealogy of the newspaper were Daniel Defoe's *Review* (1704), Steele's *Tatler* (1709), and Steele and Addison's *Spectator* (1711). The eighteenth century saw an increase in the number of English newspapers to over fifty and the circulation of these newspapers to over eleven million copies annually. In that century three of the great English dailies of today were born: the *Morning Chronicle*, the *Morning Post* and the *Times*.

In America the first newspaper is supposed to have been established in 1704 by John Campbell, Boston postmaster. It was called the *Boston News-Letter*. Other eighteenth century American newspapers included the two which engrossed Benjamin Franklin, *The New England Courant* started by his brother and the *Pennsylvania Gazette* which Benjamin himself purchased. The nineteenth century produced the so-called penny press—started by Benjamin H. Day with the *New York Sun*—and the famous journalistic names of Horace Greeley, James Gordon Bennett, Charles Anderson Dana and Whitelaw Reid. *The New York Times* was established on September 18, 1851, by Henry Jarvis Raymond, and the *New York World* on June 1, 1860. The former was brought to its high position by Adolph S. Ochs, who assumed control in 1896, and the latter to its historic reputation by Joseph Pulitzer, who gained control in 1883. Pulitzer and William Randolph Hearst competed for records in sensationalism and started what is known as "yellow journalism." The twentieth century saw the development of chains of newspapers, the largest of which was Hearst's. Other chains are those of the Scripps-Howard, Frank E. Gannett, and Paul Block groups. Another phenomenon of this century is the rise of the tabloid paper with its smaller format and greater emphasis on pictures. The *New York Daily News* boasts the

---

[3] Laura K. Martin, *Magazines for School Libraries* (rev. ed.; N.Y., Wilson, 1950), 196p.

[4] American Library Association, *Periodicals for Small and Medium-Sized Libraries* (8th ed.; Chicago, A.L.A., 1948), 106p.

[5] Guy R. Lyle and Virginia M. Trumper, *Classified List of Periodicals for the College Library* (3d ed., rev. and enl.; Boston, Faxon, 1948), 99p.

[6] For a guide to other union catalogs the reference worker is referred to "Bibliography of Union Lists of Serials," by Daniel C. Haskell and Karl Brown, p.3053-65 of *Union List of Serials*, 2d ed.

largest circulation of any United States daily. Of special significance are the news gathering syndicates and feature story enterprises that serve many newspapers. The leading one is the Associated Press. Other syndicates and services are the United Press, the International News Service, and the Newspaper Enterprise Association.

A reference librarian can contribute daily to his craftsmanship by reading *The New York Times*. It has the fullest coverage of any newspaper. Its special features—reproductions of full texts of treaties, speeches, pronouncements, and other significant documents, and departments devoted to magazine, book review, education, art, music, theater, and industrial activities—provide a mine of potential answers to current questions. On the front page of the *Times* is a box headed "World News Summarized." This provides a guide to the significant developments of the day and should be studied by reference workers regularly. *The New York Times* is the only daily newspaper with a printed index.

A rival New York paper, the *New York Herald-Tribune* is of comparable importance to the *Times*. In the opinion of many newspapermen the *Herald-Tribune* is a better edited paper with superior make-up, almost as full coverage, and features as good as if not better than the *Times*. Political affiliations of the *Times* and *Herald-Tribune* are respectively Democratic and Republican, but both newspapers have high integrity and accord gracious treatment to the opposition.

The *Christian Science Monitor* is unique among newspapers of the world. It is devoted to dignified reporting of the news of the world. Crime and violence are totally absent from its pages. National and international affairs are presented with scholarly restraint. The special features on education, art, music, and the book reviews are of high quality. Even the cartoons appear to be of an artistic caliber.

News summaries

Supplementing the daily newspapers are two weekly news services, one American and the other British. *Facts on File*, the American

---

☞ NEWS SUMMARIES

Facts on File; a Weekly Synopsis of World Events, 1940-   . N.Y., Pearson's Index.

Keesing's Contemporary Archives; Weekly Diary of World Events, 1931-   . London, Keesing's, Ltd.

service, digests and classifies from the leading newspapers the significant news of the week. Facts are recorded day by day and made accessible through an ingenious indexing system, which consists of biweekly, monthly, quarterly, and annual cumulations. The eight-page weekly issue itself consists of a two-column page lettered in the left- and right-hand margin for index reference. Summaries are grouped under world affairs, national affairs, finance and economics, arts and science, obituaries, sports, and under numerous subheads of these subjects.

Keesing's Contemporary Archives, the British service, is a looseleaf weekly record of day-to-day developments in national and international politics, economics, industry, commerce, state finance, defense, social questions, religious life, etc. Included are extensive summaries or verbatim reports of all important treaties, charters, conferences, major pronouncements of leading personages, outstanding events in art, science, sports, and other areas of human activity. Sources used are government information departments, international news agencies and selected daily, weekly, and monthly publications. Diary sheets feature statistics, tables, maps, charts, and diagrams.

Periodicals

The earliest periodical is presumed to be the *Philosophical Transactions of the Royal Society,* first issued in 1665 and still published today. As in the beginning, when issues contained a number of essays on science, the *Transactions* continues today to devote itself to scientific subjects. Among the first literary periodicals to appear were Addison's *Tatler* and *Spectator,* both in the early years of the eighteenth century. The *Gentleman's Magazine* began in 1731 and did not cease publication until 1907. Its cumulative index from 1731 to 1818 as well as its content gives reference significance to this periodical. The early years of the nineteenth century saw the birth of review periodicals such as the *Edinburgh Review* and the *Quarterly Review.* All through the nineteenth century periodicals devoted to special subjects steadily increased in number. In America, **Benjamin** Franklin started the *General Magazine* in 1741 in imitation of the *Gentleman's Magazine,* but it was short-lived. The first American periodical to survive was the *North American Review* established in 1815. Among its early contributors were John Adams, R. H. Dana, Daniel Webster, and George Bancroft. Among other famous American periodicals of the nineteenth century are the *Southern Literary Messenger* (1834), *Godey's Lady's Book* (1830), *Harper's Magazine* (1850), *Atlantic*

Monthly (1857), *Scribner's* (1870), the *Century* (1881), and the *Forum* (1885).

Weekly current events periodicals. Supplementing the daily newspapers and weekly news services are the narrative summaries in the weekly news magazines. Three of these are of especial reference value, and it is recommended that every reference worker read one carefully and at least skim the others. The one chosen will depend upon personal tastes.

Newsweek is characterized by excellent coverage, objective reporting, and a dignified style. Special departments like the Periscope and Washington Trends, consisting of short paragraphs of incidents, comments, and predictions, hold answers to many current reference questions. In the section United States National Affairs there are often excellent pictographs such as the one of December 3, 1951, showing the arms production lag, and maps like the one in the same issue showing the strategic importance of Alaskan bases. Correspondents' departments like *Washington Tides,* by Ernest K. Lindley, *Business Tides,* by Henry Hazlitt, *Sport Week,* by John Lardner, and *Perspective,* by Raymond Moley, supplement news reporting with expert interpretation. There are excellent special sections on art, science, education, music, etc.

The older and more widely circulated *Time* aims at a full coverage of the week's news, but it has always been characterized by a style which in the opinion of some is annoying. Certainly, *Time*'s method of verbal communication is distinctive and has influenced popular expression and thinking. One of its features is News in Pictures, a two-page spread of photographs in addition to the illustrations that appear throughout.

United States News and World Report is distinguished by the number of special studies of trends and current problems which it carries. The departments—Tomorrow, A Look Ahead, Whispers, Trend of American Business, and Business Around the World—contain many reference nuggets.

☞ WEEKLY CURRENT EVENTS PERIODICALS

Newsweek, 1933-   . N.Y., Weekly Publications.

Time; the Weekly Newsmagazine, 1923-   . N.Y., Time, Inc.

United States News and World Report, 1933-   (weekly). Washington, United States News Publishing Corp.

Periodicals

Quantity periodicals. Two "quantity" magazines of reference importance are the *Saturday Evening Post,* "founded in 1728 by Benjamin Franklin," and *Collier's.* Their importance stems from the apparent fidelity with which their editors interpret the current interests of the American people. For that reason the articles in these two magazines very often contain answers to current questions.

A typical issue of the *Saturday Evening Post* includes nine or ten articles of information prepared usually by authorities and sometimes in collaboration with a *Post* writer. The December 1, 1951, issue, for example, covered in its nine articles such subjects as radio, Japan, football, meteorology, China, Russia, Mustangs, toys, and week-end guests. Although citation of articles in the *Post* is difficult, both because each issue is paged separately and because folios are omitted on so many pages, the quantity of contemporary information in each issue makes of the *Saturday Evening Post* a periodical of high reference value.

Collier's averages fewer articles in each issue but covers approximately the same popular interests. Its November 10, 1951, issue, for instance, dealt with such current subjects as Argentina, Russia, football, Navy operations, biography of an archbishop, and the activities of a prominent socialite. *Collier's* is referred to frequently for its unusual cartoons and its special issues like the one of October 21, 1951, on World War III.

Pictorial periodicals. Two mass media with picture emphasis have a reference value comparable to that of the *Saturday Evening Post* and *Collier's* because of the extent to which they reflect the current interests of the general public. *Life,* with a circulation of over five million weekly, covers in text and picture such different subject interests as national and international problems, education, religion, art, fashion, television, movies, and sports. A feature is the reproduction in color of art masterpieces. The rival picture magazine *Look,* which calls itself "America's Family Magazine," covers in picture and text "the

---

❦ QUANTITY PERIODICALS
Saturday Evening Post, 1728-   . Philadelphia, Curtis.
Collier's, 1888-   (weekly). N.Y., Crowell Collier.

❦ PICTORIAL PERIODICALS
Life, 1936-   (weekly). N.Y., Time, Inc.
Look, 1937-   (fortnightly). N.Y., Cowles Magazines.

nation, the world, science and health, sports, entertainment, art and fashions, food and home living," and reviews of recordings. It is issued every other week.

Literary and review periodicals. The so-called "quality" magazine with smaller circulation presents an intellectual review of national and world affairs with an emphasis on literary subjects. Two of the three periodicals listed to represent this class are issued monthly. *Harper's* features several thought-provoking articles on contemporary problems in each issue. For example, the November, 1951, issue treated such subjects as armaments, housing, Soviet activity in Berlin, and, of course, the new books. *Atlantic Monthly* for the same month presented reports on Washington, Islam, and Poland, feature articles on the American tradition, city planning, and government spending, and a biography of a naval leader. The Atlantic Bookshelf included a series of distinguished reviews. Music and recordings were also evaluated.

Not only for its book reviews but also for its continuous attention to the background of world and national events is the *Saturday Review* valued as a reference source. Its issue on the partnership between the United States and Britain and its interviews with Nehru earned it distinguished recognition during 1951. Special issues are devoted to types of literature, including an annual reference book number.

Interpretation periodicals. *Reader's Digest* and *The New Yorker* are listed together because they present two widely different interpretations of "the American way." *Reader's Digest* prints condensations of articles that appear in other magazines—articles that consistently represent the *Reader's Digest* philosophy. Just what that philosophy is depends upon the point of view of the critic. To the favorable camp *Reader's Digest* stands for individual initiative, private enterprise, kindly Christianity at its best. To the unfavorable camp it

---

❧ LITERARY AND REVIEW PERIODICALS
Harper's Magazine, 1850-   (monthly). N.Y., Harper.
Atlantic Monthly, 1857-   . Boston, Atlantic Monthly Co.
Saturday Review, 1924-   . N.Y., Saturday Review Associates.

❧ INTERPRETATION PERIODICALS
Reader's Digest, 1922-   (monthly). Pleasantville, N.Y., Reader's Digest Assn.
The New Yorker, 1925-   (weekly). N.Y., New Yorker Magazine.

Periodicals

represents paternalism, "pollyanna-ism," anti-New Dealism. The tremendous circulation of *Reader's Digest,* over 15,500,000 copies monthly, gives it a natural reference value. Critics of the publication see a danger in this very stereotyping of the American mind through what they consider a subtle form of propaganda. Opinions of English teachers are sharply divided on its educational value, some believing in it with testimonial enthusiasm, others denouncing the digests as a further weakening of the educational fiber of the people.

The New Yorker was one of the first periodicals to refuse to permit *Reader's Digest* to condense its articles. Frequently cited as a periodical with a social conscience, *The New Yorker* has opposed demagoguery with humor. It's take-off on Westbrook Pegler and on columnists in his camp are indicative of its interpretation of the American way. But from a reference standpoint *The New Yorker's* special features—its guides to theater, art, music, movies, sports, and other cultural events—answer numerous questions. Its profiles—short biographical sketches of prominent people by prominent biographers—supplement the standard biographical sources in a distinctive way. T. S. Shaw's *Index to Profile Sketches in The New Yorker Magazine* (Faxon, 1946) indexes these biographies by biographee, occupation, and biographer. It is only fair to say that most librarians' enthusiasm for *The New Yorker* is not shared by *Reader's Digest* enthusiasts or by philosophically sympathetic readers who find *The New Yorker* emphasis provincial and its display of sophistication occasionally lacking in maturity.

Two distinguished critical and somewhat left-of-center periodicals of interpretation are *The Nation* and *The New Republic.* Both have high literary standards and attract men and women of distinction to their roster of contributors. Frequent reference to them for liberal interpretation of the week's news is made in public and college libraries.

Reading list

Hutchins, Margaret. *Introduction to Reference Work.* Chicago, A.L.A., 1944. p.69-70 (current information), 103-08 (serials), and 109-14 (pamphlets).

Kaplan, Louis. "Reference Work with Periodicals: Recent Progress and Future Needs," *College and Research Libraries,* June, 1940, v.1, p.241-50.

SERIALS

Roberts, A. D. *Introduction to Reference Books.* London, Library Association, 1948. p.40-44, 77-81. The page references are to newspaper and periodical reference sources.

Shores, Louis. "Serials in the Library School Curriculum," *Serials Slants,* October, 1950, v.1, p.4-13. Analysis of the problems that have interested serials librarians as evidenced by the programs of the Serials Round Table of the A.L.A. and its predecessors.

chapter 11

INDEXES

Introduction, Indexes to indexes,

Indexes to collections, Periodical indexes,

News indexes, Pamphlet indexes.

Introduction

Source location questions. All the classes of questions considered thus far have had one common element—they required information. Many questions asked in libraries, however, require only sources, from which the inquirers may or may not eventually seek information. For example, patrons developing bibliographies on certain subjects may require only lists of books, parts of books, pamphlets, and periodical articles. These are primarily source location questions and require two types of reference books, indexes and bibliographies. This chapter is concerned with the location of information sources in indexes.

Source location questions may involve finding poems, songs, plays, short stories, essays, speeches, orations, recitations, articles, news stories and editorials.

Examples of source location questions are: What is a suitable poem for Armistice Day? I need the words to the song, "A Perfect Day." Supply titles of plays having war and socialism as the underlying theme. A copy of Webster's Seventh of March speech is needed. Where can I find Lamb's "Essay on Roast Pig"? Parent-Teacher's Association needs a play or pageant for founder's day. Where can I find O. Henry's short story, "Phoebe"? A reader wants *The New York Times* editorial on Christmas. A teacher wants materials for a third grade unit on Indians.

Source locaters. In April, 1948, Unesco summoned a small committee preparatory to an international conference on abstracting scientific information. To clarify discussion it adopted certain definitions, two of which are important in this chapter:

> An *index* is a systematically arranged list giving enough information about each item to enable it to be identified and traced.
>
> An *abstract* is a summary of a publication or article accompanied by an adequate bibliographical description to enable the publication or article to be traced.[1]

This chapter is limited to general indexes that locate sources in more than one subject field. Indexes to books, periodicals, newspapers, and pamphlets are examined. A fifth group, indexes to indexes, are discussed first. Only one index in this chapter can be said to approach the definition of an abstract, but several abstracts will be examined in Part II.

Value of indexes. Among reference books, Dr. Wyer calls indexes "a small group, but of an importance wholly out of proportion to its numerical strength...." Unfortunately this importance, though recognized by librarians, has failed to impress itself on the reading public. Says Charles E. Rush, "Readers see indexes; they know that such things may be found in the back of many books; yet they seldom examine them. Such lists of names and numbers form for them a sort of familiar dull background along with prefaces, forewords, footnotes, appendixes and bibliographies; a faintly confusing liturgy of the book trade."[2]

Omit an index, however, from a volume crammed full with as many facts as the *World Almanac* contains, for example, and the intelligent reader will feel much as Lord Campbell felt long ago when he declared, "So essential did I consider an index to be to every book that I proposed to bring a bill into Parliament to deprive an author who published a book without an index of the privilege of copyright, and, moreover, to subject him for his offense to a pecuniary penalty."

Indexes may be classified according to arrangement as follows: (1) alphabetical, which follows a straight dictionary arrangement and is usually the most useful; (2) classified, resembling a table of contents, an attempt to bring alphabetically arranged material into logical

Introduction

order; (3) concordance, an alphabetical list of words and references to their occurrence in a particular text; (4) fact-index, which not only lists and cites but in addition briefly describes. Classified as to the types of material indexed, there are indexes of (1) books, (2) serials, (3) government publications, (4) other printed matter, (5) audio-visual materials. Classified as to forms of materials indexed, there are indexes to poems, plays, fiction, essays, orations, songs, laws, patents, trade names, and to other indexes.

For the study and evaluation of indexes the following checklist is suggested:

I. Period covered
  1. Date
  2. Frequency (if serial)—weekly, monthly, quarterly, etc.
  3. Cumulations—scheme and frequency
II. Materials indexed
  4. Number—in terms of volumes, periodicals, or articles
  5. Kinds—books, periodicals, newspapers, documents
  6. Subject—general or special
  7. Style—popular or scholarly
  8. Country—American, foreign
III. Form
  9. Complete or selective indexing (if latter, note basis of selection)
  10. Arrangement—dictionary, classified, author, title, subject
  11. Entry fulness—author, title, source, collation, date, etc.
  12. Annotation—information given
IV. Special features
  13. Distinctiveness—anything characteristic of this index and no other

Indexes in the reference department. All good reference departments supplement printed bibliographies and indexes with home-made ones. The card catalog and the shelf list will be obvious library records to use. What card indexes the reference department prepares in addition should not normally duplicate the ground of any other bibliographic tool in the library.

Some of the more usual indexes prepared by reference departments are to bibliographies, biographies, debates, directories, fiction,

---

[1] Royal Society, Scientific Information Conference, 21 June—3 July, 1948, *Reports and Papers* (London, 1948), p.557.
[2] "Cultivating the Index Habit," *Library Journal*, 1930, v.55, p.590-93.

holidays, laws, local newspapers, poetry, short stories, and to local agencies, resources, and educational opportunities.

Indexes to indexes

The number and variety of indexes in American libraries, published and on cards, are so great that it is inevitable that indexes to indexes should follow. Two such publications are cited here. Ireland's *Index to Indexes* is " a subject bibliography of published indexes assembled to aid librarians and students who wish to locate the indexsources of the various subject fields." Entries are alphabetic under subject. A frequency table of indexes most used in reference is an added feature.

Nearly 8000 unpublished indexes maintained in almost 950 different libraries listed alphabetically under subject is the scope of *Local Indexes in American Libraries* prepared as a project of the A.L.A. Junior Members Round Table and edited by Norma Ireland. In many ways this volume is also an index to what people want to know in American libraries.

Indexes to collections

Most books of information have indexes and some books of recreation could well afford them. Mark Twain once suggested indexed

---

❦ INDEXES TO INDEXES
Ireland, Norma O. An Index to Indexes. Boston, Faxon, 1942. 107p.
A.L.A. Junior Members Round Table. Local Indexes in American Libraries. Boston, Faxon, 1947. 221p.

❦ INDEXES TO COLLECTIONS
Essay and General Literature Index, 1900-1933. N.Y., Wilson, 1934. Supplements, 1934- .
A.L.A. Index; an Index to General Literature. 2d ed., greatly enl. and brought down to Jan. 1, 1900. Boston, Houghton, 1901. Supplement (1900-1910), Chicago, A.L.A., 1914.
Rue, Eloise. Subject Index to Books for Intermediate Grades. 2d ed. Chicago, A.L.A., 1950. 493p.
——— Subject Index to Books for Primary Grades. Chicago, A.L.A., 1943. 236p. First Supplement, 1946.

appendixes for "classic" descriptions of nature, man, and other things, so that the reader interested only in the narrative might read without interruption.

Every reference book, intended to be used for specific information requires an index. The better the index, the more useful the book is likely to be for reference. The quality of indexing varies greatly. Of the reference books examined thus far, encyclopedias and yearbooks have probably the best indexes. Such a comprehensive index as that in the 24th volume of the *Britannica* with its half-million entries is remarkable for its scope, if not for its form. The run-on paragraphs employed are a hindrance to rapid use. The *Compton* index, though not as extensive an undertaking, is superior in form, both from the standpoint of selection of headings and paragraph style. Such indexes as those contained in the *World Almanac*—which could be improved —and the *Lincoln Library* are vital for reference.

Indexes to composite books are vital to reference service. Among examples of this type of index the *Essay and General Literature Index* is basic. It is published semiannually, with annual, three-year and seven-year cumulations. Its basic volume for the period 1900-1933 indexes over 2000 collections containing some 40,000 essays. These 2000 volumes for indexing were selected by 36 public, 12 college, and one school library as most representative of American library holdings. Although only books published since 1900 are included it must be remembered that such composite books as are indexed include many classic essays of previous years. *Festschriften,* i.e., collections of essays, speeches, and studies in honor of a scholar, are not included. The index is arranged with all types of entries in one alphabet, with this sequence in the author entries: (1) author's works, (2) works about the author, (3) criticisms of individual works.

The *Essay and General Literature Index* supplements a previous work, the *A.L.A. Index,* which must not be confused with the *A.L.A. Catalog.* The second and last edition of the *A.L.A. Index* brought the indexing of collections down to 1900. Its purpose was "to index as far as possible all books common in our libraries which treat several subjects under one title, and to the contents of which the ordinary catalogue furnishes no guide, although they are treated analytically in the more elaborate library catalogue." Some 2800 volumes of collections of essay, travel, history, and society publications of the nineteenth century are indexed. The essay indexing sections of the *Annual Literary Index* and *Annual Library Index,* parts of the Poole periodical indexing system, were cumulated to make the *A.L.A. Index Supplement, 1900-10.*

In 1938 Eloise Rue introduced *A Subject Index to Readers,* which did for composite children's books what the *Essay and General Literature Index* did for adult collections. The popularity of the first Rue volume and the need for still further indexing of children's books on different levels resulted in two further indexes, one for intermediate grades in 1940 and one for primary grades in 1943. The latter is supplemented by a volume issued in 1946; the former and its supplement are now largely replaced by the 1950 edition. An examination of this edition of the *Subject Index to Intermediate Grades* will serve to explain the pattern for all of the titles in the series. About 1875 books are indexed by curriculum subjects. The first part of the volume is a list of the books indexed and the second part consists of references to the books under these subjects alphabetically arranged. For each entry exact reference is given to the page of the book and grade span is indicated. The following are typical subjects: Africa; Agricultural Machinery; Alaska—Stories; Birds in Winter; Carson, Christopher; Toys; Zoos.

Periodical indexes

Indexes to individual periodicals vary in quality and in period covered. Many periodicals, of course, do not have indexes; at the other extreme, some indexes to individual periodicals are significant as reference tools. Examples are the indexes to the *Book Review Digest,* to Barnard's *American Journal of Education,* to the *National Geographic Magazine.* Especially helpful are the cumulative indexes. A useful bibliography of these is D. C. Haskell's *Check Lists of Cumulative Indexes to Individual Periodicals in the New York Public Library* (1942).

Indexes to the contents of multiple periodicals comprise an important class of basic reference books. These indexes generally analyze the contents of a selected group of periodicals by subject and author and sometimes by title. Occasionally they go further and abstract, digest, or summarize periodical articles.

The two best-known and most widely used systems of general periodical indexing are Poole and Wilson, the former for the nineteenth and the latter mainly for the twentieth century.

The Poole indexes. Because of the pioneer nature of the Poole

Periodical indexes

indexes, their history is of unusual interest. The author of the system, William Frederick Poole, as a student in Yale University had noticed that old periodicals in the library were almost never used, chiefly because no one was aware of their contents. Poole, therefore, decided to index several standard sets which contained articles on many subjects about which students inquired but received very little material. His first crude index in manuscript form proved so popular that it became necessary to print the material. This first edition, a rarity now, appeared as *Index to Subjects Treated in the Reviews and Other Periodicals* (New York, 1848, 154p.). In a very short time, the 500 copies were taken up by libraries, and a second, enlarged edition, bringing the indexing down to 1852, appeared under the title, *Index to Periodical Literature* (New York, 1853, 521p.). This time one thousand copies were printed and, like the previous edition, were sold almost immediately.

The need for periodical indexing grew steadily more insistent thereafter. Libraries in desperation began indexing periodicals for themselves, much as they cataloged their books, inserting the cards for periodicals among the cards for books in the catalog. At the American Library Association's first convention in Philadelphia, 1876, the subject of periodical indexing was given top priority. Poole proposed there the following plan:

> I would print and send to all the principal libraries a list of periodicals which it was desirable to index, on which such complete sets as the library had would be checked and the lists returned to me. Having received these lists, I would make an equitable distribution of the work, taking a full share of it myself, and giving to the larger libraries more, and to the smaller libraries less. Each library would engage to index according to a code of rules, which would be furnished, the set or sets

---

☞ THE POOLE INDEXES

Poole's Index to Periodical Literature, 1802-1881. Rev. ed. Boston, Houghton, Mifflin, 1891. 2v. Supplements, 1882-1906. 5v.

Annual Literary Index, 1892-1904; Including Periodicals, American and English; Essays, Book Chapters, etc. N.Y., Publishers' Weekly, 1893-1905. 13v.

Annual Library Index, 1905-1910; Including Periodicals, American and English; Essays, Book Chapters, etc. N.Y., Publishers' Weekly, 1906-11. 6v.

INDEXES

of periodicals allotted to it, and send the references to me, who would revise, arrange, and incorporate the same with the matter of the edition of 1853 and with the work of all the other contributors. I would assume all the pecuniary responsibilities incurred, employ such assistance as was needed, print the work, and furnish a copy to each contributing library.

The plan was adopted by acclamation, and, at Poole's suggestion, Justin Winsor and Charles Ammi Cutter were appointed to assist as technical advisers. After the work had been in progress for a year, Poole appeared before the British Library Association where his plan was agreed to with misgivings in view of the failure of a similar plan for the Philological Society's dictionary. An allotment was made to English librarians, but of the 25 periodicals assigned only eight were completed in time for inclusion—on which Poole remarked in his Preface, "Perhaps the climate and social customs of England are not so favorable as they are in America for night work."

The diagram, Periodical Indexes, indicates the period covered by the Poole system of periodical indexing—about 109 years, counting the last volume of the *Annual Library Index*. When *Poole's Index* had been completed, librarians at once demanded a method for keeping

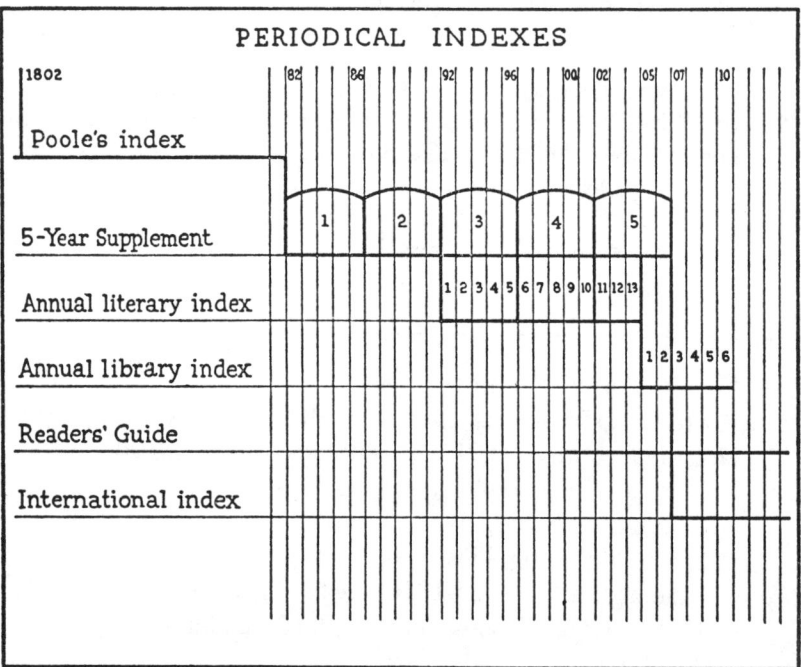

Periodical indexes

the indexing up to date. A five-year supplement for 1882-86 was undertaken, but not completed until nearly another five years had elapsed. Heroically, the librarians set out to catch up with time, and produced the second supplement, 1887-91. It then became obvious that five years comprised too long a period to wait, and so the librarians went into the business of making annual indexes. The first, for 1892, was called the *Annual Literary Index,* and with the next four was combined to form another five-year supplement, 1892-96. Five more *Annual Literary Indexes* were cumulated to form the fourth supplement, 1897-1901. The fifth and last five-year supplement saw a change in form and name for its component annuals. The 1905 annual became the *Annual Library Index,* and with the following "library" annual and the three preceding "literary" annuals formed the final five-year supplement. Four more *Annual Library Indexes* appeared before the Poole system gave way to the newer and improved Wilson indexing system.

When one considers the following statistics—590,000 articles indexed in 12,241 volumes of 470 American and English periodicals —one marvels at the achievement of Poole's co-operative venture. Primarily, the serials indexed were those English language periodicals likely to be found in public and private libraries. The year 1802 was probably chosen to begin the indexing because two important journals, *Edinburgh Review* and *Christian Observer,* were first published in that year, and only one periodical, the *Methodist Magazine,* was published earlier. All other important periodicals of the nineteenth century began after 1802.

A fairly complete job of indexing was done, Poole's instructions to the 51 co-operating libraries reading on this point, "References to trivial and inconsequential matters must be avoided." This meant omission of very brief articles and notes, minor book reviews and, because of faulty collaboration, some material from the uncompleted English journals.

Poole's basic volume is primarily a subject index. There are no entries under author unless the author is the subject of the article. In general, therefore, informational articles are entered under subject or catch title; while imaginative writings—fiction, poems, plays—are entered under the first word of the title. Book reviews of informational books are entered under subject of the book; imaginative books are entered under author, who may be considered the subject of the review.

Information given under each entry includes:
1. Title, under catchword or important word
2. Author's name when known, in parentheses
3. Title of periodical (abbreviated)
4. Volume, and first page only (not inclusive paging)

Example:
Glaciers
———Active, in United States (C. King) Atlan. 27:371
———Agency of, in the Erosion of valleys (W.H. Niles) Am. J. Sci. 116:366
———Ancient, in Auvergne (W.S. Symonds) Nature 14: 179
———and Glacier Theories. Nat. R. 9:1—Westm. 67:418

The date, not given in the entry, can be surmised from the chronological conspectus at the beginning of the volume.

The five-year supplements followed the scope and form of the original volume. When the annuals began to appear, the supplements used only the periodical indexing of the *Annuals*. Such book indexing as was done by the *Annual Literary Index* from 1892 to 1904, and by the *Annual Library Index* from 1905 to 1910, was incorporated in the revised *A.L.A. Index* of 1900, and in the *A.L.A. Index Supplement* of 1900-10.

The *Annual Literary Index* varied from the original volume in several particulars. In the matter of scope, indexing was extended to include composite books as well as periodicals, and in 1895 the "Index of Dates to Principal Events," a newspaper index in fact, was added. The contents of the *Annual Literary Index* for 1897 will indicate the scope of the work: (1) index to periodicals, including lists of periodicals and collaborators; (2) index to general literature, including list of books indexed; (3) author index to both periodicals and books; (4) bibliographies of 1897, published in England and America; (5) necrology of writers deceased in 1897; (6) index to dates of principal events for 1897.

The *Annual Library Index,* which appeared for the first time in 1905, represented more than merely a change of name. A fundamental revision in arrangement was accomplished with "entry by author and title, and subject, when not indicated in the title." Three kinds of type were used to distinguish author, title, and subject in each entry. Fiction entries appear in italics. Contents of the 1910 annual, which closed the Poole system, show how it differed from the *Annual Literary*

Periodical indexes

Index: (1) index to periodicals—dictionary arrangement; (2) index to general literature—dictionary arrangement; (3) bibliographies; (4) necrology; (5) index to dates of principal events; (6) select lists of public libraries in the United States and Canada; (7) select list of private collectors of books. The annual indexes were from the start edited by W. I. Fletcher and issued from the *Publishers' Weekly* office, even while the five-year supplements were appearing under the imprint of Houghton, Mifflin.

The Wilson indexes. In many ways, the steps which led to the establishment of the greatest current indexing system in the world paralleled those taken by its predecessor.[3] Halsey W. Wilson, while a student in the University of Minnesota, where he ran the bookstore, developed a book list, a debate index, and a selected periodical index. The first originated as an aid to his book business and became the great *United States Catalog—Cumulative Book Index* scheme. For the debating teams of the University of Minnesota Mr. Wilson prepared outlines and bibliographies, which proved very popular among students, and which ultimately grew into the series known as the *Debaters' Handbooks* and the *Reference Shelf*. The periodical index was begun in 1900, by indexing 15 popular periodicals found in most libraries, for the purpose of meeting the need which brought an abridged *Poole's*. This early Wilson index became the *Readers' Guide* and established the foundation for an indexing system which is the standard for the world.

No better statement of the principles responsible for the success of Wilson indexes can be found than that made by Miss Edith Phelps in the *A.L.A. Bulletin* in 1926:

> During the 26 years in which The Wilson Company has been engaged in the making of periodical indexes, it has found it possible to approach the ideal index most nearly by: (1) offering to all subscribers an opportunity to participate in the selection of periodicals for indexing, (2) establishing efficient methods of work, (3) establishing the service basis of charge, which, (a) enables each library to pay toward

---

[3] John Lawler, *The H. W. Wilson Company; Half a Century of Bibliographic Publishing* (Minneapolis, Univ. of Minnesota Pr., 1950), 207p. Individual Wilson publications are also described in the pamphlet, *Wilson Publications,* issued by that company free of charge and in quantity to library schools. Other desirable readings are the *Publishers' Weekly*'s salute to the *Readers' Guide* on the occasion of its fiftieth anniversary (April 7, 1951, v.159, p.1552) and Jack Harrison Pollack, "Giant of Bibliographers," *Saturday Review,* February 3, 1951, v.34, no. 5, p.32).

the indexing according to the amount it uses, and (b) permits the cost of indexing any periodical to be borne by those subscribing for that periodical and so benefiting from its indexing.[4]

Briefly, these three principles have been put into practice as follows:

First, from time to time, librarians are asked to indicate which periodicals they want indexed in any one index. The *Abridged Readers' Guide,* for example, came in response to the demand of school librarians, and as a result school librarians were asked to vote for the periodical titles they wanted indexed.

Second, a visit to the H. W. Wilson plant in New York City will convince anyone of the truth of Miss Phelps' statement about efficient methods of work. Different visitors will of course be impressed by different things there—files of entries in type, the huge presses, the system in the editorial department. But above all, everyone will come away with a feeling of work exceptionally well planned and systemized.

Third, all Wilson indexes are paid for in proportion to the amount of use made of them. In the publisher's own words:

> The problem of how to meter the service fairly to all libraries, large and small, has been a difficult one, and the present system has developed little by little over a number of years. Roughly speaking, the Wilson Company catalogs and indexes are divided into two classes— (A) the periodical indexes, where the subscription price is based on the periodicals that are indexed to which the library subscribes; and (B) the book catalogs, including the *Cumulative Book Index, Book Review Digest, Standard Catalog* series, and similar tools, where the price is determined according to the library's book fund or other reasonable basis.[5]

Besides the general periodical indexes listed as basic reference sources, the Wilson indexing system includes the following special

---

❦ THE WILSON INDEXES
Readers' Guide to Periodical Literature, 1900- .
Abridged Readers' Guide to Periodical Literature, 1935- .
International Index to Periodical Literature, 1907- .
Nineteenth Century Readers' Guide to Periodical Literature, 1890-99. 2v.

Periodical indexes

periodical indexes: *Agricultural Index,* since 1916; *Art Index,* since 1930; *Bibliographic Index,* since 1937; *Biography Index,* since 1946; *Book Review Digest,* since 1905; *Education Index,* since 1929; *Industrial Arts Index,* since 1913; and *Index to Legal Periodicals,* since 1908. These do not, of course, comprise the entire indexing system, there being in addition indexes for books (*United States Catalog* and *Cumulative Book Index*), for pamphlets (*Vertical File Service*), and for films and pictures. Only the general indexes are treated in this chapter; the subject indexes are described in the chapters on their subjects in Part II.

Readers' Guide. The first cumulation of the *Readers' Guide,* that of 1900-04, resulted from the consolidation in 1903 of the *Cumulative Index to a Selected List of Periodicals* and the Wilson *Readers' Guide.* The former index, inaugurated in the Cleveland Public Library by W. H. Brett, had been issued for 1896 and 1897 in quarterly numbers and annual cumulations. The following year the index was taken over by a commercial firm which continued to issue the index to 1903. In the meantime, the *Readers' Guide* had begun its career in Minneapolis in 1901, indexing about 20 periodicals. An annual was issued in 1901 and a two-year cumulation in 1902. After the merger of the two indexes in 1903, some new periodicals were added to the list, and the index was issued quarterly with cumulations at the end of six-, nine-, and twelve-month periods. Since the last annual cumulation of the *Cumulative Index* had been for 1899, it was decided to issue a four-year cumulation from 1900 to 1904. This first cumulation, indexing 67 periodicals, was edited by Miss Anna Lorraine Guthrie, former reference librarian of the University of Minnesota.

The second cumulation covered the period 1905-09, indexed 99 periodicals, and introduced "also in the same alphabet an index to 430 books, reports, etc., constituting a supplement to the second edition of the A.L.A. *Index to General Literature."* In the preface of neither the first nor second cumulation was there any mention of the rival Poole indexing system.

Succeeding cumulations cover periods of three or four years.

In 1935 two important features were added to the *Readers' Guide*

---

[4] "Problems Involved in Making Periodical Indexes," *A.L.A. Bulletin,* 1926, v.20, p.532.
[5] The application of this principle to specific indexes is detailed in *Wilson Publications,* 1951 ed., p.26-27.

indexing service, intended to aid both the very small and the larger libraries. For the smaller libraries, especially school libraries, an *Abridged Readers' Guide* indexing 25 selected periodicals was launched. The minimum service charge for this index is less than half the minimum service charge for the unabridged index. Thirty-five periodicals are indexed in the *Abridged Readers' Guide*. The form is the same as for the large *Readers' Guide*, but issues are monthly, except July and August, the indexing for these two issues being included in September.

Under the date of March 25, 1935, an experimental issue of the *Readers' Guide* appeared in response to a growing demand for a midmonthly issue to "shorten the gap between monthly numbers and to give subscribers even more 'up-to-the-minute' service than has been possible under the monthly schedule." The next midmonthly issue, April 25, outlined a plan for financing the increased service and again asked for votes. The third midmonthly carried the announcement of the adopted plan: (1) midmonthly issue indexes material from the 5th to the 20th of the month to be released on the 25th; (2) monthly issue indexes material from the 5th to the 5th to be released on the 10th; (3) since larger libraries profited proportionately more, the increase in cost to be assumed on a proportionate basis.

An average issue of the *Readers' Guide* now indexes more than 130 American and Canadian general serials, most of which are popular periodicals of the type found in the average American public library. Included also are a few government and society publications, like the *U.S. Office of Education Bulletins* and the *Annals of the American Academy of Political and Social Science*. Author and subject entries are given for each entry—with emphasis on subject—and title entries are included for stories. A dictionary arrangement is used.

The special feature of all Wilson indexing is the cumulation scheme. *Cumulate* as a term in library use is defined in the *New International Dictionary* as "to combine in successive issues the entries of preceding issues." Although cumulation in indexes is not a Wilson invention, the cumulative index as a reference tool has been perfected by Wilson.

International Index to Periodical Literature. The *International Index* was begun in March, 1913, in response to a need felt by the larger libraries for an index to special periodicals such as had been included in the list of periodicals indexed by the Poole system, a need

Periodical indexes

felt more sharply after the discontinuance of the *Annual Library Index* in 1910. At the time, the *Readers' Guide* was indexing about 100 general periodicals, as compared with the 470 English and American periodicals libraries had requested in 1877, when Poole's index became a co-operative venture. Of course, a great many of these publications had been suspended and some others were infrequently used by most libraries, but it could not be unimportant that the suspension of the Poole system in 1910 meant reduction of the indexing service available to libraries by at least 300 titles. Hence the appearance of the *Readers' Guide Supplement,* the name under which the *International Index* was launched, in 1913.

The first cumulation of the *Readers' Guide Supplement* was extended back to include 1907 and thus close the gap between the last five-year supplement of Poole (1902-06) and the beginning of the *Readers' Guide Supplement.* It indexed 19 special periodicals transferred from the *Readers' Guide* and 55 other periodicals. Succeeding volumes cover periods of from three to four years.

The *International Index* is now "an author and subject index to about 175 periodicals in pure science and humanities." More specifically, the subjects include anthropology, archaeology, astronomy, biology, economics, ethics, general science, geography, geology, history, literature, oceanography, paleontology, philology, philosophy, political science, physics, psychology, religion, sociology, and zoology. Since 1948 the indexing of French and German along with English language publications, dropped during the Second World War, has been resumed.

The *Nineteenth Century Readers' Guide* is the first of a projected series of indexes to periodicals of the nineteenth century. It indexes 51 selected periodicals of reference value. For those titles later included in the *Readers' Guide* indexing is carried forward from 1900 to the date when indexing in the present *Readers' Guide* began.

Other periodical indexes. Other specialized periodical indexes, some of which are described in Part II of this textbook, are issued outside the Poole and Wilson systems. *Public Affairs Information Service* (cited P.A.I.S.) is prepared in the Economics Division of the New York Public Library. Other indexes are the *Dramatic Index* (Faxon), *Engineering Index, Magazine Subject Index* (Faxon), *Quarterly Cumulative Index Medicus* (American Medical Association), and *Subject Index to Periodicals* (Library Association).

INDEXES

News indexes

A type of newspaper indexing service, as has been seen, was offered by the *Annual Literary Index* and *Annual Library Index* from 1895 through 1910. For many years before that time, however, newspapers had published their own indexes. Among them the *London Times* has probably the longest record of continuous indexing service, dating back through *Palmer's Index* to 1790. The present *Times Index* is issued quarterly and indexes all issues of the newspaper. Librarians, too, have long maintained their own newspaper index files, especially to local papers.

In this country, the oldest published index is that of *The New York Times,* whose modern era of service begins with 1913. On the shelves of the newspaper division of the New York Public Library is *The New York Times Index* for 1860-1904 as well as for 1913 to the present. The 1913 date, however, marks the beginning of most libraries' files.

Unlike a periodical index, the index to one newspaper can serve as an index to all newspapers, since major news appears in every newspaper, and minor news appears with varying degrees of emphasis in most newspapers. For this reason *The New York Times Index,* being an index to the most comprehensive daily newspaper in America, is justified in calling itself a "master-key to the news." It is a semimonthly subject index with annual cumulations, although from 1913 to 1929 it was published quarterly, and from 1930 to 1947 monthly with annual cumulations. A feature of arrangement that must be remembered is the fact that the colon in the page reference separates page from column, not, as in the periodical indexes, volume from page. Thus in *The New York Times Index* 6:1 is a reference to page six, column one; in the *Readers' Guide* it is a reference to volume six, page one.

❦ NEWS INDEXES

The Official Index to The Times, 1906-   . London, The Times.
The New York Times Index, 1913-   . N.Y., The New York Times.

❦ PAMPHLET INDEXES

Vertical File Service Catalog, 1932-   (monthly). N.Y., Wilson.

Pamphlet indexes

Several of the serial indexes list and analyze pamphlet material, but the *Vertical File Service Catalog* is the principal index devoted to ephemeral material. Begun in April, 1932, as a monthly subject catalog with annual cumulation, the *Service* has included descriptive notes, price, and conditions under which each listed pamphlet may be obtained. A title index giving the subject heading under which each title may be found is included in every issue.

There are other indexes—to audio-visual materials, to government publications, to various subjects, to foreign literature[6]—some still to be studied, others to be revealed by work on reference questions.

There is no more fitting way to close this chapter on indexes than to quote Oliver Wendell Holmes on the subject as he was quoted by the *Readers' Guide,* 1910-14:

> A great portion of the best writing and reading,—literary, scientific, professional, miscellaneous—comes to us now, at stated intervals, in paper covers. The writer appears, as it were, in his shirt-sleeves. As soon as he has delivered his message the book-binder puts a coat on his back, and he joins the forlorn brotherhood of "back volumes," than which, so long as they are unindexed, nothing can be more exasperating. Who wants a lock without a key, a ship without a rudder, a binnacle without a compass, a check without a signature, a greenback without a goldback behind it? Arranged, bound, indexed, all these at once become accessible and valuable.

---

[6] On foreign periodical indexes see A. D. Roberts, *Introduction to Reference Books* (London, Library Association, 1948), p.40-42, 88-92.

chapter 12

BIBLIOGRAPHIES

Introduction, Eclectic bibliographies,

School library eclectic bibliographies,

Public library eclectic bibliographies,

College library eclectic bibliographies,

United States national and trade bibliographies,

United States retrospective bibliography,

British national bibliography,

Other foreign national bibliographies,

Universal bibliographies, Bibliographies of bibliographies.

Introduction

Bibliographic questions. A considerable portion of the day's work in reference is concerned with bibliographic questions. These fall into three broad groups: selection, identification, and documentation.

Questions on selection require the choice of a limited number of titles to meet a specific purpose. In any one day these purposes may

Introduction

be many and varied. The reader who wants a good book to read on a certain subject challenges the reference librarian's bibliographic equipment to suggest one book to fit the individual and often peculiar needs of the inquirer from among the many available. School and college assignments necessitate at least a preliminary list of suitable works on the topic for study. The library itself, as a fundamental part of its operation, must select those books that will best serve the interests of its community. Problems of book selection, to say nothing of selection problems in nonbook materials, are therefore a continuous part of reference service.

How immense the selection type of bibliographic question really is, whether a book is being chosen for purchase or selected from the library's collection to answer a specific question, will be more readily appreciated when one considers from how many books the selection must be made. Unesco, in its preliminary statistical report on book production[1] tabulated 11,022 titles for the United States and 17,072 titles for the United Kingdom for the year 1950 alone. Disregarding for the moment the book production indicated for each of 42 other countries for that year, it is apparent that the reference librarian's choice of a limited number of books to fit the library's needs must be made from 28,000 different book titles issued in the two major English-language countries in a single year. When to that total is added the book production for every year during some five centuries of printing the universe of books reaches a number in the millions. Obviously, reference aid is required to meet inquiries of the readers' advisory type and to choose the library's own acquisitions.

A comparable problem exists in identification questions. These involve identifying or locating a book for which bibliographic information is often incomplete. Missing from the inquirer's record may be full author's name, exact title, date, paging, price, and any of several other items. Worse still, identification may be blocked by incorrect or partially correct bibliographic data. Sound bibliographic knowledge and ingenious cross-examination of the inquirer may be required to answer these questions.

The so-called documentation type of question has moved into a position of reference prominence especially since World War II. On the continent of Europe, documentation has become almost a major

---

[1] Unesco, Statistical Service, *Preliminary Statistical Report on Book Production in Various Countries* (Paris, May 14, 1951), 79p., processed.

branch of librarianship if not indeed a separate profession. In Britain a book on the subject, cited in the Reading list at the end of this chapter, was written by the late eminent librarian, Dr. S. C. Bradford, who defined documentation as "the process of collecting and subject classifying all the records of new observations or making them available, at need, to the discoverer or the inventor." It is dangerous to attempt to simplify an explanation of a subject about which there are still some differences of concept. Documentation appears to comprehend all aspects of reference that support research. It includes abstracting and disseminating the abstracts of latest researches quickly to the points where similar investigation is going on. The high aim of documentation appears to be to reduce the time lapse between discovery and application of this discovery in the effort to make new discovery. A whole new feverish sort of impetus has been given to this aspect of reference by the armament race between the East and West. In documentation probably more than in any other aspect of reference, the librarian tends to become almost a full partner in research. For that reason so many of the "documentalists," as they are called abroad, are subject specialists as well as librarians—chemists, physicists, mathematicians, engineers, biologists, agriculturists, etc.

The documentary question therefore involves a ready knowledge of the literature of a specialized field. It may at any time challenge the reference librarian's resources to locate a specific finding that will bear directly on the solution of a problem or the reduction of an obstacle that blocks new discovery. But the documentary question has an element of continuity as well as urgency. For the documentalist screens literature systematically for contribution to the researches he is hired to support.

Bibliographic sources. There have been many definitions of bibliography in the past. The word has often been used to cover every phase of book knowledge, including the art and science of book production and the business of distribution. It has been defined in a Unesco publication as "the technique of systematically producing descriptive lists of written or published records (especially books and similar materials)." Although most of the bibliographies described in this chapter are printed books, bibliography is here defined as a list of written, printed, or otherwise produced records of civilization. These records may be books, serials, pictures, maps, films, recordings, museum objects, manuscripts, and any other media of communication. A bibliography is distinguished from a catalog in the words of the *A.L.A.*

Introduction

Glossary of Library Terms as "not being necessarily a list of materials in a collection, a library, or a group of libraries."

In this chapter bibliographies are classified as (1) eclectic, (2) national and trade, and (3) universal. Bibliographies confined in scope to one subject field or area are treated in later chapters. Eclectic bibliographies are lists of records not necessarily limited by time or place, but selected for a purpose. National bibliographies are limited to the records of a single nation or language, and trade bibliographies are lists of books intended for the book trade. Universal bibliographies are lists of records that are not limited by place, time, or subject.

Study and evaluation of bibliographies. No division of library work can dispense with the use of bibliographies. The administrator needs them as guides in building his collections. In acquisitions, bibliographies give information concerning editions, publishers, dates, prices, binding, in-print and out-of-print titles. In cataloging information is verified largely with the aid of bibliographies. In the public service divisions of the library there is almost constant reference to bibliographies and catalogs.

The following evaluation checklist is suggested for the study of bibliographies:

I. Authority
  1. Compiler—qualifications—subject, bibliographic, academic
  2. Sponsor—group, publisher, or other agency responsible for production and distribution
II. Scope
  3. Purpose—as stated by compiler
  4. Limitations—subject, language, time, place, kinds of materials
III. Arrangement
  5. Primary—dictionary, author, title, publisher, subject, chronologic, regional, combination, other
  6. Index—relation to primary arrangement
IV. Entry fullness
  7. Items—author, title, imprint, collation, series, price, other
  8. Annotations—descriptive, abstract, summary
V. Special features
  9. Distinctiveness—relationship to comparable works

Good bibliographies are the work of careful compilers and reputable sponsors. Purpose and limitations should be clearly stated, either as part of the title or in a preface. Intelligent attention to arrangement enhances the reference value of a bibliography. For bibliographies which will be consulted principally for information about individual books an alphabetical arrangement is preferable; in a subject bibliography, a classified arrangement is often best. Regardless of the major arrangement, complementary indexes are an asset to use. Consistency in entry form and criteria for inclusion add to the usefulness of a list and descriptive and critical annotations save time for the research worker. Comparisons between bibliographies should bring out variations in scope and fulness of entry.

Eclectic bibliographies

Lists of "best books" have engaged the attention of bibliophiles, bibliographers, librarians, and educators for almost as long as printing itself. In recent times a more sharply focused educational significance has attached to these lists. It has been contended that an education from the reading of books would equal that offered by an institution of higher learning. One of the earliest of such self-education lists was that developed by President Charles Eliot of Harvard University which he called the Five-Foot Shelf. The author of this book in an essay on the American Library Association's annual conference theme of 1934, "Libraries Twenty Years Thence," predicted the library arts college in which guided, independent reading would largely replace classroom lectures. One college, St. John's, has indeed prepared a list of one hundred books for its students. Other colleges have introduced honors reading and independent study. *Great Books of the Western World,* identified with the University of Chicago, is still another example of an eclectic list with an educational motif.

Libraries have long been concerned with the problem of selecting

---

❦ ECLECTIC BIBLIOGRAPHIES

The Booklist, 1905-   (semimonthly). Chicago, A.L.A.

Book Review Digest, 1905-   . N.Y., Wilson.

The United States Quarterly Book Review, 1945-   . Washington, Library of Congress, 1945-1947; New Brunswick, N.J., Rutgers Univ. Pr., 1947-   .

Graham, Bessie. The Bookman's Manual. 6th ed., rev. and enl. by Hester R. Hoffman. N.Y., Bowker, 1948. 785p.

Sonnenschein, W. S. Best Books. 3d ed. London, Routledge, 1910-35. 6v.

Eclectic bibliographies

books. Limited funds have always made such selection imperative. Since 1905 the American Library Association has issued the selection aid known as *The Booklist*. It appears semimonthly (once in August) and undertakes to appraise and select from the current book output about 100-125 titles in each issue that will best meet the needs and resources of the average public library. For that reason it is also useful to the general reader. Its crisp annotations describe and discriminate, often making comparisons with similar works. Added features are the special lists of pamphlets, documents, and free and inexpensive materials on timely subjects. An annual index contributes to ready reference.

Book Review Digest evaluates about 4000 books a year by a unique plan. About eighty selected review periodicals are indexed and abstracted. Books are arranged alphabetically by author and each entry includes full bibliographic information, a brief statement of what the book is about, and critical excerpts from the indexed reviews. Following each excerpt a plus or minus indicates whether the review was favorable or unfavorable. *Book Review Digest* is published monthly, except in July. There is a six-month cumulation in August and a bound cumulated annual in February. A cumulated title and subject index is included in a separate alphabet.

The most recent addition to current bibliography is the *United States Quarterly Book Review*. It is limited to bound books of one hundred pages or more published in the United States "which are believed to make a contribution to the sum of knowledge and experience." Light fiction, manuals, and textbooks are excluded. For each book full bibliographic information, a critical annotation, and a biography of the author are given. Despite the fact that this list was prepared primarily to acquaint the other American republics with the most important United States publications it also serves the libraries of this American republic as well. The former title was *United States Quarterly Book List*.

There are numerous retrospective eclectic bibliographies. Indeed, the back volumes of both *The Booklist* and the *Book Review Digest* can now contribute to nearly a half-century of eclectic bibliography. But for the purpose of aiding in selection from among the millions of books that have been printed in the past, two eclectic general bibliographies are suggested.

One of these, Graham's *Bookman's Manual,* was originally planned for booksellers, but library school teachers of book selection courses have found it exceedingly helpful to students because of its systematic treatment of a carefully selected list of good books of all times. The sixth edition, edited by Hester R. Hoffman, presents essential information about basic books in all fields except science and social science. There are excellent chapters on dictionaries, encyclopedias, Bibles, and the various national literatures. Information about authors, editions, and publishers is especially useful.

The other retrospective eclectic bibliography, Sonnenschein's *Best Books,* though it stops at 1935, is something of a classic in the field. It includes the greatest books of all periods, languages, and subjects. Each volume covers one or more subjects and the sixth volume consists of a detailed index.

School library eclectic bibliographies

Lists of books suitable for children and young people and intended as selection aids for school libraries are issued by most of the state departments of education. As a rule these lists are classified by subject and graded by difficulty. They feature state and regional emphases not found in the national lists. Among the latter the lists issued by the H. W. Wilson Company and by the American Library Association are most often accepted as standard.

The *Children's Catalog* contains approximately 4000 titles recommended for elementary school libraries and children's departments of public libraries. About one thousand titles are starred for first pur-

---

 SCHOOL LIBRARY ECLECTIC BIBLIOGRAPHIES

Children's Catalog. 7th ed. N.Y., Wilson, 1946. 1104p.

Basic Book Collection for Elementary Grades; comp. by a Joint Committee of the American Library Association, National Education Association, Association for Childhood Education and the National Council of Teachers of English. 5th ed. Chicago, A.L.A., 1951. 130p.

Standard Catalog for High School Libraries. 5th ed. N.Y., Wilson, 1947. 1341p.

Basic Book Collection for High Schools; comp. by a Joint Committee of the American Library Association, National Council of Teachers of English, and National Education Association. 5th ed. Chicago, A.L.A., 1950. 195p.

chase. Arrangement of books is by Decimal Classification and approximate grading is noted. Easy books and picture books are specially designated. A dictionary catalog with author, title, and subject entries, including analytics, supplements the classified list, and there is also a list arranged by grades. Annual supplements are issued.

A Basic Book Collection for Elementary Grades, the work of a joint committee of the American Library Association, National Education Association, Association for Childhood Education and the National Council of Teachers of English, is a list of 1060 titles, classified, annotated, and graded from kindergarten through the eighth grade. Full buying information, Decimal Classification numbers, availability of Wilson cards, and subject headings are some of the data included. Several state departments of education have adopted this list.

The *Standard Catalog for High School Libraries* contains 4555 books, 183 of which are double starred for first purchase and 806 single starred as especially recommended. Part one of this list is a dictionary catalog with author, title, and subject entries and many analytics; part two is a classified catalog with full cataloging information and descriptive annotations. Supplements are issued in March and September of each year. A list of sources for pictures and a supplementary service on new books are added features. A Catholic supplement includes 600 books especially selected for Catholic high schools.

A Basic Book Collection for High Schools is the work of a joint committee of the American Library Association, the National Education Association, and the National Council of Teachers of English. It lists 1500 titles intended to meet curricular needs and individual reading interests of young people. Annotations, subject headings, price, and Library of Congress card numbers are included for each entry. The classified list is followed by a directory of publishers and an index. A junior high school list was published by A.L.A. in 1950.[2]

Public library eclectic bibliographies

The 1949 edition of the *Standard Catalog for Public Libraries* includes 12,300 titles selected with the needs of small and medium-sized libraries in mind. About 2500 titles are starred for first purchase, and scholarly and expensive books are cited in the notes. Arrangement is by Decimal Classification, supplemented by an analytical dic-

---

[2] *A Basic Book Collection for Junior High Schools;* comp. by Elsa R. Berner and Mabel Sacra (Chicago, A.L.A., 1950), 80p., $1.75.

tionary index. Some 2000 books have been analyzed wholly or in part. A directory of publishers is included. The *Standard Catalog* like other eclectic bibliographies has one supreme reference potential. It is a good source for answers to the questions that begin, "Can you recommend a book on —?" For the more popular books it can provide data about price, editions, publisher, exact title, and author.

The *A.L.A. Catalog* has the disadvantage of being outdated. It is, however, still useful for information on titles not in the *Standard Catalog*.

College library eclectic bibliographies

College book selection aids are in need of attention. The two basic bibliographies, both excellent in concept and execution, are now somewhat out of date. The Mohrhardt list includes 5300 books and some periodicals, arranged by main curriculum divisions. Bibliographic data include Library of Congress numbers. There is an index.

The Shaw list and supplement include together some 17,600 titles. Selection for the original volume was made by 200 college teachers, librarians, and other consultants. A feature of the supplement is the citations to reviews. *Books for Catholic Colleges; a Supplement to Shaw's List* (1948; Supplement, 1950) is the most recent aid in the series. Other good college reading lists are those prepared by the National Council of Teachers of English and St. John's College.

United States national and trade bibliographies

For bibliographic detail about most books the national and trade bibliographies are a frequent source of information. The state of na-

---

❡ PUBLIC LIBRARY ECLECTIC BIBLIOGRAPHIES

Standard Catalog for Public Libraries; 1949. N.Y., Wilson, 1950. 2057p.

A.L.A. Catalog, 1926; 1926-31; 1932-36; 1937-41. Chicago, A.L.A., 1926-1943. 4v.

❡ COLLEGE LIBRARY ECLECTIC BIBLIOGRAPHIES

Mohrhardt, F. E., comp. A List of Books for Junior College Libraries. Chicago, A.L.A., 1937. 392p.

Shaw, C. B. A List of Books for College Libraries. 2d preliminary ed. Chicago, A.L.A., 1931. Supplement (1931-38), 1940.

tional bibliographic systems in the United Nations is summarized in a recent Unesco publication.³ For many countries there is a chain of comprehensive national bibliographies that tend to record every book published from the beginning of printing. The record, of course, is not complete, but the concerted effort of bibliographers individually and collectively in such postwar efforts as those of Unesco is steadily decreasing the number of missing items.

In the United States there is a rather comprehensive chain of national bibliographies. The sources of information on current publications are reviewed first, followed by a chronological account of the retrospective sources.

Publishers' Weekly is the official organ of the book trade. Toward the back of each issue is a department called the "Weekly Record" which lists alphabetically by author every book released for publication during the week. For each entry author, title, imprint, collation, price, subject, and annotation are given. The lower half of the page lists pamphlets and lesser publications. Each month a cumulative title index is provided. Besides the "Weekly Record" there are other reference features in the *Publishers' Weekly*. Annual issues are published on reference books, business books, and other classes of books. Statistics on the year's publications, notes on publishers, editions, new titles, the book trade, and other aspects of publishing contain answers to bibliographic questions. Nor must the information value of the advertisements be overlooked.

As soon as the new monthly issue of the *Cumulative Book Index* is available it is quicker to consult it for new books than the *Publishers' Weekly*. The C.B.I., as it is referred to, lists books in the English language published in all countries in a dictionary arrangement

---

☙ UNITED STATES NATIONAL AND TRADE BIBLIOGRAPHIES
Publishers' Weekly, 1872-   . N.Y., Bowker.
Cumulative Book Index; a World List of Books in the English Language, 1898-   . N.Y., Wilson.
United States Catalog. 4th ed. N.Y., Wilson, 1928.
Publishers' Trade List Annual, 1873-   . N.Y., Bowker.

---

³ Unesco Library of Congress Bibliographical Survey, *Bibliographical Services; Their Present State and Possibilities of Improvement* (Washington, 1950), 67p. Kathrine O. Murra's *Notes on the Development of the Concept of Current Complete National Bibliography* is printed as a supplement to the survey.

of authors, titles, and subjects. Entry information includes author, title, imprint, paging, price, Library of Congress card number, and information about edition, binding, and size. Cumulations finally result in annual and multiannual volumes. These cumulations must be used to locate books published since 1928, the date of the latest edition of the *United States Catalog,* and are also used in locating books published earlier which had gone out of print by 1928.

The *U.S. Cat,* as it is referred to by librarians, is a tremendous volume listing 190,000 titles in print on January 1, 1928, in some 575,000 entries. Dictionary arrangement as in the *Cumulative Book Index* makes for easy use. Of especial reference value are the publishers' directories in both the *United States Catalog* and the *Cumulative Book Index.*

To locate books by publisher the *Publishers' Trade List Annual* is consulted. It is an annual collection of publishers' catalogs arranged alphabetically by publisher. Since 1948 an index volume, *Books in Print,* which includes authors, titles, and series, has been added to increase the usefulness of this trade bibliography immeasurably.

United States retrospective bibliography

The nearly unbroken chain of United States national bibliography begins with the two monumental sets of Evans and Sabin. Evans' *American Bibliography* covers the period from 1639 through 1799 and includes books, pamphlets, and periodicals, arranged chronologically by date of publication. Bibliographic information in each entry includes: author's name, with birth and death dates, title, imprint, collation, and frequently libraries in which the item may be found. There are three indexes in each volume: author, classified subject, and printer or publisher. Sabin's *Dictionary of Books Relating to America* includes 106,412 numbered entries. Added editions and titles cited only in the notes are not counted. Arrangement is by author and each entry includes title, imprint, format, and collation. Many entries have also bibliographic notes and library location. It is important to remember that while Evans is limited to works published in the United States, Sabin includes titles about America wherever published.

The next link after Evans and Sabin is Roorbach's *Bibliotheca Americana,* which covers the period 1820-61. This catalog of American publications is arranged alphabetically by author and title and

United States retrospective bibliography

includes reprints. Publisher, date, size, and price are the bibliographic items furnished in addition to author and title.

The Civil War years are covered by Kelly's *American Catalogue of Books,* which continues Roorbach. Kelly's special features include a list of societies and their publications, and volume one includes a list of war pamphlets, sermons, and addresses. Both Roorbach and Kelly have been found inaccurate and incomplete.

The *American Catalogue* does not quite complete the chain between Kelly and the *United States Catalog.* The first series, a list of books in print July 1, 1876, comprises two volumes, one for author and title entries and the other for subjects. Series two to four carry the record forward to June 30, 1895, and are arranged as is series one except that both the author-title list and subject index are in one volume, and there are appendixes devoted to United States government and literary and scientific society publications. Series three to four also have lists of state publications. Series five, to January 1, 1900, omits the appendixes. The remaining three series, beginning with the sixth, adopt the dictionary arrangement.

❦ UNITED STATES RETROSPECTIVE BIBLIOGRAPHY

Evans, Charles. American Bibliography; a Chronological Dictionary of All Books, Pamphlets and Periodical Publications Printed in the United States of America from the Genesis of Printing in 1639; with bibliographical and biographical notes. Chicago, Columbia Pr., 1903-34. v.1-12 (no more published).

Sabin, Joseph. Dictionary of Books Relating to America, from Its Discovery to the Present Time. N.Y., Sabin, 1868-92; Bibliographical Society of America, 1928-36. 29v.

Roorbach, O. A. Bibliotheca Americana, 1820-61. N.Y., Roorbach, 1852-61. 4v.

Kelly, James. American Catalogue of Books Published in the United States from January, 1861, to January, 1871. N.Y., Wiley, 1866-71. 2v.

American Catalogue of Books, 1876-1910. N.Y., Publishers' Weekly, 1876-1910. 9v. in 13.

American Book-Prices Current; a Record of Books, Manuscripts and Autographs Sold at Auction in New York and Elsewhere, 1895- (annual).

An attempt to inventory state by state all the publications of the United States resulted in a series known as *American Imprints Inventory*.[4] In all, some 52 projects were undertaken, of which 35 were completed. For the states that have imprints inventories, valuable supplementary bibliographical records are available, although these records stop at various points in the nineteenth century. The inventories are in processed format.

Specific types of bibliographic sources are required to answer inquiries about the market value of old and rare books. The value of a rare book—a question regularly posed by the patron cleaning an attic—is largely determined by what it will bring on the market, and that usually means the auction market. *American Book-Prices Current* records auction prices, and if the patron's "rare book" is not listed in any of its fifty or more volumes, the book probably is not really rare. The 53d annual volume, recording 131 sales held by nine auction houses from September, 1946, to July, 1947, listed alphabetically by author and title more than 17,000 priced entries. During that period the *Bay Psalm Book* fetched a price of $151,000. The top prices paid in 1946 were $50,000 each for a first folio edition of Shakespeare and the *Alice in Wonderland* manuscript; in 1945 it was $34,000 for the manuscript of Poe's *Murders in the Rue Morgue*. The 50th anniversary volume (1944) told the interesting story of *American Book-Prices Current*. Five-year cumulations speed the location of rare books, manuscripts, and autographs. Individual dealers' catalogs and auction gallery catalogs can be consulted for supplementary information.

British national bibliography

The chain of British national bibliography is much longer than ours. For current listings it must be recalled that the *Cumulative Book Index* is "a world list of books in the English language" and therefore will be useful for British publications.

❦ BRITISH NATIONAL BIBLIOGRAPHY

British National Bibliography, 1950- . London, Council of the British National Bibliography.

Whitaker's Cumulative Booklist, 1924- . London, Whitaker.

The English Catalogue of Books, Giving in One Alphabet, under Author and Title, the Size, Price, Month of Publication, and Publisher of Books Issued in the United Kingdom, 1801- . London, Low, 1864-1901; Publishers' Circular, 1906- .

Other foreign national bibliographies

The best current British list is *British National Bibliography,* issued weekly and cumulated every three, six, and twelve months. The last issue of each month includes a cumulated index of authors, titles, and subjects for the month. The list is based upon the books deposited in the Copyright Office of the British Museum and is arranged in classified order according to Decimal Classification.

Whitaker's Cumulative Booklist is based on the lists which appear in the *Bookseller. Whitaker's* is cumulated quarterly, annually, and every five years. The list is classified and indexing is by author and title.

The principal retrospective source going back to the beginning of the nineteenth century is *The English Catalogue of Books.* It is based on the weekly lists in the *Publishers' Circular,* British counterpart of the *Publishers' Weekly.* Among its special features are the supplement of society publications and the directory of publishers. The record of British publications before 1900 appears in several sources, the principal ones of which are Lowndes' *Bibliographer's Manual of English Literature,*[5] which covers the period from Caxton to 1820, and Watt's *Bibliotheca Britannica,*[6] from the beginning to 1824.

Other foreign national bibliographies

There are comparable national bibliographic chains in many countries of the world. No attempt is made here to list the national bibliographies of all countries. Instead, the chain for France is indicated and two sources for locating other national bibliographies are cited.

For French publications the links in the national bibliographic chain are approximately as follows: (1) *Biblio,* 1933 to the present, issued monthly, cumulated annually, and arranged in dictionary order; (2) *Catalogue général de la librairie française,* 1840 to the present, often referred to simply as *Lorenz,* the name of its first compiler. Authors and titles in the *Catalogue général* are in one alphabet and there is a subject index. Individual volumes in the series cover three or more

---

[4] U.S. Works Progress Administration. *American Imprints Inventory;* prepared by the Historical Records Survey, Division of Women's and Professional Projects (Washington, Historical Records Survey, 1937-42).

[5] William T. Lowndes, *Bibliographer's Manual of English Literature* (new ed., rev., cor., and enl. by H. G. Bohn; London, Bell, 1858-64), 6v. in 11.

[6] Robert Watt, *Bibliotheca Britannica; or, a General Index to British and Foreign Literature* (Edinburgh, Constable, 1824), 4v.

BIBLIOGRAPHIES

years. To locate books published prior to 1840 reference must be made to the universal bibliographies.

The two principal guides to national bibliographies are Heyl's *Current National Bibliography* (A.L.A., 1942) and the later *Current National Bibliographies* which has been appearing in the Library of Congress *Quarterly Journal of Current Acquisitions* since August, 1949.

Universal bibliographies

A general bibliography not limited by time, place, language, subject, or purpose should theoretically list all of the records of civilization. That no such complete list exists goes without saying. However, there have been individual and collective efforts to compile universal bibliographies. One of the most famous attempts by an individual resulted in Brunet's *Manuel du libraire,* which lists over 40,000 items. The Institut International de Bibliographie at Brussels has been engaged in compiling a world list of books and periodicals that may well approach the ideal of a universal bibliography.

The nearest approach to universal bibliography in the world today are the catalogs of the great national libraries. The Library of Congress *Catalog of Books* "reproduces in facsimile a complete set of the printed cards issued by the Library of Congress from the beginning of the series in August, 1898 through July 31, 1942." These cards do not represent the complete collections of the library. The 1,941,128 cards do, however, represent some four and a quarter million volumes,

---

❦ UNIVERSAL BIBLIOGRAPHIES

Brunet, J. C. Manuel du libraire et de l'amateur de livres. 5th ed. Paris, Didot, 1860-65. 6v.

U.S. Library of Congress. A Catalog of Books Represented by Library of Congress Printed Cards Issued to July 31, 1942. Ann Arbor, Mich., Edwards Brothers, 1942-46. 167v. Supplement (1941-47), 1948. 42v.

British Museum. General Catalogue of Printed Books. London, Clowes, 1931- (in progress).

Bibliothèque Nationale. Catalogue général des livres imprimés. Paris, Imprimerie Nationale, 1900- (in progress).

Universal bibliographies

mostly in the Library of Congress but also in some other American libraries.

The project which resulted in the printed catalog, sponsored by the Association of Research Libraries and aided by the Rockefeller Foundation, was begun in the spring of 1942. The first 167 volumes completed the alphabetic arrangement to July 31, 1942. The supplement of 42 volumes covered books represented by Library of Congress cards issued August 1, 1942—December 31, 1947. In January, 1947, the first number of a cumulative catalog of Library of Congress cards appeared. *Monthly Catalogs* of author entries began to appear in 1948, and of subjects in 1950. This bibliographic tool, therefore, must be understood as comprising four parts:

> *Library of Congress Catalog of Printed Cards,* August 18—July 31, 1942 (167 volumes)
> *Supplement,* August 1, 1942—December 31, 1947 (42 volumes)
> *Cumulative Catalog,* January 1947- (issued in nine monthly issues and three quarterly cumulations)
> *Monthly Catalogs*—Author (1948-); Subject (1950-)

The overlapping of the *Supplement* and the *Cumulative Catalog* was caused by the decision to include the printed cards of 1947 in the *Supplement.*

Another example of a large library catalog is the British Museum *General Catalogue of Printed Books,* the latest edition of which began appearing in 1931, and is still incomplete. A previous edition, begun in 1881, is still used; the earliest catalog was issued in 1789.

Finally, the *Catalogue* of the Bibliotheque Nationale, also incomplete, is cited as an example of a great Continental bibliography.

Closely allied to the bibliographic objective of a complete list of the records of mankind is the identification of all incunabula—that is, books printed before 1500—and of anonymous and pseudonymous works. Reference assistance on the former problem is available in several works, notably the *Gesamtkatalog der Wiegendrucke.* Problems relating to anonymous and pseudonymous works are taken to Halkett and Laing's *Dictionary of Anonymous and Pseudonymous Literature*[7] which is arranged alphabetically by title and includes notes about authorship and publication details.

---

[7] Samuel Halkett and John Laing, *Dictionary of Anonymous and Pseudonymous English Literature* (new and enl. ed.; Edinburgh, Oliver and Boyd, 1926-34), 7v.

BIBLIOGRAPHIES

Bibliographies of bibliographies

Besterman's *World Bibliography of Bibliographies* is a list of separately published bibliographies from the beginning of printing, about 1470 in this case, to date. Entries are arranged alphabetically by subject, and there is a comprehensive author and subject index in the third volume.

The Bibliographic Index is a quarterly bibliography of bibliographies with annual and four- and six-year cumulations. It indexes not only current bibliographies published separately as books and pamphlets but also those published as parts of books, pamphlets, and periodical articles. Arrangement is alphabetic by subject, and each bibliography may be indexed under several topics to which it contributes.

No type of bibliography is more important to reference than the subject bibliography. In relation to the individual subjects discussed in Part II special subject bibliographies receive first consideration.

Reading list

Bradford, S. C. *Documentation*. London, Crosby, Lockwood, 1948. 156p.

Collison, R. L. *Bibliographies, Subject and National; a Guide to Their Contents, Arrangement and Use*. N.Y., Hafner, 1951. 172p.

Hutchins, Margaret. *Introduction to Reference Work*. Chicago, A.L.A., 1944. p.41-51, 188-89.

❦ BIBLIOGRAPHIES OF BIBLIOGRAPHIES

Besterman, Theodore. A World Bibliography of Bibliographies. 2d ed. London, Besterman, 1947-49. 3v.

The Bibliographic Index, 1938- . N.Y., Wilson.

chapter 13

GOVERNMENT PUBLICATIONS

Introduction, Congressional publications,

Executive publications, Judicial publications,

Indexes and bibliographies,

Documents of state and local governments,

Foreign and international documents.

Introduction

Document questions. Questions about government—world, foreign, United States, state, local—are on the increase. Government publications are obvious sources for answers. But it is a mistake to think government publications can answer no other questions. Nearly every subject of public interest is treated somewhere in a government publication. To convince oneself one has only to examine the subjects in a volume of the *Document Catalog,* an annual index of the *Monthly Catalog,* or the titles of the *Price Lists* issued by the Superintendent of Documents.

Among areas of popular and research interest that must rely heavily on government sources, if not publications, are statistics, history, business, government, agriculture, education, defense, law and science. Statistical data in almanacs are frequently based on government sources. Government publications are often considered primary sources in historical research. From the Departments of Labor, Commerce and Agriculture come the data that answer questions of businessmen, labor unions, and farmers. Government research in such areas as nuclear physics, health, and geology is often in the vanguard of scientific investigation.

Certain bibliographic inquiries cannot be answered entirely with sources studied thus far. Identification of government publications necessitates the use of special indexes and bibliographic tools.

Government publications defined. An official definition of a government publication is given in the *Checklist of United States Public Documents, 1789-1909:*

> Any publication printed at Government expense or published by authority of Congress or any Government publishing office, or of which an edition has been bought by Congress or any Government office for division among members of Congress or distribution to Government officials or the public, shall be considered a public document.

Applied generally, this definition means that any publication issued by the authority of a government is a government publication. Even the ration books issued during the war and our income tax blanks are therefore technically government publications.[1]

Although this chapter is almost entirely devoted to United States government publications it should be pointed out that thousands of publications of importance are issued by foreign governments and by our own state and local governments.

Reference value. The value of government publications can be summarized as follows:

> 1. Authority. The government's imprint alone should insure authority, in addition to which the reputations of the many specialists regularly and specially employed permit the librarian to place specific responsibility for individual works. Many government publications are recognized by the world of scholarship as "source" or "primary" material.
> 2. Economy. Most of the publications are available to libraries free or at very little cost.
> 3. Timeliness. In many fields results of research, news of recent discoveries, latest statistics, as well as reports of government activities are presented first in documents.

Introduction

4. Readability. A great number of attractive publications planned with the general reader in mind are being issued. Indeed, at least one bookseller has been prosecuted for selling free government publications which were attractive enough in format to pass for commercial publications.

In spite of all these advantages, however, government publications have the reputation of being difficult to use. In part this is attributable to frequent changes in government organization and consequent variations in bibliographical form. But equally responsible in the past have been the method of distribution, the inadequacy of indexes, poor editing, and too little attention to format. As an example of past difficulties upon which so much of the present prejudice is based, it must be recalled that prior to 1922 depository libraries were obliged to take every document issued. Some of the smaller libraries, inadequately staffed and housed, were harried and submerged as each mail brought from Washington documents by the bagful. There was little to do with these publications but pile them in basement or attic, ceiling-high, and nourish a lasting grudge against the publisher.

History of United States government publication. Prior to 1860 Congress authorized the printing of government publications by a private printer at a set rate. The printer selected depended on the political party then in power. For example, with a Whig majority in Congress the award went to Gales and Seaton; with the Democrats or Democrat-Republicans in majority, the printing job was given to Duff Green or Blair Rives. These names on the title pages of government publications therefore are a clue to the political hue of the Congress under which they were issued. Editing and printing in this period were usually poor.

Long before 1860, however, steps toward the establishment of a national printing office had been taken. The first recommendation was made as early as 1818. Government reform moves slowly, however, and it was 1846 before a Joint Committee on Printing was created by law. Six years later an act appointing a Superintendent of Printing was passed and in 1860 the act establishing a government printing office was approved. The following year the government began its own printing.

Distribution. Although the fight for better printing has been

---

[1] A *government document* is the original and is housed in the National Archives; a *government publication* is reproduced from the document and is housed in libraries.

won, the long battle for efficient distribution still continues. At first, government publications were distributed by the Library of Congress and the Secretary of State. The authority was transferred to the Secretary of the Interior in 1857/58, and in 1861 the authority to designate depository libraries was added. The government had now set up a modern printing plant which was experimenting with and improving the art of printing. It was only natural that improvement in distribution should be sought. In 1869 a Superintendent of Documents was appointed in the Interior Department, but Congress still continued to distribute publications indiscriminately. As early as 1882 Dr. John G. Ames, then Superintendent of Documents, urged the centralization of distribution. His efforts finally gained recognition in the Printing Law of 1895 which abolished the office in the Interior Department and created a new position in the Government Printing Office, centralizing distribution there.

Over 150 million copies of government publications are distributed by the Government Printing Office during a year. Normal distribution is accomplished through the Superintendent of Documents, whose functions now include distribution to depository libraries, sales to others, compilation of bibliographies and catalogs, maintenance of a complete library of all government publications and a catalog of them, and provision of reference service through correspondence.

Many United States government publications are distributed free to depositories; that is, agencies authorized to receive and maintain such publications. The principal classes of depositories are state and territorial libraries, land grant colleges, executive departments existing in 1895, the United States Military and Naval Academies, the Alaska Historical Society, the Philippine Library, the American Antiquarian Society, and one library designated for each Congressional district and each senator. These libraries since 1922 have been allowed to select the series and separate publications they are to receive. The basic list from which they make their choices, the *Classified List of U.S. Government Publications Available for Selection by Depository Libraries,* revised from time to time and now in card form, is a useful guide to important government series of today. Depository items are also identified in the *Monthly Catalog* by a special symbol.

Non-depository libraries can secure many government publications free by one of the following methods: (1) from the overstock returned to the Government Printing Office by the issuing office; (2) from the issuing office direct, either by being placed on the mailing list

Introduction

or by request for a specific publication; or (3) through Congressmen who have an assigned quota of Congressional documents.

United States government publications may be purchased from the Superintendent of Documents. Payment must be made in advance, either with coupons, sold in sets of 20 for one dollar; by check, money order, or currency; or by a deposit account.

Guides to the use of government publications. Fortunately for the reference librarian there are a number of bibliographic guides and studies which will give him background and lead him through the intricacies of government publications. The following are particularly useful:

> Boyd, Anne M., and Rips, Rae E. *United States Government Publications.* 3d ed. N.Y., Wilson, 1949. 627p.
> Brown, E. S. *Manual of Government Publications, United States and Foreign.* N.Y., Appleton-Century-Crofts, 1950. 121p.
> Hirshberg, H. S., and Melinat, C. H. *Subject Guide to United States Government Publications.* Chicago, A.L.A., 1947. 228p.
> Schmeckebier, L. F. *Government Publications and Their Use.* 2d ed. Washington, Brookings Institution, 1939. 479p.
> Tompkins, Dorothy C. *Materials for the Study of Federal Government.* Chicago, Public Administration Service, 1948. 338p.

United States government agencies. Formidable as federal documents seem, it is possible to gain an intelligent general comprehension of them in a short time provided one does not bog down on details. The starting point is the government itself and the various agencies which constitute the issuing sources.

The frequent reorganization and rearrangement of government agencies makes it necessary to refer to handbooks like the *United States Government Manual,* which lists all federal government agencies, gives the date of their creation, authority, organization, activities and chief officials. Organizational charts for Congress and major executive departments are included and are extremely useful.

The *Congressional Directory* gives detailed information about

---

❦ UNITED STATES GOVERNMENT AGENCIES

United States Government Manual, 1935- . Washington, Govt. Print. Off.

U.S. Congress. Official Congressional Directory, 1809- . Washington, Govt. Print. Off.

Congress but is not limited to the legislative branch of the federal government. Information about the organization and personnel of the executive and judiciary branches is also included. There are also such miscellaneous data as plans of the Capitol and short biographical sketches of Congressmen, cabinet members and Supreme Court justices, rosters of foreign diplomats and consuls in the United States as well as our own foreign service abroad, names of newspaper correspondents and titles of the publications they represent, and maps of the Congressional districts.

Federal documents themselves can be roughly classified according to the divisions of our government. Beginning with the three coordinate branches of our federal system it is possible to present a classification of documents that will not only enable one to place any document in its proper relationship but at the same time provide an acquaintance with the scheme used by the Office of the Superintendent of Documents in its library and in its current index.

Congressional publications

In the last analysis Congress authorizes, directly or indirectly, all United States government publications. But there are certain classes of publications of which Congress itself is the author. These are: (1) legislation, including bills, laws, statutes and codes; (2) proceedings, including records and minutes; (3) investigations, including hearings and documents; (4) reference, including calendars, manuals of parliamentary procedure, directories and miscellany. For a detailed discussion of legislative procedure and the publications involved it is

---

❦ CONGRESSIONAL PUBLICATIONS

U.S. Congress. United States Code, 1946 ed. Containing the General and Permanent Laws of the United States, in Force on January 2, 1947. Washington, Govt. Print. Off. 1948. 5v. Supplements, 1947- .

U.S. Congress. Congressional Record, 1873- . Washington, Govt. Print. Off.

Congressional Quarterly Log News Weekly, 1945- . Washington, Congressional Quarterly News Features.

Congressional Quarterly Almanac, 1945- (annual). Washington, Congressional Quarterly News Features.

Congressional publications

recommended that a recent textbook in American government or one of the guides to the use of government publications listed above be consulted.

Legislation. When a bill is introduced into one House it is immediately given a number (for instance, H.R.367 if introduced in the House; S.367 if in the Senate) by which it is cited until it becomes a law. Bills are printed when introduced and reprinted whenever amended in their course through Congress. When passed by one House they are called acts, but carry the same number and citation (i.e., H.R.367, S.367). Bills may be traced while in progress by means of the *Daily Digest* and the biweekly index to the *Congressional Record*, described later; by the *Digest of Public General Bills* published by the Legislative Reference Service of The Library of Congress; or by a number of commercial legislative services such as *Congressional Index*, published by Commerce Clearing House.

Without tracing the detailed steps by which a bill becomes a law, it is enough to indicate here that when passed and signed by the President, it is given a new number (e.g., Public Law 197 or Private Law 197) and printed in separate or pamphlet form. These separate issues are called "slip laws."

At the end of any session of Congress all of the laws of that session are printed together in what is called the *United States Statutes at Large*. Beginning with 1937 (volume 50) each volume contains the laws enacted by one Congress. These are usually cited by title, volume and page number—for example, Printing Law of 1895, 28 *Stat.* 601-24—meaning volume 28, pages 601-24 of the *Statutes at Large*.

About every five years the *United States Code* is published. It is a collection of all permanent, public, general federal laws in force on a specified date, classified by subject. It is kept up to date by supplements.

The important legislative publications may be recapitulated as follows:

Publication	Definition	Citation
Bills	Text of a proposed law	S.367, or H.R.367
Slip law	Separate publication of a law	Public Law 197, or Private Law 197
Statutes at Large	Laws of one session of Congress	50 Stat. 197
United States Code	Laws in force on a specified date, classified	U.S.C. 24:1

213

GOVERNMENT PUBLICATIONS

Expressions of opinion or sentiment, rulings relating to internal procedure, or other action by Congress or by either House not designed to be permanent may be incorporated in a resolution. There are three kinds of resolutions. Those introduced by one House and affecting only that House are called simple resolutions. Concurrent resolutions are used for joint sessions, joint committees, and joint agreements on adjournment. Joint resolutions have the force of law, go through the same procedures as bills, including Presidential signature, are printed in slip form, and are used for matters of public interest, such as extending the thanks of the nation to individuals.

Proceedings. The current, full stenographic transcript of all speeches and proceedings in Congress is published daily for each day it is in session and is called the *Congressional Record*. Since corrections of remarks are allowed, the *Record*, though usually verbatim, is not always so. In the daily edition an appendix carries extensions of remarks, miscellaneous speeches, and editorials pertinent to the Congressmen's interests which they have "leave to print." The *Congressional Record* now also carries a most valuable feature, the "Daily Digest," which summarizes action of the previous day and records impending action, committee meetings, etc. A biweekly index is published in two sections, the first part being a name and subject index for the two weeks, the second a cumulative index, by bill number, to all action taken on each bill during that session of Congress. At the end of the session a bound edition of the *Congressional Record* is printed in several parts, with the corrections and extensions of remarks inserted in the running text where they would have occurred if actually made on the floor of the Congress, with the paging renumbered, and with an index usable only with this edition.

The whole series of proceedings from the beginning of the United States consists of: *Annals of Congress,* 1789-1824 (through Eighteenth Congress, first session); *Register of Debates,* 1824-1837 (Eighteenth Congress, second session—Twenty-fifth Congress, first session); *Congressional Globe,* 1833-1873 (Twenty-third Congress, first session—Forty-second Congress); and *Congressional Record,* 1873- (Forty-third Congress to the present).

For each session of Congress, *House* and *Senate Journals* are published. They are the official minutes of Congress, required by the Constitution. Unlike the *Congressional Record,* they include no speeches but consist of the official action taken on all bills and resolutions, including records of votes and all other proceedings.

Congressional publications

Investigations. Legislation usually proceeds through committees and committees make investigations, hold hearings, and gather data to support legislative action. When a committee has decided to recommend action on a bill, it prepares a report (or reports if there happens to be also a minority report). These reports are printed and are numbered in a *House Reports* series and in a *Senate Reports* series.

Hearings, containing the transcript of testimony given before committees who may call in experts or others to contribute to investigations made in behalf of legislation, are also published if the committee so orders, and since 1939 have been sent free to depositories on request. Many of these are extremely important for reference use. They are listed in the *Monthly Catalog.*

The *Senate Documents* and *House Documents* series contain a variety of materials, such as reports by special investigating committees and commissions, patriotic and other non-governmental agencies, and memorials to departed members.

Reference. Reference publications of Congress include such basic tools as the *Congressional Directory,* the *Biographical Directory of the American Congress, 1774-1949,* calendars of legislation, publications on parliamentary procedure, indexes to hearings, and digests of laws.

Congressional set. In many libraries a long set of Congressional publications will be found shelved together and serially numbered. This is often referred to as the "sheep set," because of the sheepskin bindings on the early volumes, or the "serial set," because of the serial numbers. The set consists of the Journals, Reports, and Documents of the House and Senate from the Fifteenth Congress, 1817, to the present. To illustrate the numbering, here is a sequence from the Seventy-ninth Congress:

Congress	Session	Serial number	Title	Sub-series number
79	1	10923	Senate Journal, 1945	
79	1	10924	House Journal, 1945	
79	1	10925-30	Senate Reports	1-199
79	1	10931-37	House Reports	1-152
79	1	10938-52	Senate Documents	1-131
79	1	10953-11011	House Documents	1-392
79	2	11012	Senate Journal, 1946	
79	2	11013	House Journal, 1946	

From this cycle it can be seen that the serial set order is Senate Journal, House Journal, Senate Reports, House Reports, Senate Doc-

215

uments, House Documents. The Journals follow the calendar sequence, since they are day-by-day records of proceedings. Each set of Reports and Documents has its own sub-series numbers, which do not always follow in the same sequence as the serial set numbers. For example, House Document 392 is in serial volume 10971; House Document 90 is in serial volume 10972.

American state papers. Selected reprints of publications of the first 14 Congresses, 1789-1816, and of certain other early executive and Congressional publications as late as 1838 were gathered together and reprinted by order of Congress under the title *American State Papers*. The contents are classified under ten headings: foreign relations, Indian affairs, finance, commerce and navigation, military affairs, naval affairs, post office, public lands, claims, miscellaneous. This set is the only readily available compilation of the early Congressional materials. A special set of serial numbers, 01-038, has been assigned to *American State Papers*.

Current information on Congressional activity is available in the *Congressional Quarterly* services which consist of the weekly *Log* and the annual *Almanac,* priced to libraries at $50 a year or at $25 a year for the *Almanac* alone. Issues of the *Congressional Quarterly Log News Weekly* are paged continuously and kept together in spring-back covers of which the publishers supply two a year. The *Almanac* replaces the *Logs* at the end of the year and reorganizes the material by broad subjects like agriculture, appropriations, education and welfare, foreign policy, labor, military and veterans, miscellaneous and administrative, taxes and economic policy. The purpose of both publications is to provide information on Congressional activities, including the work of committees, the voting and activities of individual Congressmen, and of events that affect the whole Congress, such as lobbying and elections. The first sheet of each issue of the *Log News Weekly* is an issue index, later replaced by the quarterly cumulated index. All of the reporting, although detailed, is free from bias and is readable.

Executive publications

Every executive department, agency, office, division, and section is the source of some publication, even if it is only the annual report which each unit head must make to his superior. Therefore, to know government agencies is to know likely sources of reports. To acquire

Executive publications

this knowledge it is essential to use the *United States Government Manual*. Earlier publications are described in the various guides to the use of government publications. A few representative executive agencies are mentioned here.

The Office of the President of the United States is the source of important documents: the Executive Orders and Proclamations, such as those authorizing changes in our governmental organization or declaring holidays; the Messages, such as those on the State of the Union; the Speeches, including the "fireside chats" which President Franklin D. Roosevelt developed into a radio tradition; and the annual Budget of the United States.

Any real study of the publications of the executive departments of the United States would be impossible here. It is in the thousands of periodicals, series, and separate works put out by the departments and agencies listed below that many of our most important reference works are found. These publications range from the extremely specialized, as in the Bulletins of the National Bureau of Standards, to the very elementary, as in the Farmers' Bulletins. The following outline indicates their scope briefly:

Department	Established	Representative publications
State	1789	Treaties; Directories of diplomatic and consular service; Foreign relations; *Department of State Bulletin*
Treasury	1789	Financial material; *Know Your Money; Handbook of Foreign Currencies;* Catalogs of United States coins
Defense	War, 1789[2] Navy, 1798 Air, 1947	West Point and Annapolis admission requirements; Educational publications, e.g., Army extension course texts; Manuals on care and repair of military equipment; *American Ephemeris*
Justice	1789	Uniform crime reports; Criminal identification; Naturalization and citizenship manuals
Post Office	1789[3]	*Official Postal Guide; Description of United States Postage Stamps*

---

[2] Merged 1947.

[3] Office of Postmaster General created 1789; member of cabinet, 1829; executive department, 1872.

GOVERNMENT PUBLICATIONS

Department	Established	Representative publications
Interior	1849	Indian affairs; Geological survey; *Minerals Yearbook;* Topographic maps; National Parks Service literature
Agriculture	1889[4]	All aspects of rural life; *Farmers' Bulletins* and *Leaflets; Yearbook of Agriculture;* Soil surveys; *Bibliography of Agriculture*
Commerce	1903[5]	Census; Standards; Patents; *Statistical Abstract;* Civil aeronautics; Weather; Aids for the businessman
Labor	1913	*Monthly Labor Review;* Cost-of-living figures; Occupational outlook data

In addition to the nine executive departments there are a number of independent agencies and establishments among which the following are some of the more important: Federal Security Agency, responsible for education, health, and social security, includes Children's Bureau, Office of Education, Public Health Service, and Social Security Administration; General Services Administration, established in 1949 to include Bureau of Federal Supply, Federal Works Agency, and the National Archives; Housing and Home Finance Agency; Atomic Energy Commission; Federal Communications Commission; Interstate Commerce Commission; Federal Trade Commission; Securities and Exchange Commission; Civil Service Commission; Veterans Administration; National Labor Relations Board; Selective Service System; Smithsonian Institution; Tennessee Valley Authority.

The principal source for federal regulations having the force of law is the *Federal Register* issued daily except Sunday, Monday, and days following holidays. Included are presidential proclamations and executive orders, agency organization procedures, regulations, and notices of proposed rule-making.

The 1949 *Code of Federal Regulations* makes unnecessary the use of the *Federal Register* before that time for most reference questions. Cumulative supplements to the *Code* are issued, and as a rule

❦ EXECUTIVE PUBLICATIONS

U.S. National Archives. Federal Register, 1936- . Washington, Govt. Print. Off.

——— Code of Federal Regulations of the United States. 1949 ed. Washington, Govt. Print. Off., 1949- (in progress).

only the daily issues of the *Federal Register* following these cumulations need be consulted.

Judicial publications

The judicial branch of the government includes the following courts: Supreme Court, Circuit Courts of Appeals, District Courts, Court of Claims, Court of Customs and Patent Appeals, Customs Court, and Territorial Courts. The publications of the judicial branch are primarily of interest to law librarians.

Indexes and bibliographies

The secret of successful reference use of government publications lies largely in the mastery of their indexes and catalogs. In addition to the general tools described here there are many special indexes and bibliographies of departmental publications. Lists of these may be found in detailed guides to the use of government publications.

Poore's Descriptive Catalogue, 1774-1881. Poore's *Descriptive Catalogue* carries the indexing back to the government publications of the Colonial period, listing nearly every document in chronological order as issued to March 4, 1881. The plan for the work, according to the compiler, included obtaining for each entry: "(1) The title of the book, pamphlet, or document, (2) the name of its author, (3) the date of its publication, (4) where it was to be found, and (5) a brief abstract of its contents. These were to be chronologically arranged, and accompanied by a copious, alphabetical and analytical index for convenience of reference."

The special features of this index are the abstracting of documents and the early period covered. Additional items like the names of private printers, some of the early publications of the states and related privately printed materials are also included. Documents published during each year are arranged in approximately this sequence: executive, judicial, and Congressional publications.

This catalog, though the most thorough available for the period, is not complete. Poore was greatly handicapped because no one library in the country had a comprehensive collection of early documents,

---

[4] Established as section of Patent Office, 1839; set up as independent department, 1862; recognized as major executive department, 1889.

[5] Department of Commerce and Labor until 1913.

nor were there any contemporary bibliographies or even lists of much value to help him.

Ames's Comprehensive Index, 1881-1893. Ames's *Comprehensive Index* brings the indexing of United States government documents forward from the date Poore left off, March 4, 1881, to March 4, 1893. It is arranged somewhat differently, however, being primarily an alphabetic subject or title list. The uniqueness of its arrangement is indicated by the following analysis of its three-column page:

   I. "The middle or principal column is the index itself," showing:
      A. Subject of each document (catchword form, i.e., important word first);
      B. Date;
      C. Series, if issued in editions other than the Congressional;
      D. Serial numbers of bills on which Senate and House reports are based.
  II. "The left-hand column shows the origin of documents indexed" (i.e., the source or issuing office).
 III. The right-hand column is the classification and citation.

At the end of volume two there is a personal index with this special feature: a superior figure after the page reference indicates the

---

☞ INDEXES AND BIBLIOGRAPHIES

Poore, B. P. A Descriptive Catalogue of the Government Publications of the United States, September 5, 1774—March 4, 1881. Washington, Govt. Print. Off., 1885. 1392p.

Ames, J. G. Comprehensive Index to the Publications of the United States Government, 1881-1893. Washington, Govt. Print. Off., 1905. 2v.

U.S. Superintendent of Documents. Catalog of the Public Documents of the 53d to 76th Congress and All Departments of the Government of the United States for the Period from March 4, 1893, to December 31, 1940. Washington, Govt. Print. Off., 1896-1945. 25v.

―――― United States Government Publications Monthly Catalog, 1895- . Washington, Govt. Print. Off.

―――― Checklist of United States Public Documents, 1789-1909. 3d ed. Washington, Govt. Print. Off., 1911. 1707p.

―――― Price Lists of Government Publications. Washington, Govt. Print. Off., 1898- .

Indexes and bibliographies

number of times the name indexed has been mentioned on the page referred to. The Congressional documents are listed in the main alphabet by the serial numbers which Ames himself devised.

Document Catalog, 1893-1940. The *Document Catalog* began where Ames's *Comprehensive Index* left off, March 4, 1893, and continued until December 31, 1940, when it ceased publication. After volume 22 (Seventy-third Congress) each volume covers one Congress, or two calendar years. It is the easiest document tool to use because of its dictionary arrangement by author and subject. Some features to remember are the lists of government sources in the back of each volume, both alphabetical and classified; the analytics of separates; the inclusion of serial numbers; and the Congressional documents lists which appear under that heading and include the numerical sequence of the serial set.

Monthly Catalog, 1895-   . The *Monthly Catalog* has appeared since 1895, with an annual author, title, and subject index. Its completeness and arrangement have varied through the years. Since 1947 there have been many improvements in coverage and form largely as the result of recommendations by Jerome K. Wilcox, chairman of the A.L.A. Public Documents Committee.[6] It now aims to list all government publications, including processed materials, as soon as known to the Government Printing Office. For the period of 1893-1940, the *Document Catalog* is more nearly complete and easier to use, but from that date on the *Monthly Catalog* is the only basic source. Formerly, material delayed in reaching the Documents Office was listed only in the *Document Catalog*. Two supplements to the *Monthly Catalog* covering the period 1940-46 have been issued to list materials which had been omitted in that period, and now the *Monthly Catalog* lists all material when released, even though delayed in reaching the Office.

The arrangement within issues has also varied but at present the *Monthly Catalog* is alphabetical by the key word of the name of the issuing bureau; i.e., Agricultural Economics Bureau, Agriculture Department. Congress appears in its alphabetic place with its various committees alphabetically arranged under it. Entries include complete bibliographic information, Library of Congress card number, price,

---

[6] Jerome K. Wilcox, "Report by the Chairman of the Public Documents Committee of the A.L.A. Concerning the Cataloging and Indexing Program of the Division of Public Documents," *United States Government Publications Monthly Catalog,* September, 1947, no. 632, p.iii-vi.

Documents Office classification number, and often annotations. Instructions for ordering documents are given in the front of each issue. Since July 1945, each issue has contained an author, title, and subject index, while a complete index for the year appears in the December issue. Periodicals are listed in January and July of each year.

Checklist of United States Public Documents, 1789-1909. The *Checklist of United States Public Documents, 1789-1909* (3d ed., 1911) is a shelf list of the Documents Office Library for the period indicated. This means that the documents are arranged in the order in which they appear on the shelves of any library which follows the Documents Office classification scheme. After a readable introduction on earlier indexes and lists, there follow in the *Checklist* lists of American state papers, Congressional documents (Fifteenth to Sixtieth Congresses, both with serial numbers), and departmental publications arranged alphabetically by government author. A second volume, which was to have been a subject index, has never been published. There is, however, an unofficial compilation of Superintendent of Documents classification numbers, through August, 1945, compiled by Mary E. Poole of the D. H. Hill Library, North Carolina State College, Raleigh, N. C.[7]

Price Lists. The *Price Lists of Government Publications* are free subject bibliographies, revised from time to time, listing publications in stock and for sale at the Government Printing Office. Each list is arranged, usually, alphabetically by subject and gives Documents Office classification as well as price. Among the *Price Lists* now available are the following: American History (No. 50); Census (No. 70); Education (No. 31); Engineering (No. 18); Farm Management (No. 68); Foods and Cooking (No. 11); Government Periodicals (No. 36); Handy Books; Books for Ready Reference (No. 73); Maps (No. 53); Transportation and Panama Canal (No. 37); Weather (No. 48); World War II (No. 77).

❦ DOCUMENTS OF STATE AND LOCAL GOVERNMENTS

U.S. Library of Congress. Processing Dept. Monthly Checklist of State Publications, 1910- . Washington, Govt. Print. Off.

Special Libraries Association. Basic List of Current Municipal Documents. N.Y., Special Libraries Assn., 1932. 71p.

U.S. Bureau of the Census. Checklist of Basic Municipal Documents. Washington, Govt. Print. Off., 1948.

Documents of state and local governments

Selected United States Government Publications, formerly the *Weekly List,* is now issued twice monthly by the Superintendent of Documents and includes a very brief selection of current documents likely to interest smaller general libraries and individuals. It is arranged alphabetically by subject, with brief annotations, price, and an order blank. Like the *Price Lists,* this publication is free.

Documents of state and local governments

States, counties, and municipalities in the United States publish much important material, and many foreign countries have a wealth of similar publications. The bibliographic sources for these are not as satisfactory as are those for the federal government. As an introductory guide, J. B. Childs's *Government Document Bibliography in the United States and Elsewhere* (Govt. Print. Off., 1942), which lists the principal bibliographic sources for many countries and for individual states of the United States, is helpful. Another useful aid is J. K. Wilcox' *Manual on the Use of State Publications* (A.L.A., 1940).

The federal government is responsible for the current *Monthly Checklist of State Publications,* issued since 1910 by the Library of Congress. Arranged by the states, territories, and insular possessions, the checklist includes each month a comprehensive list of state documents and each year an annual index. For the period prior to 1910, R. R. Bowker's *A Provisional List of the Official Publications; of the Several States of the United States from Their Organization* (to varying terminal dates: 1899 for New England; 1902 for North Central; 1905 for Western states and territories; 1908 for Southern states; published by Publishers' Weekly, 1899-1908) is the principal source. Wilcox' *Manual on the Use of State Publications* will be helpful as a guide. The *Book of the States* and the *Municipal Yearbook* are also of value in the search for state and local publications.

In 1932, the Special Libraries Association compiled a *Basic List of Current Municipal Documents* for 56 important cities of the United States and Canada. A subject index adds to the usefulness of this list. In 1948 the Bureau of the Census published a *Checklist of Basic Municipal Documents* as number 27 of its State and Local Government Special Studies. This covers the publications of all cities which had a population of over 100,000 in 1940.

---

[7] *Documents Office Classification* (Ann Arbor, Mich., Edwards Brothers, 1945).

GOVERNMENT PUBLICATIONS

Foreign and international documents

There is no comprehensive list of government publications of foreign countries. Brown's *Manual of Government Publications, United States and Foreign* will prove an excellent introduction. Childs's *Government Documents Bibliography* gives under each country as far as possible current and retrospective bibliographies of government publications. Gregory's *List of Serial Publications of Foreign Governments* is limited to the period 1815-1931. It is arranged by countries and under them by agencies. In all some 30,000 titles are included in this work sponsored by the American Council of Learned Societies, the National Research Council, and the American Library Association.

For United Nations publications which are mounting steadily in volume the two paper-backed issues of *Publications,* bringing the record up to January 1, 1950, and the *United Nations Documents Index,* beginning with a record of publications from that date, offer some hope of a useful continuing bibliography.

Publications includes the "official records of the various organs (the General Assembly, the Security Council, the Economic and Social Council, the Trusteeship Council and the Atomic Energy Commission), studies and reports prepared by the United Nations Secretariat and several periodicals." Under 17 numbered categories and several additional headings, publications are listed with bibliographic information, including price. A subject index follows the main listings.

The *United Nations Documents Index* lists all documents except those of a confidential nature received by the Documents Index Unit

---

☞ FOREIGN AND INTERNATIONAL DOCUMENTS

Childs, J. B. Government Document Bibliography in the United States and Elsewhere. 3d ed. Washington, Govt. Print. Off., 1942. 78p.

Gregory, Winifred. List of Serial Publications of Foreign Governments, 1815-1931. N.Y., Wilson, 1932. 720p.

United Nations. Publications, 1945-1949. Lake Success, N.Y., United Nations Dept. of Public Information, 1949-50. 2v.

United Nations Documents Index; United Nations and Specialized Agencies Documents and Publications, January 1950- . Lake Success, N.Y., United Nations Library Documents Index Unit.

Foreign and international documents

during any one month. Following an introduction and a list of abbreviations, publications are listed in a section for the United Nations and its divisions, and then successively in alphabetic order in sections for each of the agencies. Each section is arranged in three parts: (1) documents and publications; (2) revisions, addenda, corrigenda and non-English language editions; (3) republications. Full bibliographic information is given in part one; parts two and three are arranged in tabular form. There is a general index. An asterisk in front of the listing of a publication selects it as significant for reference because of bibliographies or summaries of completed projects or of the work of an Organ, as a unit of the United Nations is called.

Reading list

Hutchins, Margaret. *Introduction to Reference Work.* Chicago, A.L.A., 1944. p.122-26.

McCamy, J. L. *Government Publications for the Citizen; a Report of the Public Library Inquiry.* N.Y., Columbia Univ. Pr., 1949. 139p.

Wilcox, J. K. *Manual on the Use of State Publications.* Chicago, A.L.A., 1940. 342p.

———"New Guides and Aids to Public Documents Use, 1945-1948," *Special Libraries,* 1949, v.40, p.371-77, 406-12.

chapter 14

AUDIO-VISUAL SOURCES

Introduction, Community resources,

Museum objects, Graphics,

Projected materials, Auditory materials.

Introduction

Audio-visual questions. Inevitably some inquiries must be answered by non-verbal sources. A request for a picture of Uncle Sam full length will brook no written description, however masterly. The location of a geographic place on a map will not quite be matched by a paragraph in a gazetteer. Chapters on the making of paper may never quite convey an idea of the process as effectively as a motion picture. Identification of the main themes of a symphonic movement will be more meaningful to the layman through recorded sound than through printed score. The hardness of carborundum can probably never be impressed on the sense of the child as effectively through reading as through handling the object. Because education is increasingly recognizing the advantage of multi-sensory communication, libraries as educational institutions are expanding the scope and concept of their responsibilities. That is the meaning of the Rochester Public Library's

Introduction

film title "Not by Books Alone." Today libraries are acquiring, processing, and disseminating audio-visual materials, and modern reference service is utilizing these materials in the daily search for answers to questions.

Typical of inquiries that involve audio-visual sources are the following taken from actual questions: (1) In school libraries: costumes of South American countries; radio advertising of drugs, foods, cosmetics; picture of a louse to be used as a model for a game called "cootie"; illustrated material for "Where there's a will"; "Song of the Volga Boatman." (2) In public libraries: pictures of members of the United States Constitutional Convention; layout of tourist camp; early boats on the Great Lakes; pictures of kitchens in 1869—Dutch, Spanish, English, French, Provençal, New England, Acadian—for a commercial art studio; designs for the back of playing cards which will attract quantity sales; pictures showing various artists' interpretations of Christ preaching the Sermon on the Mount; demonstration of game of basketball. (3) In college libraries: a picture of an artist with his palette; plans for house trailers; medieval representations of the soul; the voice of Franklin D. Roosevelt; cartoons of the United States as seen by the British.

Audio-visual sources. Audio-visual materials may be defined as all media of communication other than the printed word. The ever-expanding volume and variety of audio-visual materials and equipment make any classification today almost out of date by tomorrow. The outline which follows is, therefore, only a suggestion. It sets up five classes of reference sources.

1. Community resources: including all private and public agencies—the newspaper plant, telephone company, public school system—plus such natural environmental materials as rocks, trees, rivers, hills.

2. Museum objects: including collections of such materials as paintings, sculpture, coins, stamps, scientific specimens and instruments, industrial tools and products, and archaeological and local history collections.

3. Graphics: including photographs, charts, graphs, posters, maps, cartoons, schematic drawings, models, mockups, demonstrations, breadboards.

4. Projected materials: including stereographs, slides, filmstrips, films.

5. Auditory materials: including recordings—disc, tape or

wire—transcriptions, radio and television programs, sound films and filmstrips.

Community resources

There are non-book sources of information outside the library in every community. One can read how bricks are made; one can observe their making by going to the kiln in the community to which one has been referred by the reference librarian. These non-book sources of information include the schools, the church, the newspaper, the radio station; business and industrial concerns; local government and welfare agencies; clubs and other organizations; transportation agencies; bus, railroad, air transport; surrounding natural resources; and so on, until every class of local, natural, and human resource has been accounted for. An inventory of community resources belongs in the reference library. Local indexes of community resources should be a continuing project in every library and are the legitimate function of a reference department in a large library. Local indexes can be started on cards as a directory of local agencies, with important data like address, telephone number, names of personnel, function, length of operation, and subjects to which contributions have been or can be made. Local indexes can develop into a real, local information center with the reference librarian increasingly assuming the role of information officer for the community.

Museum objects

Library exhibits in the United States have covered the major classes of man's knowledge. Stored, the materials of these exhibits are reference resources. The descriptions accompanying these exhibits are indexes to the materials. The rare specimen of a pickled scorpion, the strange seashell, the jawbone of Neanderthal man, paper in various stages of production—these are all possible reference sources. As Miss Hutchins writes: "That reference department is indeed fortunate that is located in a library having as close connections with a museum as the Newark Free Public Library."[1] Since 1944, when Miss Hutchins' book was published, an increasing number of libraries of all kinds have made these connections or started their own museums. Collections of objects in or near the library are most often found in schools, colleges, and universities. Miss Rufsvold writes of school

Graphics

libraries: "Included in the collection may be art objects, framed pictures, rocks and minerals, models of period furniture, historic vehicles, tools, textiles, national and historic costumes, flags, samples of yarn, a Roman forum or bridge, spinning and weaving tools, and so on."[2] College and university libraries often have the additional advantage of access to good campus museums, laboratories, and extension centers.

Indexes to museum objects can supplement or be a part of the community resources index. Their use in handling certain types of inquiries will be a measure of their role in reference service.

Graphics

Flat pictures, charts, broadsides, graphs, photographs, and drawings are all grouped as graphics. The October, 1946, issue of *Subscription Books Bulletin* contains one of the best lists of graphic sources in print, including the names and addresses of agencies offering free and inexpensive materials. For a discussion of the organization of the picture collection, Norma Ireland's little book, *The Picture File* (Faxon, 1952), or the pamphlet prepared for the Newark Public Library by Marcelle Frebault in 1943[3] is excellent. The *Standard Catalog for High School Libraries* also lists sources of pictures.

Among the classes of pictures useful in reference are: (1) clippings from picture magazines like *Life, Holiday, National Geographic* —or references to them by subject; (2) reproductions of art masterpieces, designs, charts, photographs; (3) photographs made from preserved negatives; and (4) portraits of persons, needed especially in connection with biographical reference.

Location of all these types of graphic materials is possible through periodical and newspaper indexes, encyclopedias and their yearbook supplements, and eclectic bibliographies, as well as through specially prepared indexes. Among notable indexes to pictures the three prepared by Jessie C. Ellis have frequent reference use. They are *General Index to Illustrations* (1931), *Travel Through Pictures* (1935), and

---

[1] Margaret Hutchins, *Introduction to Reference Work* (Chicago, A.L.A., 1944), p.115.

[2] Margaret I. Rufsvold, *Audio-Visual School Library Service* (Chicago, A.L.A., 1949), p.53.

[3] J. C. Dana, *Picture Collection* (5th ed., rev. by Marcelle Frebault; N.Y., Wilson, 1943), 86p.

Nature and Its Applications (1949), all published by the F. W. Faxon Company. Two older indexes are F. J. Shepard's *Index to Illustrations*, published in a preliminary edition by the American Library Association in 1924, and the *A.L.A. Portrait Index*, published by the Library of Congress in 1906, which is still valuable for locating the portraits of some 35,000 notables of the nineteenth century and earlier.

Charts and posters were library stock-in-trade for years before the current interest in audio-visual materials developed. Many of these graphics have been made and displayed by library staff members as an integral part of their professional work. Other graphics have been obtained from the variety of sources listed from time to time in professional library journals. One of the best recent publications is Lili Heimers' *Free Teaching Aids in 14 Subjects* (Montclair, N.J., State Teachers College, 1948), recording over 250 sources of charts and pictures as well as of maps and other publications useful to teachers. Examples of charts and posters usable in libraries are the health posters issued by the American Medical Association, the safety education posters of the National Safety Council, and *Our Democracy Charts*, published by Denoyer-Geppert.

Other examples of graphics come to us from the armed forces and from museums. During World War II much use was made of demonstrations—synthetic devices developed by industrial concerns to explain processes or mechanisms or skills. The Compton book exhibit or bindery demonstration is an application of this device to book arts. Mockups—simulations of equipment used in the war—have also been utilized by industrial museums. A miniature telephone switchboard that actually works or an amateur radio set may answer reference questions. Models and breadboards are other examples, "the latter being operating layouts of all the parts of a piece of equipment on a flat board."[4]

Projected materials

Stereographs, filmstrips, slides, films, and microtexts, which must be viewed by means of a projector, all have high potential reference value.

1. *Stereographs* are three-dimensional pictures. Since they are usually viewed by an individual, they might be thought to fall within the class of graphics. However, they do require a stereopticon or other stereoscopic viewer. The Keystone View Company is the largest pro-

Projected materials

ducer of educational stereographs and viewers and publishes a useful pamphlet on the subject, George E. Hamilton's *The Stereograph in Education* (1945).

2. *Filmstrips,* sometimes called filmslides or slidefilms, consist of a sequence of individual pictures with text photographed on 35mm. film. The pictures may be either single frame or double frame, a frame being a section of film one inch wide and three-fourths of an inch long. The average number of frames to a strip is 50 to 60, but filmstrips vary from 15 to 150 frames in length. Sound filmstrips are accompanied by recorded commentaries. Several publishers, notably McGraw-Hill; Heath; Silver, Burdett; Row, Peterson; and Macmillan, are co-ordinating books with filmstrips.

The older filmstrips may be located through Falconer's *Filmstrips* and the current ones through *Filmstrip Guide,* the first annual volume of which listed 1275 filmstrips released since Falconer was published. *Filmstrip Guide* consists of three quarterly issues and an annual volume published in September. An alphabetical title and subject list is followed by a classified, annotated list.

3. *Slides* come in two sizes, and different projection equipment is required for each. The standard slide measuring 3¼ by 4 inches consists of a photograph or drawing on glass or other material enclosed in a frame. A two by two inch slide comprises a single or double frame 35mm. film on a cardboard, glass, metal or plastic slide mount. These slides are available from various sources, the Keystone View Company in Meadville, Pennsylvania, being one of the large producers of standard lantern slides and the Society for Visual Education in Chicago being a principal source for the two by two inch slides. However, slides are available from many sources, as well as materials for creation of the library's own slides. George E. Hamilton's *How to Make Lantern Slides* (Keystone View Co., 1948) is a useful manual.

4. *Films.* Sixteen-millimeter motion picture film is standard for educational use. Both silent and sound films are produced by commercial, governmental, educational and entertainment agencies, and fall into a number of distinct types. Instructional films present factual information explaining processes, principles, skills, and concepts and are produced with the assistance of recognized authorities and educational consultants. Among the best-known producers of this type of

---

[4] J. R. Miles and C. R. Spain, *Audio-Visual Aids in the Armed Services* (Washington, American Council on Education, 1947).

AUDIO-VISUAL SOURCES

film are Encyclopaedia Britannica, McGraw-Hill, Young America, Coronet, and United World. Documentary films present social problems in the dramatic style of the photoplay. Pare Lorentz' *The River,* for instance, depicts man's efforts at flood control, and *Florida, Wealth or Waste* deals with the problems of conservation in one state. Sponsored films are those produced for promotion purposes by a commercial, industrial or other agency. Eastern Air Lines, for example, has produced a film showing the progress of aviation. Entertainment films are for the most part 16mm. reductions from the original 35mm. prints of such classics as *Great Expectations* and *Alice in Wonderland.* They are generally rented rather than sold.

The basic film bibliography is *Educational Film Guide,* published by the H. W. Wilson Company, which consists of three quarterly issues and an annual volume issued in August. Each issue consists of two parts—an alphabetical subject and title list and a list, classified by Decimal Classification, which includes descriptive notes, evaluations and gradings by educational level. Other important bibliographic and index tools are the *Educator's Guide to Free Films,* an annual list of sponsored films which contained until recently many films not included in the Wilson list; the *Blue Book of 16mm. Films,* formerly known as *1000 and One,* published annually; and the Library of Congress *Guide to United States Government Motion Pictures.* Many periodicals list and review films, among which are the audio-visual publications *Educational Screen, Film World,* and *See and Hear,* and the library and literary publications *Library Journal* and *Saturday Review.*

5. *Microtexts.* The collective term "microtext" is used to describe photographic reproductions of text so small that optical aid is neces-

---

☞ PROJECTED MATERIALS

Falconer, Vera M. Filmstrips; a Descriptive Index and User's Guide. N.Y., McGraw-Hill, 1948. 572p.

Filmstrip Guide, 1948- (quarterly). N.Y., Wilson.

Educational Film Guide, 1936- (quarterly). N.Y., Wilson.

Educator's Guide to Free Films, 1941- (annual). Randolph, Wis., Educator's Progress Service.

Blue Book of 16 mm Films, 1920- (annual). Chicago, Educational Screen.

U.S. Library of Congress. Guide to United States Government Motion Pictures. Washington, Govt. Print. Off., 1947. 104p.

sary to read or view the materials. Four kinds of microtexts are in use in libraries, two transparent and two opaque. The transparent microtexts are microfilm and flat film, the former in roll form being the most common, the latter consisting of individual film frames on mounts. Of the two opaque methods of producing microtext, microcard is steadily growing in favor. It is produced on a glazed three by five inch card. The other, microprint, is a "positive microphotograph photographically printed on paper," according to the *A.L.A. Glossary of Library Terms*. No comprehensive lists of microtexts are available.[5]

Auditory materials

Auditory materials include media that depend on sight and hearing as well as on hearing alone. In the former are included sound motion pictures and filmstrips and television; in the latter, disc, tape and wire transcriptions and recordings as well as radio programs. An increasing number of reference rooms, especially in schools, are introducing so-called "listening posts"—record players with multi-earphones so that no sound disturbs other readers.

Standard recordings are on discs of 10-inch and 12-inch size which operate on an ordinary phonograph rotating at 78 revolutions per minute. Radio transcriptions on 16-inch discs which are played on turntables rotating at $33\frac{1}{3}$ revolutions per minute are included in many library collections. These record a half-hour program on two sides whereas a 12-inch record plays only ten minutes on both sides. The newer LP (long-playing) microgroove records offer as much as 50 minutes on two sides of a 12-inch record. These records, like transcriptions, play at $33\frac{1}{3}$ revolutions per minute. A 45-revolutions-per-minute, 7-inch microgroove record, less expensive and, like the regular LP, unbreakable, is also available. Steady advances in tape recording are enabling many libraries to record and store tapes of reference value.

Music has been the subject best served by recordings in the past, but increasingly questions on speech, foreign language, drama, and

---

[5] These references will prove helpful: Blanche P. McCrum's *Microfilms and Microcards; Their Use in Research; a Selected List of References* (Washington, Library of Congress, 1950), George A. Schwegmann's *Newspapers on Microfilm; a Union Check List* (Association of Research Libraries, 1948), and the Philadelphia Bibliographic Center's *Union List of Microfilms* (rev. ed., Ann Arbor, Mich., Edwards Brothers, 1951).

AUDIO-VISUAL SOURCES

current events are being answered by transcriptions. One library has collected tape transcriptions of radio broadcasts of election campaigns and returns, including political speeches, and other special programs. Recordings are useful for recitations, folklore, games and recreation, in recording songs of birds, and for a variety of other purposes.

Recordings. A number of periodicals review recordings regularly. Among the better current sources are the *Saturday Review, Library Journal, Parents' Magazine, American Record Guide*, and *Review of Recorded Music*, as well as the audio-visual periodicals previously listed. The *Index of Record Reviews*, compiled by Kurtz Myers, indexes reviews in about 20 American and English periodicals with evaluations. It has appeared in *Notes*, published by the Music Library Association, since March, 1948.

Retrospective sources of reference value are the comprehensive *Gramophone Shop Encyclopedia*, supplemented by a monthly list which contains brief reviews; David Hall's *Records*, a comprehensive survey of recorded literature which discusses late developments in disc and tape; and the *New Guide to Recorded Music*, by Irving Kolodin, editor of the monthly *Saturday Review* record section.

Radio and television programs. It is the task of the reference librarian to provide advance information on significant radio and television programs, to record them on tape or disc, and to collect printed radio speeches. Obvious sources for programs are the daily newspapers. Monthly throughout the year the United States Office of Education publishes *Selected Radio Programs for School Listening*. Each of the major broadcasting chains offers advance notice of programs: American Broadcasting Company issues periodic outlines of programs; Columbia Broadcasting System has a monthly service schedule which is provided free; National Broadcasting System publishes a monthly service schedule free and handbooks for "University of the Air" programs at 25c each; Mutual Broadcasting Company issues free monthly schedules. Printed copies of a number of discussion broadcasts are also available.

☛ RECORDINGS

The Gramophone Shop Encyclopedia of Recorded Music. 3d ed. N.Y., Crown, 1948. Monthly Supplement, 1942- .

Hall, David. Records. N.Y., Knopf, 1950. 524p.

Kolodin, Irving. New Guide to Recorded Music. Garden City, N.Y., Doubleday, 1950.

Auditory materials

Reading list

Florida State University, School of Library Training and Service. *The Audio-Visual Way;* ed. by Charles Hoban. Tallahassee, Fla., State Dept. of Education, 1948. Compact definition and classification of audio-visual sources and services.

Gamble, B. L. "Sources of Information on Films and Filmstrips," *Wilson Library Bulletin,* 1950, v.25, p.306-07. A recent summary of basic reference tools.

Hutchins, Margaret. *Introduction to Reference Work.* Chicago, A.L.A., 1944. p.115-21, 141-45.

Miles, J. R., and Spain, C. R. *Audio-Visual Aids in the Armed Services; Implications for American Education.* Washington, American Council on Education, 1947. 96p.

Rufsvold, Margaret I. *Audio-Visual School Library Service.* Chicago, A.L.A., 1949. 116p.

part two | chapter 15

THE SUBJECT APPROACH; LIBRARIANSHIP

The subject approach, Librarianship.

The subject approach

Reference service in special fields. A very large portion of the questions asked in college, public and school libraries can be answered by the general sources reviewed thus far, and it must never be forgotten that in these general reference tools there is potential information and aid to the subject specialist. The unabridged dictionary has been prepared by some of the most distinguished subject specialists and so have many of the general encyclopedias, yearbooks, directories, handbooks, and manuals.

A large number of inquiries, however, require an early or immediate subject approach. Teachers, research workers, professional people, business and tradespeople, artists, and the clergy are likely to require special subject reference service and materials. Many public and college libraries provide for these needs by setting aside subject rooms, departments or divisions administered by librarians who are familiar with or specially trained in these fields. Thus, increasingly, law librarians are library-trained lawyers, medical librarians are library-trained students of medicine, and newspaper librarians have journalistic background as well as library training. Reference librarians with such double preparation can be expected to do effective reference work in the fields of their specialization.[1]

The subject approach

None but the very largest general libraries, however, can afford to employ specialists in all the fields represented by their collections; it therefore falls to the reference librarian in smaller libraries to know enough about the various fields of knowledge to serve the occasional specialist-reader who seeks library aid. Obviously, no one individual can hope to know much about all these subjects. The reference librarian can, however, learn the basic reference materials in each field, and thus prepare himself to give considerable assistance to the research worker. He should also try to gain at least a bibliographic acquaintance with the scholarly literature of the major subject fields whether or not his library has the actual materials available.

Subject reference. Two distinct avenues of approach should be recognized in subject reference work. One is the interpretative road directed (1) to satisfy the teacher's need for subject materials that can be used on certain educational levels—elementary, secondary, or adult, (2) to introduce a layman to the special field, or (3) to survey the present state of knowledge in a particular subject for the specialist. The other is the investigative lane that leads past present knowledge to the yet unknown or uncorrelated aspects of the subject and aids the research worker in his efforts to advance the frontiers of knowledge.

Special types of reference materials are needed both for investigation and for interpretation, but the same type is not always suitable for both groups. For example, the research worker in the field of language and literature may want to scrutinize the publications of the Modern Language Association, which is concerned with scholarly research studies of dialects, of obscure literary writers, of newer analyses of well-known books; while persons wishing interpretation may be more interested in the publications of the National Council of Teachers of English, which devotes itself to improving instruction and to studying better ways of interpreting the scholar's findings to lay adults and to young people.

To serve the subject specialists in each field, whether they be teachers or research workers, the reference librarian needs, in addition to knowledge of basic reference books, subject background and acquaintance with the most important subject reference materials.

---

[1] Special Libraries Association, *The Special Library Profession and What It Offers; Surveys of Fifteen Fields;* comp. by Marian C. Manley (N.Y., The Association, 1938), a reprint of a series of articles from *Special Libraries,* 1934-1938. Among the special libraries discussed are those connected with art museums, public utilities, municipal reference, federal departments, religion, medicine, and public health.

Subject background. The librarian will find that in the field of his undergraduate or graduate subject major he has a running start. But the librarian who has no background in a given subject need not feel discouraged. There are certain systematic steps which he can take.

An outline of the content of any subject field can be obtained quickly, in a number of ways. The Dewey Decimal and Library of Congress classification scheme outlines will indicate the main divisions of the subject. So will the table of contents of an introductory textbook or the subheads of an encyclopedia article. The general dictionary will define most commonly used technical terms and the biographical directory will identify names of persons referred to. In the general yearbooks—especially the *American Yearbook*—compact summaries of recent developments and statements about pressing problems will be found. Periodical and newspaper indexes will reveal current articles and news items. From handbooks and manuals may be obtained some of the working information essential to an understanding of the subject. The directories of agencies will indicate the principal learned societies and professional associations in the field.

Here is a suggested outline for librarians wishing to develop background in the special subject fields:

1. Prepare topical outline of subject.
    Sources: Dewey Decimal, Library of Congress and other classifications; introductory textbook; encyclopedia article.
2. Make a list of important terms, and look up definitions.
    Sources: General dictionary; subject dictionary.
3. Decide on the half-dozen or so most important names of persons, two or three significant learned societies and professional associations, and the leading periodicals of the field.
    Sources: Encyclopedia article; textbook; *Ulrich's Periodicals Directory.*
4. Get acquainted generally with kinds of data or processes important to the subject.
    Sources: Handbooks; manuals.
5. Find out whether government agencies are concerned with subject and if there are audio-visual materials.
    Sources: Document indexes; audio-visual bibliographies.
6. Locate and read a popular introduction to the subject.
    Sources: Standard Catalog series or other selected lists.
7. Indicate three or four pressing problems.
    Sources: Yearbooks; periodicals; newspapers.

The subject approach

Acquaintance with the basic literature of the field can be most economically acquired through bibliographic tools. Among these, several types will be recognized: (1) bibliographic guides or handbooks, (2) bibliographies of bibliographies, (3) abstracts and summaries, and (4) special indexes. The importance of bibliographic tools to specialized reference work has been well stated by Feipel:

> A bibliography of a subject is to the literature of that subject what an index is to a book. It shows the extent of the literature and the amount of work that has been bestowed upon it. It brings together scattered fragments of book knowledge and makes them readily accessible. Next to having knowledge is knowing where to go for it, and the only enduring guide in that direction is a bibliography.[2]

Bibliographic guides. Guides and manuals for research workers and advanced graduate students have been compiled in a number of fields. These manuals usually introduce the student to the divisions of the subject, the methods of research most commonly employed, the general nature of its literature, and the principal reference materials. Some examples of these tools, all of which are discussed elsewhere in this textbook, follow.

Subject	Author	Title
Chemistry	Soule	*Library Guide for the Chemist*
Communication	Smith, Lasswell, Casey	*Propaganda, Communication, and Public Opinion*
Education	Alexander	*How To Locate Educational Information and Data*
History	Dutcher	*Guide to Historical Literature*
Law	Notz	*Legal Research*
Mathematics and physics	Parke	*Guide to the Literature of Mathematics and Physics*
Modern language	Oliver	*Modern Language Teacher's Handbook*
Political science	Burchfield	*Student's Guide to Materials in Political Science*
Psychology	Louttit	*Handbook of Psychological Literature*
Social sciences	Tompkins	*Methodology of Social Science Research*

---

[2] Louis Feipel, *Elements of Bibliography* (Chicago, Univ. of Chicago Pr., 1916), a reprint from *Papers* of the Bibliographical Society of America, October, 1916, v.10, no. 4, p.175-207.

THE SUBJECT APPROACH; LIBRARIANSHIP

Bibliographies of bibliographies. The increasing attention now being paid to bibliographies in all subjects, both as separate undertakings and as important parts of original investigations, makes the need for a list of bibliographies or of articles and monographs featuring bibliographies imperative as the starting point for study or further research. Besterman's *World Bibliography of Bibliographies* and the *Bibliographic Index,* arranged by subject (see Chapter 12), are useful for preliminary search, as is Collison's *Bibliographies* (Hafner, 1950). Among specialized subject bibliographies of bibliographies the following, described elsewhere in this textbook, may be cited as examples:

Subject	Author	Title
Education	Monroe and Shores	*Bibliographies and Summaries in Education*
English	Northup	*A Register of Bibliographies of the English Language and Literature*
Psychology	Louttit	*Bibliography of Bibliographies on Psychology*

Abstracts and summaries. In many subject fields abstract journals or annual summaries of research are published. The abstract journal appears as a current subject bibliography with descriptive annotations. Several hundred such publications are currently being published. Some try to present truly informative digests of the material indexed. Others only indicate the nature of the content in very general terms. Well-organized abstract journals, provided with detailed indexes, either annual or cumulative over longer periods, are of value not only for current material but also as retrospective bibliographies and indexes. Summaries, or reviews of progress, serve about the same purpose, but their form is different. A summary is a running narrative account of studies and findings relating to a single problem or to several related problems, with bibliographical citations usually given to a keyed list at the end. The following titles, described elsewhere in this textbook, are examples:

Subject	Title
Biology	*Biological Abstracts*
Chemistry	*Chemical Abstracts*
Education	Gray. *Summary of Investigations Relating to Reading*
Engineering	*Electrical Engineering Abstracts*

The subject approach

English	*Year's Work in English Studies*
Mental Tests and Testing	Buros. *Mental Measurements Yearbook*
Physics	*Physics Abstracts*
Psychology	*Psychological Abstracts*

Indexes. The special serial indexes devoted to analyzing the current literature of one or of several related fields, and the form indexes to special kinds of materials, such as those to trade names, costumes, songs, poems, plays, stories, are all useful in special reference work. A few samples of subject indexes, all of which are described elsewhere in this textbook, are listed:

Subject	*Index*
Agriculture	*Agricultural Index*
Art	*Art Index*
Drama	*Dramatic Index*
Education	*Education Index*
Engineering	*Engineering Index*
Law	*Index to Legal Periodicals*
Medicine	*Index Medicus*
Science, technology	*Industrial Arts Index*
Social sciences	*Public Affairs Information Service*

Serials. Particular stress must be placed on serial publications in the special subject fields. A large proportion of reports on original work—new discoveries and interpretations of them—appear first in periodicals or other serials and sometimes are not republished. These publications take a variety of forms. In addition to the weekly, monthly or quarterly journal, serials appear as services—such as those so essential in business—monographs in series, and various irregularly issued publications from learned societies, professional associations, educational agencies and institutions, government bureaus, philanthropic foundations, and industrial and commercial firms. A good reference librarian should become familiar with the leading serial publications in many fields and be able to use them quickly and intelligently.

General reference works in subject fields. The reference librarian should not forget at this point that the pattern of reference publications in general fields followed in Part I of this textbook repeats itself in the specialized subjects. The librarian should look for and use the various types of reference books for individual subjects—dictionaries, encyclopedias, yearbooks, etc. Some examples of different types of periodicals in the subject fields, all of which are discussed in the following chapters, are:

Type	Subject	Title
Dictionary	Law	Bouvier. *Law Dictionary*
Cyclopedia	Science	Van Nostrand's *Scientific Encyclopedia*
Yearbook	Religion	*Yearbook of American Churches*
Directory	Education	Cattell. *Leaders in Education*
Handbook	Art	Gardner. *Art Through the Ages*

Reference procedure, in the majority of cases, begins as in general information questions, with classification of the question by type.

1. For language questions involving meanings, spellings, pronunciations, word usage, abbreviations, signs and symbols, slang, dialect, names, and foreign terms, consult dictionary sources first.

2. For background questions, involving "general information" or "all about" inquiries, consult encyclopedias first.

3. For trends questions, involving records of progress, last year's happenings, and current events, consult continuations and serials.

4. For fact questions, involving curiosities, statistics, documents, allusions, dates, literary items, and activity questions involving "how to do" or "how to make," consult handbooks and manuals.

5. For questions about persons, places, and agencies, involving biography, addresses, location, and distances, consult directories first.

6. For questions relating to the location of materials such as books, essays, poems, plays, short stories, speeches, articles, and original reports of research, consult bibliographies and indexes first.

Librarianship

The subject field. Librarianship is defined in the *A.L.A. Glossary of Library Terms* as: "The application of knowledge of books and certain principles, theories and techniques to the establishment, preservation, organization, and use of collections of books and other materials in libraries, and to the extension of library service." Its major divisions are: (1) bibliography, in the widest meaning of that term, including the book arts and sciences of production, distribution, recording and selection, as well as the arts and sciences relating to other media of communication; (2) library management, which includes all aspects of organization and administration such as personnel, housing, finance, promotion, etc.; (3) technical processes, such as classifi-

Librarianship

cation and cataloging, acquisition, loan, reproduction, operation of mechanical devices, preparation of materials for use, etc.; (4) reader and reference services, involving guidance, aid to research and instruction, dissemination of library materials, and diffusion of learning; (5) library foundations, including history, philosophy, ethics, organization of the profession; and (6) special librarianship, including the special problems of schools, public, college and university librarianship, as well as the literature and special problems of medicine, law, engineering, art, science and other subject fields.

More detailed outlines of the scope of librarianship are available in each of the major library classification systems and in Cannons' *Bibliography of Library Economy,* discussed later in this chapter. The most comprehensive and up-to-date classification is Stewart's *Tabulation of Librarianship* (Grafton, 1947), compiled in London during World War II.

Among current pressing problems in librarianship the following are representative: (1) bibliographic control of the mounting volume of records of all kinds by the libraries of the world—this involves not only adequate indexing and cataloging, but allocation of rare and specialized materials in such a way as to ensure accessibility to scholars; (2) documentary reproduction by microphotography and the comparative advantages of the different forms; (3) audio-visual materials and their relation to print; and (4) library integration with instruction on both the school and college levels. Important professional terms are included in the *A.L.A. Glossary of Library Terms* referred to frequently in this book.

Persons of importance in librarianship to whom frequent reference is made include the American pioneers, many of whom were honored in connection with the 75th anniversary of the American Library Association, and contemporaries whose innovations in practice or whose writings and research stimulate investigation. Among the former must be included all the names represented in the A.L.A. series of American library pioneers.[3] For example, Melvil Dewey, Charles Cutter, John Cotton Dana, W. H. Brett are names associated with library subjects like classification, author members, service to business,

---

[3] This series includes: H. M. Lydenberg, *John Shaw Billings* (1924); Linda A. Eastman, *Portrait of a Librarian, William Howard Brett* (1940); W. P. Cutter, *Charles Ammi Cutter* (1931); Chalmers Hadley, *John Cotton Dana* (1943); Fremont Rider, *Melvil Dewey* (1944); R. K. Shaw, *Samuel Swett Green* (1936); J. A. Borome, *Charles Coffin Jewett* (1950).

and open shelves and offer therefore potential clues to reference inquiries.

Similarly certain movements, clusters of statistics, processes, divisions of work, and peripheral trades and professions must be recognized by the reference librarian if he is to handle inquiries in the special subject field of librarianship intelligently. Examples of current movements with reference potential are documentation, library cooperation, Heritage of America, microphotography, modular construction, and audio-visual services. Clusters of statistics for which reference calls are frequent include library holdings, budgets, salaries, circulation, and public library service to rural areas. Questions relating to divisions of work can be illustrated by those concerning reclassification, cataloging of corporate entries, varieties of self- or automatic-charging, posters and bulletin boards. Finally, the scope of such peripheral fields as printing, publishing, binding, archives, museums, and architecture must be known in order to supplement reference service to librarianship.

General reference sources. Almost all of the basic reference books reviewed to this point have something to contribute to reference service in library science or librarianship. Compilers of the leading dictionaries, for example, have given careful attention to the definition of library terms. Encyclopedia publishers have employed librarians to write their articles on library subjects. Yearbooks provide data and summaries of interest to librarians; the *American Yearbook* summaries are particularly effective. Statistics in the almanacs are more recent than those in professional literature. These examples illustrate the necessity of consulting general reference tools to answer special inquiries on libraries and librarianships such as come to the Headquarters Library of the American Library Association and to library school libraries.

Bibliographies and indexes. The basic retrospective bibliography is Cannons' *Bibliography of Library Economy,* which covers the

---

❦ BIBLIOGRAPHIES AND INDEXES

Cannons, H. G. T. Bibliography of Library Economy; a Classified Index to the Professional Periodical Literature in the English Language. Chicago, A.L.A., 1927. 680p.

Library Literature, 1921-   (semiannual). N.Y., Wilson.

Library Science Abstracts, 1950-   (quarterly). London, Library Assn.

period from 1876 to 1920. It is a classified list of references and includes publishing, printing and bibliography as well as library science. From 1920 to the present the record of professional writings is found in *Library Literature,* which is issued semiannually and cumulated annually and triennially. It is an author and subject index to periodicals, books and pamphlets relating to the library profession. Entries are generally annotated, and articles of professional interest appearing outside regular library publications are included.

Library Science Abstracts, issued quarterly since 1950, aims "to present a conspectus of current activity and thought in the field of interest . . . to enable every member of our varied profession to feel closely linked with all branches of the profession. . . ." Abstracts are numbered and arranged by major subject divisions. There is an annual author, name and subject index. Although this is a British publication, representation is world-wide.

There is no up-to-date bibliographic manual at present, although Burton and Vosburgh's *A Bibliography of Librarianship* (Library Association, 1934) is useful for the period covered.

These special bibliographic tools can often be supplemented by the use of general bibliographic and index tools and by consulting special subject bibliographies for peripheral fields. Examples of what is meant are Bigmore and Wyman's *Bibliography of Printing,*[4] Monroe and Shores's *Bibliographies and Summaries in Education,* or *London Bibliography of the Social Sciences* (see Chapter 17). The catalogs of the publications of the American Library Association, the H. W. Wilson Company, the F. W. Faxon Company, the R. R. Bowker Company and others who publish in the field of librarianship are useful.

Serials. As in most other subject fields, the body of knowledge in librarianship is developed through serial literature. The number of professional periodicals now published throughout the world is large enough to make a respectable section in the latest edition of *Ulrich's Periodicals Directory.* The seven selected for listing are probably those most often subscribed to by American librarians and represent fairly wide professional coverage. Of these, the *A.L.A Bulletin, Library Journal* and *Wilson Library Bulletin* are universally present even in small libraries. The first, as the official organ of the

---

[4] E. C. Bigmore and C. W. H. Wyman, *A Bibliography of Printing* (London, Quaritch, 1880-86), 3v.

national association, carries professional news, significant articles and summaries of conferences and meetings. *Library Journal* is the oldest professional journal and is distinguished by a most attractive format, emphasis on personal news, controversial articles, and abundant illustrations. Its professional annotations of books, films, and recordings are other features. *Wilson Library Bulletin,* published by the H. W. Wilson Company, emphasizes the smaller library and gives considerable attention to school library needs. Regular departments covering reference book reviews, publicity and other library interests together with a monthly Readers' Choice of Best Books are notable features. Illustrations are plentiful and good.

Of the remaining four periodicals, three are specialized in scope. *Library Quarterly* emphasizes research studies; *College and Research Libraries,* articles of interest to the sections of the Association of College and Reference Libraries; and *Special Libraries,* materials, articles, and reviews dealing with the problems of the various subject specialties. The *Library Association Record* is the British counterpart of the *A.L.A. Bulletin.*

Other special serials of importance are the *Bulletin of Bibliography,* which includes notes on the births and deaths of periodicals as well as bibliographies and biographies of librarians, the *American Archivist, American Documentation,* and regional publications like the *Southeastern Librarian.*

Other reference books. Selection of representative reference books in the field of librarianship is made more difficult by the fact that most professional books have reference value. Consequently the

---

❦ SERIALS

American Library Association. Bulletin, 1907-   (monthly). Chicago, A.L.A.
Library Journal, 1876-   (semimonthly). N.Y., Bowker. $6.
Wilson Library Bulletin, 1914-   (monthly). N.Y., Wilson.
Library Quarterly, 1931-   . Chicago, Univ. of Chicago Pr. $5.
College and Research Libraries, 1939-   (quarterly). Chicago, A.L.A. $4.
Special Libraries, 1910-   (monthly). N.Y., Special Libraries Assn. $7.
Library Association Record, 1899-   (monthly). London, Library Assn.

Librarianship

titles listed are merely intended to illustrate with a single example five types of reference books.

The *A.L.A. Glossary of Library Terms,* frequently quoted in this book, is an example of a subject dictionary. It "includes technical terms used in American libraries, except those purely, or largely, of local significance" and some terms from related fields like archives, bibliography, printing, etc. The work dates back to 1926 when the Board of Education for Librarianship planned to meet the professional need for a more comprehensive collection of definitions of library terms than was available in print. Volunteer readers searched the literature under the guidance of two committees. The resulting glossary is an alphabetical list of professional terms with compared definitions.

There is no subject encyclopedia, nor is there a systematic summary of the year's developments in librarianship. The British *Year's Work in Librarianship* and the *A.L.A. Handbook* have at various times been the nearest approaches to an annual professional summary. The former through bibliographic comments and lists, annual examination questions, and summaries of Library Association activities presents a partial year's record of librarianship. At present, summaries of American Library Association activities can be found in the *A.L.A. Bulletin.* Encyclopedia supplements and the *American Yearbook,* however, still provide the best annual summaries.

Who's Who in Library Service, though somewhat out of date, gives biographical data on 8000 librarians in active service in 1943. Arrangement is alphabetic and sketches are of the "who's who" type. There is a geographical index.

❦ OTHER REFERENCE BOOKS

A.L.A. Glossary of Library Terms, with a Selection of Terms in Related Fields; prepared under the direction of the Committee on Library Terminology by Elizabeth H. Thompson. Chicago, A.L.A., 1943. 159p. $3.50.

Year's Work in Librarianship, 1928- . London, Library Assn.

Williamson, C. C. and Jewett, Alice L. Who's Who in Library Service. 2d ed., rev. and enl. N.Y., Wilson, 1943. 612p.

American Library Directory; comp. under the direction of Karl Brown. 18th ed. N.Y., Bowker, 1948. 731p.

Dewey, Melvil. Decimal Classification and Relative Index. 15th ed., rev. N.Y., Wilson, 1951, 661p. $16.

The eighteenth edition of the *American Library Directory* is "a classified list of 11,334 libraries with names of librarians and statistical data." Its major divisions are United States public, college and junior college, law, medical, institutional, hospital, federal, state, and special libraries; United States territorial libraries; Canadian and Newfoundland libraries; library schools; library organizations; state and provincial extension agencies; special collections and libraries; an index of memorial names. Data included for each library are name, personnel, size of the collection, finances and special collections. Major arrangement is by state and locality. The index of special collections, special subjects and special libraries is helpful but difficult for quick reference because citation is to page and not to library.

There are many examples of handbooks and manuals. The one chosen to illustrate this type is a professional classic. Most American libraries still use the Dewey *Decimal Classification* for book stock arrangement and the fifteenth edition of this manual, known as the "Standard Library Edition," is "designed to meet the needs of the greatest number of libraries." Simplified spelling has been abandoned and new numbers provided for new subjects. The introduction is a manual for classification with general instructions on how to classify books.

Reading list

Butler, Pierce, ed. *The Reference Function of the Library.* Chicago, Univ. of Chicago Pr., 1943. Includes papers by reference library specialists in social science, p.163-78; geography, p.144-62; science and technology, p.180-201; etc.

Hutchins, Margaret. *Introduction to Reference Work.* Chicago, A.L.A., 1944. Includes sections on subject reference work in biography, p.56-63; history and geography, p.64-68; bibliography, p.41-55; etc.

chapter 16

HISTORY AND AUXILIARY SUBJECTS

Introduction, Bibliographies, Serials,

Cyclopedias, Handbooks and atlases,

Cyclopedic sets, Geography, Biography,

Local history, Genealogy.

Introduction

The subject area. History has been defined as a record of all human events. The acceptance of such an inclusive definition means that history reference may well involve the sources of almost any area of human knowledge, since all subjects have a history, and history is itself the summation or record of events in all areas of human life.

The subject of history is generally divided by periods: ancient, medieval, modern; by geography: continent, nation, region, state, community; and by aspect and topic: political, military, economic, cultural. A representative outline of the subject includes: (1) historiography, including history of history, study and writing of history, philosophy of history, great historians; (2) general history, covering the history of the world as a whole; (3) ancient history, to about A.D.

HISTORY AND AUXILIARY SUBJECTS

476, including Far East, Near East, Greece and the Hellenistic World, Rome (both the Republic and the Empire), Christianity, Mohammedanism and the Moslem Peoples; (4) medieval times, to about 1450; (5) modern Europe; (6) British Empire; (7) Union of Soviet Socialist Republics; (8) Latin America; (9) United States; (10) two world wars.[1]

Sources for history questions. Dates, events, allusions and names represent the kinds of historical information most frequently wanted; documents and maps are the materials most often requested.

Date questions are a part of chronology and are closely related to the calendar. Identification of an event, person or place from the past can be made through a general background approach in encyclopedias or through the special handbooks of dates described in Chapter 8. Current dates involve the trends tools—the *Britannica Book of the Year,* which begins with a calendar of events, the almanacs, and the records of progress such as the *Annual Register.* The longer the period of time covered by the source the relatively more significant must a date or event be for inclusion. A recent, comparatively minor event must therefore be located in the contemporary serial—annual, periodical, or newspaper.

Events can be arranged in reference books either alphabetically or chronologically. Encyclopedias, history cyclopedias, and allusion books are alphabetically arranged, as is the index to the handbook of dates. If a chronological source will serve, the procedure is the same as for dates. Historical allusions not easily identified in historical reference sources can at times be discovered in the curiosity books and the literary allusion books described in Chapter 8. The periodical and newspaper indexes should never be overlooked, no matter how ancient the event or allusion. Names can be located in many of the general sources and in such added special tools as are included in the biography and other checklists of this chapter.

Historical maps are in great demand: European boundaries in the fifteenth century, the Near East in ancient times, the Roman Empire at its height. Historical atlases are a part of the general encyclopedias. The commercial firms mentioned in the section on maps in Chapter 6 also publish wall-size historical maps. Recent boundary changes are a special feature of *Statesman's Yearbook.*

Documents of historical significance have been brought together in handbooks like Monaghan's *Heritage of Freedom* and Commager's *Documents of American History* described in Chapter 8. Other sources

Introduction

for documents are encyclopedias, the publications of the State Department, and certain serials which feature reproduction of documents in full—*Annual Register, Current History, The New York Times,* and *United States News and World Report.*

Closely related to historical reference are the requests for pictures of flags, seals, emblems, mottoes, insignia, and medals, which may be found in the many plates in the two unabridged dictionaries—*Webster's New International* and *Funk and Wagnalls' New Standard.* Encyclopedias, as well as special handbooks issued privately and by the government, are added sources.

General reference books useful in history. The so-called reference editions of the two American unabridged dictionaries include a chronology of world history. Biographical and gazetteer features in these and many other dictionaries should not be forgotten. The *Oxford English Dictionary* because of its chronological sequence for definitions identifies historical allusions, especially in English history. Foreign language dictionaries and Mawson's *Dictionary of Foreign Terms* give meanings of words important in the history of other nations.

All the basic encyclopedias are strong in history. Of particular note are the summaries of centuries in the *Encyclopedia Americana,* entered alphabetically under the name of the century, and the comprehensive articles on each nation. In addition to national history, sections dealing with the economic, cultural, social and other aspects of a nation's life are included. The *Americana*'s article on the U.S.S.R. by Ernest J. Simmons has been published as a separate volume by Cornell University Press. Chronologies for the year can be found in the encyclopedia supplements, in the almanacs, and in certain issues of periodicals and newspapers which summarize the happenings of the past years. Each year the Associated Press publishes a list of the ten most significant events of the year as judged by newsmen.

The *Statesman's Yearbook* contains answers to many reference questions in recent world history: maps showing disputed boundaries, information on the United Nations and international relations, a bibliography on each country, and summaries of military potential, resources, education, and government. The other yearbooks all have a bit of world or United States history in them. *American Yearbook*

---

[1] For another outline of historical studies that has aroused wide interest, see Table V and p.567 of D. C. Somervell's abridgment of Arnold J. Toynbee, *A Study of History* (London, Oxford Univ. Pr., 1947).

is particularly valuable for narrative summary by subject, *Annual Register* for a scholarly review of world history, and the almanacs for journalistic summaries.

Of the curiosity fact books Kane's *First Facts* answers reference questions dealing with origins. Mulhall's *Dictionary of Statistics* and Webb's *New Dictionary of Statistics* are sources for historical statistics from ancient times to the beginning of this century; for later statistics the United States census and other national and international censuses must be used.

Biographical dictionaries, gazetteers, atlases, maps, and globes contribute to reference in history. De Ford's *Who Was When* with its tables of contemporaries from ancient times to the present is a reference tool for quick identification of historical figures. Primarily, it answers the question: Who were the contemporaries in the arts, sciences, military service, and statesmanship at any particular time in world history?

For the location of representative, distinguished works in world and United States history the eclectic bibliographies are fruitful. Among the more comprehensive lists the *United States Catalog, Cumulative Book Index* and *Publishers' Weekly* are helpful. These and other national bibliographies will provide bibliographic information about the more specialized titles. For the location of serial literature, periodical and newspaper indexes will supplement the bibliographic sources already named.

Historical agencies. The principal historical agencies useful in filling specialized reference demands are the learned societies, certain government agencies, and libraries known for their special collections. The American Historical Association is the most important national learned society. An example of a regional society is the Mississippi Valley Historical Association. All of the states and many of the counties and municipalities have local historical societies.

Some examples of government agencies that may be helpful in historical reference because of their publications, collections or services are the Library of Congress, the National Archives, the Departments of State, Defense, Treasury, Justice, and indeed many other cabinet departments and independent establishments.

The American Antiquarian Society in Worcester, Massachusetts, the John Carter Brown Library in Providence, Rhode Island, the William L. Clements Library in Ann Arbor, Michigan, the Hoover Library on War and Peace in Palo Alto, California, and the Newberry Library in Chicago house some of the strong history collections in the United States.

Bibliographies

History is rich in bibliographic sources. It is a subject with an exemplary bibliographic guide, a bibliography of bibliographies for general history, and both retrospective and current bibliographic tools for American history. There are in addition many national, period and subject bibliographies touching a great many phases of history. Allan Nevins' *The Gateway to History* (Appleton, 1938) affords a readable introduction to the literature of history, and Homer C. Hockett's *Introduction to Research in American History* (Macmillan, 1948) and the report of the Social Science Research Council's Committee on Historiography, *Theory and Practice in Historical Study* (1946), provide background study and investigation in historical research.

In co-operation with the American Library Association, the American Historical Association undertook in 1919, through a special committee appointed for that purpose, to prepare a basic bibliography in history. The result was the *Guide to Historical Literature* published in 1931 and reissued in 1937. It is a selective list containing the fundamental source materials for historical research classified largely by the divisions indicated at the beginning of this chapter. Each list is the work of a specialist. Under each of the general classes, for which letters are used (e.g., L–Great Britain), subdivisions are numbered so as to give the whole system certain mnemonic features. For example: 1-20 Bibliographies; 21-40 Reference works; 41-50 Geography and atlases; 51-60 Ethnography. Thus L 51 designates Great Britain—

❦ BIBLIOGRAPHIES

Guide to Historical Literature. N.Y., Macmillan, 1937. 1222p.

Coulter, Edith M., and Gerstenfeld, Melanie. Historical Bibliographies; a Systematic and Annotated Guide. Berkeley, Univ. of California Pr., 1935. 206p.

Beers, H. P. Bibliographies in American History. Rev. and enl. ed. N.Y., Wilson, 1942. 500p. $4.75.

Writings on American History, 1906-   (annual). N.Y., Macmillan, v.1-3; New Haven, Yale Univ. Pr., v.7-12; Washington, Govt. Print. Off., v.4-6, 13- .

Ethnography. There is an index to authors, periodicals, and academy publications.

Coulter and Gerstenfeld's *Historical Bibliographies,* prepared in collaboration by a librarian and a historian, brings "together in convenient form the important retrospective and current bibliographies of history and those general bibliographical manuals which are deemed essential as a basis in bibliographical investigation." Emphasis has been placed on fields of investigation favored in American universities. Thirteen volumes of the *International Bibliography of Historical Sciences* covering 1926-1938 and published by the Oxford University Press offer detailed, classified access to world historical research during that period. Frewer's *Bibliography of Historical Writings Published in Great Britain and the Empire,* 1940-1945 (Basil Blackwell, 1947) has been prepared as far as possible in the same manner and format.

Beers's *Bibliographies in American History* is classified and contains a subject index. *Writings on American History,* an annual bibliography of books and articles on United States history, "with some memoranda on Canada and the British West Indies," is a government publication and forms volume two of the Annual Report of the American Historical Association. Classified, indexed, annotated and comprehensive, *Writings on American History* is a full record of scholarly and popular writings in the field.

Handbook of Latin American Studies, an annual bibliography published by Harvard University Press since 1936, is an outgrowth of a conference of scholars interested in Latin American studies held on April 27, 1935. It includes, in addition to history, the fields of literature, archives, ethnology, geography, economics, archaeology, sociology, law, music, and other phases of Latin American life. The lists are classified, annotated and indexed.

Jerome K. Wilcox' *Official War Publications,* a "guide to state, federal and Canadian publications" to May, 1945, is a set of nine mimeographed lists issued by the Bureau of Public Administration, University of California. The set lists approximately 19,000 items and is indexed by subject.

Serials

Among general serials the newspapers like *The New York Times,* news services like *Facts-on-File* and *Keesing's Contemporary Archives,* and the news magazines like *Newsweek, Time* and *United States News*

Cyclopedias

and World Report are sources for current history. Nor should the *Congressional Record* be overlooked for its contribution to United States history. Two additional semipopular periodicals for history reference are *Current History* and *Foreign Affairs,* which feature documents and bibliographies as well as significant articles.

Among the scholarly historical journals four have been selected for special attention. Of these the quarterly *American Historical Review* is first in importance in American libraries. A single issue may contain nearly 200 pages of book reviews, annotations and listings in addition to important articles. Of nearly equal bibliographic significance is the *Mississippi Valley Historical Review* which features in addition to reviews and listings notices of "selected recent acquisitions" by libraries of historically important materials. Nearly every state has a historical society which issues a journal. Examples of important journals on other than United States history are the *English Historical Review* and the *Hispanic American Historical Review*.

Cyclopedias

Two historical cyclopedias, one for world events and the other for the United States, are in frequent reference use. *The New Larned History for Ready Reference,* "the actual words of the world's best historians, biographers and specialists," is arranged alphabetically under historical topics. Instead of a specially prepared article on each subject there is a quoted extract from the work of a great historian.

❦ SERIALS

Current History, 1914-   (monthly). Philadelphia, Events Pub. Co. $4.

Foreign Affairs; an American Quarterly Review, 1922-   . N.Y., Council on Foreign Relations. $5.

American Historical Review, 1895-   (quarterly). N.Y., Macmillan. $5.

Mississippi Valley Historical Review; a Journal of American History, 1914-   (quarterly). Lincoln, Nebr., Mississippi Valley Historical Assn.

English Historical Review, 1886-   (quarterly). London, Longmans, Green. 40s.

Hispanic American Historical Review, 1918-   (quarterly). Durham, N.C., Duke Univ. Pr. $4.

Each quoted extract is cited exactly so that to some extent *Larned* fulfills the functions of a bibliography as well. Among the great historians quoted are Herodotus, Froissart, Voltaire, Gibbon, Macaulay, Ranke, Parkman, Rhodes, Ferrero, Breasted, Aulard, Treitschke, Stubbs, Renan, Lavisse. If one were compiling a list of the important historians of the past one could do no better than to select those cited by Larned, who declared the object of his undertaking to be:

> to represent and exhibit the better Literature of History in the English Language and to give it an organized body—a system—adapted to the greatest convenience in any use, whether for reference or for reading, for teacher, student, or casual inquirer.

The work abounds in special features. Besides the quotations from famous historians, the system of cross references, the illustrations, the accurate citations and the chronologic arrangement of articles under topics, mention should be made of the maps, which if brought together in one volume would comprise a splendid historical atlas. There is no readier reference for historical background.

The *Dictionary of American History* offers quick answers to questions about "specific facts, events, trends, policies in our American past." The 6245 topics of popular interest are covered by short dictionary-type articles, with an occasional long article on a general subject. All contributions are signed and brief bibliographies are provided. The index is analytical. Since this is a companion volume to the *Dictionary of American Biography,* biographical articles are not included.

Handbooks and atlases

Historical handbooks identify documents, dates, events, allusions and miscellaneous facts quickly. Sources of documents have been discussed in the chapter on handbooks; for dates and events Langer's *Encyclopedia of World History* cited in the same chapter is an example of a chronology handbook arranged by period. In contrast, Keller's

---

❦ CYCLOPEDIAS
Larned, J. N. The New Larned History for Ready Reference, Reading, and Research. Springfield, Mass., Nichols, 1922-24. 12v.
Dictionary of American History; ed. by James Truslow Adams. 2d ed., rev. N.Y., Scribner, 1942. 5v. and Index. $60.

Handbooks and atlases

Dictionary of Dates presents chronology under a regional arrangement. It is "a record from earliest times through the year 1930." The first volume covers the old world and the second the new. A special feature is the treatment of large subjects like Balkan wars and international affairs in chronological order like the histories of countries. Both old and new style calendar dates are given.

Allusions have been discussed in the handbook chapter. In addition to Benét's *Reader's Encyclopedia* several special historical allusion handbooks, the oldest of which is Brewer's *Historic Notebook,* will be helpful in identifying obscure persons, places, events, and nicknames. *Harper's Dictionary of Classical Literature and Antiquities* is a source for facts about Greek and Roman life and culture. It undertakes "to give the student . . . the essential facts concerning . . . the literature, the religion, and the art of classical antiquity . . . [and] to indicate the sources whence a fuller and more critical knowledge of these subjects can be most readily and most accurately gained." The kinds of information included are biography, mythology, amusements, art, costume, domestic life, law, music, coins, and Greek and Roman tables of weights. Illustrations and bibliographies are important features.

Historical maps are available in a variety of sources—history textbooks, encyclopedias, wall maps produced by educational map makers —in addition to the special historical atlases. Shepherd's *Historical Atlas* is a collection of historical maps representing political divisions from 2100 B.C. to 1929 A.D. For every important period there are one

---

HANDBOOKS AND ATLASES

Keller, Helen R. The Dictionary of Dates. N.Y., Macmillan, 1934. 2v. $15.

Peck, H. T. Harper's Dictionary of Classical Literature and Antiquities. N.Y., American Book Co., 1923. 1701p.

Shepherd, W. R. Historical Atlas. 7th ed., rev. and enl. N.Y., Holt, 1929. 216 + 115p.

Paullin, C. O. Atlas of the Historical Geography of the United States; ed. by John K. Wright. Washington, Carnegie Institution; New York, American Geographical Soc., 1932. 162p., 688 maps on 166 plates. $15.

Adams, J. T. Atlas of American History. N.Y., Scribner, 1943. 360p. $10.

257

HISTORY AND AUXILIARY SUBJECTS

or more maps indicating historical changes. The index is primarily a list of towns with reference to the maps. Location on the maps is by means of a large letter, which refers to the space between two lines of longitude, and a small letter, which refers to the space enclosed by two lines of latitude. Thus, the index entry "Madrid 83Kg" locates the city on map 83 between 5° and 0° longitude and 40° to 45° latitude. Maps showing military campaigns, treaty results and commercial developments are special features.

American historical maps of reference value are found in Paullin's *Atlas of the Historical Geography of the United States,* covering such frequently requested subjects as: Indians, 1867-1930; colleges, universities and churches, 1775-1890; boundaries, 1607-1927; political parties and opinions, 1788-1930; industries and transportation, 1620-1931; distribution of wealth, 1799-1928; plans of American cities, 1775-1803; military history, 1689-1919. The atlas contains reproductions of old maps and maps prepared from original sources. It is especially strong on exploration, settlements, and population movement and includes other statistical data on American life.

James Truslow Adams' *Atlas of American History* is a companion volume to the *Dictionary of American History* for which it aims to serve as a location guide to all places mentioned. Maps are in black and white.

E. F. Brown's *The War in Maps* (Oxford Univ. Pr.) is an atlas of *New York Times* maps for World War II, showing the shifting battle lines on all fronts.

The *Encyclopaedia Britannica* atlas *March of Man* (1935) provides 64 plates covering history from prehistoric times to the present.

Cyclopedic sets

Certain historical sets are reference masterpieces. The Cambridge Histories—ancient, medieval, modern, British Empire—are in that class. They are of encyclopedic proportions. Various chapters have been written by different authorities. Of these four sets, that for the British Empire is still in progress.

For United States history, *Chronicles of America* and *The American Nation*[2] are strong in text; *Pageant of America* and *Album of American History,* outstanding in pictures. The first two sets are standard histories, each volume by a different author and covering a separate period or phase. Bibliographies are a feature of *The Ameri-*

Cyclopedic sets

can *Nation,* and compactness a characteristic of the *Chronicles of America.* Each of the 15 volumes of *Pageant of America* presents a pictorial chronology of the development of one phase of American life: drama, industry, transportation, religion and education, politics, the great names. Volume 15, *Sports,* is one of the basic reference tools in that area.

"To tell the history of America through pictures made at the time the history was being made" is the purpose of the *Album of American History,* a companion volume in the series which includes *Dictionary of American Biography, Dictionary of American History* and *Atlas of American History.* The arrangement is chronological: volume one covers the colonial period; volume two, 1783-1853; volume three, 1853-1883; volume four is entitled *End of an Era;* and volume five is the index. There are over 5000 pictures in the 1649 pages of the first four volumes. Reproductions are clear and the selection of illustrations pertinent and dramatic. The index, which was completed just before the death of the editor-in-chief in May, 1949, includes over 14,000 entries and gives the *Album* an advantage over the *Pageant of America* in reference use, although the latter is more comprehensive. Main entries in the *Album* index are arranged alphabetically by subject and cover such items as persons, ships, streets, buildings, organizations and book titles. Entries usually give date and identification of picture.

☞ CYCLOPEDIC SETS

Cambridge Ancient History. Cambridge, Univ. Pr., 1923-39. 12v. and 5v. plates.

Cambridge Mediaeval History. Cambridge, Univ. Pr., 1911-36. 8v.

Cambridge Modern History. Cambridge, Univ. Pr., 1902-26. 13v. and Atlas.

Cambridge History of the British Empire. Cambridge, Univ. Pr., 1929-41. v.1-8 (in progress).

Chronicles of America; ed. by Allen Johnson. New Haven, Yale Univ. Pr., 1921. 50v.

Pageant of America; ed. by Ralph Henry Gabriel. New Haven, Yale Univ. Pr., 1925-29. 15v.

Album of American History; James Truslow Adams, editor-in-chief. N.Y., Scribner, 1944-49. 4v. and Index.

---

[2] *The American Nation: A History from Original Sources by Associated Scholars;* ed. by Albert Bushnell Hart (N.Y., Harper, 1904-18) 28v.

HISTORY AND AUXILIARY SUBJECTS

Geography

Geography as a study auxiliary to history has its own bibliographic and other reference tools. A number of these have already been examined in the chapter on geographical sources. The more specialized titles are treated here.

Wright and Platt's *Aids to Geographical Research* is a bibliographic handbook providing a guide to the literature of the subject including landmarks in bibliographies, journals, society publications and maps. Jensen and Wright's *Bibliography of the Best References for the Study of Geography* is a teacher's tool intended to help prepare lessons at elementary and higher levels of learning. The arrangement and selection of materials relate to study units found in school curricula. Thiele's *Official Map Publications,* a third type of geographical bibliography, is concerned with the listing of maps or sources for maps.

The *Sixth Report* of the United States Geographic Board and its supplements are geographical dictionaries of fundamental value for the location of places and the pronunciation of place names. They include a discussion of geographic names, a history of the Board, by-laws of the Board, and a dictionary of geographic names. The last gives pronunciation, location (by latitude and longitude), definitions (that

---

GEOGRAPHY

Wright, J. K., and Platt, Elizabeth T. Aids to Geographical Research (American Geographical Society Research Series, no. 22). 2d ed. N.Y., Columbia Univ. Pr., 1947. 331p. $4.50.

Jensen and Wright. Bibliography of the Best References for the Study of Geography. The Authors, 1945. 31p.

Thiele, Walter. Official Map Publications. Chicago, A.L.A., 1938. 356p.

U.S. Board on Geographical Names. Sixth Report, 1890-1932. Washington, Govt. Print. Off., 1933. 834p. 80c.

National Geographic Magazine, 1889-   (monthly). Washington, National Geographic Soc. $5.

Geographical Review, 1916-   (quarterly). N.Y., American Geographical Soc. $5.

Journal of Geography, 1902-   (monthly September to May). Chicago, A. J. Nystrom for National Council of Geography Teachers.

is, hill, city, district, lake, etc.), and various translations of names given.

Three geography periodicals have been selected as representative of popular, educational, and research interests. The *National Geographic Magazine* with its excellent illustrations, popular treatment of near and distant lands—frequently accompanied by good maps—and its cumulative index is a periodical of high reference value for layman and scholar. For instruction the *Journal of Geography,* official organ of the National Council of Geography Teachers, features articles and teaching materials. The *Geographical Review* is the scholarly journal of the American Geographical Society, oldest geographical association in the United States.

Biography

Another important auxiliary to the study of history is biography. A review of the chapter on biographical dictionaries is important in connection with special reference service. In addition to biographical dictionaries the following classes of biographical sources must be considered: (1) books in the general collection; (2) serials; (3) audio-visual materials; (4) local and other agencies; (5) primary materials.

The most obviously useful books in the general collection are individual and collected biographies in the "92," "B," or "920" section of a Dewey-arranged library, including diaries, letters, reminiscences and autobiography. But it is also well to remember that there is much biographical information in histories, literary anthologies and collected works of individual authors, and in the histories and introductory works for the fields to which the biographee contributed. Biographical information on the great psychologist Wundt, for example, will be included in a discussion of his contribution in some of the standard introductory textbooks on psychology.

All of the news magazines, *Time* and *Newsweek* especially, present colorful sketches of people in the news. "Success" stories in the *American, Saturday Evening Post* and *Readers' Digest,* profiles in the *New Yorker,* and reviews in the *Saturday Review* are also useful. Increasingly, periodicals include with the article or near the masthead sketches and portraits of their contributors. Newspaper sketches of prominent people can be found on the dates of significant events in their lives.

Sleuthing for biographies involves a variety of approaches. Pamphlet series like those issued by publishers for their authors, book

HISTORY AND AUXILIARY SUBJECTS

jacket blurbs, pamphlets of Carnegie hero medalists, lists of contributors to reference sets, college alumni directories and monthly magazines, and other serial sources may be used. Lodge, company, professional and trade organs all print news about people. So does the society column of the local newspaper.

Calls for portraits are frequent. Many of the sources already suggested will yield results. In addition, paintings—available through the art reference tools—family albums, newspaper morgues, and the "vanity" biographical directories may yield results. Occasionally the film will produce an animated portrait, and the sound film, radio transcription or recording the voice of a great speaker or singer or actor. The local newspaper morgue is often productive. Excellent picture collections, including portraits, are maintained in some state libraries and in the photographic libraries of the armed forces, notably the Navy, Army Signal Corps, and Air Force Photographic Division.

Primary materials for biography include manuscript letters, diaries, records of transactions, and scrapbooks. Many reference departments systematically develop local collections of these materials.

Here is a summary of biographical sources other than biographical dictionaries found in reference departments:

1. Dictionaries. Both *Webster* and *Funk and Wagnalls* unabridged dictionaries include brief, identifying sketches. If the library has a set of the old *Century Dictionary* in 12 volumes, volume 11 is the *Century Cyclopedia of Names*.

2. Encyclopedias. To the large collections of biographies in *Americana, Britannica,* and the other general sets add the many biographies found in subject cyclopedias like the *Encyclopedia of the Social Sciences,* Hackh's *Chemical Dictionary,* and Grove's *Dictionary of Music and Musicians*.

3. Continuations and serials. All of the encyclopedia supplements will be useful, not only under the biographee's name but under the subject with which his name is associated. The *United States Congressional Directory* and the yearbooks summarizing developments in one area of human activity or thought—such as the *Radio Annual,* which lists announcers, "disc jockeys," singers, comedians and news commentators, often with portrait—are helpful for contemporaries.

4. Handbooks and manuals. The curiosity books and the handbooks in special subjects, notably Mary E. Hazeltine's *Anniversaries and Holidays* (A.L.A., 1944), the sports handbooks, and the literary and historical allusion books are examples of useful handbooks and manuals.

5. Bibliographies and indexes. Bibliographies and indexes serve biography reference in identifying the writings or other contributions of a person. In addition, dates of birth and death, pseudonym, maiden name, and forenames may be revealed. In this connection, the library card catalog is a most useful bibliography.

Local history

Local history is history of the community served—campus, school, neighborhood, city, county, and state. It includes every aspect of history—biographical, social, cultural, and scientific. Its boundaries are defined largely by the interests of those who comprise the locality. Representative questions are: verification of local events or places; ancestry of family; trace descendants for probation of will; Indian customs and legends of area; part played in the various wars; weather records; monuments; origin of street names; calendar of coming and past events; history of local enterprises; biographies of residents.

To develop a working collection the following classes of materials are needed: (1) community histories, published or manuscript, about the city, county, and state (an increasing number of graduate schools are encouraging theses about the social, economic, educational, and cultural aspects of a community; reference workers should be alert to such studies in progress); (2) books of local authors, publishers, and printers, and with local background; (3) newspaper and periodical files of local publications;[3] (4) club, church, school and other local agency publications, including house organs of industry; (5) clippings, programs and various memorabilia; (6) directories—city, telephone and of local groups; (7) letters, manuscripts, diaries, papers of local residents, scrapbooks; (8) government publications, county and city; (9) prints, pictures, stereographs, slides, films; (10) the library's own records, annual reports, forms; (11) college or school records and forms.

In addition to these collections of materials, local indexes and citation files will prove helpful. Representative local indexes that have proved useful are those to—(1) biographies in books, periodicals, clippings, scrapbooks, local publications; (2) pictures in vertical files, local publications, books and periodicals; (3) local topics: in a public library, files on buildings, agencies, local issues; in a college library,

---

[3] Doris Wells, "Local History Clipping File," *Library Journal*, March 1, 1938, v.63, p.189-91, offers valuable suggestions.

HISTORY AND AUXILIARY SUBJECTS

files on faculty activities, alumni, commencement programs; (4) recreational, educational, and health agencies and opportunities; (5) calendar of events, past and future; (6) speakers and speeches; (7) maps; (8) materials owned by individuals; (9) "who knows what" —where to get answers to questions; (10) courses of study.

The following 21 sources for local history are discussed in Donald Dean Parker's excellent little volume:[4] (1) local published histories—village, town, city, county, region, and state; (2) family histories and biographies; (3) military records; (4) directories—county, city, telephone, commercial, and fraternal; (5) maps; (6) atlases, gazetteers; (7) travelers' accounts; (8) anniversary addresses and sermons; (9) photographs, pictures; (10) stories and reminiscences of old residents; (11) private letters, diaries, account books; (12) keepsakes, heirlooms, relics; (13) local newspapers and periodicals; (14) census reports; (15) abstracts and title deeds; (16) surveyors' notes; (17) school records; (18) public records—village, town, city, county, and state; (19) business records; (20) church registers, denominational minutes and reports; (21) cemetery inscriptions.

When the above classes of sources are considered in relation to the model outline for a local history proposed by Mr. Parker, some notion of the scope of local history reference requests can be gained. His skeleton outline covers geography; antiquities; pioneer settlement; economic, political, and religious developments; population; the family; education; publications and libraries; social and fraternal organizations; other cultural activities; science and technology; law; social problems and reform; recreation; and folklore.

Genealogy

Genealogy is concerned with ancestry. Every reference librarian knows the avidity with which would-be members of first families trace their lineage back through the Revolution and across with the *Mayflower,* and the gleam in the eye of the patron who has just traced his line back to the ninth century is enthusiastic evidence of public recognition for library service. Genealogical societies and commercial investigators in various parts of the world are engaged in continuous research and are therefore enlarging genealogical literature. The use of genealogical reference tools requires a skill all its own.

G. H. Doane's *Searching for Your Ancestors* (Univ. of Minne-

Genealogy

sota Pr., 1948) is especially good as an introduction to genealogical reference. For American genealogy these titles are representative:

American Genealogical Index; Fremont Rider, ed.; Published by a Committee Representing the Cooperating Subscribing Libraries. Middletown, Conn., 1942-   (in progress).

Doane, Gilbert H. *Searching for Your Ancestors; the How and Why of Genealogy.* Rev. ed. Minneapolis, Univ. of Minnesota Pr., 1948. 176p. Written by a librarian for librarians. Chapter four, "Digging in Books and Libraries," is extremely valuable.

U.S. Bureau of the Census. *Heads of Families at the First Census, 1790.* Washington, Govt. Print. Off. 1907-09. 12v. Names are given of those who were counted as being in the United States in 1790.

Virkus, Frederick A. *Compendium of American Genealogy; the Standard Genealogical Encyclopedia of the First Families of America.* Chicago, Institute of American Genealogy, 1925-42. 7v.

Useful sources for foreign genealogy and heraldry include:

Almanach de Gotha, annuaire genealogique, diplomatique et statistique, 1763-   . Gotha, Perthes. This annual has long been known as the source for genealogies for the houses of Europe.

Bolton, Charles K. *Bolton's American Armory; a Record of Coats of Arms Which Have Been Used within the Present Bounds of the United States.* Boston, Faxon, 1927. 223p.

Boutell, Charles. *Boutell's Manual of Heraldry;* rev. and illus. by V. Wheeler-Holohan. London, Warne, 1931. 332p.

Cokayne, George E. *The Complete Peerage; or, A History of the House of Lords and All Its Members from the Earliest Times.* Rev. and much enl. ed. London, St. Catherine Pr., 1910-   (in progress).

Who's Who includes the reigning royal family in a special introductory section. Genealogies of the English kings, and biographies of other sovereigns, may be found in Langer's *Encyclopedia of History.*

Reading list

Hutchins, Margaret. *Introduction to Reference Work.* Chicago, A.L.A., 1944. p.56-68.

---

[4] *Local History; How To Gather It, Write It and Publish It;* rev. and ed. by Bertha E. Josephson for the Committee on Guide for Study of Local History of the Social Science Research Council (The Council, 1944).

chapter 17

SOCIAL SCIENCES

Introduction, Sociology, anthropology, social work, Political science, government, law, Economics and business, Psychology and education.

Introduction

The subject area. Social sciences may be defined as those sciences concerned with the study of man's relationships with man, in individuals and in groups. For a fuller definition of the social sciences, their history, relations and status, a reading of the first 349 pages of volume one of the *Encyclopedia of the Social Sciences* is recommended. The classification of articles in the *Encyclopedia* (v.15, p.547-57) gives the best quick concept of the scope of the sprawling social sciences, from "Administration of Justice" to "War." In historical order, the essential social sciences are listed as politics, economics, history, jurisprudence, anthropology, penology, sociology, social work, ethics, education, and psychology. In this chapter the social sciences, excluding history, are grouped in four clusters: (1) sociology, anthropology, and the applied field of social work; (2) political science and the applied fields of government and law; (3) economics and the applied field of business; and (4) psychology and the applied field of education.

Social science questions. The heavy emphasis in types of questions in the social sciences is on trends, statistics, laws, bibliography

Introduction

and biography. Trends questions may relate to banking, business, commerce, consumption, co-operation, credit, crime, government, housing, industry, insurance, international relations, labor, marriage and the family, occupations, public opinion, health, welfare, social discrimination, taxation, transportation, and war. Statistics questions involve averages, births, census, child mortality, consumption, crime, crop and livestock reporting, demography, family budgets, forecasting in business, national income, prices, and production. Questions of other types also range through the subject area of the social sciences.

General reference sources and the social sciences. Because the subject range of the social sciences is so wide almost the entire reference collection can contribute to questions within this area. The two unabridged American dictionaries have enlisted authoritative editorial aid in their continuous revision programs to insure up-to-date definitions of legal and business terms, as well as of words used in sociology, anthropology, social work, political science, government, education and psychology, economics and business. The continuous revision programs for encyclopedias also stress social science material. Compact factual data are featured in the *Lincoln Library,* originally conceived by and for school people. Pictographs, charts and diagrams for the social sciences in *Compton's* and *World Book* are notable. All of the encyclopedia supplements, almanacs and subject yearbooks belong in the repertoire of the social science reference worker. The indexes to periodicals, pamphlets and newspapers are the key to reference help from serials.

Among handbooks the *Statistical Abstract of the United States* and Bureau of the Census publications are of first importance. Also important on social issues are the volumes of the *Reference Shelf* with their selected bibliographies. Taintor and Monro's *Secretary's Handbook* is useful for business correspondence and forms, and *Henley's Twentieth Century Book of Formulas* for industrial processes.

Besides the general biographical dictionaries, certain special directories of persons have potentialities for social science reference: the government personnel registers—civil service, armed forces, state department, *Congressional Directory;* and telephone and city directories. *Ayer's Directory of Newspapers and Periodicals* is an excellent index to American towns and cities, their principal industries, transportation, and publications. The eclectic bibliographies are sources for reading guidance in the social sciences.

Among the learned societies in the field of the social sciences two should be noted here because their scope is as broad as the whole area. The Social Science Research Council, organized in 1923 for the purpose of furthering closer co-operation between students of politics and of other social sciences, is composed of three representatives from each of seven learned societies in the fields of political science, economics, sociology, history, anthropology, psychology, and statistics. Its major interest is in research. Among recent studies sponsored by the Council is the Public Library Inquiry. The other learned society, the National Council for the Social Studies, is concerned primarily with the teaching and study of the many subjects in this area that have now been included in our school and college curricula. It is the publisher of a yearbook, each issue of which is centered on one significant theme. The annual for 1948, "Geographic Approaches to Social Education," is full of useful information on the effective use of audiovisual materials in the teaching of the social studies.

Bibliographies, indexes, encyclopedias. The nearest approach to a comprehensive bibliography in English for all the social sciences is the *London Bibliography of the Social Sciences,* issued by the London School of Economics. The foundation set of four volumes including publications to May 31, 1929, contains approximately 600,000 entries arranged alphabetically by subject with an author index. The compilation is based on the holdings of nine London libraries and indicates the location of materials in these libraries. Of the four volumes in the foundation set, three are arranged by subject, and under subject alphabetically by author, personal authors preceding corporate authors. Volume four includes author index, periodicals list, and table of subject headings. The first supplement carries the listings through May 31, 1931; the second, larger supplement continues through May 31, 1936; the third supplement extends from June 1, 1936, to June 1, 1950. Items containing bibliographies are

---

❦ BIBLIOGRAPHIES, INDEXES, ENCYCLOPEDIAS

London Bibliography of the Social Sciences, 1931-50. London, London School of Economics, 1931-52. 9v.

Public Affairs Information Service. Bulletin, 1915-   (weekly). N.Y., Public Affairs Information Service.

Tompkins, Dorothy C. Methodology of Social Science Research; a Bibliography. Berkeley, Univ. of California Pr., 1936. 159p. $2.

Encyclopedia of the Social Sciences; ed.-in-chief, E. R. A. Seligman. N.Y., Macmillan, 1930-35. 15v.

Introduction

marked with a "Z"; items starred are those not available in the London School of Economics.

An unincorporated co-operative association of libraries, organized by a group of special librarians at the Kaaterskill conference of the Special Libraries Association in 1913, launched *Public Affairs Information Service,* a weekly indexing service of useful library materials in the field of economics and public affairs. The weekly *PAIS Bulletin,* as it is usually cited, indexes over 1000 periodicals plus books, government documents, pamphlets, and processed material. Publications from all English-speaking countries, and in English from many other countries, are included. Originally designed for the use of legislative and municipal reference librarians, *Public Affairs Information Service* now finds its way into some 600 libraries.

The index is arranged alphabetically by subject. Cumulated bulletins superseding the weekly issue are published five times a year, and the fifth cumulation is the annual bound volume which supersedes the previous issues for that year. A special feature is the directory of publishers and organizations, which is often useful in locating obscure agencies. The final section indexes selected typewritten material. *Public Affairs Information Service* is a basic current social science bibliography, indispensable to research worker and student.

Tompkins' *Methodology of Social Science Research* is a classified and selected bibliography of the fundamental tools arranged in the order of research steps under such headings as "Selection and Definition of Problem" and "Collection of Data." Author and subject indexes are provided.

The *Encyclopedia of the Social Sciences,* although rapidly going out of date on changing subjects, is still the great reference tool in its field. Its threefold purpose is (1) to provide for the scholar a synopsis of the progress that has been made in the various fields of social science in the broadest sense of the term; (2) to furnish an assemblage or repository of facts and principles which will subserve the interests of all those who are keeping abreast of recent investigation and accomplishment; and (3) to constitute a center of authoritative knowledge for the creation of a sounder and more informed public opinion on the major questions which lie at the foundation of social progress and world development.

Except for the first and last volumes the materials are arranged alphabetically by topic, with a generous number of cross references. The first volume contains besides the first part of the "A" topics a

349-page introduction including E. R. A. Seligman's essay, "What Are the Social Sciences?" Part one of this essay has 11 articles on Development of Social Thought and Institutions; part two describes the status of the social sciences in the various countries. The last volume, in addition to the end of the alphabetical topics, has three indexes: classified or schematic subject, dictionary subject, and contributors.

There can be no question of the authority of this work. Outstanding scholars from all parts of the world have signed their names to individual articles. Since the work is American, scholars in this country were chosen as contributors when their reputation was equal to that of anyone abroad. When the foreign scholar was more outstanding, however, he was asked to write the article in his native tongue to be subsequently translated for the *Encyclopedia*. Although 50 per cent of all articles are biographical, these take up only 20 per cent of the total space. The wide range of subjects, the excellence of the materials, and the appended bibliographies, sometimes classified by country, make the *Encyclopedia of the Social Sciences* the basic reference tool for all of the subjects designated as pure social sciences and semisocial sciences, and for some of the others as well.

Sociology, anthropology, social work

The subject fields. The social sciences of sociology and anthropology embrace such major divisions as anthropometry, criminology, population, and race and are here combined with the applied science of social work. Sociology is the study of society. Anthropology is a comparative study of man's physical characteristics and behavior from the earliest times. Social work is an application of sociological principles to relieve or prevent poverty, disease, crime and other conditions that prevent the good life.

Representative questions in these fields deal with such subjects as socialized medicine, juvenile delinquency, prison reform, birth control, miscegenation, minority groups, and old-age pensions. These inquiries are selected from some actually made in libraries: What is an Aryan? Some good books on preparation for marriage are wanted. Newspaperman wants statistics on wages, living costs, rents, food, "broken down as far as possible for smaller cities and towns in this region." What is the Ethical Culture Movement? "My Ideal Girl"—for a young people's meeting. What was the purchasing power of the dollar from the end of World War I to the end of World War II?

Sociology, anthropology, social work

Reference sources. The *General Index to Annual Reports* of the Bureau of American Ethnology is a significant tool for anthropology because of the outstanding contributions to the study of American Indians and other aborigines found in the reports themselves. Author, title and subject entries are included in the index. A special bibliographic tool is Work's *Bibliography of the Negro,* a classified list of references in periodicals as well as books.

The *Social Work Yearbook* is "a description of organized activities in social work and in related fields" issued by the Russell Sage Foundation. The book, created in 1929 and issued biennially since 1933, is divided into two alphabetical parts: (1) about 75 signed articles, alphabetically arranged, on such subjects as alcoholism, adoption, camping, disaster relief, housing, recreation; (2) directory of national agencies, governmental and voluntary. In the latter part, for example, the Russell Sage Foundation, established in 1907, is described as having for its purpose: "To promote the improvement of social and living conditions in the United States." The index covers both parts.

Two other "yearbooks," neither one of which appears regularly, is *The Negro Handbook* of approximately biennial frequency and the *Negro Yearbook,* which has been published at Tuskegee Institute since 1914 at irregular intervals. The *Handbook* brings together scattered data on the Negro's progress, including information on achievements, awards, welfare, education, religion, housing, business, government, vital statistics, sports, books, civil rights, riots and other subjects.

The *Dictionary of Sociology,* compiled by a staff of 93 contributors, three advisory editors and one associate editor under the direction of Dr. H. P. Fairchild, gave sociology a needed glossary. Terms in anthropology, economics, psychology, political science, statistics and history have been included when they had "genuine sociological significance." A briefer dictionary is Panunzio's *Student's Dictionary of Sociological Terms.*[1] Young's *Dictionary of Social Welfare* aims "to supply the busy social worker with a usable clue to the meaning of those technical terms which he is most apt to encounter in daily practice." Terms have been chosen from the following fields: social work, social case work, social science, law, psychology, psychiatry, psychoanalysis, medicine, biology, chemistry, statistics, folklore, and folk language.

---

[1] Constantine Panunzio, *Student's Dictionary of Sociological Terms* (Berkeley, Univ. of California Pr., 1937), 49p., $1.

SOCIAL SCIENCES

Kurtz and Edgerton's *Statistical Dictionary of Terms and Symbols*[2] was prepared by an advisory council of thirty members. Council representation indicates the statistical areas represented: biology and zoology, business, economics and sociology, education, mathematics, and psychology.

Handbooks which contribute to reference work in this area are the *Statistical Abstract of the United States, Historical Statistics of the United States, 1789-1945,* and *U.S.A.: Measure of a Nation.*

Among serial publications the *Survey Graphic* and *Midmonthly* contain general articles on most of the social sciences, but especially on sociology. The principal journals in sociology are the American Sociological Society's *American Sociological Review,* bimonthly since 1936, *The American Journal of Sociology,* bimonthly since 1895, and *Social Forces,* quarterly since 1922. Anthropology has several important journals, notably the two quarterlies, *American Anthropologist,* issued by the American Anthropological Association, and *Journal of American Folklore,* by the American Folklore Society, both published since 1888. Among the social work serials, *Social Service Review,* quarterly since 1927, and *Social Work,* quarterly since 1943, are important. The National Conference of Social Work, which held its 75th anniversary meeting in Atlantic City in 1948, publishes a collection of papers, summary of business and an index to publications in its annual *Proceedings.* Each volume provides a summary of developments which amplifies the general yearbook summaries.

☞ REFERENCE SOURCES

U.S. Bureau of American Ethnology. General Index to Annual Reports, 1876-1931. Washington, Govt. Print. Off., 1933. (In its 48th Annual Report, 1930/31.)

Work, M. N. Bibliography of the Negro in Africa and America. N.Y., Wilson, 1928. 698p. $12.

Social Work Yearbook, 1929- (biennial). N.Y., Russell Sage Foundation.

The Negro Handbook, 1942- . N.Y., Current Books.

Dictionary of Sociology; ed. by H. P. Fairchild. N.Y., Philosophical Library, 1944. 342p. $6.

Young, E. F., ed. Dictionary of Social Welfare. N.Y., Social Sciences Pub., 1948. 218p.

Political science, government, law

The subject fields. The late E. R. A. Seligman called politics the oldest of the social sciences. Pure political science is concerned with such problems as the origin and theory of the state, sovereignty, bicameral legislation, political parties, and civil service. From the field of government come these subjects on which reference questions are asked: local, state, federal and world governments; constitutionalism; empire; legislation; police power; anarchism; autocracy; socialism; fascism; plebiscite; referendum; initiative; recall.

Questions in law have a strong bibliographic flavor. Location of laws, decisions, and cases dominate legal reference, but there are also questions relating to definition of legal terms, to legal procedures, to information about persons for probating wills, and to places and agencies. Some representative topics in law from which questions are derived are: text of organic law; meaning and significance of the social contract; habeas corpus; military courts-martial; articles of war; citizenship requirements and procedures for application; federal district courts, their location and jurisdiction; state laws on grounds for divorce; North Atlantic Treaty Organization; Magna Carta; Bill of Rights.

Bibliographies and indexes. Burchfield's *Student's Guide to Materials in Political Science* is designed to introduce the student to the more important source materials, finding devices, bibliographic and general reference works. The book is one of the projects of the Sub-Committee on Research of the Committee on Policy of the American Political Science Association. Sections on political science research, national, state, and municipal government in the United States, law

---

☞ BIBLIOGRAPHIES AND INDEXES

Burchfield, La Verne. Student's Guide to Materials in Political Science. N.Y., Holt, 1935. 426p. $3.

Tompkins, Dorothy C. Materials for the Study of Federal Government. Chicago, Public Administration Service, 1948. 338p.

Hicks, F. C. Materials and Methods of Legal Research. Rochester, N.Y., Lawyers Cooperative Publishing Co., 1942. 659p. $6.

Index to Legal Periodicals, 1908-   (monthly). N.Y., Wilson.

---

[2] Albert Kurtz and H. Edgerton, *Statistical Dictionary of Terms and Symbols* (N.Y., Wiley, 1939), 191p., $2.

and jurisprudence, political theory and international relations indicate the scope of the bibliography. There are also sections on general and special reference works.

Tompkins' *Materials for the Study of Federal Government* is a descriptive guide to materials useful for the study of organization and function of the various branches of the United States government and their publications. World War II and the New Deal are treated in separate sections. Examples of bibliographies on phases of political science are *Foreign Affairs Bibliography* (Council on Foreign Relations, 1933-45), an annotated list in two volumes, one by Langer and Armstrong, for the years 1919-31, and the other by Woolbert for 1932-42; and *Propaganda, Communication and Public Opinion,* by Bruce Smith, Harold Lasswell and Ralph Casey (Princeton Univ. Pr., 1946), a classified, annotated list of objective studies and analyses in books and periodicals.

Hicks's *Materials and Methods of Legal Research* is the basic bibliographical manual for law. It contains, in addition to instructions on the methods and art of legal research, bibliographies and an abridged law dictionary. The compiler is a lawyer and a librarian. Other bibliographic handbooks of law and legal literature are Notz's *Legal Bibliography and Legal Research* (National Law Book Co., 1947) and Eldean's *How To Find the Law* (West, 1949). The latter features reproduction of parts of legal reference tools as well as directions for their use.

Index to Legal Periodicals is an author and subject index compiled by the American Association of Law Libraries to more than one hundred legal magazines and bar association reports. It is issued monthly and cumulated annually and triennially.

Serial publications of reference value include the *American Political Science Review,* published bimonthly since 1906 by the American Political Science Association, and the *Political Science Quarterly,* issued since 1886 by the Academy of Political Science. *The American City,* issued monthly, contains popular articles on municipal government. Of especial reference value to all the social sciences is the bimonthly *Annals of the American Academy of Political and Social Science,* each issue of which is devoted to a major social or political problem.

Reference books. A number of special reference tools are available in political science, government and law. Smith and Zurcher's *New Dictionary of American Politics* identifies a variety of terms,

Political science, government, law

phrases, slogans and nicknames in popular, brief articles. Legal terms will be found in a standard law dictionary such as Bouvier, Ballentine or Black.[3] Theimer's *Encyclopedia of Modern World Politics* will help in the identification of such current terms as communism, fascism, and economic aid in brief articles about political movements and thought.

Handbooks to world and national governments have already been described in such works as the *Statesman's Yearbook* and the *United States Government Manual*.

The biennial *Book of the States* is a combined handbook and directory for the 48 states. It includes a list of the chief officials, description of the legislative reference service and reference to the state handbook. Each of the states has its own handbook—called variously "Manuals," "Red Books," or "Blue Books"—summarizing the activities of that state. The handbook for the home state is basic in every library.

The *Municipal Year Book* is "an authoritative résumé of activities and statistical data" issued annually by the International City Managers Association. "To provide municipal officials with discussions of the current problems of cities throughout the country, with facts and statistics on individual city activities, and with analyses of trends by population groups" is the chief purpose of the *Year Book*. Information is given for all urban places of over 5000 population. Besides a host of statistical data, the suggestions on how to interpret statistics and the bibliographies on municipal government are worth noting. Thumb guides and a full index aid reference use.

☞ REFERENCE BOOKS

Smith, E. C., and Zurcher, A. J. New Dictionary of American Politics. N.Y., Barnes & Noble, 1949. 437p. $3.25.

Theimer, Walter. Encyclopedia of Modern World Politics. N.Y., Rinehart, 1950. 696p.

Book of the States, 1935-   (biennial). Chicago, Council of State Governments.

Municipal Year Book, 1934-   . Chicago, International City Managers Assn.

---

[3] John Bouvier, *Bouvier's Law Dictionary and Concise Encyclopedia* (3d revision; Kansas City, Mo., Vernon, 1914), 3v. James Ballentine, *Law Dictionary with Pronunciations* (1948 ed.; Rochester, N.Y., Lawyers Cooperative Pub. Co., 1948), 1494p. H. C. Black, *Black's Law Dictionary* (3d ed.; St. Paul, West, 1933), 1944p.

SOCIAL SCIENCES

Economics and business

The subject fields. In the field of pure economics, the major divisions are consumption, production, distribution and exchange. Some of the aspects of these divisions are business cycles, capitalism, competition, cost, exploitation, income, individualism, theory of international trade, money, monopoly, national wealth, overproduction, price theory and statistics, profit, public finance, rent, supply and demand, taxation, unearned increment, labor, wages, and labor unions.

Business, the application of economic principles, is the subject of reference questions on accounting, advertising, business education, cartels, corporation finance and taxes, employers' associations, Federal Trade Commission, foreign exchange, government regulation, holding companies, insurance, management, investments, products, retailing and wholesaling, real estate, salesmanship, and utilities.

Typical questions in economics and business are on meanings of business terms and symbols; trends in stocks, prices, wages, taxes; statistics on sales, production, profits, income, costs; how to correspond, keep books, sell, advertise; background of business cycles, unions, corporations; and names of products, manufacturers, and distributors.

Bibliographies and indexes. *Sources of Business Information,* by Edwin T. Coman, librarian of the Stanford School of Business, is one of the fine subject bibliographic guides. This 415-page volume has a twofold purpose: to provide a key to sources for specific facts and to present a broad picture of the literature of business. Sources are grouped under subjects like management, advertising, real estate, and under a general heading, "Basic." A good index locates titles easily.

Although the Wilson *Industrial Arts Index* also indexes science

---

❦ BIBLIOGRAPHIES AND INDEXES

Coman, E. T. Sources of Business Information. N.Y., Prentice-Hall, 1949. 415p. $6.

Industrial Arts Index, 1913-   . N.Y., Wilson.

American Institute of Accountants. Accountants' Index; a Bibliography of Accounting Literature. N.Y., The Institute, 1912-48. v.1-7 (in progress). $10 per vol.

periodicals, its analysis of more than 200 periodicals in industry, finance, public administration, advertising, insurance, aviation, engineering, economics, printing and other related fields earns for it recognition here as a basic bibliography. It is issued monthly, cumulated annually in December, and equipped with the handy arrangement features that characterize the other Wilson indexes.

Business Literature, issued monthly—except July and August—at the Newark Public Library, is a good current bibliography. It lists books, magazine articles, government publications, and pamphlets. The 1934-44 ten-year volume with cumulative index is an important bibliographic tool.

From Dartmouth College's Amos Tuck School of Business Administration comes *A Reading List on Business Administration* (5th ed., 1947), which attempts to present the landmarks in business literature by subject divisions. Annotations are brief, and magazines as well as books are included.

The *Accountants' Index* is a bibliography of the literature found in books, periodicals, and pamphlets, arranged by author and subject. The basic volume covers the period 1912-1920, and supplements cover periods of three or four years each.

Services. Business reference service leans heavily on two types of sources—the so-called business services, like Poor's and Moody's, and directories. Business services are serial in form, but because of their special format and devices are here described separately from business periodicals and continuations. Most frequently these services are loose-leaf and follow the insert plan described under encyclopedia supplements; that is, new pages are sent to replace old ones to keep rapidly changing information constantly up to date. Sometimes there is also a basic volume containing less frequently changing facts.

Need for loose-leaf services in business has been more keenly felt in recent years because of the trend toward government regulation. Imperative in the businessman's operation of his enterprise is up-to-the-minute knowledge of changes in laws and regulations. But there are other reasons, too, for this kind of flexible reference format: stock

---

❦ SERVICES

Moody's Manual of Investments, American and Foreign, 1909- .
   N.Y., Analyses Pub. Co., 1909-14; Moody's Investors Service, 1915- .

SOCIAL SCIENCES

market changes, price fluctuations, reorganizations of business firms.

For a compact description of loose-leaf reference services, readers are referred especially to Coman's *Sources of Business Information,* p.23-30. Some representative services in different business areas are:

Advertising. *Standard Rate and Data Service,* 536 Lake Shore Drive, Chicago. Issued monthly in four sections: newspapers, business papers, magazines, radio. Information includes rates for various types of advertising, individuals concerned with advertising, and other data.

Investments and financial information. Of the many services available these are probably best known: (1) *Babson's Statistical Service,* Wellesley, Massachusetts. The *Confidential Barometer Letter* is a weekly forecast concerned with general business conditions, commodities, inventory, and stock market trends. (2) *Moody's Investors Service,* 65 Broadway, New York, has been selected as typical. It includes a *Stock Survey* and a *Bond Survey,* both weekly, a *Dividend Record,* semiweekly, a *Bond Record,* semimonthly, and a *Manual,* annually. The last is kept current by semiweekly bulletins. Subdivisions of the security field include government stocks and bonds; banks, insurance, real estate, investment trusts; industrial stocks and bonds; public utilities, railroads. Each company is described in detail and a complete record of dividends reported. (3) *Standard and Poor's Corporation,* 345 Hudson Street, New York. Services offered by Standard and Poor are the *Weekly Outlook for the Securities Market, Monthly Earnings and Ratings Stock Guide,* a daily *Facts and Forecasts,* and *Records,* six loose-leaf volumes, revised monthly, that provide factual information on about 6000 major and 5000 smaller firms. This, like Moody's, is a comprehensive service.

Laws, regulations, taxes. Commerce Clearing House, 214 North Michigan Avenue, Chicago, issues a number of loose-leaf services. Some of the more important are the *State Tax Guide, All State Tax Reports, Federal Tax Guide Reports, Federal Securities Law Reports, Labor Law Guide,* and *Labor Law Reports.*

Ratings. *Dun and Bradstreet Reference Book* supplies credit information on firms and individuals, and a description of each business listed. Although it is not available to libraries it is of considerable reference value.

Directories. A large number of questions in economics and business involve locating firms and products, and names and addresses of

Economics and business

people. Hence the extraordinary stress on directories and the necessity of guides to their use. Some useful keys to directories are:

>Davis, Marjorie V. *Guide to American Business Directories.* Washington, Public Affairs Pr., 1948. 242p. $3.75. Substantially this is a reissue of the United States Department of Commerce *American Business Directories.* The 1468 directories listed are arranged under 127 business headings.
>
>Manley, Marian C. *Business Directories: a Key to Their Use.* Newark, N.J., Newark Free Public Library, 1934. 63p. $2.20. Although this was compiled earlier than Davis, it contains more detailed information. It is the work of the head of the Newark Public Library's famous Business Library.
>
>Special Libraries Association. Business Group. *Directories for the Business Man;* comp. by Laura A. Eales. N.Y., Special Libraries Assn., 1938. 66p. $1. Lists 975 directories classified by subjects.

Who's Who in Labor includes some 5000 biographies. Special features are lists of international unions, publications, educational and research directory, glossary of labor terms, chronology of labor legislation and the constitutions of the A.F.L. and C.I.O. *Who's Who in Commerce and Industry* has a wide coverage, including less prominent businessmen; and the directory of corporations is helpful in locating top-level officers of a company.

For identifying manufacturers and their products, the basic reference book is *Thomas' Register of American Manufacturers.* It lists more than 70,000 products under the name of the manufacturer, the product, and the trade name. Some of the facts supplied by this annual are addresses, names of company officers, capital invested, and commercial associations. The British counterpart, *Kelly's Directory,* is an

---

DIRECTORIES

Who's Who in Labor; the Authorized Biographies of the Men and Women Who Lead Labor in the United States and Canada and of Those Who Deal with Labor. N.Y., Dryden Pr., 1946. 480p. $12.

Who's Who in Commerce and Industry. 6th international ed. Chicago, Marquis, 1948. 1552p.

Thomas' Register of American Manufacturers, 1905- (annual). N.Y., Thomas. $15.

Kelly's Directory of Merchants, Manufacturers and Shippers, 1880- (annual). London, Kelly's Directories, Ltd. $22.50.

SOCIAL SCIENCES

annual guide to export, import and shipping industries as well as to manufacturers.

Aside from these business directories the telephone and city directory are of importance. Some business libraries maintain files of out-of-town directories which will be helpful in identifying both individuals and firms. For individuals only, the general biographical dictionaries like *Who's Who in America* and *Who Knows—and What* will include a generous representation of business and labor leaders. However, the special biographical directories will have more names in the fields of economics and business.

Yearbooks, dictionaries, cyclopedias, handbooks. The literature of business is voluminous and many books in the field can be used as reference sources. Of the eight titles listed here, five are yearbooks and three are dictionaries and cyclopedias. In addition some handbooks are cited. Such lists as *A Reading List on Business Administration*, already described, will be useful for additional suggestions.

The Economic Almanac, issued by the National Industrial Conference Board, is "a handbook of useful facts about business, labor and government in the United States and other areas." The Board, founded in 1916, is an "institution for scientific research, practical service and public information in connection with economic and management

---

YEARBOOKS, DICTIONARIES, CYCLOPEDIAS, HANDBOOKS

The Economic Almanac, 1940-   (annual). N.Y., National Industrial Conference Board. $5.

The Commodity Yearbook, 1939-   . N.Y., Commodity Research Bureau.

U.S. Office of International Trade. Foreign Commerce Yearbook, 1922-   . Washington, Govt. Print. Off.

Exporters' Encyclopaedia, 1904-   (annual). N.Y., Exporters' Encyclopaedia Corp.

Labor Research Association. Labor Fact Book, 1931-   (biennial). N.Y., International Pubs.

Crobaugh, C. J. Handbook of Insurance. N.Y., Prentice-Hall, 1949. v.1-   (in progress). v.1, $7.50.

Horton, B. J., and others. Dictionary of Modern Economics. Washington, Public Affairs Pr., 1948. 365p. $5.

Munn, G. G. Encyclopedia of Banking and Finance. 5th ed. Cambridge, Mass., Bankers Pub. Co., 1949. 727p. $12.

problems." The Board's work is supported by subscriptions for its publications and services from labor, management, governmental, educational and other agencies. The *Almanac* is "designed to meet the need for a compact, convenient handbook of the latest, most significant and trustworthy statistical and other data useful to business executives, labor leaders, educators . . . and others concerned with current economic problems." Some 24 sections supply significant facts and figures on population, debt, finance, banking, prices, manufacturing, mining, transportation, trade, construction, utilities, communication, agriculture, industries, resources, income, savings, etc. A selective glossary and a list of alphabetical designations of government agencies are special features. The index, arranged by commodity, contributes to quick reference.

The Commodity Yearbook describes "virtually all the important raw and semi-finished products that serve to make up our national economy" arranged alphabetically by commodity.

The *Foreign Commerce Yearbook* appeared as part two of the *Commerce Yearbook* issued by the Bureau of Foreign and Domestic Commerce from 1922 to 1932, was suspended during World War II, resumed publication in 1948. It includes important statistical data on agriculture, mining, manufacture, trade and transportation.

Comparable in many ways is the *Exporters' Encyclopaedia* with its information on shipping, mail and passport regulations, consulates, ports, and sailings from American cities, as well as language, area, currency, weights and measures, legal holidays, and many other facts about the countries which exporters are interested in.

More restricted is the *Labor Fact Book* which provides information on such subjects as trade unions, political movements, legislation, social conditions, and labor abroad. Statistics are included in many of the summary articles.

An example of a handbook concerned with one aspect of business is Crobaugh's *Handbook of Insurance.* Volume one includes life, accident and health insurance terms which are explained clearly and fully enough to be understood by prospective policy holders. Other handbooks are *Handbook of Business Administration,*[4] an overview of the whole field, including marketing, finance, personnel, office management, etc., with each subject treated by a specialist, and Brown

---

[4] American Management Association, *Handbook of Business Administration;* W. J. Donald, ed.-in-chief (N.Y., McGraw-Hill, 1931), 1753p., $10.

and Doris' *Business Executive's Handbook*,[5] concerned with the daily problems of running a business and emphasizing correspondence and sales promotion.

The *Dictionary of Modern Economics* by Byrne J. Horton and others defines terms in economics like *distribution, marginal return,* and *deficit financing.* Other terms are defined in Munn's *Encyclopedia of Banking and Finance* which emphasizes the vocabulary relating to money, credit, securities, investment, banking history, and trusts. Another work in the field is *Crowell's Dictionary of Business and Finance* (1930), and libraries with copies of the *New Century Dictionary* should not overlook the separate list of business terms found there.

Serials. The serials most frequently consulted are the two dailies, *Wall Street Journal* issued by Dow-Jones and Company, with its reports on current business conditions, market quotations, and dividend news, and the *Journal of Commerce,* issued by B. J. Ridder, which emphasizes commodities, commerce, and manufacturing news; the *Kiplinger Washington Letter,* a weekly roundup of trends and opinions in business and government; the monthly *United States Federal Reserve Bulletin* with its statistics on finance, production, employment, sales, cost of living; and *American Economic Review,* issued five times a year by the American Economic Association and presenting the theoretical aspects of economics and business. Other important serials are the semiweekly *Commercial and Financial Chronicle* and weekly *Business Week* with news and current summaries; the two government publications, the *Survey of Current Business* prepared by the United States Bureau of Foreign and Domestic Commerce and the *Monthly Labor Review* by the United States Bureau of Labor Statistics; the National Chamber of Commerce's monthly *Nation's Business,* and *Fortune* with its forecasts and startling surveys.

Psychology and education

The subject fields. Some of the important research areas in psychology are abnormal, adolescent, animal, child, experimental, physiological, and educational psychology. Certain movements and fields of investigation like behaviorism, Gestalt psychology, psychoanalysis, and extra-sensory perception stimulate reference questions. Aspects of psychology like character, guidance, consciousness, **genius,**

Psychology and education

mental hygiene, mental tests, play, psychiatry, and emotion are likely to create many inquiries.

Psychology and the other social sciences are applied in education. Some of the principal divisions of education are: administration, including finance, personnel, quarters and equipment; curriculum, including subject content for every age; teaching methods; education on the elementary, secondary, higher and adult levels; instructional materials; the student and the psychology of learning. In these fields of psychology and education, questions are asked about: meanings of terms and phrases, like *instinct, frame of reference;* addresses of institutions, agencies, publishers; biographies of educators; statistics on enrollment; finance, materials, equipment, personnel; activities; instructions on teaching methods, coaching, guidance; bibliographies of investigation, theses, texts, courses of study; problems of academic freedom; intercollegiate athletics; history of Chautauqua; information about correspondence courses; sex education; colleges and universities; sororities and fraternities; and summer camps.

Bibliographies and indexes. There are more than 4000 bibliographic references in Monroe and Shores' *Bibliographies and Summaries in Education* extending over the period from the beginning of modern educational research in 1910 through June, 1935. The arrangement is alphabetic by subject and author.

For the period subsequent to 1935 as well as for the years back to 1929 the *Education Index* will be useful not only for bibliographies but also for locating educational literature generally. *Education Index* appears monthly with frequent cumulations. It is a key to more than 120 leading educational periodicals in the United States, Canada, and foreign countries. Each issue is in six parts: (1) notes on new publications and educational meetings; (2) list of periodicals and books indexed; (3) key to abbreviations; (4) directory of publishers; (5) checklist of professional books, relevant association reports, and government documents; and (6) main author and subject index. A forerunner, the *Loyola Educational Index,* was issued for one year, 1928, and was then replaced by the *Education Index.*

Carter Alexander's *How To Locate Educational Information and Data* is the outgrowth of his work in library use with graduate students at Teachers College, Columbia University. It is an excellent survey

---

[5] Stanley M. Brown, *Business Executive's Handbook;* rev. by Lillian Doris (3d ed.; N.Y., Prentice-Hall, 1947), 1600p., $7.50.

of the important educational bibliographic and reference tools and of method in investigating educational problems. Chapters on the publications of the National Education Association, the United States Office of Education and other educational agencies are important to reference work with teachers and research workers.

For psychology, *Psychological Abstracts* is the current and continuing bibliographic source. Each issue abstracts some 350 to 400 books and periodicals under broad subjects and has an author index. There is a cumulated index in the December issue. Although the coverage is not as full as that provided by the *Psychological Index,* 1894-1935, which the *Abstracts* superseded, the latter has the advantages of more thorough analysis, more frequent issue, and cumulated indexing.[6]

Louttit's *Handbook of Psychological Literature,* although in need of revision, is still helpful as an introduction to the literature of psychology. Among its useful features are the notes on journals, government and society publications, indexes, and other reference books relating to psychology, and on library classifications of the subject.

Buros' *Mental Measurements Yearbooks*[7] lists and annotates tests and reviews and provides indexes and directories of periodicals, publishers, titles, names, and subjects. It is the basic guide to tests and testing. Although the 1949 volume covering the period 1940-47 is called the third, it is actually the sixth in the series.

Serials and continuations. Of the large number of education periodicals three are specified for reference attention: *School Life* is issued monthly, except for July-September, by the United States Office of Education. Among features of note are the lists of selected

---

BIBLIOGRAPHIES AND INDEXES

Monroe, W. S., and Shores, Louis. Bibliographies and Summaries in Education to July, 1935. N.Y., Wilson, 1936. 470p.

Education Index, 1929- (monthly). N.Y., Wilson.

Alexander, Carter, and Burke, Arvid. How To Locate Educational Information and Data. 3d ed., rev. and enl. N.Y., Teachers College, Columbia Univ., 1950. 441p. $4.50.

Psychological Abstracts, 1927- (monthly). Lancaster, Pa., American Psychological Assn.

Louttit, C. M. Handbook of Psychological Literature. Bloomington, Ind., Principia Pr., 1932. 273p. $2.50.

theses in education and educational aids from governmental agencies. *N.E.A. Journal,* published monthly, except June-August, by the National Education Association, has many features, including lists of free and inexpensive materials, news and trends, and idea exchange. *School and Society,* a weekly, is published by the Society for the Advancement of Education, and is especially useful for reports of research, news of events and people, and lists of books.

There are 29 departments of the National Education Association, all of which issue some kind of publication: proceedings, yearbook, processed material. Among these publications are found some of the most important education continuations. The following table is a selection of N.E.A. serial publications.

Department	Date Established	Publication
Adult Education	1924	Bulletin
American Association for Health, Physical Education and Recreation	1937	Journal; Research Quarterly
American Association of School Administrators	1870	Yearbook
American Educational Research Association	1930	Review; Encyclopedia
Association for Supervision and Curriculum Development	1929	Educational Leadership
Audio-Visual Instruction	1923	Educational Screen
Classroom Teachers	1913	Yearbook
Elementary School Principals	1921	Yearbook; National Elementary Principal
Higher Education	1870	College and University Bulletin
National Council for Social Studies	1925	Social Education
National Science Teachers Association	1895	The Science Teacher

---

[6] There is, however, an index to *Psychological Index* as a whole: H. L. Ansbacher, *Psychological Index: Abstract References, Volumes 1-35* (Columbus, Ohio, American Psychological Assn. 1940-41), 2v. Abstracts are cited for each entry if any are available.

[7] Oscar K. Buros, ed., *Third Mental Measurements Yearbook* (New Brunswick, N.J., Rutgers Univ. Pr., 1949), 1047p., $12.50. Earlier editions were published in 1938 and 1940.

SOCIAL SCIENCES

Dictionaries and cyclopedias. Good's *Dictionary of Education,* sponsored by the education honorary fraternity, Phi Delta Kappa, aims "to make available a comprehensive dictionary of professional terms in education." One hundred specialists have written 20,000 definitions of 16,000 terms, including supplementary terms used in other countries.

Warren's *Dictionary of Psychology* was prepared by an advisory board and a list of collaborators including over a hundred outstanding psychologists, among whom the following names are notable: Watson, Terman, Boring, Gates, Jastrow, MacDougall, Murchison, Peterson, Pintner, Poffenberger. These men set forth their purpose as "to explain the meaning of technical terms which the reader will meet in psychological literature or which the psychologist may wish to use in his writings." Each definition has been passed on by at least two authorities in the special field to which the term belongs. The dictionary includes an alphabetic list of terms followed by an appendix of 18 tables, including: color-vision tests, complexes—a list of fundamental types, glands frequently treated in psychological literature, phobias—a list of the most common types, statistical formulas useful in psychology and education, symbols and technical abbreviations, and the topography of the human central nervous system. There are also glossaries of French and German terms and a bibliography of technical dictionaries and vocabularies.

Monroe's *Encyclopedia of Educational Research,* prepared under the auspices of the American Educational Research Association, aims to present a "critical evaluation, synthesis, and interpretation of re-

---

DICTIONARIES AND CYCLOPEDIAS

Good, Carter V., ed. Dictionary of Education. N.Y., McGraw-Hill, 1945. 495p. $4.

Warren, Howard C. Dictionary of Psychology. Boston, Houghton, Mifflin, 1934. 372p. $4.50.

Monroe, W. S. Encyclopedia of Educational Research. Rev. ed. N.Y., Macmillan, 1950. 1520p. $17.50.

Monroe, Paul. Cyclopedia of Education. N.Y., Macmillan, 1911-13. 5v. in 3.

Encyclopedia of Modern Education; ed. by Harry N. Rivlin; associate ed., Herbert Schueler. N.Y., Philosophical Library, 1943. 902p. $10.

Psychology and education

ported studies in the field of education." Articles are arranged alphabetically, are signed, and contain bibliographies. Entries are restricted to subjects on which sufficient research literature has been written to justify an article. Because of this restricted purpose it is necessary to use two other educational cyclopedias.

Paul Monroe's *Cyclopedia of Education,* although somewhat out of date, is still useful for questions on the history and philosophy of education. Its material is arranged alphabetically by small topics, and volume five includes an analytical index arranged as follows: history, philosophy, educational psychology, teaching methods, educational sociology, administration, elementary education, secondary education, higher education, physical education, and school architecture. Major emphasis is placed on American education, but considerable material on foreign systems is included. The articles are signed and are enhanced by illustrations and bibliographies.

Rivlin and Schueler's *Encyclopedia of Modern Education* is the work of about 200 authorities. This 900-page volume stresses present-day problems, trends, theories, and practice. Brief bibliographies accompany the articles and there is a system of cross references.

Handbooks and directories. Two handbooks to supplement the almanacs and yearbooks for statistical and other educational information are the *Biennial Survey of Education* of the U.S. Office of Education and the *N.E.A. Handbook and Manual.* The former, though never up to date, is a thorough statistical analysis of schools, school population, finance and other data. The latter, a newer publication, summarizes current educational developments and includes much help to teachers on methods and devices.

To supplement *Who's Who in America* and *Who Knows—and What* there are several directories of psychologists and educators. Murchison's *Psychological Register,* though out of date, is still useful. It includes brief biographies and full bibliographies of psychologists throughout the world, arranged by country. The plan of the work calls for volume one to include psychologists not now living and as far back as the Greeks. Volume two included 1250 psychologists from 29 countries. It was revised, expanded, and published as volume three with 2400 biographies of psychologists from 40 countries.

Of the directories of educators, the two issued by Science Press are most useful. One of these is *Leaders in Education* which includes "who's who" biographical sketches of college presidents, deans, school administrators, professors of education and other distinguished people in the American educational world. The other is the *Directory of American Scholars*,[8] published under the auspices of the American Council of Learned Societies in 1942, which includes scholars in the fields of the humanities and social sciences.

There are a great many directories of educational agencies. The *Educational Directory*, issued by the United States Office of Education, and *Patterson's Educational Directory* have already been described. A number of other directories are concerned with special classes of educational agencies.

The American Council on Education issues three directories of higher education. *American Colleges and Universities,* which has been issued once for every college generation of four years, in its fifth edition describes 820 degree-conferring institutions arranged alphabetically. For each institution the following data are given: type, history, admission requirements, fees, departments and staff analyzed by rank, degrees given, enrollment, library statistics, publications, finances, buildings, grounds, and administrative officers. General articles on phases of higher education such as professional education, accreditation and foreign students in the United States are included. *American Junior Colleges*,[9] edited by Jesse P. Bogue, is a directory to 564 accredited junior colleges. Carter V. Good's *Guide to Colleges, Universities and Professional Schools in the United States*[10] gives its information in tabular form. A fourth Council publication, *Universities of the World Outside U.S.A.*,[11] completes a shelf of higher educational directories that supplements the data found in encyclopedias, almanacs and other general sources. For additional information the

---

❦ HANDBOOKS AND DIRECTORIES

U.S. Office of Education. Biennial Survey of Education, 1916/18-   . Washington, Govt. Print. Off.

National Education Association of the U.S. N.E.A. Handbook and Manual, 1945-   (annual). Washington, N.E.A.

Murchison, Carl. Psychological Register. Worcester, Mass., Clark Univ., 1929-32. v.2-3 (v.1 not published).

Leaders in Education. 3d ed. Lancaster, Pa., Science Pr., 1951.

American Council on Education. American Colleges and Universities. 5th ed., ed. by A. J. Brumbaugh. Washington, The Council, 1948.

Baird, W. R. Baird's Manual of American College Fraternities. 15th ed. Menasha, Wisc., George Banta, 1949. 966p. $6.75.

foreign directories like *World of Learning* and the older French *Index generalis* and German *Minerva Jahrbuch,* still found on reference shelves, should not be forgotten.

An important special directory by the late Porter Sargent is *A Handbook of Private Schools* now in its 32d edition (1950).[12] Of especially high reference value on college campuses is Baird's *Manual of American College Fraternities,* which includes social, honorary, and professional sororities and fraternities, with lists of chapters, general information on the "Greek" world, and a list of distinguished fraternity men and women. It does not, however, answer the question that recently kept one college library reference staff busy: What was the name of the original "Sweetheart of Sigma Chi"?

Reading list

Griffith, Ernest S. "Special Reference Problems in the Social Sciences." In Pierce Butler, *The Reference Function of the Library.* Chicago, Univ. of Chicago Pr., 1943. p.163-79.

Kaplan, Louis. *Research Materials in the Social Sciences; an Annotated Guide for Graduate Students.* Madison, Univ. of Wisconsin Pr., 1939.

Manley, Marian C. *Library Service to Business; Its Place in the Small City.* Chicago, A.L.A., 1946. 85p.

"What Are the Social Sciences?" In *Encyclopedia of the Social Sciences.* N.Y., Macmillan, 1930. v.1, p.1-349.

---

[8] Jaques Cattell, *Directory of American Scholars, a Biographical Directory* (Lancaster, Pa., Science Pr., 1942), 928p., $10.

[9] American Council on Education, *American Junior Colleges;* ed. by Jesse P. Bogue (2d ed.; Washington, The Council, 1948), 537p., $6.50.

[10] Carter V. Good, *A Guide to Colleges, Universities, and Professional Schools in the United States* (Washington, American Council on Education, 1945), 681p., $5.

[11] *Universities of the World Outside U.S.A.;* ed. by M. M. Chambers (Washington, American Council on Education, 1950), 924p.

[12] *Handbook of Private Schools for American Boys and Girls;* by Porter Sargent (Boston, Sargent, 1915-   ), annual.

chapter 18

THE SCIENCES—
PURE AND APPLIED

Introduction, Physical sciences, Applied physical sciences: engineering and technology, Biological sciences, Applied biological sciences.

Introduction

The subject areas. The word *science* has been given many meanings, varying from the all-encompassing definition "any department of systematized knowledge"[1] to a much more limited one, "the systematized knowledge of nature and the physical world."[2] It is within the limits of this latter definition that materials discussed in this chapter lie. Also included are materials devoted in whole or in part to the practical applications of that systematized knowledge in the technologies and applied sciences.

Many subjects which are called sciences, such as psychology and the other social sciences, have already been discussed. In this chapter, covering in large part the 500's and 600's in the Dewey Classification, reference sources in the pure sciences—mathematics, physics, chemistry, geology and the biological sciences—and in certain of the applied sciences—engineering and practical trades, medicine, agriculture and home economics—are considered.

The literature of the sciences, both pure and applied, is extremely

Introduction

large and much of it is very specialized. The research literature in many fields can only be interpreted adequately by those who have a detailed knowledge of the subject. Many librarians with limited science background feel actual terror when they attempt any type of reference work in scientific and technical subjects. It is true, perhaps, that to make a complete search of the literature in a scientific field, one would need a thorough foundation in its subject matter, but it is also true that there are excellent technical librarians who are not science specialists, but who have learned the bibliographical tools, the terminology and the literature resources of their subjects and know how to use them intelligently.

It is not the purpose of this chapter to cover completely the reference sources for the research librarian in the sciences, but rather to consider some of the most widely useful tools, with emphasis on those of most importance for the general library. In the sciences perhaps more than in any other field, publications go out of date rapidly. For that reason, in many cases types of publications rather than individual titles are stressed.

Science and technology questions. In the present day, with its profound dependence on scientific and technological progress, there has been a great increase in the demand made on libraries for materials which were long regarded as highly specialized. Children talk glibly of atomic fission and want to know about living conditions in outer space; gardeners investigate the pH concentration in their soils and want the latest formulas for fertilizers; homemakers inquire about the vitamin B complex. Any day may bring questions like these even to the small library: What is the diameter of human hair? Which heats faster from the rays of the sun—the earth or the water? How does one remove whitewash? Is the powder given off by broken fluorescent tubes harmful to inhale? What is the effect of magnesium chloride on steel? What is the bright star in the west tonight? What makes a jet engine work? We have found a big green bug that looks like a grasshopper from Mars. What is it? My husband has brought home six rabbits. How do I prepare them for freezing? Where can I find a wiring diagram for a 1931 Chevrolet? Many of the questions are of the "how to" or the "why" variety. Many are practical, and their answers will be of concrete value to the inquirer. Since most of them can be answered

---

[1] *Webster's New Collegiate Dictionary* (Springfield, Mass., Merriam, 1949).

[2] *Webster's New World Dictionary of the American Language* (Cleveland, World Pub., 1951).

291

by definite factual statements, the librarian can be reasonably sure whether he has found what the patron wanted.

Much information in these fields is provided by general reference tools, but it is seldom detailed enough for the specialist. The unabridged dictionaries have made particular efforts to include scientific terms and have asked experts to prepare the definitions. An examination of the "New Words Supplement" to *Webster,* for instance, will show a very high percentage of scientific, technical and trade terms. That publishers of general encyclopedias are very conscious of the popular demand for accurate and up-to-date scientific information is proved by the fact that a great number of the new or revised articles advertised with each reprinting of an encyclopedia are in these areas. It is important for the librarian to remember, however, that for current information the encyclopedias must be supplemented by the encyclopedia yearbooks which try to keep up with recent developments. The annual summaries of progress in the sciences which appear in the *American Yearbook* are excellent. The general periodical indexes do not, with the exception of the *International Index,* cover the sciences even at an elementary level; the *Readers' Guide* indexes only a few popular scientific periodicals. Government publications are, of course, of great importance in science and technology, and the *Monthly Catalog* and the various bibliographies and indexes of the publications of specific agencies such as the Department of Agriculture, the Bureau of Mines, the Office of Technical Services, and the National Bureau of Standards are essential reference tools.

Bibliographies and indexes. A number of types of bibliographies and indexes are available to aid in book selection and identification of titles, both retrospective and current.

Book selection aids. Because the judgment of subject specialists is needed to evaluate the accuracy of scientific and technical books and because the demand for the books is limited often to specialists, the

---

❦ BOOK SELECTION AIDS

Hawkins, R. R., ed. Scientific, Medical and Technical Books Published in the United States of America, 1930-1944. N.Y., Bowker, 1946. 1114p. $20. Supplement (1945-1948), 1950.

Technical Book Review Index; comp. and ed. in the Technology Department, Carnegie Library of Pittsburgh, 1935-   (monthly except July and August). N.Y., Special Libraries Assn. $7.50.

Introduction

general book selection aids are not always adequate. Though some publications in science and technology are included in the *Book Review Digest,* many are not. The basic selection aids like the *Standard Catalog,* the *A.L.A. Catalog* and *Booklist,* though they are helpful for popular science, do not include highly technical publications.

During the Second World War, at the request of the State Department, the National Research Council prepared *Scientific, Medical and Technical Books Published in the U.S.A., 1930-1944,* under the editorship of R. R. Hawkins, chief of the Science and Technology Division, New York Public Library. A highly competent committee of specialists made the selection of over 6000 titles in print at the time of publication. To this a supplement has added 2583 titles published in 1945-48. This basic bibliography is limited to American publications, but is outstanding in its standards of selection and in its excellent annotations. It is kept informally up to date by an annual list of new technical books which appears in the *Library Journal* for May 15 of each year, and by other short lists during the year.

The *Technical Book Review Index,* published since 1935 by the Special Libraries Association, is a counterpart of the *Book Review Digest* in the technical field. Now prepared by the Technology Department of the Carnegie Library in Pittsburgh, it appears monthly, except in July and August, and indexes and quotes from reviews appearing in scientific, technical and trade journals. There is an annual author-title index, but no subject approach. The user wishing to locate reviews of new books in a special subject would first need to get his titles from the *Cumulative Book Index,* for instance, and then turn to the *Technical Book Review Index.* Another useful annotated list of new materials is *New Technical Books,* which is published bimonthly by the New York Public Library.

A number of valuable bibliographic guides have been prepared for subject specialists in the individual sciences. These publications are helpful to librarian and patron alike for bibliographic guidance and for book and periodical selection. Several of these guides, such as Soule's *Library Guide for the Chemist* and Parke's *Guide to the Literature of Mathematics and Physics,* are discussed later in this chapter.

Retrospective bibliographies. A large proportion of the original contributions in science appear in periodical and serial publications. In recent years scientific publications have been appearing increasingly in the form of technical reports filed only in government bureaus and private industry. Even during the nineteenth century much material appeared first in journals and dissertations rather than in full-length books. Science has always been international in its scope, and hence it has always been necessary for scientists to keep track of discovery and invention all over the world. Many international efforts have been made to index and list scientific publications. Perhaps the earliest of these major efforts was that of the Royal Society of London, with its *Catalogue of Scientific Papers, 1800-1900*. Appearing in four series, this catalog provides a complete author index to the scientific publications of the nineteenth century. It covers material from many languages and includes books, periodical articles, materials from proceedings of scientific institutions, and doctoral dissertations. It was the intention also to publish subject indexes to each large field. However, only those for pure mathematics, mechanics, and physics have appeared.[3]

By the beginning of the twentieth century the research literature of the sciences was increasing tremendously and becoming more and more specialized. Until World War I caused its cessation, the *International Catalogue of Scientific Literature,* also published under the auspices of the Royal Society, attempted to record the literature of science. Annual bibliographies in 17 subject fields were prepared by international teams of indexers. Each volume contains schedules of classification, indexes in four languages, and an author and subject catalog. The increase in publication in the sciences in the early twentieth century is indicated by the fact that the Royal Society *Catalogue* for the nineteenth century fills 19 volumes, while the *International Catalogue* for the first fourteen years of the twentieth century occupies 142 volumes, including the elaborate subject indexes.

With the completion of the volumes for 1914 the *International Catalogue* ceased publication, and since that time no general, complete international bibliography of this field has been attempted. The bibliographies and indexes of science and technology have for the most part become highly specialized, and many are limited to minute

---

❦ RETROSPECTIVE BIBLIOGRAPHIES

Royal Society of London. Catalogue of Scientific Papers, 1800-1900.
    London, Clay, 1867-1902; Cambridge, Univ. Pr., 1914-25. 19v.
International Catalogue of Scientific Literature, 1900-1914. Pub. for
    the International Council by the Royal Society of London, 1902-19. 14v. in 142.

Introduction

subject fields. A survey made in 1939 by a committee of the American Library Association listed over 500 indexing and abstracting services covering all fields of knowledge published at that time.[4] A *Preliminary Title List of Current Scientific Abstracting and Indexing Services in the U.S.,* compiled in the Reference Department of the Library of Congress and dated March 17, 1952, includes 198 titles. A similar British list[5] includes 127 indexes published in Great Britain.

Current bibliographies. The most useful index to current periodical literature in science and technology is the *Industrial Arts Index,* which has appeared since 1913 with monthly issues cumulating throughout the year. It is primarily devoted to the applied sciences, trade and business. However, some material in the so-called pure sciences such as chemistry and physics is also included. The *Industrial Arts Index* is a subject index only, but its wide scope and useful selection of periodicals make it of great value. Most of the publications covered are in English.

The *International Index to Periodicals* also includes a number of journals in the pure sciences, many of them scholarly. Especially featured are geology, anthropology, history of science, and publications of academies of science.

A more specialized publication, *Chemical Abstracts,* is considered here because of its international importance, and because its coverage touches not only chemistry, but also physics, biology, medicine, engineering and other sciences related to chemistry. The most extensive of all current scientific abstracting and indexing publications, *Chemical Abstracts* is world-wide in scope, appears twice each month. Each

---

☞ CURRENT BIBLIOGRAPHIES
Industrial Arts Index, 1913-   (monthly). N.Y., Wilson.
Chemical Abstracts, 1907-   (semimonthly). Easton, Pa., American Chemical Soc.

---

[3] An important retrospective bibliography of early writings on science is George Sarton, *Introduction to the History of Science* (Baltimore, pub. for the Carnegie Institution by Williams & Wilkins, 1927-48), v.1-3 in 4. Volumes 1-3 cover in a thoroughly documented running text the history of science up to the fourteenth century. Many references to original materials are included.

[4] A.L.A. Serials Section, "Tabular Analysis of 550 Titles in the Field of Periodicals Indexing and Abstracting," *Library Journal,* May 1, 1939, v.64, p.354-57.

[5] Royal Society of London, *A List of Periodicals and Bulletins Containing Abstracts Published in Great Britain* (London, The Society, 1949).

issue is arranged by large standardized topics and contains an author index. Books, periodicals, serials, pamphlets, and patents of all sorts and from all countries are covered, so long as they are judged to contain new material or important reviews of developments in any application of chemistry. All articles giving new information are abstracted, and as far as possible the actual data are included in the abstract. Often, therefore, for factual information, *Chemical Abstracts* will provide not only a source reference but also the desired facts themselves. The annual indexes, by author, subject, patent number, and chemical composition, are exhaustive, and four cumulative decennial indexes have been published. *Chemical Abstracts* is not a tool for quick reference consultation and a knowledge of chemistry is essential for its full use, but many questions can be answered from it by the non-specialist.

Two works described in the chapter on bibliographies are of particular help in scientific and technical bibliographic searching. The *Bibliographic Index* is heavily weighted with scientific and technical sources, and Besterman's *World Bibliography of Bibliographies* has analyzed hundreds of bibliographies in various scientific fields, including patent abridgments. Other more specialized indexes and bibliographies are mentioned with the discussion of individual sciences.

Union lists. A number of special union lists of periodicals and serials in this field can be used to supplement or partially to substitute for the *Union List of Serials*.

Periodically *Chemical Abstracts* publishes a *List of Periodicals Abstracted*. The latest of these lists appeared in 1951, gave the titles of over 5000 serials which are covered by the *Abstracts,* and included such data about each title as publisher and address, number of volumes per year, price, and many cross references. There are notes of discontinued or changed titles, and an indication of the holdings of 280

UNION LISTS

Chemical Abstracts. List of Periodicals Abstracted by Chemical Abstracts. Easton, Pa., American Chemical Soc., 1951.

Special Libraries Association. Science-Technology Group. Union List of Technical Periodicals in Two Hundred Libraries of the Science-Technology Group. 3d ed. N.Y., Special Libraries Assn., 1947. 285p.

World List of Scientific Periodicals Published in the Years 1900-1933. 2d ed. Oxford, Univ. Pr., 1934. 779p.

Introduction

libraries in the United States, its possessions, and Canada is given. This list is sometimes difficult to use, since the serials are alphabeted by the abbreviation used in *Chemical Abstracts* and not by actual title.

The Science-Technology Group of the Special Libraries Association has prepared a useful *Union List of Technical Periodicals* in some 200 special libraries, most of which did not have their holdings included in the *Union List of Serials*. An English publication, different in format, but giving full information about 36,000 periodicals and showing location in 187 British libraries, is the *World List of Scientific Periodicals . . . 1900-1933*. The *World List* is not merely a union list for Great Britain, but also includes many titles not available in the British Isles. It is often extremely difficult to use because the method of alphabeting by title is confusing and inconsistent.

Dictionaries. The scientist and engineer have developed extensive languages of their own in specialized fields. Many terms are coined for trade use, for identification of trade products, or for new natural species. Frequently words having a common general meaning have an entirely different one in science. *Pattern making* is a part of dressmaking to a woman, but of foundry work to a man. *Chattering, reducing agents,* and *dish pan idler* might also be mentioned as examples of terms with different masculine and feminine connotations. Many

---

❦ DICTIONARIES

Beadnell, C. M. Dictionary of Scientific Terms As Used in the Various Sciences. London, Watts, 1942. 232p. 2s.

Chambers's Technical Dictionary; ed. by C. F. Tweney and L. E. C. Hughes. Rev. ed. with supplement. N.Y., Macmillan, 1948. 976p. $6.50.

Henderson, Isabella F., and Henderson, W. D. Dictionary of Scientific Terms. 4th ed. N.Y., Van Nostrand, 1949. 480p. $10.

De Vries, Louis. French-English Science Dictionary. N.Y., McGraw-Hill, 1940. 546p. $4.50.

—— German-English Science Dictionary. 2d ed. N.Y., McGraw-Hill, 1946. 558p. $4.50.

—— German-English Technical and Engineering Dictionary. N.Y., McGraw-Hill, 1950. 928p. $20.

Zimmerman, O. T., and Lavine, Irwin. Scientific and Technical Abbreviations, Signs and Symbols. 2d ed. Dover, N.Y., Industrial Research Service, 1949. 54p. $8.

specialized dictionaries have been compiled, both for slang and for the more serious scientific terminology. Glossaries of terms found in handbooks and in general textbooks will also be extremely useful.

The majority of these dictionaries are limited to single fields, such as geology and biology, and several are discussed later. Among the more general is an English publication, Beadnell's *Dictionary of Scientific Terms As Used in the Various Sciences,* which is perhaps the most inclusive for the physical and biological sciences. Definitions are brief, and pronunciations or derivations are not given. A few terms are explained in more detail, or quotations given. *Chambers's Technical Dictionary* includes words in both pure and applied science. Trade, engineering, and medical terms also are carefully defined. Henderson's *Dictionary of Scientific Terms* is limited to the biological sciences. It gives not only concise definitions but also indicates pronunciation and derivation of terms.

Because of the international aspects of the literature of science, another type of dictionary in great demand is the bilingual or polyglot dictionary. Many of these exist in the various sciences.[6] Among these dictionaries three edited by Louis De Vries—a *French-English Science Dictionary,* a *German-English Science Dictionary,* and a *German-English Technical and Engineering Dictionary*—are excellent modern aids for those wishing to translate into English. They do not have an English language alphabet or index. Other useful titles are to be found in Winchell's *Guide to Reference Books.*

Abbreviations and symbols are other sources of questions in the sciences. In mathematics, chemistry, or engineering, for instance, these are used continually, and often much searching must be done to identify them. The lists of abbreviations and symbols in the general dictionaries are useful, as are those in handbooks in the special fields. Zimmerman and Lavine's *Scientific and Technical Abbreviations, Signs and Symbols* has wide coverage, including many tables and lists in all fields of science and technology, most of which are arranged in order of the phrase itself followed by the abbreviation. Though there are some lists of abbreviations in particular fields, there is no cross-indexing from abbreviation to phrase. The De Vries *German-English Technical and Engineering Dictionary* has a 30-page list of abbreviations with German and English equivalents.

Encyclopedias and yearbooks. The general field of science does not have any exhaustive encyclopedia in English, though some exist in subdivisions of the sciences, such as chemistry. *Van Nostrand's Scien-*

Introduction

tific Encyclopedia is useful for its wide scope. It covers material in "aeronautics, astronomy, botany, chemical engineering, chemistry, civil engineering, electrical engineering, electronics and radio, geology, mathematics, mechanical engineering, medicine, metallurgy, meteorology, mineralogy, navigation, photography, physics, statistics, zoology." The information it gives is brief but recent and well selected. It contains many tables and a few small, clear illustrations. In many cases articles are graded, beginning with elementary material and progressing to the more technical. Articles are initialed and are written by qualified authors. There are no biographies or bibliographies.

Progress in science is reported not only in general yearbooks, but also in several specialized ones. *Science in Progress,* edited by G. A. Baitsell, contains scholarly articles by experts, with lengthy bibliographies. Another useful publication is the *Annual Report* of the Smithsonian Institution, which contains each year not only the official reports of that outstanding scientific institution but also a series of authoritative articles written for the layman on various aspects of scientific and technological progress. These articles are also available separately. Annual summaries are frequently prepared for individual subjects: for instance, the *Annual Reports on the Progress of Chemistry* published by the Chemical Society of Great Britain.

Biographical dictionaries and directories. The eighth edition of *American Men of Science* contains over 50,000 names of scientists,

---

❦ ENCYCLOPEDIAS AND YEARBOOKS

Van Nostrand's Scientific Encyclopedia. 2d ed. N.Y., Van Nostrand, 1947. 1600p. $15.

Baitsell, G. A., ed. Science in Progress, 1939-   (annual). New Haven, Yale Univ. Pr.

Smithsonian Institution. Annual Report, 1846- . Washington, Smithsonian Institution.

❦ BIOGRAPHICAL DICTIONARIES AND DIRECTORIES

American Men of Science. 8th ed. Lancaster, Pa., Science Pr., 1949. 2836p. $17.

Who's Who in Engineering. 6th ed. N.Y., Lewis Historical Pub. Co., 1948. $10.

---

[6] J. E. Holstrom, *Bibliography of Interlingual Scientific and Technical Dictionaries* (Unesco, 1951) lists 1044 dictionaries under 224 subjects in 45 languages.

with brief biographical data supplied by each biographee. In the earlier editions, outstanding leaders were starred, but this practice, the validity of which had been subject to severe criticism, has been abandoned in this edition. A similar type of publication for engineers —*Who's Who in Engineering*—contains some 16,000 biographies. *Chemical Abstracts* indexes biographical information under individual name and also under the general heading Biographies. Directories of various scientific organizations often give biographical data.

Also important in science and technology are the directories of societies, industrial research organizations, and trade associations, both national and international, some of which have already been discussed in Chapter 7. Of particular usefulness is the National Research Council's *Handbook of Scientific and Technical Societies and Institutions of the United States and Canada*, which may be used to locate societies either by name or by their subject field. It is helpful in understanding the activities and publications of important individual scientific and technical societies. For instance, it includes the information that the American Association for the Advancement of Science, the largest of these groups, has over 200 affiliated societies, publishes the two journals *Science* and *The Scientific Monthly*, is a sponsor of *Science News Letter*, also publishes a useful *Current Proceedings and Directory* and a group of symposia on scientific subjects, and offers rewards for outstanding scientific achievements.

Periodicals and serials. The reference librarian in science should have a clear conception of the pattern of serial publication and should know the nature of the leading periodicals in all the fields in which he works. Ulrich's *Periodical Directory* is a very helpful guide to current publications by subject.

All sciences have their professional journals, usually published under the auspices of a society or institution, characterized by long, documented articles which present full results of research. Examples are the *Journals* of the *American Chemical Society*, the *Franklin Institute*, and the *National Bureau of Standards*, the *Astrophysical Journal*, and the *Journal of Home Economics*. Another type of periodical may be characterized as semiresearch. Articles are shorter and frequently more popular. The publisher may still be a national society, but usually advertising is accepted. Examples are *Science, Industrial and Engineering Chemistry,* and *Mechanical Engineering*. A third characteristic periodical is the trade journal, such as *Iron Age* or *Power,* commercially published and carrying survey and progress articles, news,

Physical sciences

and many advertisements. A fourth type is the news journal, a few of which are published by professional societies—for example, *Science News Letter* and *Chemical and Engineering News*. Others—like *Engineering News Record* and *Nature*—are published by commercial publishers. A fifth example is the journal for popular consumption, such as *Popular Mechanics, Scientific American, Nature Magazine,* and *Sky and Telescope*.

Still another useful, large group of periodicals are the house organs, many of which are valuable sources of reference material. Outstanding are the *General Electric Review* and the *Du Pont Magazine*. Many engineering colleges and scientific research organizations publish journals. *Technology Review,* from the Massachusetts Institute of Technology, and *Natural History,* from the American Museum of Natural History, may be cited as examples. Also, scientific societies, government bureaus, engineering and agricultural experiment stations, and industrial research laboratories produce bulletins, research papers, and proceedings, published more or less irregularly, many of which are necessary for reference work.

Physical sciences

The subject fields. The physical sciences as considered here include mathematics (really a tool of the sciences), astronomy, physics, chemistry, geology, and meteorology. For the specialist and the research worker the important reference sources in these sciences are bibliographies, journals, and reports. The needs of the layman are met by dictionaries of technical terms and factual handbooks. In this presentation, though guides and a few important bibliographies for specialists in individual fields are mentioned, the emphasis is on more elementary materials.

Mathematics. Few reference books in mathematics are essential to the general library. A representative collection of textbooks in the conventional fields of arithmetic, algebra, geometry, trigonometry, calculus and probability; a history of mathematics; and several collections of mathematical tables will probably suffice. Questions usually arise from problems of everyday life. Weights, measures, conversion tables, business arithmetic, and compound interest computations are typical of the subjects most requested by public library patrons. Unfortunately there are frequent requests for actual help in working problems (sometimes over the telephone). The librarian, even though an expert in mathematics, should refuse this type of aid unless he is willing to be imposed upon unmercifully.

Astronomy. Astronomy is a popular subject for the amateur and many questions of fact are asked. A mystery story writer may want the time of sunrise in Havana on March 13, 1889. An amateur astronomer may desire to build a telescope. A comet or brilliant planetary configuration often brings queries. Information on surveying, navigation, time and tide, each of which has astronomical background, is frequently requested of the librarian and requires reference to specially prepared tables. The chief tools of the professional astronomer have been star charts, tables, and the serial publications of astronomical observatories, but he is making an increasing use of the research literature of physics and chemistry, and is himself contributing to the development of these subjects by his investigations of the constitution of the universe.

Physics. The great recent developments in atomic physics, electronics and other subdivisions of physics have resulted in a large increase in research publication in this area. The many practical applications of these new principles have excited great popular interest, and the layman, as well as the specialist, wants to know more about the Einstein theory, quantum mechanics, and light and radio waves. Furthermore the practical applications of these principles in radio, television, lighting, sound, heat, and air conditioning bring frequent questions. Many may be answered by means of up-to-date textbooks; the handbooks of facts are also important sources.

Chemistry. The literature of chemistry is by far the most prolific and, with the exception of geology, the best organized of all the scientific literatures. Chemists are more dependent upon their books and periodicals than are other scientists, and formal instruction in the use of these materials is given in many colleges and universities. The interest of the layman in chemistry is usually restricted either to general background reading or to practical information for a specific purpose. Formula and recipe books, which give instruction on how to make everything from soap to plaster casts, are largely chemical in their content, and are in constant use. Factual data found in handbooks and tables and descriptions of small- and large-scale manufacturing processes are frequently requested.

Geology. The geological sciences are partly physical and partly biological. In contrast to the literatures of physics and chemistry, many of the topics are within the scope of the layman's comprehension and

Physical sciences

interest. Inquiries about rocks, fossils, mineral resources, water supply, gems, mountains, glaciers and other physical features of the earth all come to the library. Amateur collectors live in the hope of finding gold, and the librarian may want to learn to identify fool's gold, or pyrite, when he sees it!

Much of the basic investigation in geology and related sciences has been done under government auspices, and the publications of national and state geological surveys and bureaus of mines are important sources of information for expert and layman alike. Maps, too, are of basic importance and have unusually thorough bibliographic coverage.

Meteorology. The science of meteorology has progressed greatly with modern advances in rapid communication and in aviation. Weather forecasts and weather post-mortems are topics of general conversation and universal curiosity. To the farmer, airplane pilot, or highway maintenance engineer weather information is vital. As is true of geology, much of this information is governmental in origin.

Bibliographies and indexes. A number of useful guides have been published which show the searcher how to find his way through the mazes of specialized literature in the physical sciences. The field of chemistry, in particular, has had several guides of importance, though all are now rather out of date. Soule's *Library Guide for the Chemist*

📚 BIBLIOGRAPHIES AND INDEXES

Soule, B. A. Library Guide for the Chemist. N.Y., McGraw-Hill, 1938. 302p. $3.

Parke, N. G. Guide to the Literature of Mathematics and Physics. N.Y., McGraw-Hill, 1947. 205p. $5.

Pearl, R. M. Guide to Geologic Literature. N.Y., McGraw-Hill, 1951. 239p. $4.50.

Mathematical Reviews, 1940- (monthly). Lancaster, Pa., American Mathematical Soc.

Science Abstracts... Section A, Physics Abstracts, 1898- (monthly). London, Institution of Electrical Engineers.

Nickles, J. M. Geologic Literature of North America, 1785-1918. Washington, Govt. Print. Off., 1931-44. 2v.

Bibliography of North American Geology, 1919-1928, 1929-1939. Washington, Govt. Print. Off., 1931-44. 2v. Biennial supplements, 1940- .

not only discusses the general nature of reference tools in chemistry, but also describes in detail the methods of using some of them. Parke's *Guide to the Literature of Mathematics and Physics* may be consulted successfully by librarian or student wishing to understand the organization of scientific literature and the methods of bibliographic searching. Half the book is devoted to this subject and the remainder is a very useful selected bibliography of recent materials in mathematics and physics. The author's observations on the scope of many of the subjects are quite helpful. Pearl's *Guide to Geologic Literature,* like Parke, discusses general library searching and contains an analysis of the nature of geologic literature as well as bibliographies of important materials.

Of the current sources, *Chemical Abstracts* has already been described as the most important index to chemistry and related fields. Among other chemical abstracting services are *British Abstracts* and the *Chemisches Zentralblatt.* In the physical sciences there are many more. Each subject has some medium for the reporting of its current literature.[7] *Mathematical Reviews,* published monthly (except August) by the American Mathematical Society, has world-wide coverage and offers signed abstracts. It is interesting that many of the articles listed in *Mathematical Reviews* are available only on microfilm because of the impossibility of finding regular publishers for this highly theoretical material.

Science Abstracts, published in England since 1898 and sponsored by American and British physical and electrical engineering societies, appears in two sections: Section A, *Physics Abstracts,* and Section B, *Electrical Engineering Abstracts. Physics Abstracts* covers several hundred journals of interest to physicists. It appears monthly; the material is arranged by Universal Decimal Classification number and each entry gives complete bibliographic information and an abstract. Mathematics, astronomy, physical chemistry, geophysics and biophysics are also included. There is an author index in each issue and there are annual author and subject indexes. The American Institute of Physics completed in 1950 an exhaustive study of physics abstracting which should not only improve the quality of the abstracts but at the same time minimize duplication with *Chemical Abstracts.*

As has been mentioned previously, geology is unusually well indexed. In the United States a series of bibliographies and indexes cover all types of geologic publication from 1785 to the present. Nickles' *Geologic Literature of North America, 1785-1918* and its supplement, *Bibliography of North American Geology,* which includes two

Physical sciences

decennial volumes for 1919-1939 with biennial cumulations since that time, published by the United States Geological Survey, are excellent and basic. Material is arranged alphabetically by author, supplemented by detailed subject indexes. It is important in using this work to remember that the listings are indexed first by place (usually by state) and then by subordinate subjects. A companion publication, *Bibliography and Index of Geology Exclusive of North America,* is published by the Geological Society of America. Important in geology, too, are the *List of Publications* of the United States Bureau of Mines and *Publications* of the Geological Survey. Separate lists of topographic and geologic maps are also available from the Survey.

Dictionaries and encyclopedias. Special dictionaries of technical terms in the physical sciences are numerous and often contain formulas and tables of physical and chemical properties. Though mathematical terms are hard to define briefly, James's *Mathematics Dictionary* is helpful to the non-specialist because of its coverage of both popular and scientific terms. Useful tables, symbols and formulas are also included. In chemistry two valuable dictionaries, the *Condensed Chemical Dictionary* and *Hackh's Chemical Dictionary* have progressed through several editions. The *Condensed Chemical Dictionary* is devoted specifically to chemicals and chemical products, including trade names, and gives all types of essential data about them. *Hackh's* defines not only chemicals but process terms, and, as indicated in its subtitle, related words in "physics, astrophysics, mineralogy, pharmacy, agriculture, biology, medicine, engineering, etc." It also contains many brief biographical citations. Weld's *Glossary of Physics*

❦ DICTIONARIES AND ENCYCLOPEDIAS

James, Glenn, and James, R. C. Mathematics Dictionary. Rev. ed. N.Y., Van Nostrand, 1949. 432p. $7.50.

Condensed Chemical Dictionary. 4th ed. N.Y., Reinhold, 1950. 721p. $10.

Hackh, I. W. D. Hackh's Chemical Dictionary. 3d ed. Philadelphia, Blakiston, 1944. 925p. $8.50.

Encyclopedia of Chemical Technology; ed. by R. E. Kirk, D. F. Othmer, and others. N.Y., Interscience Encyclopedias, 1947-50. v.1-7 (in progress). $25 per vol.

---

[7] Dwight E. Gray and Robert S. Bray, "Abstracting and Indexing Services of Physics Interest," *American Journal of Physics,* May, 1950, v.18, p.274-99.

(McGraw-Hill, 1937), Rice's *Dictionary of Geological Terms* (Edwards Bros., 1945), *Mineralogical Dictionary* (Chemical Pub. Co., 1948), and Thiessen's *Weather Glossary* (Govt. Print. Off., 1946) are examples of useful dictionaries in their respective fields.

Truly encyclopedic works in English are few, but there are a number in German. Chemistry has many encyclopedias, and some, such as the many-volumed Beilstein *Handbuch der Organischen Chemie*, attempt to provide a complete survey of the literature of the field they represent, thus serving also as bibliographies. A modern American encyclopedia, still in progress, is Kirk and Othmer's *Encyclopedia of Chemical Technology*. This excellent work, to appear in 14 volumes when completed, presents signed articles, which, though written by specialists, are generally quite intelligible to the layman. A well-known similar English publication, now appearing in its fourth edition, is *Thorpe's Dictionary of Applied Chemistry* (Longmans, 1937-   ).

Handbooks and yearbooks. The handbook is probably the most characteristic reference book of the pure and applied sciences. The need for much factual data in concise form, available at all times, has encouraged publication of many such works. A number of these are revised constantly, and annual or biennial editions are common. Libraries find that a collection of ready reference handbooks in the various fields supplies answers to a large majority of the inquiries on science.

In astronomy and geology, where handbooks are needed by amateur as well as by specialist, two levels of guides may be identified.

❦ HANDBOOKS AND YEARBOOKS

Barton, S. G., and Barton, W. H. Guide to the Constellations. 3d ed. N.Y., McGraw-Hill, 1943. 80p. $4.

Loomis, F. B. Field Book of Common Rocks and Minerals. N.Y., Putnam, 1923. $3.50.

Tannehill, I. R. Weather around the World. Princeton, N.J., Princeton Univ. Pr., 1943. 200p. $2.50.

Chemical Rubber Co., Cleveland. Handbook of Chemistry and Physics. 33d ed. Cleveland, Chemical Rubber Pub. Co., 1951.

Bennett, Harry. Chemical Formulary. N.Y., Chemical Pub. Co., 1933-50. v.1-9 (in progress).

U.S. Bureau of Mines. Minerals Yearbook. Washington, Govt. Print. Off., 1932-   .

Physical sciences

Barton and Barton's *Guide to the Constellations* is a useful, rather elementary handbook for the layman, giving star charts and interesting data about the stars. Norton's *Star Atlas and Reference Handbook* is more advanced, and gives charts and lists of astronomical phenomena requiring the use of small telescopes as well as those visible to the naked eye. In geology and meteorology there are handbooks for the amateur such as Loomis' *Field Book of Common Rocks and Minerals,* with its excellent descriptions, and Tannehill's *Weather around the World,* which gives records of weather for nearly 200 places and much other useful information for travelers and students of geography. For the specialist, Berry's *Handbook of Meteorology* (McGraw-Hill, 1945) and the classic Dana *System of Mineralogy* (Wiley, 1944) are examples of basic standard reference tools.

In chemistry and physics an exceedingly useful handbook is the *Handbook of Chemistry and Physics.* Originally prepared as a small pamphlet for advertising purposes, it has developed into a book of nearly 3000 pages, revised annually and containing tables and other compilations of essential physical, chemical and mathematical information. Lange's *Handbook of Chemistry* (Handbook Pub., 1946), also revised frequently, is prepared more specifically for chemistry, while for the engineering aspects of chemistry the *Chemical Engineers' Handbook* (McGraw-Hill, 1950) by John H. Perry provides much useful material.

Henley's *Twentieth Century Book of Formulas* has already been described in the chapter on manuals. A more elaborate publication and one that is kept up to date with frequent new volumes is Bennett's *Chemical Formulary,* which includes recipes for the manufacturing of chemical products, many of which are patented. There are useful indexes to sources of chemicals and trade-named materials.

The *Minerals Yearbook,* published annually by the United States Bureau of Mines, has much handbook information on developments in mineral production, and in addition contains useful statistical tables.

Tables. In the physical sciences there are many important compilations of tables supplemented by little or no textual information. For mathematics, the *Index of Mathematical Tables,* compiled by Alan Fletcher and others, provides a guide to these publications.[8] The first

---

[8] Examples of useful books of tables are Barlow's *Tables of Squares, Cubes, Square Roots and Reciprocals* (N.Y., Chemical Pub. Co., 1941) and R. S. Burington's *Handbook of Mathematical Tables and Formulae* (3d ed.; Sandusky, Ohio, Handbook Pub., 1949).

part of the book is arranged by mathematical function, the second part is a bibliography arranged by authors' names, and there is a subject index.

The *American Ephemeris and Nautical Almanac* which appears annually gives basic data several years in advance for astronomer, surveyor and navigator. Another classical work in this field is Bowditch's *American Practical Navigator* (Govt. Print. Off.), and similar publications are now prepared for aviators. For physics and chemistry an important basic collection of tables is the National Research Council's *International Critical Tables*. For this encyclopedic compilation, groups of experts selected the most reliable values from the mass of physical and chemical data appearing in the literature and prepared elaborate tables. References to original sources for the data are given. In meteorology two useful examples of tables may be mentioned: *Smithsonian Meteorological Tables,* which appeared in a sixth revised edition in 1951, is prepared for the professional meteorologist. Clayton's *World Weather Records,* also published by the Smithsonian Institution, presents meteorological records from all parts of the world covering the period to 1940.

Applied physical sciences: engineering and technology

The subject fields. The applied sciences derive directly from the pure sciences, and, as has already been observed, it is impossible to separate entirely the literature of the two fields.[9] Engineering has been

---

❦ TABLES

Fletcher, Alan, and others. Index of Mathematical Tables. N.Y., McGraw-Hill, 1946. 450p. $16.

U.S. Nautical Almanac Office. American Ephemeris and Nautical Almanac. 1855-   (annual). Washington, Govt. Print. Off.

National Research Council. International Critical Tables. N.Y., McGraw-Hill, 1926-33. 7v. and Index.

Smithsonian Meteorological Tables. 6th ed. Washington, Smithsonian Institution, 1951.

Clayton, H. H. World Weather Records (Smithsonian Miscellaneous Collections, v.79, 90, 105). Washington, Smithsonian Institution, 1927-47. 3v.

Engineering and technology

defined as "the science dealing with the design, construction, and operation of various structures, machines, engines and other devices used in industry and everyday life."[10] It has many branches and a prolific literature. Advanced and theoretical engineering publications are often highly mathematical, though there are also many "how to" publications prepared for the mechanic and the craftsman in the useful arts and manufactures.

Engineering includes such specializations as civil engineering, which deals largely with public works, construction and transportation, and mechanical engineering, which concerns itself with the production and use of power and machinery. Important branches are aeronautical and automobile engineering, shipbuilding and machine shop work. Electrical engineering considers the generation, transmission and use of electric power; lighting, radio, electronics and television are all important subdivisions. Metallurgical and chemical engineering treat of the manufacture and use of metals and chemical products.

Closely related to engineering is the group of subjects called the useful arts, or the practical technologies, including such topics as manufacturing and building.

Reference material sought in the applied sciences is largely factual and often very practical. The engineer seldom asks for historical material but wants the latest information available. The collections of data in engineering handbooks are his most essential reference tools.

Bibliographies and indexes. Blanche Dalton's *Sources of Engineering Information* was originally prepared to accompany lectures on the use of the engineering library at the University of California. It lists, with some annotations, the principal indexes, abstracts, bibliographies and reference materials in all fields of engineering, but there is no accompanying text. In 1951 the long-promised manual *Technical Libraries* was published by the Special Libraries Association. Lucille Jackson, the editor, in collaboration with a number of members of the Science-Technology Division of the Special Libraries Association, has prepared a very useful manual on all phases of technical library man-

---

[9] For a discussion of the relationships of the pure and applied sciences see "Divisions of Natural Science and Technology," by H. J. T. Ellingham, in *Royal Society Scientific Information Conference Reports and Papers*, 1948, p.477-84, one of the charts from which is reproduced as the frontispiece in Lucille Jackson's *Technical Libraries* (N.Y., Special Libraries Assn., 1951).

[10] *Columbia Encyclopedia* (2d ed., 1950).

agement. There are excellent bibliographies, as well as an appendix of "Basic reference publications and specimen subject field bibliographies."

For many libraries the *Industrial Arts Index,* mentioned earlier in this chapter, is an adequate guide to technical periodical literature, but the oldest index in this field in the United States is the *Engineering Index,* which appears annually and has been published since 1884. In its present form it both indexes and abstracts with brief annotations all the engineering material added to the Engineering Societies Library in New York. It analyzes many more foreign periodicals than does *Industrial Arts Index,* its entries are arranged by subject, and there is an author index each year. Users should remember that in the *Engineering Index* each article is indexed under one subject only, and it may be necessary to check the numerous cross references thoroughly to discover all pertinent material. The annual volumes of *Engineering Index* are supplemented by a current card service available in whole or in part through subscription. The expense of this service, however, makes it practicable for only a few libraries.

At the close of World War II military forces in Europe captured thousands of valuable technical and research reports from enemy sources. Tons of documents were gathered and brought to this country, and similar collections were made by England and France. In 1946 the Office of the Publication Board (now called the Office of Technical Services) was established within the Department of Commerce to make much of this information available to American industry. The Office was also charged with responsibility for distributing thousands of research reports prepared during the war in this country and released at the close of hostilities for public use. The *Bibliography of*

☞ BIBLIOGRAPHIES AND INDEXES

Dalton, Blanche H. Sources of Engineering Information. Berkeley, Univ. of California Pr., 1948. 109p. $4.

Jackson, Lucille, ed. Technical Libraries. N.Y., Special Libraries Assn., 1951. 202p. $6.

Engineering Index, 1884-   (annual). N.Y., Engineering Magazine, 1892-1919; American Soc. of Mechanical Engineers, 1920-34; Engineering Index, 1934- .

U.S. Dept. of Commerce. Office of Technical Services. Bibliography of Technical Reports, 1946-   (monthly). Washington, Govt. Print. Off.

Engineering and technology

Technical Reports is the medium used to list this material. Published at first as a weekly, with the title *Bibliography of Scientific and Industrial Reports,* it became a monthly in 1948. For each report listed, a description and price are given, and for many there are abstracts. The material in each issue is arranged by large subjects and each item carries a serial number by which it is identified. These numbers are all preceded by the letters PB, and the publications themselves are frequently referred to as PB reports. Subject indexes have been prepared for some of the volumes, but they are not yet current. To use this bibliography requires a great deal of patience, but it is important because of the volume of original research represented. In 1949 the Special Libraries Association published a helpful numerical index to the PB numbers contained in the first ten volumes.

Dictionaries and cyclopedias. Many specialized technical dictionaries are available for radio, electronics, aviation, metallurgy, machine shop and other subjects. A few of the more general dictionaries are mentioned here. It is useful to remember that many textbooks and technical handbooks supply helpful glossaries.

Crispin's *Dictionary of Technical Terms,* as described in its subtitle, contains "definitions of commonly used expressions in aeronautics, architecture, woodworking and building trades, electrical and metal-working trades, printing, chemistry, etc." It includes abbreviations and defines terms in simple non-technical language. *Engineering Terminology* by Brown and Runner stresses engineering rather than trades. There are 372 pages of definitions in one alphabet and several useful supplements, including lists of English-Spanish, Spanish-English, and German-English equivalents.

A separation of cyclopedias from dictionaries of technology is perhaps unnecessary, for the dividing line between the two types is

---

❦ DICTIONARIES AND CYCLOPEDIAS

Crispin, F. S. Dictionary of Technical Terms. 8th ed. Milwaukee, Bruce, 1948. 440p. $3.25.

Brown, V. J., and Runner, D. G. Engineering Terminology. 2d ed. Chicago, Gillette, 1939. 439p.

Brady, G. S. Materials Handbook. 7th ed. N.Y., McGraw-Hill, 1951. 913p. $8.

Jones, F. D. Engineering Encyclopedia. 2d ed. N.Y., Industrial Pr., 1943. 2v. $8.

often very obscure. There are in English no large up-to-date encyclopedias of general engineering. Among smaller cyclopedias Brady's *Materials Handbook* and the *Engineering Encyclopedia* by F. D. Jones may be mentioned. Both are arranged in dictionary form but give more than dictionary definitions. The *Materials Handbook,* which is designed to provide the busy executive with information about materials, lists all kinds of industrial substances from Abrasives to Zirconium. Concise information on each material is given, including its properties, uses, sources and trade names. There is a detailed subject index. The *Engineering Encyclopedia* emphasizes information on mechanical engineering terms and includes definitions and factual data.

Handbooks and manuals. A complete list of useful technical handbooks would require many pages. Two well-known publishers, McGraw-Hill and John Wiley, have an extensive and excellent series of handbooks for almost all branches of engineering. There is much overlapping between the two series, and it is difficult to recommend one title in preference to another. Examples of useful titles published by John Wiley are:

> *Kent's Mechanical Engineer's Handbook.* 12th ed. 1950. 2v.
> *Kidder-Parker Architects' and Builders' Handbook.* 18th ed. 1931.
> Peele, Robert, and Church, J. A. *Mining Engineers' Handbook.* 3d ed. 1941. 2v.
> Pender, Harold, and Del Mar, W. A. *Electrical Engineers' Handbook.* 4th ed. 1950. 2v.

Similar handbooks published by McGraw-Hill are:

> Croft, T. W. *American Electricians' Handbook.* 6th ed. 1948.
> Henney, Keith. *Radio Engineering Handbook.* 4th ed. 1950.
> Marks, L. S. *Mechanical Engineers' Handbook.* 5th ed. 1951.
> Perry, J. H. *Chemical Engineers' Handbook.* 3d ed. 1950.

❦ HANDBOOKS AND MANUALS

Machinery's Handbook for Machine Shop and Drafting Room. 14th ed. N.Y., Industrial Pr., 1949. $7.

Metals Handbook. 1948 ed. Cleveland, American Soc. for Metals, 1948. 1444p. $15.

Tressler, D. K., and others. Marine Products of Commerce. 2d ed. N.Y., Reinhold, 1951.

Engineering and technology

Other publishers also provide excellent handbooks. One that is frequently revised is *Machinery's Handbook for Machine Shop and Drafting Room*. The tables and factual information in this publication are very compact, and are planned for the practical man rather than the theorist. Occasionally a librarian finds himself asked to read tables of tolerances or screw-thread dimensions over the telephone, but fortunately the inquirer usually knows how to interpret the data, and can tell the librarian just where it may be found.

Useful handbooks are often prepared by technical societies, and the authority of those organizations is a guarantee of their accuracy. An important example is the *Metals Handbook* of the American Society for Metals. Articles and tables were prepared by a great number of specialists, whose names add to the prestige of the work. An example of another type of handbook in technical and manufacturing fields is *Marine Products of Commerce* by Tressler. This is a truly encyclopedic publication, covering all aspects of the subject—methods of obtaining salt and bromine from sea water, cultivating pearls, freezing fish, extracting oil from whales. There are extensive bibliographies and an excellent index.

Manuals for the practical man. For the man operating or caring for a machine or practicing a trade a different type of publication is often needed. Operator's manuals for refrigerators, automobiles, radios, etc., are much in demand and many may be obtained free from the manufacturers. Elaborate services such as John F. Rider's *Perpetual Trouble Shooter's Manual* are frequently requested. This is a loose-leaf service, now in many volumes, covering wiring diagrams for all known radio models. Similar works are now appearing for television sets. An old favorite of the automobile repair man is *Dyke's Automobile and Gasoline Engine Encyclopedia,* which appeared in its 21st edition in 1949.

Standards and specifications. Reference librarians in industrial cities become quite familiar with requests for specifications for materials, standards for sizes, and approved methods of testing. Purchasing agents from government and industry set up standards for materials which they require, and in turn the companies must satisfy such demands for the products they sell. The National Bureau of Standards of the Department of Commerce has done much work in this field, and the American Standards Association has promoted cooperation of interested groups in agreement on uniform standards. The American Society for Testing Materials, a large and very active organization, publishes triennially its *Book of A.S.T.M. Standards,* covering ferrous and non-ferrous metals, fuels, soaps, textiles, paper, plastics, rubber and many other materials. These standards are supplemented by tentative standards published annually.[11]

Patents. A brief mention of patents must be made in any discussion of reference materials in science and technology, since the chemist and engineer use patent literature frequently. The United States Patent Office publishes a pamphlet, *General Information Concerning Patents,* which should be available in every library. The weekly *Official Gazette* of the Patent Office, which lists, with brief abstracts, all the patents issued in the United States, is available in many libraries. The annual *Index of Patents,* also issued by the Patent Office, contains an alphabetical list of patentees and a title list of patents, but lacks a real subject list. Patents, both American and foreign, of interest to the chemist, are abstracted in *Chemical Abstracts,* but there is no similar index for other patents, except within the Patent Office itself. A true patent search requires both a knowledge of patent law and of the subject, and should not be attempted by a librarian who lacks such skills.[12]

Biological sciences

The subject fields. The biological sciences deal with life and living matter. They are commonly divided into two main areas, that dealing with plants, or botany, and that concerned with animals, or zoology. As with the physical sciences, the boundary that separates the pure from the applied branches cannot always be precisely defined. Closely related to both botany and zoology are the applied biological sciences of medicine and of agriculture.

Man's interest in biological facts dates from prehistoric time, and much of our knowledge has grown from the observations of natural historians made through centuries of inquiry. Early natural history was largely a composite of personal narratives of explorers, discoveries of backyard zoologists and botanists, and the writings of a few naturalists who sought an orderly classification of plants and animals. The persistent interest of the layman in these subjects is still familiar to every reference librarian.

Questions deal frequently with identification of plants and animals or with their life habits. Many problems are seasonal, and librarians find an aid file a great help with such recurring topics as schedules of

Biological sciences

bird migration and life histories of such spectacular insects as the praying mantis and luna moth.

The natural history museums of the country have done much to encourage amateur interest in the biological sciences, and a local museum may frequently be of considerable help to the reference librarian. The popular publications of such organizations as the American Museum of Natural History and the Smithsonian Institution are invaluable. Professional biologists are usually connected with universities and with government agencies. Many, of course, are actually working with applications of biology in medicine or agriculture. As with the physical sciences, the professional literature is highly specialized. Research publications in the biological sciences are extensive but are not easy for the layman to interpret. Their purchase is therefore customarily limited to large research, reference, and special libraries. General library reference tools in the biological sciences are primarily handbooks for identification and popular expositions of natural wonders.

Bibliographies and indexes. A practical guide to the literature on animal life is the *Guide to the Literature of the Zoological Sciences* by Roger Smith. Its emphasis is on tools for the professional zoologist. For early American publications the *Bibliography of American Natural History,* by Max Meisel, covers the period from 1769 to 1865. This is an annotated work, and though not organized for easy consultation it has a wealth of bibliographical information. The current general abstracting journal is *Biological Abstracts.* It has been published since 1926 and is "a comprehensive abstracting and indexing journal of the world's literature in theoretical and applied biology, exclusive of clinical medicine." Since 1939 it has appeared in nine

---

❦ BIBLIOGRAPHIES AND INDEXES

Smith, R. C. Guide to the Literature of the Zoological Sciences. Rev. ed. Minneapolis, Burgess, 1945. 114p. $2.

Meisel, Max. Bibliography of American Natural History ... 1769-1865. Brooklyn, Premier Pub. Co., 1924-29. 3v. $20.

Biological Abstracts, 1926-   . Philadelphia, Biological Abstracts.

---

[11] For a brief list of other sources of standards and specifications see Jackson, *op. cit.*, p.161.

[12] Useful information on patent searching is found in B. A. Soule, *Library Guide for the Chemist* (N.Y., McGraw-Hill, 1938), p.207-49, and in Jackson, *op. cit.*, p.135-41.

THE SCIENCES—PURE AND APPLIED

sections covering such topics as general biology (section A), animal sciences (section E), and cereals and cereal products (section J). The sections may be subscribed to separately, but there is also a combined edition. Annual author, subject, systematic, and geographical indexes are prepared.

Specialized bibliographies also exist for subject areas within biology. For example, the *Zoological Record,* published annually since 1865, is an exhaustive bibliography of world literature. Even more specialized is the *Index to the Literature of American Economic Entomology.* Other useful current sources are the various agricultural and medical abstracts and indexes.

Dictionaries. The specialized nomenclature of the biologist has developed in response to his need for precision, hence most plants and animals have "official" or scientific names as well as quite different popular names. The general dictionaries are useful, since they include many biological terms and are frequently illustrated. The handbooks and field guides, mentioned later, are also essential. Since much of the work of the biologist is describing plants and animals which he is observing, he must be able to establish their names; and since new species are still being discovered, new names for them must be invented. Two helpful guides to the meaning of biological terms, useful for interpreting existing names and devising new ones, are Jaeger's *Source Book of Biological Names and Terms,* and Woods's *The Naturalist's Lexicon,* "a list of classical Greek and Latin words used, or suitable for use, in biological nomenclature, with abridged English-classical supplement." The *Dictionary of Scientific Terms* by Henderson, already mentioned, emphasizes biological terminology. Other

---

DICTIONARIES

Jaeger, E. C. A Source Book of Biological Names and Terms. 2d ed. Springfield, Ill., C. C Thomas, 1950. 287p. $4.50.

Woods, Robert S. The Naturalist's Lexicon. Pasadena, Calif., Abbey Garden Pr., 1944. 282p. $2.75. Addenda, 1947.

American Joint Committee on Horticultural Nomenclature. Standardized Plant Names. 2d ed. Harrisburg, Pa., J. H. McFarland, 1942. 675p. $10.50.

Rehder, Alfred. Manual of Cultivated Trees and Shrubs Hardy in North America. 2d ed., rev. N.Y., Macmillan, 1940. 996p. $10.50.

Biological sciences

more specialized dictionaries are *Standardized Plant Names,* prepared by the American Joint Committee on Horticultural Nomenclature, which lists both common and approved scientific names for plants and plant products, and Rehder's *Manual of Cultivated Trees and Shrubs Hardy in North America,* which gives brief descriptions under the scientific name and also indexes trees and shrubs by their popular equivalents.

Field books and handbooks. The librarian has a wide variety of guides to plants and animals from which he may choose. Clear illustrations, good indexes to popular as well as scientific names, and a descriptive, non-technical text are criteria for evaluation. The pocket size of many of these field books contributes to the librarian's missing book problem, and manuals of plants are apt to be returned with leaf and flower specimens (even poison ivy) pressed between the pages.

Two recent general handbooks are *Fieldbook of Natural History,* by Palmer, and *The Amateur Naturalist's Handbook* (Little, Brown, 1948), by Brown. Palmer covers a wide variety of natural history topics—astronomy, geology, mineralogy, botany and zoology. There are hundreds of small, clear line drawings, some photographs, and descriptions for identification, and other useful field data. Brown's handbook is really an elementary guide to the "what and how" of nature study rather than a guide for identification.

There are several excellent series of handbooks for the study and identification of plants and animals. *Putnam's Nature Field Books* is a series of established reputation. Such titles as *Field Book of American Wild Flowers,* by F. S. Mathews, *Field Book of Ponds and Streams,* by Morgan, and *Field Book of the Stars,* by Olcott, are examples of the

---

FIELD BOOKS AND HANDBOOKS

Palmer, E. L. Fieldbook of Natural History. N.Y., Whittlesey House, 1949. 664p. $7.

Putnam's Nature Field Books. N.Y., Putnam.

Handbooks of American Natural History. Ithaca, N.Y., Comstock Pub. Co.

Peterson, R. T. A Field Guide to the Birds. 2d ed. Boston, Houghton, Mifflin, 1947. 290p. $3.50.

Gray, Asa. Manual of Botany. 8th centennial ed., largely rewritten and expanded by Merritt Lyndon Fernald. N.Y., American Book Co., 1950. 1632p. $9.50.

variety to be found among the nearly thirty titles in the series, which maintains a high standard of quality both in illustration and in text. Another series, *Handbooks of American Natural History,* was inaugurated more recently, but its publisher, the Comstock Publishing Company of Ithaca, New York, has long been active in biological fields. Included in this series are such titles as *Handbook of Frogs and Toads,* by Wright, and *Handbook of the Mosquitoes of North America,* by Matheson.

The handbooks on birds, animals, fish, butterflies, etc., published by the National Geographic Magazine are also well known, and many others are published jointly under the sponsorship of one of the scientific organizations and a commercial publisher. An outstanding example is Roger Tory Peterson's *Field Guide to the Birds,* sponsored by the National Audubon Society and published by Houghton, Mifflin. For the student and the specialist important reference works are such standard treatises as Gray's *Manual of Botany,* which has been a bible for the botanist for over one hundred years, and the systematic catalogs and indexes of plants and animals, of which many are truly encyclopedic in character. A selection of the important titles is listed in Winchell's *Guide to Reference Books.*

Applied biological sciences

The subject fields. The applied biological sciences include agriculture, gardening, home economics, and medicine. Just as the various branches of engineering derive largely from the application of the principles of the physical sciences to the practical needs of everyday life, so are agriculture and medicine related to the biological sciences. Home economics, which is mentioned briefly, is actually closely related both to physical and to biological science.

Agriculture and gardening. In a city, reference work in agricultural topics deals largely with backyard farming, landscaping, indoor and outdoor gardening, control of pests, and care of pets. In a rural community, the emphasis may be quite different. As in other subjects, there is a distinct division of material into that for specialist or research worker and that for the layman. A wealth of material at all levels is published by the United States Department of Agriculture and the extension agencies and experiment stations of the several states. These make available to the librarian excellent reference material at moderate cost. Garden clubs, pet clubs, growers of specialties, and the various

Applied biological sciences

rural organizations such as Farm Bureau, the Grange, and 4-H Clubs all publish helpful materials and give practical assistance.

Bibliographies and indexes. Much agricultural information appears in bulletins and miscellaneous serial publications as well as in periodicals. Each bulletin usually deals with a single topic. Also, since agriculture is more affected by climate than by political boundaries, foreign publications are often desirable, though many libraries find that their most useful reference materials are those which are quite local in application.

The *Agricultural Index* of H. W. Wilson has been published in the company's usual cumulative pattern since 1916. It is a subject index of wide scope and covers all aspects of agriculture and gardening. Since agricultural extension programs are also concerned with home management, nutrition, consumer information, and a wide variety of other domestic activities, the *Agricultural Index* is of value to the home economist and supplies much practical "how to" information as well. The checklist of materials indexed which appears in each issue may be used as a buying guide.

For listing of new materials published by the Department of Agriculture the *Monthly Catalog, United States Public Documents* must be remembered. The Department also publishes its own *Monthly List of Publications,* distributed free, an annual *List of Available Publications,* arranged by subject, and a detailed subject and author *Index to Publications* which analyzes each publication exhaustively. The *Index* covers the period from 1901 to 1940, and five-year supplements can be expected.

The Department of Agriculture library publishes the exhaustive *Bibliography of Agriculture,* which appears monthly and indexes all published material on agriculture and related fields. It is international in coverage, is arranged in classified order, and has a detailed author and subject index, which is cumulated twice a year. It is now

---

BIBLIOGRAPHIES AND INDEXES

Agricultural Index, 1916-   (monthly). N.Y., H. W. Wilson Co.

U.S. Dept. of Agriculture. Index to Publications ... 1901-25; 1926-30; 1931-35; 1936-40. Washington, Govt. Print. Off., 1932-43. 4v.

——— Library. Bibliography of Agriculture, 1942-   (monthly). Washington, Govt. Print. Off.

regarded as the most important of all bibliographic sources for the specialist in this field. Although its tremendous coverage makes it too elaborate for the small library, it is not so complex that the layman cannot use it.

Dictionaries, encyclopedias and handbooks. The library needs a representative and up-to-date collection of ready-reference publications for the farmer and gardener. In addition to the general titles discussed here, there are numerous handbooks devoted to individual topics, ranging from those on farm animals or house pets to those on tree culture and the raising of African violets.

Liberty Hyde Bailey, famous for his contributions in agriculture and horticulture, has been the editor of many important publications. His *Cyclopedia of American Agriculture* in four volumes (Macmillan, 1907-10) and *Standard Cyclopedia of Horticulture* in six (Macmillan, 1914-17), though old, are still frequently useful. His *Hortus Second* is an extremely helpful dictionary of cultivated plants of North America. It also gives brief information on methods of cultivation and propagation. Another such compilation with wide scope is *Taylor's Encyclopedia of Gardening, Horticulture and Landscape Design,* which includes more practical information than Bailey and covers material not only on plants but also on pest control, soilless gardens, plant hormones and the like. Wilcox' *Modern Farmers' Cyclopedia of Agriculture* is a compact, well-indexed, one-volume handbook for the farmer rather than for the horticulturalist. It includes animal care and feeding, crop management, fruit culture and gardening.

Many questions are asked about the care of pets, for people seem interested in raising everything from earthworms to elephants. A multitude of books and pamphlets are available, of which a recent

---

DICTIONARIES, ENCYCLOPEDIAS AND HANDBOOKS

Bailey, L. H., and Bailey, Zoe. Hortus Second. N.Y., Macmillan, 1941. 778p. $6.

Taylor's Encyclopedia of Gardening, Horticulture, and Landscape Design; ed. by Norman Taylor. Boston, Houghton, Mifflin, 1948. 1225p. $5.

Wilcox, E. V. Modern Farmers' Cyclopedia of Agriculture. 2d ed. N.Y., Judd, 1946. 511p. $4.50.

Davis, H. P. The Modern Dog Encyclopedia. Harrisburg, Pa., Stackpole and Heck, 1949. 626p. $10.

Applied biological sciences

useful example is *The Modern Dog Encyclopedia* by H. P. Davis. Information on over one hundred breeds is given, and there are practical instructions on breeding, care and training. The American Kennel Club breed standards and a brief history of dogs are included.

Yearbooks and maps. The *Yearbook of Agriculture,* which has been published since 1894 by the Department of Agriculture, has, since 1936, become an annual encyclopedia on some aspect of agriculture. Each issue is devoted to one specific subject and many are truly outstanding. For example, the Yearbook for 1941, *Climate and Man,* and that for 1949 on *Trees* should be in any reference collection. Prior to 1936 the statistical information concerning agriculture was included in the Yearbook, but since that time it has been published separately as *Agricultural Statistics.*

Information about the distribution of soils, maps showing climate variations, and the location of principal crops are frequently desired. The *Atlas of American Agriculture,* which was co-operatively prepared by several bureaus of the Department of Agriculture, has excellent general maps. For detailed information on soils, the series of soil survey maps prepared by the same agency is very important. Several hundred have been issued, usually covering one county. Each has a brief description of the soils of the county as well as an extensive soil map in colors. A list of these is to be found in the *List of Available Publications* of the United States Department of Agriculture.

Home economics. Among subjects in the useful arts none is more popular in the library than home economics. Telephone calls come frequently as the result of domestic emergencies—such as stopped-up plumbing or ink on the new carpet—and there is frequent demand for more specialized information such as diet for diabetic children. New recipes, new ideas for remodeling the kitchen are sought continually. Cookbooks and practical manuals on care and repair of the home have already been discussed in Chapter 9. It is wise

---

❦ YEARBOOKS AND MAPS

U.S. Dept. of Agriculture. Yearbook of Agriculture, 1894-   . Washington, Govt. Print. Off.

——— Agricultural Statistics, 1936-   (annual). Washington, Govt. Print. Off.

——— Atlas of American Agriculture. Washington, Govt. Print. Off., 1936. 6v. in 1. $17.

to keep a few standard manuals of this type for reference use only. Tables giving analyses of foods, such as Alice Bradley's *Tables of Food Values* (Manual Arts Pr., 1942), are often needed for quick reference work.

The professional home economist is partly chemist, partly biologist and partly technologist. Her literature like that of the scientist is technical. The bibliographic tools of agriculture, medicine and chemistry all have material applicable to her needs.

Medicine. Medical reference work presents a special problem in most libraries. Much of the published material is extremely technical and expensive and is not suitable for use in the general library. Too often the layman seeks such books in order to try self-medication or diagnosis, or he pesters the librarian, who has no medical qualification, for health advice. The public library must refuse this type of aid and generally reject for purchase books intended for the physician.

Many questions, however, are legitimately asked and answered. Material on general health, child care, nutrition, medical history, state medicine and home nursing should be available. The *Standard Catalog* has well-selected lists in these fields. The Government Printing Office *Price Lists* No. 51, "Health," and No. 71, "The Children's Bureau," include many authoritative publications useful to the layman. The popular magazine *Today's Health* (formerly *Hygeia*), sponsored by the American Medical Association, has frequent reviews and carries occasional lists of recommended books. Some useful manuals on health and first aid have been mentioned in Chapter 9.

Bibliographies and indexes. The *Handbook of Medical Library Practice* edited by Janet Doe for the Medical Library Association (A.L.A., 1943) is an excellent handbook and guide not only for medical libraries but also for anyone needing an introduction to medi-

---

❦ BIBLIOGRAPHIES AND INDEXES

U.S. Army Medical Library. Index-Catalogue of the Library of the Surgeon General's Office. Washington, Govt. Print. Off., 1880-1948. Series 1-3 complete. Series 4 ceased publication with v.10, M-Mez, 1948.

———— Author Catalog, 1949- (annual). Washington, Library of Congress.

Current List of Medical Literature, 1941- (monthly). Washington. Army Medical Library.

Applied biological sciences

cal literature. The Medical Library Association *Bulletin* has supplemented this with frequent useful bibliographies and articles.

Medicine has a series of famous indexes and bibliographies and a tremendous periodical literature. The *Index-Catalogue of the Library of the Surgeon General's Office* was planned as a complete analytical dictionary catalog to the books, pamphlets and periodical articles in the largest medical library in the world. Three series have been completed covering material from 1880 through 1932. Series 4 unfortunately was discontinued in 1950 when it had reached volume 10, M-Mez, chiefly because of its expense and lack of timeliness.

The *Index-Catalogue* is being superseded by two publications which will be less expensive in format and which can be kept more nearly up to date. The *Army Medical Library Catalog*, which will cover books, has appeared annually since 1949 as a supplement to the Library of Congress author and subject catalogs. In 1949 only an author catalog was prepared, but in 1950 and 1951 subject indexes were added. Periodicals and serials are included in the *Current List of Medical Literature*, which now appears monthly, with a cumulated issue in December. Every effort is being made to produce this index as promptly and inexpensively as possible. Each issue is divided into two main sections, the first containing a table of contents arranged alphabetically by title of periodical with each item numbered, the second providing an author and a subject index. The pattern of subject headings has been set up so that IBM coding can be used.

Another important index is the *Quarterly Cumulative Index Medicus*, published by the American Medical Association. It appears quarterly and indexes by author and subject more than 1200 periodicals from all over the world. Like many other indexes, its appearance is often delayed.

Dictionaries and directories. At least one medical dictionary is almost a necessity in any reference collection. The *American Illustrated Medical Dictionary*, edited by Dorland, is frequently revised, and includes not only terms in medicine, nursing, dentistry, pharmacy and other subjects, but also brief medical biographies. Pronunciations are indicated and there are many excellent illustrations. Another excellent title is *Blakiston's New Gould Medical Dictionary*, which has a similar scope but gives definitions in simpler language. A number of useful charts and tables appear in appendixes, including a list of over 600 different phobias!

Libraries should make it an established policy to refer all inquiries about physicians to the local medical society or hospital. However, medical directories have an important place in a library collection. The biennial *American Medical Directory,* a register of legally qualified physicians, also contains information on medical schools, hospitals, libraries, and societies. The *Directory of Medical Specialists* lists certified specialists and gives brief biographical facts about them.

Formularies and pharmacopeias. Handbooks containing lists of medicinal substances with instructions for their preparation, called formularies, and pharmacopeias, which describe approved or standard drugs and chemicals, are important reference books even in nonmedical libraries. The *Pharmacopeia of the United States of America* (14th ed., 1950) is an official work, giving accepted drug standards and including actual methods of testing or assay. It will be referred to often by chemist and pharmacist. The *USP*, as it is commonly cited, is revised frequently and supplemented by other publications for new drugs, such as the annual *New and Non-Official Remedies,* published by the American Medical Association, and the monthly publication *Unlisted Drugs,* issued by the Pharmaceutical Section of the Science-Technology Division, Special Libraries Association.

Reading list

Fussler, H. H. "Characteristics of the Research Literature Used by Chemists and Physicists in the United States," *Library Quarterly,* 1949, v.19, p.19-35, 119-43.
Gray, D. E. "Physics Abstracting," *American Journal of Physics,* October, 1950, v.18, p.417-24.
Henkle, H. H. "The Natural Sciences, Characteristics of the Literature, Problems of Use and Bibliographic Organization in the Field."

❦ DICTIONARIES AND DIRECTORIES

Dorland, W. A. N. American Illustrated Medical Dictionary. 22d ed. Philadelphia, Saunders, 1951.
Blakiston's New Gould Medical Dictionary. Philadelphia, Blakiston, 1949. 1294p. $8.50.
American Medical Directory, 1906- (biennial). Chicago, American Medical Assn.
Directory of Medical Specialists, Holding Certification by American Boards, v.5. Chicago, Marquis, 1951.

Applied biological sciences

In J. H. Shera, *Bibliographic Organization*. Chicago, Univ. of Chicago Pr., 1951. p.140-60.
Jackson, Lucille. "Reference Procedures—Literature Searches." In her *Technical Libraries*. N.Y., Special Libraries Assn., 1951. p.120-43.
Leidecker, K. F. "How To Write a Technical Dictionary," *Library Journal*, August, 1947, v.72, p.1096-97, 1113.
Taylor, K. L. "Special Reference Problems in Science and Technology." In Pierce Butler, *The Reference Function of the Library*. Chicago, Univ. of Chicago Pr., 1943. p.180-201.

chapter 19

THE HUMANITIES

Introduction, Visual arts,

Auditory arts—music, Recreatory arts,

Literature, Philosophy and religion.

Introduction

The subject areas. The area in American higher education called the humanities embraces the subjects of the fine arts, literature, philosophy, and religion. Libraries have always emphasized materials in these fields, and to many people a library persists in the mind as a collection of books of literature. Even though the use of the library for practical information is growing, and demand for utilitarian materials is also increasing, the librarian finds that a steady and important part of his reference work has to do with the humanities, and with the aesthetic and philosophical aspects of literature. He is expected by his patrons to know literature, to understand much of philosophy and religion, and to be an intelligent appreciator of the fine arts, if not a practitioner of one of them.

The area of the fine arts. From the standpoint of reference service and organization many libraries have found it practicable to separate their fine arts collections from the rest of the library, even though they are not otherwise departmentalized. The extreme variations in the form of fine arts materials—which include pictures, folios, sheet music and records, as well as books—the relative expensiveness

Visual arts

of individual items, and the problems of their adequate housing and servicing make some special segregation advantageous. Some libraries not only maintain a fine arts department but also have separate quarters for the music collection, listening aids for those wishing to hear phonograph records, and a piano on which to try out compositions.

The topics usually included under *fine arts* are extremely varied. They comprise not only materials on the aesthetic side of art appreciation but on that of the actual performance of the various arts.[1] In this study of library sources in the field it seems best to divide the material into visual, auditory, and recreatory arts.

Visual arts

Art appreciation and education, including history and theory, and the several visual arts of architecture, painting, sculpture, drawing, design, decoration and photography are considered in this section on the visual arts. Smaller subjects in this area that involve considerable reference effort are antiques, ceramics, color, costume, furniture, insignia, postage stamps, and uniforms.

Questions in the visual arts. Appreciation and performance dominate reference requests in the visual arts. Fact questions, general information and background inquiries are prominent. Common types of reference questions involve identification of masterpieces; reproduction of masterpieces; biography of artists; location of paintings, sculpture, other works of art; pronunciation of artists' names; definition of art terms; and material on costumes. Some representative subjects of questions asked in college, public and school libraries are: Name, address and information about Cleveland's leading art school are needed. Is it true that the "Mona Lisa" was stolen? Does the library have pictures of spirals taken from nature? How are plaster of Paris molds for kewpie dolls made? What are the precise dimensions of the captain's quarters in a Spanish galleon? A reader wants a series of Alma-Tadema's pictures appearing in some periodical. Designs based on geometry are needed. What was the color of the insignia of Eddie Rickenbacker's squadron in World War I? A reader wants to see costumes of South American countries. What were various artists' interpretations of Saint Sebastian's martyrdom?

---

[1] A thought-provoking analysis of the nature of the materials of the fine arts and the contrast with those in the field of chemistry was made by J. I. Wyer in his *Reference Work* (Chicago, A.L.A., 1930), p.141-67.

THE HUMANITIES

General reference sources for the visual arts. Visual materials become steadily more important. Lantern slides, Kodachromes, stereographs, photographs, film strips, films, and facsimiles are but some of the classes of non-book materials. In the general circulation books the Dewey 700-779 classes and biography are continually referred to. Among general reference sources the following should be reviewed for their visual arts potentialities:

1. Dictionaries. Both American unabridged dictionaries are strong in art terms. Roget's *Thesaurus* or Mawson's dictionary version of Roget will provide many synonyms and antonyms for hackneyed adjectives of criticism. For foreign equivalents Mawson's *Dictionary of Foreign Terms* and bilingual foreign-language dictionaries are useful.

2. Encyclopedias. Reproductions of masterpieces in *Collier's, Compton's, World Book,* and other encyclopedias are notable. Identification of artists, masterpieces, and movements, and explanation of technical terms can often be accomplished for the inquirer without going to any other source.

3. Continuations and serials. All the encyclopedia supplements and almanacs summarize recent art developments, as does the *American Yearbook. Life* magazine features reproductions in color from time to time, reprints of which are available separately. *The New Yorker* provides a current guide to art galleries. There are good art sections in *The New York Times, Christian Science Monitor, New York Herald-Tribune,* and other major metropolitan dailies.

4. Handbooks and manuals. Art curiosities abound in the curiosity handbooks. There are many suggestions for interior decoration and design in the *Woman's Home Companion Household Book.* Henley and other formula books give recipes for artists' colors, molding materials, photographic formulas, etc.

5. Directories. All the general biographical tools include famous and notable artists. *Current Biography* frequently features people in the arts.

6. Bibliographies and indexes. Art books, periodicals, pamphlets, bibliographies, and visual materials can be located through the general bibliographies and indexes. The eclectic bibliographies are helpful for readers' advisory service in art appreciation.

7. Audio-visual sources. All but the auditory sources are essentially visual arts tools. Increased use of projected materials—slides, filmstrips, and films—can be expected in future art reference work.

Bibliographies and indexes. The art field has not been well

Visual arts

covered, especially the earlier periods, in bibliographic tools. Since 1929 the *Art Index,* indexing by author and subject some 120 periodicals, museum bulletins and annuals devoted to painting, sculpture, architecture, archaeology, ceramics, graphic arts, crafts, decoration and ornament, industrial design, and landscape architecture, has been the principal current source for bibliography in the field. Book reviews and exhibitions are listed. For earlier bibliography, the biobibliographies found under artists' names in Thieme and Becker's *Allgemeines Lexikon der Bildenden Künstler* are most useful. This work, of equal importance for biographical information, is now complete in 36 volumes, and covers a world-wide selection of artists, both living and dead. Though each volume aims to bring the material on its subject up to date, because the work has been under way since 1911 more recent information is found on artists whose names are near the end of the alphabet.

Continuations and serials. The *American Art Annual,* part one, appearing biennially, serves as a general yearbook, summarizing recent developments, records of art sales, and exhibitions, and as a directory of art organizations, schools, periodicals, and museum publications. The *Annual of Advertising Art* (Longmans, Green) publishes, with no text, reproductions of all advertising material shown at the annual exhibition of the Art Directors Club, New York. It is most useful to commercial artists. Many of the illustrations are in full color.

There are many fine arts periodicals for scholar, artist and layman. *Connoisseur* and *Studio,* both published in England, are beautifully illustrated and contain articles for expert and for layman. In this country the quarterly *Art Bulletin* and the *College Art Journal,* both published by the College Art Association, contain scholarly illustrated articles and book reviews. The *Art Digest* supplies news and general articles, and the *Magazine of Art,* published by the American Federation of Arts and appearing monthly, October through May, covers all

---

❦ BIBLIOGRAPHIES AND INDEXES

Art Index, 1929-   (quarterly). N.Y., Wilson.

Thieme, Ulrich, and Becker, F. Allgemeines Lexikon der Bildenden Künstler. Leipzig, Seemann, 1911-47. 36v. Supplement, 1950.

❦ CONTINUATIONS AND SERIALS

American Art Annual. Washington, American Federation of Arts, 1898- .

THE HUMANITIES

phases of the fine arts in a semipopular manner. *School Arts Magazine* is a mine of information for teachers, particularly in the elementary grades. Among useful periodicals in more specialized fields are *Antiques,* with its many illustrations and valuable cumulated index covering its material in detail from 1922 through 1946, the *American Collector* and *Hobbies,* for the gatherer of art objects of all sorts, and *Design,* specializing in creative design. *Architectural Forum* with its emphasis on public, school and commercial buildings and the many magazines for domestic architecture and design, such as *House Beautiful, American Home,* and *Better Homes and Gardens,* all contain considerable material on the fine arts.

Dictionaries and cyclopedias. Adeline's *Art Dictionary,* though old and unattractive in format, is still a full guide to the terminology of art, architecture, heraldry, and archaeology. It has many small black-and-white illustrations. *Harper's Encyclopedia of Art,* published in 1937, was based on a famous French work by Louis Hourticq. The material is arranged alphabetically, with many illustrations, and the coverage is comprehensive.[2] Runes and Schrickel's *Encyclopedia of the Arts* is also comprehensive in its coverage and is arranged alphabetically under broad topics. The articles are written by a number of experts, are quite uneven in quality, and, unfortunately for an art work, are not illustrated.

Handbooks and manuals. Reinach's *Apollo* is a compact handbook full of valuable information and profusely illustrated with tiny

---

❦ DICTIONARIES AND CYCLOPEDIAS

Adeline, Jules. Art Dictionary; tr. from the French and enl. N.Y., Appleton, 1910. 422p. $3.50.

Hourticq, Louis. Harper's Encyclopedia of Art. N.Y., Harper, 1937. 2v. $30.

Runes, D. D., and Schrickel, H. G., eds. Encyclopedia of the Arts. N.Y., Philosophical Library, 1945. 1064p. $10.

❦ HANDBOOKS AND MANUALS

Reinach, Salomon. Apollo; an Illustrated Manual of the History of Art Throughout the Ages; tr. from the French by Florence Simonds; with 600 illustrations. N.Y., Scribner, 1935. 378p. $3.

Gardner, Helen. Art Through the Ages; an Introduction to Its History and Significance. 3d ed. N.Y., Harcourt, Brace, 1948. 851p. $4.50.

Visual arts

but clear photographs and drawings. It has been revised many times and is well indexed. Gardner's *Art Through the Ages,* planned as a college textbook in art appreciation and history, is also an excellent basic reference handbook, with many illustrations, bibliographies and a glossary of terms. "How-to-paint" manuals such as are exemplified by Getten and Stout's *Painting Materials* (Van Nostrand, 1942) or by Mayer's *Artist's Handbook of Materials and Techniques* (Viking, 1940) may be found in the stack collection.

Directories. Biographical information is sought continually on both contemporary and historical artists. *Who's Who in American Art,* published in alternate years as part two of the *American Art Annual,* covers contemporary American artists, editors, critics and executives. A directory of art materials and a bibliography of recent art publications are included. *Mallett's Index of Artists* has ambitious coverage with brief facts given on over 27,000 workers in every field of art in all times and countries. A supplement adds some 14,000 more names. The reader is referred by symbols to sources of other information—organizations, museums or printed information. Unfortunately, some of these references are vague or inaccurate and are difficult to locate. Thieme and Becker's *Allgemeines Lexikon,* mentioned previously as a bibliographical source, is also extremely useful, and there are many other biographical compilations. Another helpful tool is Kaltenbach's *Dictionary of Pronunciation of Artists' Names,* produced by the Art Institute of Chicago for student use.

American museums, schools and other agencies are listed and described in the *American Art Annual.* Many are publishers of important guides, periodicals, exhibition catalogs, and separate prints. Librarians should become familiar with the names and special interests of such museums as the Metropolitan Museum of Art and the Museum

---

❦ DIRECTORIES

Who's Who in American Art, 1936-37-   . Washington, American Federation of Arts.

Mallett, D. T. Mallett's Index of Artists. N.Y., Bowker, 1935. 493p.

Kaltenbach, G. E. Dictionary of Pronunciation of Artists' Names, with Their Schools and Dates. 2d ed. Chicago, Art Institute, 1938.

---

[2] This work has been reprinted by Garden City Publishing Company under the title *New Standard Encyclopedia of Art.*

THE HUMANITIES

of Modern Art in New York, the Fogg Museum at Harvard, the Boston Museum of Art, and the Art Institute in Chicago. Among art associations the American Federation of Arts and the College Art Association of America are sponsors of many important reference and popular publications.

Paintings, prints and illustrations. Because of recent improvements in color printing, many more books reproducing art masterpieces and many more fine color prints are available than formerly. An extremely detailed index to these is Monro's *Index to Reproductions of American Paintings,* analyzing more than 520 books and 300 exhibition catalogs widely duplicated in libraries. Each illustration is entered under artist's name and title of picture, and many under subject also. *Ars una; species mille,* an encyclopedic history of art in seven volumes, devotes each volume to a different country and is extensively illustrated with reproductions of paintings. Zigrosser's *Book of Fine Prints,* previously published under the title *Six Centuries of Fine Prints,* discusses the development of the graphic arts and presents a fine collection of plates, with an index giving dimension, medium and artist. As aids in location of illustrations, which are sought by artist as well as layman, Jessie Ellis' indexes are important, especially *Nature and Its Applications* (Faxon, 1949), which indexes over 200,000 nature forms shown in illustrations. Others of her titles are *General Index to Illustrations* (Faxon, 1931) and *Travel Through Pictures* (Faxon, 1935).

Costume. The perennial interest in costumes of all countries may

---

❦ PAINTINGS, PRINTS AND ILLUSTRATIONS

Monro, Isabel S., and Monro, K. M. Index to Reproductions of American Paintings. N.Y., Wilson, 1948. 731p. $8.50.

Ars una; species mille; General History of Art. N.Y., Scribner, 1909-28. 7v. in 8.

Zigrosser, Carl. The Book of Fine Prints. N.Y., Crown, 1948. 499p. $5.

❦ COSTUME

Davenport, Millia. The Book of Costume. N.Y., Crown, 1949. 2v. $15.

Planché, J. R. A Cyclopaedia of Costume; or, Dictionary of Dress. London, Chatto, 1876-79. 2v.

Visual arts

be satisfied by Davenport's *Book of Costume,* a chronological survey of dress of all countries through the middle of the nineteenth century, with 300 illustrations, some in color. Planché's *Cyclopaedia of Costume,* with its charming illustrations, is an older encyclopedic work. Leeming's *Costume Book for Parties and Plays* (Stokes, 1938), gives clear black-and-white drawings and brief text, suitable both for younger readers and for mothers wishing simple diagrams to follow in making costumes.

Photography. There are many handbooks and manuals for the photographer, whether professional or amateur, and a steady interest in the topic is shown by library patrons. Most of the books are of the practical or "how to" type, and recommendation of specific titles as those most desirable is difficult. Many are listed in the *Standard Catalog* series and similar tools. Pamphlets published by the leading manufacturers of photographic equipment and materials also serve as useful reference aids. Wall's *Dictionary of Photography and Reference Book for Amateur and Professional Photographers* (Fountain Pr., 1948) fulfills the function of a cyclopedia, is frequently revised, but is British in background. As a yearbook with coverage both of the artistic and technical sides of photography, the *American Annual of Photography* (American Photographic Pub. Co.) presents survey articles, many fine illustrations, and information on new techniques, formulas, and materials, as well as a directory of societies and exhibitions. *International Motion Picture Almanac* (Quigley) performs a comparable service for the moving picture world.

Architecture. Architecture, like photography, has an extremely technical as well as an artistic side. From the technical aspect, Corkhill's *Concise Building Encyclopedia* and the *Kidder-Parker Architects' and Builders' Handbook* (Wiley, 1931) are very valuable. For the person wishing to understand architectural history or to obtain descriptions of famous buildings or of architectural details, Fletcher's

---

❦ ARCHITECTURE

Corkhill, Thomas. A Concise Building Encyclopedia. London, Pitman, 1945. 287p. $3.

Sturgis, Russell. Dictionary of Architecture and Building; Biographical, Historical and Descriptive. N.Y., Macmillan, 1901. 3v.

Hamlin, T. F. Architecture Through the Ages. Rev. ed. N.Y., Putnam, 1944. 680p. $6.

History of Architecture on the Comparative Method (Scribner, 1945) is a basic one-volume work, many times revised, with excellent glossaries, bibliographies and illustrations. An older, still much-referred-to work is Sturgis' *Dictionary of Architecture and Building,* illustrated with numerous engravings. Those wishing a more popular introduction with reference value may find Hamlin's *Architecture Through the Ages* helpful.

Crafts. In the field of general craftsmanship, S. G. Williamson's *The American Craftsman* (Crown, 1940) is a well-illustrated and interesting guide to the works of famous craftsmen in many fields, containing also check lists and bibliographies. Arthur Train's *Story of Every Day Things* (Harper, 1941), though emphasizing American history, describes all types of articles, from Indian canoes and moccasins to the furniture, costumes, and household items of the nineteenth century. Aronson's *Encyclopedia of Furniture* (Crown, 1938), arranged alphabetically, has many short articles and a few longer ones on the principal types of furniture. The book is well illustrated with photographs and line drawings. Bond's *Encyclopedia of Antiques* (Tudor, 1945) contains sections devoted to furniture, pottery, porcelain, glass, textiles, and metals. Bibliographies are included. Books on identification of old silver, glass and porcelain are in continual demand. Litchfield's *Pottery and Porcelain* (Macmillan, 1925) emphasizes the historical background, while Chaffers' *Marks and Monograms on European and Oriental Pottery and Porcelain* (Reeves, 1932) is one of several guides for identification. McKearin's *American Glass* (Crown, 1948) and S. B. Wyler's *The Book of Old Pottery* are other popular examples.

Philately and numismatics. For the stamp collector, Scott's *Standard Postage Stamp Catalog,* published annually in two parts bound as one volume, covers—with illustrations, description, and approximate current value—the stamps of the whole world. It is the bible of the philatelist. The United States Post Office Department publishes a *Description of United States Postage Stamps,* frequently revised, well illustrated and covering all issues. The United States Treasury Department in 1928 published quite a complete *Catalogue of Coins,* unfortunately not illustrated. Among helpful catalogs of coins and currency are several volumes edited and published by Wayte Raymond: *The Annual Standard Catalogue of United States Currency and Tokens; Coins of the World, Nineteenth Century Issues* (1947); and *Coins of the World, Twentieth Century Issues* (1948).

Auditory arts—music

Questions in music. There is considerable request for materials in music reference, especially scores, sheet music and recordings. Identification of musical literature—songs, symphonies, chamber music, popular tunes, and stories of operas—is emphasized in the information questions. Biographies of composers, history of musical trends, and criticisms of works are the subjects of frequent reference questions. Definitions of musical terms like *counterpoint, arpeggio,* and *fugue* are in demand. Earphones and acoustically-treated listening booths are an asset to the use of auditory sources for identification and appreciation of musical masterpieces.

Bibliographies and indexes. The National Association of Schools of Music publishes *A List of Books on Music* with supplements which appear in their *Bulletin.* The sixth supplement for 1948 gives an excellent selected list of materials, primarily titles in print. Another selected bibliography is Gleason and Luper's *A Bibliography of Books on Music and Collections of Music* (Eastman School of Music, 1948). The quarterly magazine *Notes,* the official organ of the Music Library Association, is rich in bibliographic material. Darrell's *Guide to Books on Music and Musicians* is an annotated list of English and selected foreign publications.

Until very recently musical periodicals were not covered in any indexing service, but *The Music Index,* which appeared first in January, 1949, now provides a much-needed index to over 40 music periodicals. The Gramophone Shop *Encyclopedia of Recorded Music* (3d ed., Crown, 1948) serves with its *Record Supplement* (monthly) as an index by composer to phonograph records from all producers. Frank and perceptive reviews are included in the supplement. Sears's *Song Index* and Cushing's *Children's Song Index* analyze songs in many collections by author, composer, title and first line. As a special-

---

❦ BIBLIOGRAPHIES AND INDEXES

Darrell, R. D., comp. Schirmer's Guide to Books on Music and Musicians. N.Y., Schirmer, 1951. 440p.
The Music Index, 1949-   (monthly). Detroit, Information Service.
Sears, Minnie E. Song Index. N.Y., Wilson, 1926. 650p. Supplement, 1934.
Cushing, H. G. Children's Song Index. N.Y., Wilson, 1936. 798p.

ized bibliographical tool, the music section of the *Catalog of Copyright Entries* published by the United States Copyright Office must be remembered.

Continuations and serials. There have been various attempts to provide a yearbook of music. The *Billboard Encyclopedia of Music,* formerly called *Billboard Music Yearbook* and last published in 1947/48, is a combination yearbook and trade directory emphasizing the field of popular music. Articles on musical progress in various fields are accompanied by many lists of performances and much advertising matter. *The Year in American Music,* edited by David Ewen, contains useful chronicles of events, lists of musicians in the news and of performances, and other helpful material.

Music periodicals show a wide variety in type. Now that the *Music Index* is being published, they will probably be found more permanently useful in many libraries. Among those requested by the music teacher are *Etude* and the *Music Educators Journal,* published by Music Educators National Conference. For the serious student of music theory *Musicology* and *Musical Quarterly* are excellent. *Notes,* previously mentioned for its bibliographies, is devoted to music and its literature and contains many reviews of books, records and music. A new publication, *Film Music Notes,* covers a field of much popular interest. Of the more general periodicals, *Musical America,* published sixteen times a year, and *Billboard,* a weekly devoted to all fields of entertainment, including the often-requested popularity ratings of current song hits, are frequently helpful in reference work.

Dictionaries and cyclopedias. A good quick reference work on musical topics, excluding biographical data, is Apel's *Harvard Dictionary of Music,* while an older publication, Baker's *Dictionary of Musical Terms,* gives concise explanation of technical words and phrases, including terms in foreign languages. The *Dictionary of Musical Themes* by Barlow and Morganstern identifies 10,000 or more themes by the use of an ingenious notation index. The first part of the book, arranged by composer and compositions, reproduces the themes. The

---

❦ CONTINUATIONS AND SERIALS

Billboard Encyclopedia of Music, 1946/47-   (annual). N.Y., Billboard Pub. Co.

The Year in American Music, 1946/47-   . N.Y., Allen, Towne and Heath.

Auditory arts—music

notation index follows. The same authors' *Dictionary of Vocal Themes* catalogs some 8000 "basic melodies from all important operas, operettas, oratorios, cantatas, etc., as well as lieder, art songs, and standard compositions for the voice." An index to songs and first lines is included.

The standard musical cyclopedia is *Grove's Dictionary of Music and Musicians,* published in six volumes, of which the last is an American supplement. There are signed articles with excellent bibliographies by international authorities on all aspects of music. A most useful one-volume work is Thompson's *International Cyclopedia of Music and Musicians,* which contains lists of compositions, bibliographies, and opera plots as well as excellent general articles.

Handbooks and manuals. *The Oxford Companion to Music* by Percy A. Scholes is designed for the musician and the layman. It consists primarily of concise articles, including 1500 biographies, but there are some long articles, carefully organized, and abundant cross references make the work self-indexing. A pronouncing glossary at

---

❦ DICTIONARIES AND CYCLOPEDIAS

Apel, Willi. Harvard Dictionary of Music. Cambridge, Harvard Univ. Pr., 1944. 824p. $8.50.

Baker, Theodore. A Dictionary of Musical Terms. N.Y., Schirmer, 1923. 257p. $1.50.

Barlow, Harold, and Morganstern, Sam. A Dictionary of Musical Themes. N.Y., Crown, 1948. 656p. $5.

——— A Dictionary of Vocal Themes. N.Y., Crown, 1950. 547p. $5.

Grove, Sir George, ed. Grove's Dictionary of Music and Musicians. 4th ed. London, Macmillan, 1940. 6v. $65.

Thompson, Oscar. The International Cyclopedia of Music and Musicians. 5th ed., rev. and enl. by Nicolas Slonimsky. N.Y., Dodd, Mead, 1949. 2380p. $16.

❦ HANDBOOKS AND MANUALS

Scholes, P. A. The Oxford Companion to Music. 8th ed. N.Y., Oxford Univ. Pr., 1950. 1228p. $17.50.

McSpadden, J. W. Operas and Musical Comedies. N.Y., Crowell, 1946. 607p. $3.50.

Ewen, David. Encyclopedia of Musical Masterpieces. N.Y., Grossett, 1949. 692p. $2.98.

the end and many illustrations are helpful. One example among a number of similar handbooks is McSpadden's *Operas and Musical Comedies*. A useful handbook for those interested in performances at the Metropolitan Opera House is *Metropolitan Opera Annals* (Wilson, 1947), compiled by W. H. Seltsam, which includes summaries of seasons and casts and titles of each performance from 1883 to February 1, 1947. Some press reviews are also included. Ewen's *Encyclopedia of Musical Masterpieces*, the sixth edition of his *Music for the Millions*, comments on composers and their principal works and features recommendations of recordings.

Directories. There is much reference demand for biographical tools on composers, performers and conductors. David Ewen has written a number of popular biographical guides, such as *American Composers Today* (Wilson, 1949), *Living Musicians, Dictators of the Baton, Twentieth Century Composers* (Crowell, 1937), and *Composers of Yesterday*. The material is in somewhat the style of the biographies in *Current Biography*. Each is illustrated with a photograph and contains lists of works, performances and recordings, and a bibliography. An older work is *Baker's Biographical Dictionary of Musicians,* covering both performers and composers. Pronunciation of names is indicated in many cases and coverage is world wide and of all periods. Such works as *Grove's Dictionary of Music and Musicians* and Thompson's *International Cyclopedia of Music and Musicians* have much biographical information. For current or recent musicians the *ASCAP Biographical Dictionary of Composers, Authors, and Publishers* is an invaluable tool. Included are short sketches

---

✯ DIRECTORIES

Ewen, David. Book of Modern Composers. N.Y., Knopf, 1942. 560p. $6.
——— Composers of Yesterday. N.Y., Wilson, 1937. 488p. $5.
——— Dictators of the Baton. N.Y., Prentice-Hall, 1948. 310p. $4.
——— Living Musicians. N.Y., Wilson, 1940. 390p. $5.
——— Men of Popular Music. Chicago, Ziff-Davis, 1944. 213p. $3.
Baker, Theodore. Baker's Biographical Dictionary of Musicians. 4th ed. N.Y., Schirmer, 1940. 1240p. $6.
ASCAP Biographical Dictionary of Composers, Authors, and Publishers; ed. by Daniel I. McNamara. N.Y., Crowell, 1948. 483p. $5.

of 1890 writers of both music and lyrics, and of over 300 publishers. All biographees are or were members of the American Society of Composers, Authors, and Publishers, one of whose major purposes is to protect the copyrights and performance rights of its members. The publishers estimate that about one listing in six is of a deceased person. There are indexes by birthplace, birthday, and place of residence.

Apart from those already mentioned, many types of associations and agencies of musicians, from labor unions (American Federation of Musicians) to associations devoted to the theory of music (American Musicological Society), are found in the world of music. Among those interested in music education are Music Teachers National Association and the National Association of Schools of Music.

Recreatory arts

The recreatory arts include the dance, indoor games, and outdoor sports. There is a rich popular reference interest in this area. Although the "do-how" questions may outnumber the "know-what" there is an increasing number of both kinds in academic, community and school libraries. Examples of "know-what" questions are: Is Walter Johnson or Christy Mathewson considered the greatest pitcher? Who were the four horsemen of Notre Dame? What is the difference between the T and split-T formations in football? Who are the greatest living ballerinas? What is the Blackwood system of bridge bidding? Examples of "do-how" questions are: How is jai alai played? What is a good book on jiujitsu? How does one perform a pirouette?

General reference sources for the recreatory arts. Terms for all subjects in the recreatory arts are authoritatively defined in the two unabridged American dictionaries. Encyclopedias are generally strong in these subjects—the adult encyclopedias are particularly helpful for historical background and the school encyclopedias in ingenious explanation by word and picture. Identification of games, diagrams of playing fields, and stories of performers and players may also be found in school encyclopedias. Volume 15 of the *Pageant of America* (see Chapter 16) is a history of sports in the United States. Summaries of the past year in sports may be found in the encyclopedia supplements, and comparative statistics in the almanacs. News magazines and newspapers report current happenings and can be used for contemporary accounts of past performances, games and contests. *The New York Times Index* locates events in the athletic world quickly.

THE HUMANITIES

The dance. The dance is a field of general interest and frequent inquiry. Subjects of questions range from information on the latest dance step to a complete history of the ballet. An important list of old and recent materials on all phases of the subject is Magriel's *Bibliography of Dancing,* a classified bibliography with author, subject and analytical index. An *Index to Folk Dances and Singing Games* which analyzes about one hundred collections by title, type and nationality has been compiled at the Minneapolis Public Library. Among periodicals on the dance are *Dance Observer,* which prints semi-technical articles by authorities and reviews important performances, and *Dance Magazine,* also a monthly, which is concerned with ballroom dancing, dance bands, etc. Periodicals are indexed in Belknap's *Guide to Dance Periodicals.* For those wishing instruction in dancing there are a number of manuals. An example is *Popular Ballroom Dances for All* (Barnes & Noble, 1947) by T. E. Parson. For the ballet follower, Beaumont's *Complete Book of Ballets* (Putnam, 1938) is a delightfully illustrated guide to the principal ballets of the nineteenth and twentieth centuries, giving biographical data, lists of characters, and synopses. A supplement was published in 1942. *Collier's Encyclopedia* has an unusually effective article on the ballet for quick reference. *The Dance Encyclopedia,* edited by Anatole Chujoy, gives definitions of dance terms, biographical sketches of people famous in the dance, and history and description of all kinds of dancing in all periods.

Games, sports and athletics. Practical information on how to perform, biographical data on famous athletes, and fact information on records seem to lead the field of questions in the area of games, sports and athletics. Much valuable data, as already mentioned, may be found in general reference tools. Among handbooks in the special field are the annual *Spalding Official Athletic Almanac* and the many

---

☞ THE DANCE

Magriel, P. D. A Bibliography of Dancing. N.Y., Wilson, 1936. 229p. $4.75. 4th Cumulated Supplement, 1941.

Minneapolis Public Library. Index to Folk Dances and Singing Games. Chicago, A.L.A., 1936. 216p. Supplement, 1949.

Belknap, S. Y., comp. Guide to Dance Periodicals, 1948-   (annual). Asheville, N.C., Stephens Press.

Chujoy, Anatole, comp. The Dance Encyclopedia. N.Y., A. S. Barnes, 1949. 546p. $7.50.

Recreatory arts

guides in the *Spalding Athletic Library* series published by the American Sports Publishing Company, which contain official rules for basketball, football and other sports, and instructions for all types of gymnastics and athletic contests. The *Official Handbook* of the Amateur Athletic Union[3] is another annual of importance. Excellent definitions of terms in all sporting fields may be found in Cummings' *Dictionary of Sports.* Appendixes group terms under the game to which they apply and give data on scorekeeping, diagrams of signals used by officials, and tournament rules. Menke's *All-Sports Record Book* covers history, records, rules, and personalities of many sports. Unusual items such as a list of the speeds of birds and animals may be found.

There are numerous manuals and other publications on fishing, hunting, golf, and other outdoor recreational activities. Excellent selections may be found in the *Standard Catalog for Public Libraries* and other general book selection aids. The handbooks published by the Boy Scouts of America and the Girl Scouts are full of recreational suggestions and instructions of interest to younger inquirers. Among general titles on games which need to be on the reference shelves are Bancroft's *Games,* a comprehensive guide to play activities, games, and sports, with an index arranged by age groups, and Wood's *Complete Book of Games* (Garden City, 1948), which includes indoor and outdoor games, many card games, dances, and stunts. There are diagrams, rules, and clear instructions, but though it has a detailed table of contents, it suffers from the lack of an alphabetical index.

Among periodicals for the sportsman and athlete are *Amateur Athlete,* official organ of the Amateur Athletic Union, *Recreation,* that of the National Recreation Association, and *Journal of the American Association for Health, Physical Education and Recreation,* for-

---

❦ GAMES, SPORTS AND ATHLETICS

Cummings, Parke. Dictionary of Sports. N.Y., A. S. Barnes, 1949. 572p. $7.50.

Menke, F. G. All-Sports Record Book. N.Y., A. S. Barnes, 1950. 326p. $5.

Bancroft, J. H. Games. N.Y., Macmillan, 1937. 685p. $7.

[3] Amateur Athletic Union of the U.S., *Official Athletic Rules and Official Handbook,* Spalding's Athletic Library, Group XII, No. 12A (annual; N.Y., American Sports Pub. Co.).

341

THE HUMANITIES

merly called *Journal of Health and Physical Education*. Among popular magazines for the outdoor man is *Field and Stream*.

Instructions for card games are essential in reference collections. *Foster's Complete Hoyle*,[4] which is periodically revised, covers all kinds of indoor games. Handbooks such as Culbertson's *Contract Bridge for Beginners* (Winston, 1943) and the latest rules on canasta are often needed. Many librarians supplement the general manuals with free pamphlet materials from manufacturers of playing equipment, cards, etc.

Literature

The subject field. Reference work in literature requires a fund of information and a wide acquaintance with the subject, but librarians traditionally have a workable store of knowledge in this field. Probably more librarians approach their professional training with a college major or minor in literature than in any other subject area. Certainly library patrons, even in a highly specialized technical library, expect the librarian to help them with requests for information in literary fields.

World literature, English language and literature, and other national languages and literatures are the three broad divisions of literature reference service. Under each of these divisions, literary form—poetry, plays, fiction, essays, speeches, toasts, and anecdotes—is important. Questions cluster about form and about history, criticism, and reviews. There are also questions about characters in fiction and in mythology, about quotations on certain subjects and by certain authors, and about proverbs and inscriptions; and of course there are thousands of requests for reading advice. Examples of specific subjects of questions are: newspaper and periodical editing or writing; poetry writing; selling short stories; speech making; novel with historical figures of Queen Elizabeth's time as characters; fiction on sports, on vocations; sequence of Galsworthy's *Forsyte Saga;* examples of metaphors and similes; origin and meaning of "to drink of the Castalian spring"; Ruskin's and Kipling's opinions on imperialism; list of one-eyed characters in legend and mythology; interesting recipes found in fiction; humanism and contemporary literature; short stories about the American Revolution; influence of Whitman on modern poetry; and word usage among the Appalachian mountaineers.

General reference sources for literature. Needless to say, al-

Literature

most all the types of reference tools already discussed have potential usefulness in the field of literature. Dictionaries—unabridged, abridged, or of special nature—are referred to constantly. Encyclopedias have many biographies and articles on literary criticism and history and may include plots of literary works.

Reports of annual progress, recipients of literary awards, and titles of best sellers may be found in the yearbooks. Particularly good are the surveys in the *Annual Register* and the *American Yearbook*. Authors are conspicuously present in the biographical dictionaries, both current and retrospective.

Among the handbooks, collections of quotations—perhaps the most used of literary reference tools—have already been discussed. The miscellaneous fact books are full of answers to questions on literary curiosities, facts and allusions. Bibliographies and indexing sources locate criticism and have many other uses. The standard book selection aids answer many questions on series, sequels, content, and other subjects.

Bibliographies. A number of useful guides to reference materials in literature have been compiled for graduate students. These will also serve as bibliographic aids for the librarian. An example is Cross's *Bibliographical Guide to English Studies* (Univ. of Chicago Pr., 1947).

The great *Cambridge Bibliography of English Literature* covers to 1900 the materials by and about authors in what was then considered the British Empire. It includes listings both of books and of critical and biographical articles. Two annual bibliographies published in England help to bring the *Cambridge Bibliography* up to

---

❦ BIBLIOGRAPHIES

Cambridge Bibliography of English Literature; ed. by F. W. Bateson. N.Y., Macmillan, 1941. 4v. $37.50.
The Year's Work in English Studies, 1919/20-   ; ed. for the English Association. London, Oxford Univ. Pr.
Modern Humanities Research Association. Annual Bibliography of English Language and Literature, 1920-   . Cambridge, Univ. Pr.
Spiller, R. E., and others. Literary History of the United States. N.Y., Macmillan, 1948. 3v. $20.

---

[4] Robert F. Foster, *Foster's Complete Hoyle; an Encyclopedia of Games* (rev. and enl.; Philadelphia, Lippincott, 1950), 720p., $3.

343

date. *The Year's Work in English Studies* is a critical summary of materials arranged in running paragraph form, published for the English Association. The *Annual Bibliography of English Language and Literature,* a classified bibliography with index published for the Modern Humanities Research Association, has a wider scope and is regarded as essential by American and English scholars. Much delayed by the war, it is not up to date at present.

In this country, a recent important work edited by R. E. Spiller and others, *Literary History of the United States,* has as its third volume detailed bibliographies classified by period, author, and literary type for the whole of United States literary history. Current bibliography is recorded primarily by two publications: a bibliography of American literature appears each year in one issue of *Publications of the Modern Language Association,* cited as *PMLA;* and *American Literature* carries a current bibliography in each of its quarterly issues. This material for the period 1920-1945 was gathered and edited by Lewis Leary in his *Checklist of Articles on American Literature Appearing in Current Periodicals, 1920-1946* (Duke Univ. Pr., 1947).

Bibliographic tools of help in advising on choice of reading are usually studied thoroughly in book selection courses and are not covered in any detail here. Useful guides include *A Guide to Good Reading* by the Committee on College Reading, Graham's *Bookman's Manual, The Booklist, United States Quarterly Book Review, Book Review Digest,* and of course the eclectic bibliographies such as the *Standard Catalog for Public Libraries* and the *Children's Catalog.*

Cyclopedias, handbooks, histories. The series of Oxford Companions described in Chapter 8 are basic handbooks for literature reference. *Annals of English Literature, 1475-1925* (Oxford Univ. Pr., 1935) has a purpose and arrangement similar to the tabular outline in the *Oxford Companion to American Literature* showing year-by-year literary history in one column and social progress in another. Benét's *Reader's Encyclopedia,* also discussed in Chapter 8 as an example of a general handbook, is primarily devoted to literary material. Another useful handbook is the *Columbia Dictionary of Modern European Literature* in which 31 literatures are treated by 239 contributors in articles alphabetically arranged.

The great histories of English and American literature are useful in many aspects of literary reference work. The *Cambridge History of English Literature* and its companion, the *Cambridge History of American Literature,* have very full bibliographies in addition to the text. Spiller's *Literary History of the United States*, listed under bibliographies of literature, is a more recent authoritative work in the field. An older English work is Garnett and Gosse's *English Literature*, still valuable for its autographs, facsimiles and other illustrations, though its text is unreliable.

Compilations of an extensive nature still referred to frequently, though published many years ago, are Moulton's *Library of Literary Criticism of English and American Authors* and the *Warner Library of the World's Best Literature*. Moulton treats each author chronologically, giving brief factual information on each author followed by quotations selected from criticisms both of individual works and of a general nature. Exact references are given. The *Warner Library*, which gives biographical sketches of the world's writers followed by representative excerpts from their works, is still used not only for the selections themselves, but also for criticism, biographies, and synopses of the works included.

Poetry. Reference work in poetry is frequently interesting, sometimes tantalizing or trying. Identification of imperfectly remembered

---

❦ CYCLOPEDIAS, HANDBOOKS, HISTORIES

Columbia Dictionary of Modern European Literature; ed. by Horatio Smith. N.Y., Columbia Univ. Pr., 1947.

Cambridge History of English Literature. Cambridge, Univ. Pr. 1907-27. 15v.

Cambridge History of American Literature. N.Y., Putnam, 1917-21. 4v.

Garnett, Richard, and Gosse, Edmund. English Literature; an Illustrated Record. N.Y., Macmillan, 1923. 4v.

Moulton, C. W. Library of Literary Criticism of English and American Authors. Buffalo, N.Y., Moulton Pub. Co., 1901-05. 8v.

Warner Library of the World's Best Literature. N.Y., Warner Library, 1917. 30v.

❦ POETRY

Granger, Edith. Index to Poetry and Recitations. 3d ed., rev. and enl. Chicago, McClurg, 1940. 1525p. Supplement (1938-44), N.Y., Columbia Univ. Pr., 1945.

Brewton, John. Index to Children's Poetry. N.Y., Wilson, 1942. 965p.

Bruncken, Herbert. Subject Index to Poetry. Chicago, A.L.A., 1940. 220p. $3.25.

THE HUMANITIES

poems may require hours of search. Some librarians have a gift for this work, and staff members so talented should be known by the reference librarian and called on when needed. The principal indexes to poetry require that the searcher know either author, first line, or title. This is true of Granger's *Index to Poetry and Recitations* which covers, with its three editions and supplements, hundreds of anthologies. Special lists of poems for holidays and other occasions are included in appendixes. Brewton's *Index to Children's Poetry* not only indexes 130 collections by title, author, and first line, but also provides a subject index. Bruncken's *Subject Index to Poetry* provides a topical guide to 215 adult anthologies. For approaching many poems by subject or for identifying a poem when the part remembered is not the first line, the handbooks of quotations are invaluable.

Plays and the theater. Wide public interest in the drama results in continual calls on the reference librarian for information in this

---

❦ PLAYS AND THE THEATER

Baker, Blanch M., comp. Dramatic Bibliography. N.Y., Wilson, 1933. 320p.

Dramatic Index, 1909-   (annual). Boston, Faxon.

Mantle, Burns. Best Plays of 1899/1909-   and Yearbook of the Drama in America. Boston, Small, 1920-25; N.Y., Dodd, 1926-   .

International Motion Picture Almanac, 1929-   (annual). N.Y., Quigley.

Firkins, Ina Ten Eyck. Index of Plays, 1800-1926. N.Y., Wilson, 1927. 307p. Supplement (1927-34), 1935.

Ottemiller, J. H. Index to Plays in Collections. N.Y., Wilson, 1943. 130p. $2.50.

Logasa, Hannah, and Ver Nooy, W. Index to One-Act Plays. Boston, Faxon, 1924-50. 4v. $6 ea.

Thomson, Ruth G. Index to Full Length Plays, 1926-1944. Boston, Faxon, 1946. 305p. $4.

Ireland, Norma O. An Index to Monologs and Dialogs. Rev. and enl. ed. Boston, Faxon, 1949. 171p. $4.50.

Sobel, Bernard. The Theatre Handbook and Digest of Plays. Rev. ed. N.Y., Crown, 1948. 897p. $4.

Parker, John. Who's Who in the Theatre. London, Pitman, 1947. 2014p.

Literature

field. Of particular importance in the wealth of reference material available are the bibliographies and indexes, the critical reviews, biographical data, and history. Blanch Baker's *Dramatic Bibliography, an Annotated List of Books on the History and Criticism of the Drama and Stage and on the Allied Arts of the Theatre,* is the basic annotated bibliography, and contains an author and analytical subject index. The *Dramatic Index,* which has appeared annually since 1910, indexes periodical articles on the drama—criticism, individual productions, players and playwrights—and many illustrations of actors and scenes. It is supplemented by a section in the quarterly *Bulletin of Bibliography.* The *New York Times Index* entries under the heading Theatre are useful in locating current reviews.

Several yearbooks are available which analyze the theater output of the year. The annual Burns Mantle *Best Plays* includes condensations of the outstanding successes, information on performances, casts and statistics, and biographical material. Among other annuals are *Theatre World,* edited by Daniel Blum, with annual reviews of plays, players, producers, directors and designers, the *Theatre Annual,* published under the auspices of the Theatre Library Association, interested in research on the theater, and the highly personalized *Theatre Book of the Year* prepared by George Jean Nathan. *Billboard* and *Variety,* typical trade magazines, give weekly summaries and reports. *Theatre Arts Monthly* is a beautifully illustrated magazine with reviews, criticisms and historical articles. A weekly loose-leaf service, the *New York Theatre Critics' Reviews,* which reproduces the actual text of reviews in the New York papers, is a valuable tool for the library able to afford it. In the motion picture field the *International Motion Picture Almanac* gives much data on all aspects of the film industry, as does the *Motion Picture Production Encyclopedia.*

A number of analytical indexes to plays have been compiled. Firkins' *Index of Plays, 1800-1926* and its supplement analyze nearly 8000 plays in English from collections and individual volumes. The author list gives complete bibliographical information and indicates the type of play—comedy, tragedy, etc.—while a title and subject list refers to the author listing. Ottemiller's *Index to Plays in Collections* covers only full-length plays and includes 3844 plays by 890 authors. The collections indexed were published in the period 1900-1942, but of course include many older works. There are editor, author and title lists. Logasa and Ver Nooy's *Index to One-Act Plays* is a boon to the amateur theatrical group wishing lists of plays for certain sizes and

THE HUMANITIES

types of casts, as well as for those wishing to identify a title. Ruth Thomson's *Index to Full Length Plays, 1926-1944* includes author and subject information for 1340 titles. A specialized tool is Ireland's *Index to Monologs and Dialogs.*

Among available cyclopedias and handbooks, Nathan's *Encyclopedia of the Theatre* (Knopf, 1940) is especially valuable for information on the modern theater, though heavily flavored by personal opinion. Bernard Sobel's *Theatre Handbook and Digest of Plays* is helpful for brief information on plots, play construction, biographies, and definitions of theatrical terms. A practical handbook for the producer, Cornberg and Gebauer's *Stage Crew Handbook* (Harper, 1941) is an excellent, well-illustrated guide to the technical processes behind the scenes.

Biographical information about actors and actresses abounds in the biographical sources already described. But one special source of value is the British *Who's Who in the Theatre,* which includes such features as genealogies of theatrical families as well as biographies of actors, actresses, dramatists, composers, critics, managers, scenic artists, and historians of the theater and its people.

Fiction. Outstanding among bibliographies and selective guides to fiction are the indispensable *Fiction Catalog* with its annotations of over 5000 selected novels, entered under author, title and subject, and Baker's *Guide to the Best Fiction.* For aid in finding novels about particular periods of history, Nield's *Guide to the Best Historical Novels and Tales* and Logasa's *Historical Fiction and Other Reading References for Classes in Junior and Senior High Schools* are of value. Lenrow's *Reader's Guide to Prose Fiction* and Van Nostrand's *Subject Index to High School Fiction* are particularly helpful for a subject approach.

Short stories as well as novels require reference work, predominantly bibliographic. The long series of *Best American Short Stories* not only includes each year a selection of outstanding works but also summarizes information on the output of that year. Firkins' *Index to Short Stories* lists the works of over two thousand writers of many countries and indicates collections in which they are available. Eastman's *Index to Fairy Tales, Myths and Legends* is primarily a title index to stories in many collections, with cross references from variant titles to the titles best known.

Information on myths is often requested. *Mythology of All Races,* arranged by race, in contrast to Frazer's *Golden Bough* which is ar-

Literature

ranged by subject, is encyclopedic in nature. One-volume sources are Gayley's *Classic Myths in English Literature and in Art* (Ginn, 1911) and Bulfinch's *Age of Fable,* available in a number of editions. The *Funk and Wagnalls Standard Dictionary of Folklore, Mythology and Legend* is a notable aid.

Essays and speeches. Sutton's *Speech Index* analyzes the contents of 64 collections of speeches. It guides the inquirer to examples of speeches for certain occasions, as well as to authors and subjects.

❦ FICTION

Fiction Catalog; comp. by Dorothy E. Cook and others. N.Y., Wilson, 1942. Supplement, 1942-46; annual supplements, 1947-   .

Baker, E. A., and Packman, J. Guide to the Best Fiction, English and American, Including Translations from Foreign Languages. New and enl. ed. N.Y., Macmillan, 1942. 634p. $10.50.

Nield, Jonathan. Guide to the Best Historical Novels and Tales. 5th ed. N.Y., Macmillan, 1929. 424p.

Logasa, Hannah. Historical Fiction and Other Reading References for Classes in Junior and Senior High Schools. 4th rev. and enl. ed. Philadelphia, McKinley, 1949. 232p. $3.50.

Lenrow, Elbert. Reader's Guide to Prose Fiction. N.Y., Appleton, 1940. 371p. $3.50.

Van Nostrand, Jeanne. Subject Index to High School Fiction. Chicago, A.L.A., 1938. 67p. 75c.

Best American Short Stories of 1915-   and the Yearbook of the American Short Story. Boston, Houghton, Mifflin.

Firkins, Ina. Index to Short Stories. 2d enl. ed. N.Y., Wilson, 1923. 537p. Supplements, 1929 and 1936.

Eastman, Mary H. Index to Fairy Tales, Myths and Legends. Boston, Faxon, 1926. 610p. $6. Supplement, 1937.

Mythology of All Races. Boston, Marshall Jones, 1916-32. 13v.

Frazer, Sir J. G. The Golden Bough; a Study in Magic and Religion. N.Y., Macmillan, 1907-15. 12v.

Funk and Wagnalls Standard Dictionary of Folklore, Mythology and Legend; ed. by Maria Leach. N.Y., Funk & Wagnalls, 1949-51. 2v.

❦ ESSAYS AND SPEECHES

Sutton, Roberta D. Speech Index. N.Y., Wilson, 1935.

THE HUMANITIES

A number of tools already described in the chapter on indexes are useful in locating essays. The *Essay and General Literature Index* and its predecessor the *ALA Index* with their wide coverage are used continually in locating essays by author and subject. The wealth of critical material to be located through these works is of especial importance. Eloise Rue's *Subject Index to Readers* and *Subject Index to Books for Intermediate Grades* make available material otherwise hard to find.

Quotations. Quotation handbooks, discussed in Chapter 8, should be mentioned here again. No library can have too many of them. When the elusive quote is requested, all types of sources must be used. Dictionaries, especially the *Oxford English Dictionary,* concordances to the Bible, Shakespeare, and other authors, indexed collections of authors' works—all may be necessary.

Serials and agencies. All types of periodicals may from time to time be used in literature reference work. The general and "literary" magazines, some of which have been described in Chapter 10, are given constant use. The professional, scholarly journals in the field of language and literature have considerable significance, especially for their bibliographic features and their specialized reviews. *American Literature* and *PMLA* have already been mentioned as important for their bibliographical materials. They also carry many excellent critical articles. *PMLA,* as the official journal of the Modern Language Association of America, also carries reports of its activities, meetings, and research projects. *College English* and *English Journal* are both organs of the National Council of Teachers of English and carry news of that organization as well as articles, results of research, and reviews. Another publication of this type is the *Modern Language Journal* of the National Federation of Modern Language Teachers. Annually this periodical includes an *Annotated Bibliography of Modern Language Methodology.*

Philosophy and religion

The subject area and the field of service. In the series of articles on opportunities in special libraries sponsored by the Special Libraries Association some years ago, Hollis W. Hering of the Missionary Research Library stated that there are some 198 seminary libraries in the United States, seven with collections in excess of 100,000 volumes. There are, besides, departmental libraries in philosophy and religion

Philosophy and religion

in our university and public libraries. A small but interesting part of the general reference collection in smaller libraries includes materials in these fields, and serves a stimulating group of teachers and ministers as well as members of the lay public.

Popular reference subjects in the field are the Bible, missions, churches, comparative religion, symbolism, ethics, great philosophies, philosophers, and religious leaders. Considerable bibliographic search and text analysis is involved.

Sample questions in religion and philosophy are: What missions are located in Allahabad, India? Supply comparative statistics on American Baptist and Methodist Churches. What are the principal tenets of the Jain religion? What is the address of the American Missionary Society? Are there any Greek Orthodox Churches in Tennessee? What are the differences between the "high" and "low" Church of England? What did Hitler borrow from Hegel's philosophy? Material on the life of Gautama Buddha is needed. Where can one read about scholasticism? Is John Dewey considered a great philosopher abroad? Supply a suitable scriptural reading for the anniversary of V-J day. What is the significance of the story of Sodom and Gomorrah? In how many religions is there reference to the Deluge? A Sunday school instructor needs teaching aids. What is the meaning of *existentialism?*

General reference sources in philosophy and religion. The unabridged dictionaries and the general encyclopedias carefully present all religious and philosophical terms and subjects to insure utmost objectivity. As a rule, editorial advisers representing Catholic, Jewish and Protestant faiths pass on all religious material. The yearbooks summarize trends in religion and philosophical thought authoritatively, and the almanacs provide statistics about church memberships. The *Statesman's Yearbook* names the major religions of each nation of the world. Church pages in the daily newspapers and sections and articles on religion in the magazines are sources of current information. Philosophers and religious leaders are well represented in the biographical dictionaries. All general bibliographies and indexes include religion and philosophy. Of the general periodical indexes, the *International Index* seems to have the best coverage, though very few religious journals are included in any general index service.

The Bible. Questions on the Bible are frequent and a representative collection of versions of the Bible, concordances, handbooks and dictionaries is necessary in the reference collection. An excellent discussion of the various versions of the Bible may be found in chapter eight of Graham's *Bookman's Manual*. Copies of at least the following versions should be on hand for reference purposes: King James (Authorized), Douay (Roman Catholic), Jewish, and the American translation by Goodspeed and Smith. A copy of the *Revised Standard Version of the New Testament* and a good parallel edition containing both the King James and the Revised versions will be helpful. Library reference copies need to be firmly bound and clearly printed on good paper.

Concordances which index the actual words of the Bible are essential. Strong's *Exhaustive Concordance of the Bible* is one of the most frequently used, and serves as an index to both the Authorized and the Revised versions, which do not include the Apocrypha. Other well-known concordances are those by Cruden (including the Apocrypha)[5] and *Complete Concordance to the Bible (Douay)*, prepared by Thompson and Stock. Topical or subject guides to Biblical writings are *Harper's Topical Concordance* by Charles R. Joy (Harper, 1940) and Stevenson's *Home Book of Bible Quotations* (Harper, 1949). General quotation books include many Biblical sayings.

James Hastings has edited two works, both called *Dictionary of the Bible*. One, a five-volume work, is a true Biblical encyclopedia, with special articles, bibliographies and maps. The other, in one volume (Scribner, 1909), is a quite independent, useful handbook, not a condensation of the larger work. Among more modern handbooks are Miller's *Encyclopedia of Bible Life,* which is excellent for Sunday school teachers and others wanting concise information on Biblical times and backgrounds, and the *Westminster Historical Atlas*

❦ THE BIBLE

Strong, James. Exhaustive Concordance of the Bible. N.Y., Methodist Book Concern, 1890.

Thompson, N. W., and Stock, Raymond. Complete Concordance to the Bible (Douay). St. Louis, Herder, 1945. 1914p. $10.

Hastings, James. Dictionary of the Bible. N.Y., Scribner, 1898-1904. 5v.

Miller, Madeleine S., and Miller, J. L. Encyclopedia of Bible Life. N.Y., Harper, 1944. 497p. $4.95.

Wright, G. E., and Filson, Floyd. Westminster Historical Atlas of the Bible. Philadelphia, Westminster Pr., 1945. 114p. $4.

of the Bible by G. E. Wright, whose excellent maps and very good explanatory text begin with early archaeological discoveries. Stimpson's *Book about the Bible* (Harper, 1945) is similar in format to his other curiosity books, being arranged in question and answer form, with a good index.

Dictionaries and cyclopedias. Religion has been characterized as the field of the great subject encyclopedias, and several outstanding works in the English language give weight to this claim. For example, both Hastings' *Encyclopaedia of Religion and Ethics* and the *New Schaff-Herzog Encyclopedia of Religious Knowledge* are very comprehensive and rich in bibliographical material. They cover all types of religious and ethical beliefs. A small, one-volume work, *An Encyclopedia of Religion* edited by Vergilius Ferm, is a modern handbook including a wide variety of material. It is especially useful for biographical data on current and obscure persons. The *Catholic Encyclopedia*,[6] the *Jewish Encyclopedia*,[7] and the more recent *Universal Jewish Encyclopedia*[8] cover all aspects of the history and activities of their respective faiths, and are really general encyclopedias with a

---

👉 DICTIONARIES AND CYCLOPEDIAS

Hastings, James, ed. Encyclopaedia of Religion and Ethics. N.Y., Scribner, 1908-27. 12v. and Index.

Schaff, Philip. New Schaff-Herzog Encyclopedia of Religious Knowledge. N.Y., Funk & Wagnalls, 1908-12. 12v. and Index.

Ferm, Vergilius, ed. An Encyclopedia of Religion. N.Y., Philosophical Library, 1945. 844p. $10.

Julian, John. Dictionary of Hymnology. Rev. ed. N.Y., Scribner, 1925. 1768p.

Baldwin, J. M. Dictionary of Philosophy and Psychology. N.Y., Macmillan, 1901-05. 3v. in 4.

---

[5] Alexander Cruden, *Complete Concordance to the Old and New Testament . . . with . . . a Concordance to the Apocrypha* (London, Warne), 719p.

[6] *Catholic Encyclopedia; an International Work of Reference on the Constitution, Doctrine, Discipline and History of the Catholic Church* (N.Y., Catholic Encyclopedia Pr., 1907-22), 17v.

[7] *Jewish Encyclopedia; a Descriptive Record of the History, Religion, Literature, and Customs of the Jewish People from the Earliest Times to the Present Day* (N.Y., Funk & Wagnalls, 1901-06), 12v.

[8] *Universal Jewish Encyclopedia . . . an Authoritative and Popular Presentation of Jews and Judaism Since the Earliest Times* (N.Y., Universal Jewish Encyclopedia, 1939-44), 10v.

religious bias, rather than subject works devoted to the exposition of their beliefs. All are rich in religious subject content, however, and in bibliography.

Encyclopedic in a very special field is Julian's *Dictionary of Hymnology,* giving the origin and history of Christian hymns of all nations and information on their authors and translators.

In the field of philosophy, Baldwin's *Dictionary of Philosophy and Psychology* is still a classic, though badly out of date. A certain amount of useful encyclopedic material on philosophy is found in Hastings' *Encyclopaedia of Religion and Ethics* and in the *Encyclopedia of the Social Sciences.*

Bibliographies and indexes. Religion is sadly lacking in organized bibliographical tools. Though efforts have been made for many years to sponsor a general index to religious periodicals—like the *Catholic Periodical Index* in its special field—they have so far been unsuccessful. The religious encyclopedias have much bibliographical material, but librarians needing to keep up with current periodicals find it necessary to do their own indexing.

In philosophy, the basic retrospective bibliography is volume three of Baldwin's *Dictionary of Philosophy and Psychology.* Issued in two parts and edited by Benjamin Rand, it is comprehensive for books and articles which appeared before 1900. Available for recent years are the *Bibliography of Philosophy, 1933-1936*[9] and *Philosophical Abstracts,* published four times a year since 1939. The *International Index* includes some philosophical journals.

Yearbooks, handbooks and directories. Many religious groups publish yearbooks and directories which may be obtained from the headquarters of the organizations. The *Yearbook of American Churches* is published biennially and gives general information about

---

YEARBOOKS, HANDBOOKS AND DIRECTORIES

Yearbook of American Churches, 1915- . N.Y., Round Table Pr., for Federal Council of the Churches of Christ in America.

U.S. Bureau of the Census. Religious Bodies, 1936. Washington, Govt. Print. Off., 1941. 2v. in 3.

Sacred Books of the East; tr. by various oriental scholars and ed. by F. M. Muller. Oxford, Clarendon Pr., 1879-1910. 50v.

Holweck, F. G. Biographical Dictionary of the Saints. St. Louis, Herder, 1924. 1053p. $10.

Philosophy and religion

the activities of all organized groups. Included are statistics, directory information and lists of publications. The United States Census Bureau for several decades published *Religious Bodies,* a statistical and factual summary about all such organizations in the United States. The latest edition is that of 1936.

Handbook compilations on comparative religion are frequently found on reference shelves. *Sacred Books of the East,* edited by F. M. Muller, is a documentary handbook containing translations of the most important books of seven non-Christian religions. Ferm's *Religion in the Twentieth Century* (Philosophical Library, 1948) contains descriptions of 27 religious faiths as presented by adherents. *One God,* by Florence Mary Fitch (Lathrop, 1944), is an excellent illustrated introduction to the Jewish, Catholic and Protestant faiths, written for children but also useful for adults. Still another handbook is Hume's *World's Living Religions* (Scribner, 1924) containing concise surveys of religious groups which have existed for at least a century and which are active today. Much tabular material is included.

Biographical material may be found in many of the encyclopedic works. For a helpful list see "Biography—Religion" in Hirshberg's *Subject Guide to Reference Books.* For current material, directories of various churches are available. A comprehensive, much-used, one-volume biographical dictionary of the saints of all Christian churches is Holweck's *Biographical Dictionary of the Saints. Religious Leaders of America*[10] includes some 7500 biographies of living clergymen. A current reference work in philosophy is Runes's *Who's Who in Philosophy* (Philosophical Library, 1942).

Serials and agencies. Many individual sects publish their own periodicals, which are often simply news bulletins. Of those offering more general coverage, *Christian Century* is a Protestant non-sectarian weekly; *Commonweal,* also weekly, is a popular Catholic periodical not only presenting religious news but also showing much interest in international affairs. *Commentary,* published by the American Jewish Committee, presents international ethical and some religious material from the Jewish point of view. *Religious Education,* the official organ of the Religious Education Association, is also generally useful.

Most philosophical periodicals are primarily for the specialist.

---

[9] *Bibliography of Philosophy, 1933-36* (N.Y., Journal of Philosophy, 1934-37), 4v., $1 each. These bibliographies are reprinted from the *Journal of Philosophy.*

[10] *Religious Leaders of America,* v.2, 1941-43, ed. by J. C. Schwarz (N.Y., The Author, 1941), 1147p., $12.50.

Two well-known titles are the *Journal of Philosophy,* a fortnightly with articles, book reviews, notes and discussions, and *Philosophical Review,* the official journal of the American Philosophical Association which appears bimonthly and includes excellent articles and reviews.

The professional organization of philosophers in this country is the American Philosophical Association, which promotes study and teaching of philosophy in all its branches.[11] Most religious societies of a scope wider than a single religious faith are co-operative organizations rather than professional organizations promoting research. They publish informational material, bulletins, and sometimes statistics. Examples are the Federal Council of Churches of Christ in America, made up of Protestant and Eastern Orthodox communions, the National Conference of Christians and Jews, and the World Council of Churches, the official co-operative organization of 150 denominations in over 40 countries.

Reading list

Graham, Bessie. *Bookman's Manual.* N.Y., Bowker, 1948. p.143-65, 166-91.

Gwynn, S. E. "Special Reference Problems in Art and Music." In Pierce Butler, *Reference Function of the Library.* Chicago, Univ. of Chicago Pr., 1943. p.124-43.

Hering, H. W. "Religious Libraries," *Special Libraries,* December, 1935, v.26, p.294-98.

Hutchins, Margaret. *Introduction to Reference Work.* Chicago, A.L.A., 1944. p.48-55.

"The Library's Picture Collection," *Subscription Books Bulletin,* October, 1946, v.17, p.41-69.

---

[11] The American Philosophical Society, the oldest learned society in America, is, in spite of its name, primarily a scientific society.

INDEX

Italicized page numbers indicate the location of complete bibliographical information for the title listed.

A.C.L.S. *Newsletter,* 132
A.L.A. *Bulletin,* 245, 246
A.L.A. *Catalog,* 198
A.L.A. *Cataloging Rules,* 16
A.L.A. *Glossary of Library Terms,* 2, 18, 89, 127, 137, 192-93, 247
A.L.A. *Index,* 176, 177, 350
A.L.A. *Portrait Index,* 230
A.S.T.M. *Standards,* 313-14
Abbreviations, 49-50; used in footnotes, 16
Abbrevs, 49, 50
Abridged Readers' Guide, 184, 186
Abstract of the Census, 146-47
Abstracts, 174, 240-41
Academia Española, *Diccionario de la lengua española,* 54
Académie Française, *Dictionnaire de l'Académie Française,* 54
Accountants' Index, 276, 277
Acquisitions, 1
Adams, *Atlas of American History,* 257, 258
Adeline, *Art Dictionary,* 330
Advanced Atlas of Modern Geography, 120, 121
Advertising, 278
Age of Fable, 349
Agricultural Index, 319
Agricultural Statistics, 321
Agriculture, 318-21
Aids to Geographical Research, 119, 260
Album of American History, 258, 259

Alexander, *How to Locate Educational Information,* 283, 284
All-Sports Record Book, 341
Allen, *Dictionary of Abbreviations,* 49, 50
Allgemeines Lexikon der Bildenen Künstler, 329, 331
Allusions, 140-44
Almanach de Gotha, 265
Almanacs, 92-94
Alterslund, B., 138
Amateur Athletic Union, *Official Athletic Rules and Official Handbook,* 341
Amateur Naturalist's Handbook, 317
American Annual of Photography, 333
American Art Annual, 329, 331
American Association for the Advancement of Science, 300
American Automobile Association, 124
American Bibliography, 200, 201
American Book of Days, 142, 143
American Book-Prices Current, 201, 202
American Business Directories, 279
American Catalogue of Books, 201
American College Dictionary, 42, 43
American Council of Learned Societies, 131-32; *A.C.L.S. Newsletter,* 132
American Council on Education, *American Junior Colleges,* 288; *American Universities and Colleges,* 133, 134, 288
American Craftsman, 334

357

Index

American Dialect Dictionary, 50, 51
American Educator Encyclopedia, 78, 84, 92
American Electricians' Handbook, 312
American English, 40
American Ephemeris, 89, 308
American Federation of Arts, 332
American Genealogical Index, 265
American Glass, 334
American Guide Series, 118, 119
American Historical Association, 253
American Historical Review, 255
American Illustrated Medical Dictionary, 323, 324
American Imprints Inventory, 202
American Institute of Accounts, *Accountants' Index*, 276, 277
American Joint Committee on Horticultural Nomenclature, *Standardized Plant Names*, 316, 317
American Junior Colleges, 288
American Library Association, 2, 224, 253; *A.L.A. Bulletin*, 245, 246; *A.L.A. Catalog*, 198; *A.L.A. Cataloging Rules*, 16; *A.L.A. Glossary of Library Terms*, 2, 18, 89, 127, 137, 192-93, 247; *A.L.A. Index*, 176, 177, 350; *A.L.A. Portrait Index*, 230; *Booklist*, 21, 194, 195; *Classification and Pay Plans*, 3; *Descriptive List of Professional and Non-Professional Duties in Libraries*, 4; *Local Indexes in American Libraries*, 176; *Periodicals for Small and Medium-Sized Libraries*, 164; *Subscription Books Bulletin*, 20, 21, 62-63, 66, 87, 97, 110, 125
American Library Directory, 247, 248
American Management Association, *Handbook of Business Administration*, 281
American Medical Association, 324
American Medical Directory, 324
American Men of Science, 108, 299, 300
American Nation, 258
American Newspapers, 164
American Notes and Queries, 138, 141
American Oxford Atlas, 122
American Peoples Encyclopedia, 76, 77
American Political Science Review, 274
American Practical Navigator, 308
American Pronouncing Dictionary of Troublesome Words, 51, 52
American Red Cross, *First Aid Textbook*, 156
American Society for Testing Materials, *Book of A.S.T.M. Standards*, 313-14
American Society of Composers, Authors and Publishers, *ASCAP Biographical Dictionary*, 338, 339
American Standards Association, 313
American State Papers, 216
American Thesaurus of Slang, 50, 51
American Universities and Colleges, 133, *134*, 288
American Yearbook, 95, 96, 127, 292
Americana Annual, 90
Americana Encyclopedia, 61, 70, 72-74
Americanisms, 51
America's Needs and Resources, 145-46
Ames, J. G., 210; *Comprehensive Index to the Publications of the United States Government*, 220, 221
Anniversaries and Holidays, 143
Annual Bibliography of English Language and Literature, 343, 344
Annual Library Index, 179, 181-83
Annual Literary Index, 179, 181-82
Annual of Advertising Art, 329
Annual Register, 96, 252
Annual Standard Catalogue of United States Currency and Tokens, 334
Annuals, 88
Anthologies, indexes, 345-47
Anthropology, 270
Antiques, 334
Apel, *Harvard Dictionary of Music*, 336, 337
Apollo, 330, 331
Appel, *Bibliographical Citation in the Social Sciences*, 16
Appleton's New English-Spanish Spanish-English Dictionary, 54
Applied science, 308-14
Architecture, 333-34
Architecture Through the Ages, 333, 334
Army Medical Library Catalogue, 323
Aronson, *Encyclopedia of Furniture*, 334
Ars Una, 332
Art, 326-32
Art Dictionary, 330
Art Index, 329
Art Through the Ages, 330, 331
Artist's Handbook of Materials and Techniques, 331
ASCAP Biographical Dictionary of Composers, Authors, and Publishers, 338, 339
Astronomy, 302
Athletics, 339-42
Atlantic Monthly, 170
Atlas of American Agriculture, 321
Atlas of American History, 257, 258
Atlas of the Historical Geography of the United States, 257, 258

Index

Atlases, 112, 120-22; evaluation, 113
Audio-Visual School Library Service, 235
Audio-visual sources, 4, 226-35
Auditory arts, 335-39
Automobile Encyclopedia, 313
Ayer, *Directory of Newspapers and Periodicals,* 162, 163

Babson's Statistical Service, 278
Baedeker Guide Books, 118
Bagley, *Facts and How To Find Them,* 20, 21
Bailey, L. H., *Cyclopedia of American Agriculture,* 320; *Hortus Second,* 320
Bailey, N., *Universal Etymological Dictionary,* 25
Baird's Manual of American College Fraternities, 288, 289
Baitsell, *Science in Progress,* 299
Baker, B., *Dramatic Bibliography,* 346, 347
Baker, E., *Guide to the Best Fiction,* 348, 349
Baker, T., *Dictionary of Musical Terms,* 336, 337
Baker's Biographical Dictionary of Musicians, 338
Baldwin, *Dictionary of Philosophy and Psychology,* 353, 354
Bancroft, *Games,* 341
Barlow, *Dictionary of Musical Themes,* 336, 337; *Dictionary of Vocal Themes,* 337
Bartholomew, *Advanced Atlas of Modern Geography,* 120, 121
Bartlett, *Familiar Quotations,* 142, 143
Barton, M., *Reference Books,* 20
Barton, S., *Guide to the Constellations,* 306, 307
Basic Book Collection for Elementary Grades, 196, 197
Basic Book Collection for High Schools, 196, 197
Basic List of Current Municipal Documents, 222, 223
Basic Reference Forms, 17
Bayle, Pierre, 58-59
Beadnell, *Dictionary of Scientific Terms,* 297, 298
Beaumont, *Complete Book of Ballets,* 340
Becker, *Allgemeines Lexikon der Bildenen Künstler,* 329, 331
Beers, *Bibliographies in American History,* 253, 254
Beilstein, *Handbuch der Organischen Chemie,* 306

Belknap, *Guide to Dance Periodicals,* 340
Bender, *NBC Handbook of Pronunciation,* 51, 52
Bénét, *Reader's Encyclopedia,* 140
Bennett, *Chemical Formulary,* 306, 307
Berrey, *American Thesaurus of Slang,* 50, 51
Berry, *Handbook of Meteorology,* 307
Best American Short Stories, 348, 349
Best Books, 194, 196
Best Plays, 346, 347
Besterman, *World Bibliography of Bibliographies,* 206, 296
Better Homes and Gardens, 153; *Cook Book,* 152; *Garden Book,* 154
Betty Crocker's Picture Cook Book, 152
Bible, 351-53; concordances, 352
Biblio, 203
Bibliographer's Manual of English Literature, 203
Bibliographic form, 12-17
Bibliographic guides, subject, 239-40
Bibliographic Index, 206, 296
Bibliographical Citation in the Social Sciences, 16
Bibliographical Guide to English Studies, 343
Bibliographical Services, 199
Bibliographies, 190-206; arrangement, 14; bibliographies of, 206, 240; eclectic, 194-99; evaluation, 193; foreign national, 202-04; subject, 239-40; U. S. national, 198-202; universal, 204-06
Bibliographies in American History, 253, 254
Bibliography, 11, 12, 14; definition, 192
Bibliography and Footnotes, 16.
Bibliography of Agriculture, 319, 320
Bibliography of American Natural History, 315
Bibliography of Best References for the Study of Geography, 260
Bibliography of Dancing, 340
Bibliography of Historical Writings Published in Great Britain and the Empire, 1940-1945, 254
Bibliography of Library Economy, 244, 245
Bibliography of North American Geology, 303
Bibliography of Philosophy, 1933-36, 354
Bibliography of Technical Reports, 310, 311
Bibliography of the Negro in Africa and America, 271, 272

359

Index

Bibliotheca Americana, 200, 201
Bibliotheca Britannica, 203
Bibliothèque Nationale, *Catalogue général des livres imprimés*, 204, 205
Bibliotherapy, 10-11
Biennial Survey of Education, 287, 288
Billboard Encyclopedia of Music, 336
Biographical dictionaries, 98-110; current, 106-08; retrospective, 102-05; universal, 101-02
Biographical Dictionary of the Saints, 354, 355
Biographical directories, 108
Biographical sources, 99-101; evaluation, 100-01; indexes, 108-09; types, 99-100, 261-63
Biography, *see* entries beginning Biographical
Biography in Collections, 109
Biography Index, 109
Biological Abstracts, 315, 316
Biological sciences, 314-24
Birds, 317-18
Blakiston's New Gould Medical Dictionary, 323, 324
Blue Book of 16 mm Films, 232
Blum, *Theatre World*, 347
Bogue, *American Junior Colleges*, 288
Bol'shaia sovetskaia entsiklopediia, 85, 86
Bolton's American Armory, 265
Bond, *Encyclopedia of Antiques*, 334
Book of Costume, 332, 333
Book of Fine Prints, 332
Book of Knowledge, 61, 84, 85
Book of Knowledge Annual, 91, 92
Book of Modern Composers, 338
Book of Old Pottery, 334
Book of the States, 223, 275
Book Review Digest, 194, 195, 293
Booklist, 21, 194, 195
Bookman's Manual, 194, 195-96, 352
Boston Cooking-School Cook-Book, 152
Botany, 314-18
Boutell's Manual of Heraldry, 265
Bowditch, *American Practical Navigator*, 308
Bowker, *List of American Learned Journals*, 132
Boyd, *United States Government Publications*, 211
Bradford, *Documentation*, 192
Bradley, *Tables of Food Values*, 322
Brady, *Materials Handbook*, 311, 312
Bread and Butter, 156
Breul, *Heath's New German-English, English-German Dictionary*, 54
Brewer, *Historic Notebook*, 257

Brewton, *Index to Children's Poetry*, 345, 346
Brief Facts, 138, 139
Britannica Book of the Year, 72, 90, 91
Britannica Encyclopaedia, 57, 61, 69-72, 70, 122, 177
Britannica Junior, 78, 83
British Museum, *General Catalogue of Printed Books*, 204, 205
British National Bibliography, 202, 203
Brockhaus' Konversations-Lexikon, 85, 86
Brown, *Amateur Naturalist's Handbook*, 317
Brown, E. F., *War in Maps*, 258
Brown, E. S., *Manual of Government Publications*, 211, 224
Brown, S. M., *Business Executive's Handbook*, 282
Brown, V. J., *Engineering Terminology*, 311
Bruncken, *Subject Index to Poetry*, 345, 346
Brunet, *Manuel du Libraire*, 204
Bulfinch, *Age of Fable*, 349
Burchfield, *Student's Guide to Materials in Political Science*, 273
Burke, *How to Locate Educational Information*, 283, 284
Buros, *Mental Measurements Yearbook*, 284
Business, 276-82
Business Directories, 134, 135, 279
Business Executive's Handbook, 282
Business Literature, 277
Business ratings, 277-78
Business services, 277-78
Butler, *Reference Function of the Library*, 20, 21, 248

Calendar handbooks, 143
Cambridge Ancient History, 259
Cambridge Bibliography of English Literature, 343
Cambridge History of American Literature, 344, 345
Cambridge History of English Literature, 344, 345
Cambridge History of the British Empire, 259
Cambridge Mediaeval History, 259
Cambridge Modern History, 259
Cannons, *Bibliography of Library Economy*, 244, 245; *Classified Guide to 1700 Annuals*, 89
Card games, 342
Card records, 15
Carnegie Endowment for International

Index

Peace, *Handbook of International Organizations in the Americas,* 128, 129
Carpenter, Helen, 7, 56
Carskadon, *U. S. A.: Measure of a Nation,* 145, 146
Catalog of Books Represented by Library of Congress Printed Cards, 204, 205
Catalog of Copyright Entries, 336
Catalog of the Public Documents of the 53d to 76th Congress, 220, 221
Cataloger and reference, 1-2
Cataloging Rules for Author and Title Entries, 16
Catalogue général de la librairie française, 203-04
Catalogue général des livres imprimés, 204, 205
Catalogue of Coins, 334
Catalogue of Scientific Papers, 294
Catholic Encyclopedia, 353
Catholic Periodical Index, 354
Cawdrey, Robert, 25
Caxton, William, 58
Census, U. S., 146-47
Century Dictionary and Cyclopedia, 32, 40, 102
Ceramics, 334
Certain, *Handbook of English for Boys and Girls,* 48
Chaffer, *Marks and Monograms on European and Oriental Pottery and Porcelain,* 334
Chambers, Ephraim, *Cyclopaedia,* 59
Chambers's Biographical Dictionary, 101, 102
Chambers's Encyclopaedia, 85
Chambers's Technical Dictionary, 297, 298
Champion, *Racial Proverbs,* 143
Checklist of Basic Municipal Documents, 222, 223
Checklist of United States Public Documents, 220, 222
Chemical Abstracts, 295, 296, 300, 304; *List of Periodicals Abstracted,* 296, 297
Chemical Engineers' Handbook, 312
Chemical Formulary, 306, 307
Chemical Rubber Co., *Handbook of Chemistry and Physics,* 306, 307
Chemistry, 302
Chicago. University. *Manual of Style,* 12, 16
Children's Book of the Year, 92
Children's Catalog, 196, 197
Children's Song Index, 335
Childs, *Government Document Bibliography in the United States and Elsewhere,* 223, 224
Christian Science Monitor, 164, 166
Chronicles of America, 258, 259
Chujoy, *Dance Encyclopedia,* 340
Church, *Mining Engineers' Handbook,* 312
Circle of the Sciences, 61
Circulation, 1-2
Citations, 14-15
City directories, 109-10
Classic Myths, 349
Classification and Pay Plans (A.L.A.), 2
Classified List of Periodicals for the College Library, 164
Clayton, *World Weather Records,* 308
Clippings, 229
Code of Federal Regulations, 218, 219
Coins, 334
Coins of the World, Nineteenth Century Issues, 334; *Twentieth Century Issues,* 334
Cokayne, *Complete Peerage,* 265
Colby, *American Pronouncing Dictionary of Troublesome Words,* 51, 52
Cole, Dorothy, 6, 7, 8
Collation, 14
College and Research Libraries, 162, 246
Collier's, 169
Collier's Encyclopedia, 70, 74-75, 121
Collier's Yearbook, 90, 91
Columbia Dictionary of Modern European Literature, 344, 345
Columbia Encyclopedia, 77
Coman, *Sources of Business Information,* 276
Comenius, *Orbis Pictus,* 79
Commager, *Documents of American History,* 148
Commerce Yearbook, 281
Commodity Yearbook, 280, 281
Compendium of American Genealogy, 265
Complete Book of Ballets, 340
Complete Book of Games, 341
Complete Concordance to the Bible (Douay), 352
Complete Concordance to the Old and New Testament (Cruden), 352
Complete Peerage, 265
Complete Pronouncing Gazetteer (Lippincott), 116, 117
Complete Rhyming Dictionary and Poet's Craft Book, 52
Composers of Yesterday, 338
Comprehensive Index to the Publications of the United States Government, 220, 221

361

Index

Compton, F. E., 79, 86
Compton Fact-Index, 80, 122
Compton's Pictured Encyclopedia, 78, 79-81, 92
Concise Building Encyclopedia, 333
Concise Dictionary from the Beginnings to 1921 (D.N.B.), 102, 105
Concordances, 352
Condensed Chemical Dictionary, 305
Congressional Directory, 211, 212
Congressional Quarterly, 212, 216
Congressional Record, 212, 213, 214
Conner, Martha, 5
Conover, *Manual for Bibliographers in the Library of Congress,* 17
Consumers' Guide, 155
Consumers' Research, 155; *Bulletin,* 155
Consumers Union, 155; *Bread and Butter,* 156; *Buying Guide,* 155; *Consumer Reports,* 155
Continuous revision, 69, 86
Contract Bridge for Beginners, 342
Cookbooks, 151-52
Corey, *McCall's Complete Book of Dressmaking,* 154
Corkhill, *Concise Building Encyclopedia,* 333
Cornberg, *Stage Crew Handbook,* 348
Correspondence, 157
Costume, 332-33
Costume Book, 333
Coulter, *Historical Bibliographies,* 253, 254
Courtis-Watters Illustrated Golden Dictionary for Young Readers, 46
Cowley, *Use of Reference Materials,* 20, 21
Crafts, 334
Craigie, *A Dictionary of American English,* 32, 40
Cram, G. F., & Co., 123
Crispin, *Dictionary of Technical Terms,* 311
Crobaugh, *Handbook of Insurance,* 280, 281
Croft, *American Electricians' Handbook,* 312
Cross, *Bibliographical Guide to English Studies,* 343
Crowell's Dictionary of Business and Finance, 282
Cruden, *Complete Concordance to the Old and New Testament,* 352
Culbertson, *Contract Bridge for Beginners,* 342
Cummings, *Dictionary of Sports,* 341
Cumulation, 186
Cumulative Book Index, 199, 293

Currency, 334
Current Abbreviations, 49, 50
Current Biographical Reference Service, 106, 107
Current Biography, 106, 107-08
Current History, 255
Current List of Medical Literature, 322, 323
Current National Bibliographies, 204
Current Reference Books, 21, 138
Cushing, *Children's Song Index,* 335
Cuyas, *Appleton's New English-Spanish Spanish-English Dictionary,* 54
Cyclopaedia of Costume, 332, 333
Cyclopedia of Education, 286, 287

D.A.B. (*Dictionary of American Biography*), 102, 103-04
Dallas News Almanac, 94
Dalton, *Sources of Engineering Information,* 309, 310
Dana, *System of Mineralogy,* 307
Dana, J. C., *Picture Collection,* 229
Dance, 340
Dance Encyclopedia, 340
Darrell, *Schirmer's Guide to Books on Music and Musicians,* 335
Darsie, Helen, 7
Dartmouth College, *Reading List on Business Administration,* 277
Davenport, *Book of Costume,* 332, 333
Davis, H. P., *Modern Dog Encyclopedia,* 320, 321
Davis, M. V., *Guide to American Business Directories,* 279
Decimal Classification and Relative Index, 247, 248
DeFord, *Who Was When,* 101, 102
Del Mar, *Electrical Engineers' Handbook,* 312
Denoyer-Geppert, 123-24, 230
Depository libraries, 210
Descriptive Catalogue of the Government Publications of the United States (Poore), 219, 220
Deutsches Wörterbuch, 27, 54
De Vries, *French-English Science Dictionary,* 297, 298; *German-English Science Dictionary,* 297, 298; *German-English Technical and Engineering Dictionary,* 297, 298
Dewey, Melvil, *Decimal Classification and Relative Index,* 247, 248
Dewhurst, *America's Needs and Resources,* 145-46
Diccionario de la lengua española, 54
Dictators of the Baton, 338

Index

Dictionaries, 23-55; abridged, 41-47; authority, 28-29; bilingual, 53-54; classes, 24; college, 42-44; evaluation, 27-31; foreign language, 53-55; format, 29; high school, 44-45; history, 25-27; intermediate, 45-46; picture, 46-47; polylingual, 53; primary, 46-47; reviews, 31; scope, 27-28; unabridged, 31-40; word treatment, 29-30
Dictionary of Abbreviations, 49, 50
Dictionary of American Biography, 102, 103-04
Dictionary of American English, 32, 40
Dictionary of American History, 256, 258, 259
Dictionary of Americanisms, 50, 51
Dictionary of Anonymous and Pseudonymous English Literature, 205
Dictionary of Architecture and Building, 333, 334
Dictionary of Books Relating to America, 200, 201
Dictionary of Dates, 144, 256, 257
Dictionary of Education, 286
Dictionary of Foreign Terms Found in English and American Writings, 52, 53
Dictionary of Geological Terms, 306
Dictionary of Hymnology, 353, 354
Dictionary of Modern American Usage, 48
Dictionary of Modern Economics, 280, 282
Dictionary of Modern English Usage, 48
Dictionary of Music, 337
Dictionary of Musical Terms, 336, 337
Dictionary of Musical Themes, 336, 337
Dictionary of National Biography, 102, 104-05
Dictionary of Philosophy and Psychology, 353, 354
Dictionary of Photography, 333
Dictionary of Pronunciation of Artists' Names, 331
Dictionary of Psychology, 286
Dictionary of Scientific Terms, 297, 298
Dictionary of Slang and Unconventional English, 50, 51
Dictionary of Social Welfare, 271, 272
Dictionary of Sociology, 271, 272
Dictionary of Sports, 341
Dictionary of Statistics, 147
Dictionary of Technical Terms, 311
Dictionary of the Bible, 352
Dictionary of the Noted Names of Fiction, 141
Dictionary of the Spanish and English Languages, 54
Dictionary of Vocal Themes, 336, 337
Dictionnaire de l'Académie Française, 54
Diderot, Denis, Encyclopédie, 59-60
Directories, 109-110, 126-35, 278-80
Directories for the Business Man, 279
Directory of Directories, 134, 135
Directory of International Scientific Organizations, 128, 129
Directory of Medical Specialists, 324
Directory of Newspapers and Periodicals, 162, 163
Doane, Searching for Your Ancestors, 264-65
Document Catalog, 220, 221
Documentation, 191-92
Documents, 147, 251
Documents of American History, 148
Documents Office Classification, 222
Doris, Business Executives' Handbook, 282
Dorland, American Illustrated Medical Dictionary, 323, 324
Douay Bible, concordance, 352
Doubleday's Encyclopedia, 77
Douglas, American Book of Days, 142, 143
Drama, 346-48
Dramatic Bibliography, 346, 347
Dramatic Index, 346, 347
Duden, Pictorial Encyclopedia, 52, 53
Dyke, Automobile Encyclopedia, 313

Eastman, Index to Fairy Tales, 348, 349
Eclectic bibliographies, 194-98
Economic Almanac, 280, 281
Economics, 276-77
Edgerton, Statistical Dictionary of Terms and Symbols, 272
Education, 283-89
Education Index, 283, 284
Educational Directory, 133, 134, 288
Educational Film Guide, 232
Educator's Guide to Free Films, 232
Effective English, 47, 48
Electrical Engineers' Handbook, 312
Eliot, C. W., 194
Ellis, General Index to Illustrations, 229; Nature and Its Applications, 230; Travel Through Pictures, 229
Emily Post Cook Book, 152
English Catalogue of Books, 202, 203
Enciclopedia italiana, 85, 86
Enciclopedia universal illustrada, 85, 86
Encyclopaedia Britannica, 57, 61, 69-72, 70, 122, 177

363

Index

Encyclopedia Americana, 61, 70, 72-74
Encyclopedia of Antiques, 334
Encyclopedia of Banking and Finance, 280, 282
Encyclopedia of Bible Life, 352
Encyclopedia of Chemical Technology, 305, 306
Encyclopedia of Educational Research, 286, 287
Encyclopedia of Furniture, 334
Encyclopedia of Modern Education, 286, 287
Encyclopedia of Modern World Politics, 275
Encyclopedia of Musical Masterpieces, 337, 338
Encyclopedia of Religion, 353
Encyclopedia of Religion and Ethics, 353
Encyclopedia of the Arts, 330
Encyclopedia of the Social Sciences, 268, 269, 270
Encyclopedia of the Theatre, 348
Encyclopedia of World History, 142, 144
Encyclopedias, 56-87; adult, 69-78; classes, 57; evaluation, 65-69; foreign, 85-86; one-volume, 77-78; school, 78-85; supplements, 68, 89-92
Encyclopédie, 59-60
Encyclopedists, 60
Engineering, 308-14
Engineering Encyclopedia, 311, 312
Engineering Index, 310
Engineering Terminology, 311
English Historical Review, 255
English Literature; an Illustrated Record, 345
Epitome of History, 144
Espasa (Enciclopedia universal illustrada), 85, 86
Essay and General Literature Index, 176, 177, 350
Essays, 349-50
Etiquette, 157
Evans, American Bibliography, 200, 201
Ewen, Book of Modern Composers, 338; Composers of Yesterday, 338; Dictators of the Baton, 338; Encyclopedia of Musical Masterpieces, 337, 338; Living Musicians, 338; Men of Popular Music, 338
Exhaustive Concordance of the Bible, 352
Exporters' Encyclopaedia, 280, 281

Fact books, 136-49

Fact sources, 137
Facts and How To Find Them, 20, 21
Facts-on-File, 166, 167, 254
Falconer, Filmstrips, 231, 232
Familiar Allusions, 141
Familiar Quotations, 142, 143
Family Physician, 156
Famous First Facts, 138, 139
Farmer, Boston Cooking-School Cook-Book, 152
Federal Council of Churches, 356
Federal documents, 207-23
Federal Register, 218
Federal Statistical Directory, 147
Federal Writers' Project, American Guide Series, 118, 119
Ferm, An Encyclopedia of Religion, 353; Religion in the Twentieth Century, 355
Fiction, 348-49
Fiction Catalog, 348, 349
Field Book of Common Rocks and Minerals, 306, 307
Field Book of Ponds and Streams, 317
Field Book of the Stars, 317
Field Book of Wild Flowers, 317
Field books, 317-18
Field Guide to the Birds, 317, 318
Fieldbook of Natural History, 317
Films, 231-32
Filmstrip Guide, 231, 232
Filmstrips, 231, 232
Filson, Westminster Historical Atlas of the Bible, 352, 353
Finance, 278
Fine arts, 327-32
Firkins, Index of Plays, 346, 347; Index to Short Stories, 348, 349
First aid, 156-57
First Aid Textbook, 156
Fitch, One God, 355
5,000 New Answers to Questions, 138, 140
Fletcher, History of Architecture, 333-34
Fletcher, A., Index of Mathematical Tables, 307, 308
Folklore, 348-49
Footnotes, 15-16, 17
Foreign Affairs, 255
Foreign Affairs Bibliography, 274
Foreign Commerce Yearbook, 280, 281
Foreign language dictionaries, 53-55
Foreign terms, 52-53
Foster's Complete Hoyle, 342
Fowler, Dictionary of Modern English Usage, 48
Frasier, Right Word, 46
Fraternities, 289

364

Frazer, *Golden Bough*, 348, 349
Free Teaching Aids in 14 Subjects, 230
French-English Science Dictionary, 297, 298
Frewer, *Bibliography of Historical Writings*, 254
Frogs, 318
"Fugitives," 138
Fuller, *Thesaurus of Book Digests*, 142
Funk and Wagnalls New College Standard Dictionary, 42, 44
Funk and Wagnalls New Standard Dictionary, 32, 35-37
Funk and Wagnalls Standard Dictionary of Folklore, 349
Funk and Wagnalls Standard High School Dictionary, 44, 45
Funk and Wagnalls Standard Junior Dictionary, 45, 46
Furniture, 334

Gable, *Manual of Series Work*, 161-62
Games, 341
Gardening, 154, 320
Gardner, *Art Through the Ages*, 330, 331
Garnett, *English Literature, an Illustrated Record*, 345
Gateway to History, 253
Gaver, *The Research Paper*, 16
Gayley, *Classic Myths*, 349
Gazetteers, 116-18
Gebauer, *Stage Crew Handbook*, 348
Genealogy, 264-65
General Catalogue of Printed Books (British Museum), 204, 205
General Index to Illustrations, 229
General Mills, *Betty Crocker's Picture Cook Book*, 152
Geographical Review, 260, 261
Geographical sources, 111-25, 260-61; atlases, 120-22; evaluation, 112-14; gazetteers, 116-18; globes, 124; guidebooks, 118-20; maps, 123-24
Geography, 260-61
Geologic Literature of North America, 303, 304-05
Geology, 302-03
German-English Science Dictionary, 297, 298
German-English Technical and Engineering Dictionary, 297, 298
Gerstenfeld, *Historical Bibliographies*, 253, 254
Gesamtkatalog der Wiegendrucke, 205
Getten, *Painting Materials*, 331
Givens, *Modern Encyclopedia of Cooking*, 152

Globes, 124
Glossary, 24-25
Glossary of Physics, 305
Golden Bough, 348, 349
Golden Dictionary, 46, 47
Golden Encyclopedia, 78, 84
Good, *Dictionary of Education, 286; Guide to Colleges*, 288
Good Food and How To Cook It, 151-52
Goode's School Atlas, 120, 122
Gosse, *English Literature; an Illustrated Record*, 345
Government, 273-75
Government Document Bibliography in the United States and Elsewhere, 223, 224
Government publications, 207-25; definition, 208; distribution, 209-11; evaluation, 208-09; foreign, 224-25; guides, 211; indexes, 219-23; local, 223; state, 223; U.N., 224-25
Government Publications and Their Use, 211
Gradus, 25
Graham, *Bookman's Manual*, 194, 195-96, 352
Gramophone Shop Encyclopedia of Recorded Music, 234, 335
Grand Dictionnaire universel du XIXe siècle français, 86
Grande encyclopédie, 86
Granger, *Index to Poetry*, 345, 346
Gray, *Manual of Botany*, 317, 318
Great Books of the Western World, 194
Greek-English Lexicon, 54
Greet, *World Words*, 51, 52, 117
Gregory, *International Congresses and Conferences, 1840-1937*, 130; *List of Serial Publications of Foreign Governments*, 224
Grimm, *Deutsches Wörterbuch*, 27, 54
Grolier Encyclopedia, 76, 77, 91
Gross technique, 162-63
Grove, *Dictionary of Music*, 337
Guerrier, Edith, 7
Guidance, 9-10
Guide to America, 118, 119
Guide to American Business Directories, 279
Guide to Colleges, Universities, and Professional Schools in the United States, 288
Guide to Dance Periodicals, 340
Guide to Geologic Literature, 303, 304
Guide to Good Reading, 344
Guide to Historical Literature, 253
Guide to Reference Books, 19, 20, 97

365

Guide to the Best Fiction, 348, 349
Guide to the Best Historical Novels and Tales, 348, 349
Guide to the Constellations, 306, 307
Guide to the Literature of Mathematics and Physics, 303, 304
Guide to the Literature of the Zoological Sciences, 315
Guide to United States Government Motion Pictures, 232
Guidebooks, 118-20

Hackh's Chemical Dictionary, 305
Halkett, *Dictionary of Anonymous and Pseudonymous English Literature,* 205
Hall, D., *Records,* 234
Hall, R. M., *Index to Handicrafts,* 158
Hamlin, *Architecture Through the Ages,* 333, 334
Hammond's Comparative Wall Atlas, 123-24
Hammond's Complete World Atlas, 120, 121
Handbook of Business Administration, 281
Handbook of Chemistry, 307
Handbook of Chemistry and Physics, 306, 307
Handbook of English for Boys and Girls, 48
Handbook of Insurance, 280, 281
Handbook of International Organizations in the Americas, 128, 129
Handbook of Latin American Studies, 254
Handbook of Meteorology, 307
Handbook of Private Schools, 289
Handbook of Psychological Literature, 284
Handbook of Scientific and Technical Societies and Institutions of the United States and Canada, 131, 132
Handbook of Social Correspondence, 157
Handbook of the Learned and Scientific Societies and Institutions of Latin America, 130
Handbook on the International Exchange of Publications, 128, 129
Handbooks, 136-49; calendar, 142-43; curiosities, 138-40; documentary, 147-48; evaluation, 137-38; statistical, 144-47
Handbooks of American Natural History, 317, 318
Handbuch der Organischen Chemie, 306

Handicrafts, 158
Hanson, *New World Guide to the Latin American Republics,* 118, 120
Harmsworth's Universal Encyclopedia, 77
Harper's Dictionary of Classical Literature, 257
Harper's Encyclopedia of Art, 330
Harper's Latin Dictionary, 54
Harper's Topical Concordance, 352
Harris, John, 59
Hart, *Oxford Companion to American Literature,* 140, 141
Harvard Dictionary of Music, 336, 337
Harvey, *Oxford Companion to Classical Literature,* 140, 141; *Oxford Companion to English Literature,* 140, 141
Haskins, *5,000 New Answers to Questions,* 138, 140
Hastings, *Dictionary of the Bible,* 352; *Encyclopaedia of Religion and Ethics,* 353
Hawkins, *Scientific, Medical and Technical Books Published in the United States of America,* 292, 293
Haydn, *Dictionary of Dates,* 144
Haydn, H., *Thesaurus of Book Digests,* 142
Hazeltine, *Anniversaries and Holidays,* 143
Heads of Families at the First Census, 1790, 265
Heal, *Teen Age Manual,* 157
Health, 156-57
Heath's New German-English, English-German Dictionary, 54
Hefling, *Index to Contemporary Biography and Criticism,* 109
Heimer, *Free Teaching Aids in 14 Subjects,* 230
Henderson, *Dictionary of Scientific Terms,* 297, 298
Henley's Twentieth Century Formulas, 153, 154
Heritage of Freedom, 148
Heyl, *Current National Bibliographies,* 204
Hicks, *Materials and Methods of Legal Research,* 273, 274
High school abridged dictionaries, 44-45
Highways in the Sky, 112
Hirshberg, *Subject Guide to Reference Books,* 20, 135, 355; *Subject Guide to United States Government Publications,* 211
Hiscox, *Henley's Twentieth Century*

Index

Formulas, 153, 154
Hispanic American Historical Review, 255
Historic Notebook, 257
Historical Atlas, 257, 258
Historical Bibliographies, 253, 254
Historical Fiction, 348, 349
Historical Statistics of the United States, 145, 272
History, 144-45, 249-59; atlases, 256-58; bibliographies, 253-54; handbooks, 256-58, 263-64; local, 263-64; sources, 250-52, 263
History for Ready Reference, 255, 256
History of Architecture, 333-34
Hoare, Short Italian Dictionary, 54
Hobbies, 158
Hockett, Introduction to Research in American History, 253
Holidays, 143
Holweck, Biographical Dictionary of the Saints, 354, 355
Home Book of Bible Quotations, 352
Home Book of Quotations, 142, 143
Home economics, 321-22
Home maintenance, 153
Home making, 153
Home planning, 153
Hook, Research Paper, 16
Horticulture, 318-21
Horton, Dictionary of Modern Economics, 280, 282
Horwill, Dictionary of Modern American Usage, 48
Hotels, 119, 127
Hourticq, Harper's Encyclopedia of Art, 330
How-to books, 158
How To Do It Books, 158
How to Locate Educational Information, 283, 284
Hoyle, Foster's Complete Hoyle, 342
Hoyt, New Encyclopedia of Practical Quotations, 142, 143
Hubbell, Writing Documented Papers, 16
Hulbert, A Dictionary of American English, 32, 40
Humanities, 326-56
Hume, World's Living Religions, 355
Hurt, Bibliography and Footnotes, 16-17
Hutchins, Introduction to Reference Work, 20, 21, 110
Hutchinson, Standard Handbook for Secretaries, 157
Hygeia, 322

Illustrations, 332

Index-Catalogue of the Library of the Surgeon General's Office, 322, 323
Index Generalis, 289
Index Medicus, 323
Index of Mathematical Tables, 307, 308
Index of Plays, 346, 347
Index of Record Reviews, 234
Index to Children's Poetry, 345, 346
Index to Contemporary Biography and Criticism, 109
Index to Fairy Tales, 348, 349
Index to Folk Dances and Singing Games, 340
Index to Full Length Plays, 346, 348
Index to Handicrafts, 158
Index to Indexes, 176
Index to Legal Periodicals, 273, 274
Index to Monologs and Dialogs, 346, 348
Index to One-Act Plays, 346, 347-48
Index to Plays in Collections, 346, 347
Index to Poetry and Recitations, 345, 346
Index to Reproductions of American Paintings, 332
Index to Short Stories, 348, 349
Index to the Literature of American Economic Entomology, 316
Indexes, 173-89, 241; composite book, 177; evaluation, 174-75; home made, 175; library, 175; newspaper, 188; periodical, 178-87
Industrial Arts Index, 276, 295, 310
Infant Care, 156, 157
Information desk, 4
Information Please Almanac, 92, 93, 138-39
Information Roundup, 138, 139
Inquirers, 4-5
Instruction, 11
Insurance, 280-81
Interlibrary loans, 4
International Bibliography of Historical Sciences, 254
International Catalogue of Scientific Literature, 294
International Congresses and Conferences, 1840-1937, 130
International Critical Tables, 308
International Cyclopedia of Music and Musicians, 337
International Index to Periodical Literature, 184, 295, 354
International Motion Picture Almanac, 333, 346, 347
International Thesaurus, 49
International Who's Who, 106, 107

367

Index

Introduction to Reference Books, 20, 135, 172
Introduction to Reference Work, 20, 21, 110
Introduction to Research in American History, 253
Investments, 278
Ireland, Index to Indexes, 176; Index to Monologs and Dialogs, 346, 348; Picture File, 229

Jackson, Technical Libraries, 309, 310
Jaeger, Source Book of Biological Names and Terms, 316
James, Mathematics Dictionary, 305
Jensen, Bibliography of Best References for the Study of Geography, 260
Jewett, Who's Who in Library Service, 247
Jewish Encyclopedia, 353
Johnson, Samuel, Dictionary, 25-26
Jones, Engineering Encyclopedia, 311, 312
Joughlin, Basic Reference Forms, 17
Journal of Commerce, 282
Journal of Geography, 260, 261
Journals, See Serials
Joy, Harper's Topical Concordance, 352
Julian, Dictionary of Hymnology, 353, 354

Kallett, Arthur, 155
Kaltenbach, Dictionary of Pronunciation of Artists' Names, 331
Kander, Settlement Cook Book, 152
Kane, Famous First Facts, 138, 139; More First Facts, 139
Keesing's Contemporary Archives, 166, 167, 254
Keller, Dictionary of Dates, 144, 256, 257
Kelly, American Catalogue of Books, 201
Kelly's Directory of Merchants, Manufacturers and Shippers, 279
Kent's Mechanical Engineer's Handbook, 312
Kenyon, Pronouncing Dictionary of American English, 52
Kidder-Parker Architects' and Builders' Handbook, 312, 333
Kill, Family Physician, 156
Kingery, How To Do It Books, 158
Kiplinger Washington Letter, 282
Kirk, Encyclopedia of Chemical Technology, 305, 306
Knott, Pronouncing Dictionary of American English, 52

Kolodin, New Guide to Recorded Music, 234
Kroeger, Alice, 19
Kurtz, Statistical Dictionary of Terms and Symbols, 272

Labor Research Association, Labor Fact Book, 280, 281
Laing, Dictionary of Anonymous and Pseudonymous English Literature, 205
Lange, Handbook of Chemistry, 307
Langer, Encyclopedia of World History, 142, 144
Language sources, supplementary, 47-53
Larned, History for Ready Reference, 255, 256
Larousse, Grand dictionnaire universel du XIXe siècle français, 86
Larousse du XXe siècle, 85, 86
Lavine, Scientific and Technical Abbreviations, 297, 298
Law, 273-75
Law dictionaries, 275
Law directories, 134-35
Laws, 278; U.S., 212-13
Leaf, Manners Can Be Fun, 157
Learned societies, 131-33
Leeming, Costume Book, 333
Legal Bibliography and Legal Research, 274
Lenrow, Reader's Guide to Prose Fiction, 348, 349
Lexicography, 25-27
Lexicon, 25
Librarianship, 242-48; bibliographies, 244-45; serials, 245-46
Library Association Record, 246
Library Guide for the Chemist, 293, 303, 304
Library instruction, 11
Library Journal, 245, 246
Library Literature, 244, 245
Library of Congress, See U.S. Library of Congress
Library of Literary Criticism, 345
Library organization, 1-2
Library Quarterly, 246
Library science, 242-48
Library Science Abstracts, 244, 245
Liddell, Greek-English Lexicon, 54
Life, 169
Lincoln Library, 77, 78
Lippincott's Biographical Dictionary, 101, 102
Lippincott's Gazetteer, 116, 117
List of American Learned Journals De-

368

Index

voted to Humanistic and Social Studies, 132
List of Books for College Libraries, 198
List of Books for Junior College Libraries, 198
List of Periodicals Abstracted (Chemical Abstracts), 296, 297
List of Serial Publications of Foreign Governments, 224
Listening posts, 4
Litchfield, *Pottery and Porcelain*, 334
Literary History of the United States, 343, 344
Literature, 342-50; bibliographies, 343-44; cyclopedias, 344-45; handbooks, 344-45; histories, 344-45; serials, 350; sources, 342-43
Living Musicians, 338
Local History, 264
Local Indexes in American Libraries, 176
Logasa, *Biography in Collections*, 109; *Historical Fiction*, 348, 349; *Index to One-Act Plays*, 346, 347-48
London Bibliography of the Social Sciences, 268
London Times Survey Atlas of the World, 122; See also *Times* (London)
Look, 169
Loomis, *Field Book of Common Rocks and Minerals*, 306, 307
Loose-leaf insertions, 68
Lorenz, *Catalogue général de la librairie française*, 203
Lorge-Thorndike semantic count, 42
Louttit, *Handbook of Psychological Literature*, 284
Lovell, *Index to Handicrafts*, 158
Lowndes, *Bibliographer's Manual of English Literature*, 203
Loyola Educational Index, 283
Lyle, *Classified List of Periodicals for the College Library*, 164

MLA Style Sheet, 17
McCall's Complete Book of Dressmaking, 154
Machinery's Handbook for Machine Shop and Drafting Room, 312, 313
McKearin, *American Glass*, 334
Macmillan Modern Dictionary, 42, 44, 45
McSpadden, *Operas and Musical Comedies*, 337, 338
Magazines for School Libraries, 164
Magriel, *Bibliography of Dancing*, 340
Mallett's Index of Artists, 331

Manley, *Business Directories*, 134, 135, 279
Manners Can Be Fun, 157
Mansion's Shorter French and English Dictionary, 54
Mantle, *Best Plays*, 346, 347
Manual for Bibliographers in the Library of Congress, 17
Manual for Writers of Dissertations, 17
Manual of Botany, 317, 318
Manual of Cultivated Trees and Shrubs, 316, 317
Manual of Government Publications, 211, 224
Manual of Serials Work, 161-62
Manual of Style (Chicago), 12, 16
Manual on the Use of State Publications, 223, 225
Manuals, 150-58; evaluation, 151; home maintenance, 153
Manuel du Libraire, 204
Maps, 123-24; classes, 112; evaluation, 113-15; projection, 113; scale, 113
March of Man, 258
Marine Products of Commerce, 312, 313
Marks, *Mechanical Engineers' Handbook*, 312
Marks and Monograms on European and Oriental Pottery and Porcelain, 334
Marquis, A.N., & Co., 106-08
Martin, *Magazines for School Libraries*, 164
Martindale-Hubbell Law Directory, 134-35
Masters, *Handbook of International Organizations in the Americas*, 129
Materials and Methods of Legal Research, 273, 274
Materials for the Study of Federal Government, 211, 273, 274
Materials Handbook, 311, 312
Mathematics, 301-02
Mathematics Dictionary, 305
Mathews, *Field Book of Wild Flowers*, 317
Mawson, *Dictionary of Foreign Terms*, 52, 53; *Thesaurus of the English Language in Dictionary Form*, 49
Mayer, *Artist's Handbook of Materials and Techniques*, 331
Mechanical Engineers' Handbook, 312
Medicine, 322
Meisel, *Bibliography of American Natural History*, 315
Melinat, *Subject Guide to United States Government Publications*, 211
Men of Popular Music, 338

369

Index

Menke, *All-Sports Record Book*, 341
Mental Measurements Yearbook, 284
Merriam-Webster, See entries under Webster's
Metals Handbook, 312, 313
Meteorology, 303
Methodology of Social Science Research, 268, 269
Metropolitan Opera Annals, 338
Microtexts, 244
Miller, *Encyclopedia of Bible Life*, 352
Mills, John, 59
Mineralogical Dictionary, 306
Minerals Yearbook, 306, 307
Minerva Jahrbuch, 289
Mining Engineers' Handbook, 312
Minneapolis Public Library, *Index to Folk Dances and Singing Games*, 340
Minto, *Reference Books*, 20
Mississippi Valley Historical Review, 255
Modern Dog Encyclopedia, 320, 321
Modern Encyclopedia of Cooking, 152
Modern English Usage, 48
Modern Farmers' Cyclopedia of Agriculture, 320
Modern Humanities Research Association, *Annual Bibliography of English Language and Literature*, 343, 344
Modern Portuguese-English, English-Portuguese Dictionary, 54
Modley, *U.S.A.: Measure of a Nation*, 145, 146
Mohrhardt, *List of Books for Junior College Libraries*, 198
Monaghan, *Heritage of Freedom*, 148
Monro, I. S., *Index to Reproductions of American Paintings*, 332
Monro, K. M., *Handbook of Social Correspondence*, 157; *Secretary's Handbook*, 157
Monroe, P., *Cyclopedia of Education*, 286, 287
Monroe, W. S., *Bibliographies and Summaries in Education*, 283, 284; *Encyclopedia of Educational Research*, 286, 287
Monthly Catalog, United States Government Publications, 220, 221, 292, 319
Monthly Checklist of State Publications, 222, 223
Moody's Manual of Investments, 277
More First Facts, 139
Moreri, Louis, 58-59
Morgan, *Field Book of Ponds and Streams*, 317
Morganstern, *Dictionary of Musical Themes*, 336, 337; *Dictionary of Vocal Themes*, 337
Mosquitoes, 318
Motion pictures, 231-32, 346-47
Mottoes, 143
Moulton, *Library of Literary Criticism*, 345
Mudge, Isadore G., 19
Mulhall, *Dictionary of Statistics*, 147
Municipal documents, 223
Municipal Year Book, 223, 275
Munn, *Encyclopedia of Banking and Finance*, 280, 282
Murchison, *Psychological Register*, 287, 288
Museums, art, 331-32; science, 315
Music, 335-39
Music Index, 335
Music Library Association, *Notes*, 335
My First Dictionary, 46
Myers, *Index of Record Reviews*, 234
Mythology, 348-49
Mythology of All Races, 348

NBC Handbook of Pronunciation, 51, 52
Nathan, *Encyclopedia of the Theatre*, 348; *Theatre Book of the Year*, 347
Nation, 171
National Archives, See U.S. National Archives
National Associations of the United States, 134
National Cyclopaedia of American Biography, 102, 104
National Education Association, 285; *N.E.A. Handbook and Manual*, 287, 288; *N.E.A. Journal*, 285
National Geographic Society, 123; *National Geographic Magazine*, 123, 260, 261, 318
National Research Council, 131, 224; *Handbook of Scientific and Technical Societies*, 131, 132; *International Critical Tables*, 308
Naturalist's Lexicon, 316
Nature and Its Applications, 230
Negro Handbook, 271, 272
Negro Yearbook, 271
Nevins, *Gateway to History*, 253
New Century Dictionary, 41, 282
New Complete Russian-English Dictionary, 54
New Dictionary of American Politics, 274, 275
New Dictionary of Statistics, 147
New Encyclopedia of Practical Quotations, 142, 143
New Etiquette, 157

Index

New Garden Encyclopedia, 154
New Guide to Recorded Music, 234
New International Encyclopedia, 61, 70, 75-76
New International Yearbook, 90
New Republic, 171
New Schaff-Herzog Encyclopedia of Religious Knowledge, 353
New Winston Dictionary for Young People, 44, 45
New World Guide to the Latin American Republics, 118, 120
New Worlds of English Words, 25
New York Herald-Tribune, Home Institute Cook Book, 152
New York Times, 108, 138, 164, 165-66; *Index,* 188, 347
New Yorker, 170, 171
Newbery, John, 61
Newill, *Good Food and How To Cook It,* 151-52
News services, 165-66
News summaries, 166-67
Newspapers, 164-66
Newsweek, 168
Nickles, *Geologic Literature of North America,* 303, 304-05
Nield, *Guide to the Best Historical Novels and Tales,* 348, 349
Nineteenth Century Readers' Guide, 184, 187
Norton, *Star Atlas and Reference Handbook,* 307
Notables, 98
Notes and Queries, 138
Notz, *Legal Bibliography and Legal Research,* 274
Numismatics, 334
Nystrom, A. J., & Co., 123

O'Brien, Lucy, 72
Ochs, Adolph S., 103
Official Athletic Rules, 341
Official Guide of the Railways and Steam Navigation Lines, 116, 117, 127
Official Hotel Red Book and Directory, 118, 119, 127
Official Index to The Times, 188
Official Map Publications, 260
Official Railroad Guide, 116, 117, 127
Official War Publications, 254
Oftedahl, *My First Dictionary,* 46
Olcott, *Field Book of the Stars,* 317
Old Farmer's Almanack, 94
One God, 355
Operas and Musical Comedies, 337, 338
Orbis Pictus, 79
Ottemiller, *Index to Plays in Collections,* 346, 347
Oxford Advanced Atlas, 122
Oxford Companion to American Literature, 140, 141
Oxford Companion to Classical Literature, 140, 141
Oxford Companion to English Literature, 140, 141
Oxford Companion to Music, 337
Oxford Dictionary of Quotations, 143
Oxford English Dictionary, 27, 32, 37-40, 142, 350
Oxford Junior Encyclopedia, 84, 85

PAIS, See Public Affairs Information Service
Packman, *Guide to the Best Fiction,* 348, 349
Pageant of America, 258, 259, 339
Paging, 14
Painting, 332
Painting Materials, 331
Palmer, *Fieldbook of Natural History,* 317
Palmer's Index, 188
Pamphlets, 188-89
Panunzio, *Student's Dictionary of Sociological Terms,* 271
Parke, *Guide to the Literature of Mathematics and Physics,* 303, 304
Parker, D. D., *Local History,* 264
Parker, J., *Who's Who in the Theatre,* 346, 348
Parker, W. R., *MLA Style Sheet,* 17
Parliamentary law, 148-49
Parson, *Popular Ballroom Dances for All,* 340
Partridge, *Dictionary of Slang,* 50, 51
Patents, 314
Patterson's American Educational Directory, 133, 134
Paullin, *Atlas of the Historical Geography of the United States,* 257, 258
Pearl, *Guide to Geologic Literature,* 303, 304
Peck, *Harper's Dictionary of Classical Literature,* 257
Peele, *Mining Engineers' Handbook,* 312
Pender, *Electrical Engineers' Handbook,* 312
Periodical indexes, 178-87
Periodical revision, 69
Periodicals, 159-72
Periodicals for Small and Medium-Sized Libraries, 164
Perpetual Trouble Shooter's Manual, 313

Index

Perrin, *Writer's Guide and Index to English,* 47, 48
Perry, *Chemical Engineers' Handbook,* 312
Peterson, *Field Guide to the Birds,* 317, 318
Pets, 318
Pharmacopeia of the United States of America, 324
Pharmacy, 324
Phelps, Edith, 183
Philately, 334
Phillips, *New Worlds of English Words,* 25
Philosophical Abstracts, 354
Philosophy, 350-56
Photography, 333
Physical Sciences, 301-14
Physics, 302
Pickens, *Sewing for Everyone,* 154; *Sewing for the Home,* 154
Picture Collection, 229
Picture Dictionary for Children, 46
Picture File, 229
Pilkington, Walter, 138
Planché, *Cyclopaedia of Costume,* 332, 333
Platt, *Aids to Geographical Research,* 119, 260
Plays, 346-49
Pliny, 58
Ploetz, *Epitome of History,* 144
Poetry, 345-46
Political science, 273-75
Pomeranz, *Family Physician,* 156
Poole, E., *Documents Office Classification,* 222
Poole, W. F., 179; indexes, 178-83
Poole's Index to Periodical Literature, 179
Poore, *Descriptive Catalogue of the Government Publications of the United States,* 219, 220
Poor's, 277-78
Popular Ballroom Dances for All, 340
Porcelain, 334
Post, Emily, *Cook Book,* 152; *Etiquette,* 157
Pottery, 334
Pottery and Porcelain, 334
Price Lists of Government Publications, 220, 222
Prints, 332
Projected materials, 230-33
Pronouncing Dictionary of American English, 52
Pronunciation, 51-52
Propaganda, 274

Proverbs, 143
Psychological Abstracts, 284
Psychological Register, 287, 288
Psychology, 282-84, 354
Public Affairs Information Service, 162, 187, 268, 269
Public documents, 207-25
Public libraries, 3
Publishers' Circular, 203
Publishers' Trade List Annual, 199, 200
Publishers' Weekly, 21, 199
Putnam's Nature Field Books, 317

Quarterly Cumulative Index Medicus, 323
Quarterly Journal of Current Acquisitions (L.C.), 204
Questions, 5-10, 242; activities, 150; agency, 126; analysis, 9; audio-visual, 226; background, 56; bibliographic, 190-91; biographical, 98; classes, 5-9, 242; contemporary, 159; curiosity, 139; current, 88; document, 207; examples, 5, 23, 56, 88, 126, 136, 150, 159, 191, 226, 270, 273; fact, 136; handling, 9-10; history, 250; how-to-do, 150; language, 23; literature, 342; music, 335; organization, 126; philosophy, 351; places, 111; religion, 351; science, 291; social science, 266, 270, 273; source location, 173; sports, 339; technology, 291; trends, 88; visual arts, 327
Quotation books, 142-43
Quotations, 350

Racial Proverbs, 143
Radio, 312
Railroad Guide, 116, 117, 127
Rainbow Dictionary, 46, 47
Rand McNally & Co., 123, 124; *Commercial Atlas,* 122; *Cosmopolitan World Atlas,* 120, 121
Ratings, financial, 278
Raymond, *Annual Standard Catalogue of United States Currency and Tokens,* 334; *Coins of the World, Nineteenth Century Issues,* 334; *Twentieth Century Issues,* 334
Reader's Digest, 170
Reader's Encyclopedia, 140
Readers' Guide to Periodical Literature, 164, *184,* 185-87
Reader's Guide to Prose Fiction, 348, 349
Reading List on Business Administration, 277
Recordings, 233-34

Index

Records, 234
Recreatory arts, 339-42
Red Cross, 156
Reference, 1-22, 236-42; definition, 2; department, 2-5; functions, 2-21; instruction, 11; literature, 19-21; organization, 3-4; personnel, 4; practice, 1-2; questions, *See* Questions; ready, 5; records, 15; room, 3-4; staff, 4; subject approach, 236-42; supervision, 2-5
Reference books, 4, 17; classes, 18; definition, 17-18; evaluation, 18-19; reviews, 19-21
Reference Books, 20
Reference Function of the Library, 20, 21, 248
Reference Shelf, 148, 149
Reference staff, 4
Reference Work, 20, 21
Rehder, *Manual of Cultivated Trees and Shrubs,* 316, 317
Reinach, *Apollo,* 330, 331
Religion, 350-55
Religion in the Twentieth Century, 355
Religious Bodies, 354, 355
Religious Leaders of America, 355
Reproduction equipment, 4
Research and reference, 236-42
Research librarian, 191-92, 236-38
Research Paper, 16
Rhymes, 52
Rhyming Dictionary of the English Language, 52
Rice, *Dictionary of Geological Terms,* 306
Richards, *Index to Contemporary Biography and Criticism,* 109
Richardson, *Modern Portuguese-English, English-Portuguese Dictionary,* 54
Rider, *Perpetual Trouble Shooter's Manual,* 313
Right Word, 46
Rips, *United States Government Publications,* 211
Rivlin, *Encyclopedia of Modern Education,* 286, 287
Robert, *Rules of Order,* 148, 149
Roberts, *Introduction to Reference Books,* 20, 135, 172
Roget, Peter, 49; *International Thesaurus,* 49
Roorbach, *Bibliotheca Americana,* 200, 201
Roosevelt, F. D., 217
Royal Society of London, *Catalogue of Scientific Papers,* 294
Rue, *Subject Index to Books for Intermediate Grades,* 176, 178, 350; *for Primary Grades,* 176, 178; *Subject Index to Readers,* 178, 350
Rufsvold, *Audio-Visual School Library Service,* 235
Rules of Order, 148, 149
Runes, *Encyclopedia of the Arts,* 330; *Who's Who in Philosophy,* 355
Runner, *Engineering Terminology,* 311
Rush, C. E., 174

Sa Pereira, *Modern Portuguese-English, English-Portuguese Dictionary,* 54
Sabin, *Dictionary of Books Relating to America,* 200, 201
Sacred Books of the East, 354, 355
Sargent, *Handbook of Private Schools,* 289
Saturday Evening Post, 169
Saturday Review, 21, 108, 170
Schaff, *New Schaff-Herzog Encyclopedia of Religious Knowledge,* 353
Schirmer's Guide to Books on Music and Musicians, 335
Schlinck, F. J., 155
Schmeckebier, *Government Publications and Their Use,* 211
Scholes, *Oxford Companion to Music,* 337
School and Society, 285
School encyclopedias, 61
School libraries, 3-4, 196
School Life, 284
Schrickel, *Encyclopedia of the Arts,* 330
Science, 290-324
Science Abstracts, 303, 304
Science in Progress, 299
Scientific and Learned Societies of Great Britain, 128, 130
Scientific and Technical Abbreviations, 297, 298
Scientific, Medical and Technical Books Published in the United States of America, 292, 293
Scott, *Standard Postage Stamp Catalog,* 334
Searching for Your Ancestors, 264-65
Sears, *Song Index,* 335
Secretary's Handbook, 157
Segal, *New Complete Russian-English Dictionary,* 54
Selected Radio Programs for School Listening, 234
Seltsam, *Metropolitan Opera Annals,* 338
Serial set, 215
Serials, 159-72
Series note, 15

373

Index

Service basis, 184
Settlement Cook Book, 152
Severance, *Handbook of the Learned and Scientific Societies and Institutions of Latin America*, 130
Sewing for Everyone, 154
Sewing for the Home, 154
Seymour, *New Garden Encyclopedia*, 154
Shankle, *Current Abbreviations*, 49, 50
Shaw, *List of Books for College Libraries*, 198
Sheep set, 215
Shepherd, *Historical Atlas*, 257, 258
Shores, Louis, 172; *Bibliographies and Summaries in Education*, 283, 284; *Highways in the Sky*, 112
Short Italian Dictionary, 54
Short stories, 348-49
Shorter Oxford Dictionary, 41, 42
Slang, 50-51
Slides, 231
Slogans, 143
Smith, B., *Propaganda*, 274
Smith, E. C., *New Dictionary of American Politics*, 274, 275
Smith, R. C., *Guide to the Literature of the Zoological Sciences*, 315
Smithsonian Institution, *Annual Report*, 299; *Smithsonian Meteorological Tables*, 308
Sobel, *Theatre Handbook*, 346, 348
Social Science Research Council, 132-33; Committee on Historiography, *Theory and Practice in Historical Study*, 253
Social sciences, 266-89
Social work, 270
Social Work Yearbook, 271, 272
Socialites, 99
Societies, learned, 131-33
Sociology, 270
Song Index, 335
Sonnenschein, *Best Books*, 194, 196
Soule, *Library Guide for the Chemist*, 293, 303, 304
Source Book of Biological Names and Terms, 316
Sources of Business Information, 276
Sources of Engineering Information, 309, 310
Spalding Athletic Library, 341
Special Libraries Association, *Basic List of Current Municipal Documents*, 222, 223; *Directories for the Business Man*, 279; *Special Libraries*, 246; *Union List of Technical Periodicals*, 296, 297

Specialists, 98
Specifications, 313-14
Speech Index, 349
Speeches, 349
Spiller, *Literary History of the United States*, 343, 344
Sports, 340-42
Staats, *The Right Word*, 46
Stage Crew Handbook, 348
Stamps, 334
Standard and Poor's Corporation, 278
Standard Catalog for High School Libraries, 196, 197
Standard Catalog for Public Libraries, 197, 198, 341
Standard Handbook for Secretaries, 157
Standard Postage Stamp Catalog, 334
Standardized Plant Names, 316, 317
Standards, 313-14
Star Atlas and Reference Handbook, 307
State documents, 223
State manuals, 275
Statesman's Year-Book, 95, 96, 251, 351
Statistical Abstract of the United States, 146, 272
Statistical Dictionary of Terms and Symbols, 272
Statistics, 144-47
Statutes at Large, 213
Stephenson, *Abbrevs*, 49, 50
Stereographs, 230-31
Stevenson, *Home Book of Bible Quotations*, 352; *Home Book of Quotations*, 142, 143
Stewart, *Tabulation of Librarianship*, 243
Stimpson, *Book About the Bible*, 353; *Information Roundup*, 138, 139
Stock, *Complete Concordance to the Bible* (Douay), 352
Story of Every Day Things, 334
Story of Our Time, 90, 91
Stout, *Painting Materials*, 331
Stratton, *Effective English*, 47, 48
Strong, *Exhaustive Concordance of the Bible*, 352
Student's Dictionary of Sociological Terms, 271
Student's Guide to Materials in Political Science, 273
Sturgis, *Dictionary of Architecture and Building*, 333, 334
Style Manual (G.P.O.), 17
Style manuals, 16-17
Subject Guide to Reference Books, 20, 135, 355
Subject Guide to United States Government Publications, 211

Index

Subject Index to Books for Intermediate Grades, 176, 178, 350
Subject Index to Books for Primary Grades, 176, 178
Subject Index to High School Fiction, 348, 349
Subject Index to Poetry, 345, 346
Subject Index to Readers, 178, 350
Subscription books, 62-65, 87
Subscription Books Bulletin, 20, 21, 62-63, 66, 87, 97, 110, 125
Summaries, 240
Sunday Times Travel and Holiday Guide to the Continent of Europe and to the British Isles, 118, 119
Supplementary word books, 47-53
Sutton, Speech Index, 349
Synonyms, 48-49
System of Mineralogy, 307

Tables of Food Values, 322
Tabulation of Librarianship, 243
Taintor, Handbook of Social Correspondence, 157; Secretary's Handbook, 157
Tannehill, Weather Around the World, 306, 307
Taube, Manual for Bibliographers in the Library of Congress, 17
Tavenner, Brief Facts, 138, 139
Taxes, 278
Taylor's Encyclopedia of Gardening, 320
Teaching and reference, 11
Teaching library use, 11
Technical Book Review Index, 292, 293
Technical Libraries, 309, 310
Technology, 308-14
Teen Age Manual, 157
Telephone directories, 109
Telephone service, 4
Television, 234
Ten Eventful Years, 91
Theater, 346-48
Theatre Book of the Year, 347
Theatre Handbook and Digest of Plays, 346, 348
Theatre World, 347
Theimer, Encyclopedia of Modern World Politics, 275
Theory and Practice in Historical Study, 253
Thesaurus, 25
Thesaurus of Book Digests, 142
Thesaurus of the English Language in Dictionary Form, 49
Thiele, Official Map Publications, 260
Thieme, Allgemeines Lexikon der Bildenen Künstler, 329, 331

Thiessen, Weather Glossary, 306
Thomas, Old Farmer's Almanack, 94
Thomas, J., Universal Pronouncing Dictionary of Biography and Mythology, 101, 102
Thomas' Register of American Manufacturers, 279
Thompson, N. W., Complete Concordance to the Bible (Douay), 352
Thompson, O., International Cyclopedia of Music and Musicians, 337
Thomson, Index to Full Length Plays, 346, 348
Thorndike, E. L., 42, 45, 55
Thorndike - Barnhart Comprehensive Desk Dictionary, 44
Thorndike-Century Beginning Dictionary, 46; Junior Dictionary, 45, 46; Senior Dictionary, 44, 45
Thorpe's Dictionary of Applied Chemistry, 306
Time, 168
Time tables, 117
Times (London) index, 188; Sunday Times Travel and Holiday Guide to the Continent of Europe and to the British Isles, 118, 119; Survey Atlas of the World, 122
Today's Health, 322
Tompkins, Materials for the Study of Federal Government, 211, 273, 274; Methodology of Social Science Research, 268, 269
Train, Story of Every Day Things, 334
Travel, 118-20
Travel Through Pictures, 229
Trees, 317
Trench, Richard, 27
Tressler, Marine Products of Commerce, 312, 313
Turabian, A Manual for Writers of Dissertations, 17

U.S.A.: Measure of a Nation, 145, 146, 272
Ulrich's Periodicals Directory, 162, 163, 245, 300
Unesco, 162; Bibliographical Services, 199; Directory of International Scientific Organizations, 128, 129; Handbook on the International Exchange of Publications, 128, 129
Union List of Serials, 164, 296
Union List of Technical Periodicals, 296, 297
United Nations, Documents Index, 224, 225; Publications, 224; Statistical

375

Index

Yearbook, 146; Yearbook, 96, 97, 127; *See also* Unesco
U.S. Department of Agriculture, *Agricultural Statistics, 321; Atlas of American Agriculture, 321; Bibliography of Agriculture, 319, 320; Consumers' Guide,* 155; *Yearbook of Agriculture, 321*
U.S. Bureau of American Ethnology, *Annual Reports,* 271; *General Index to Annual Reports,* 271, 272
U.S. Army Medical Library, *Index-Catalogue of the Library of the Surgeon General's Office,* 322, 323
U.S. Bureau of the Budget, *Federal Statistical Directory,* 147
U.S. Bureau of the Census, 146-47; *Abstract of the Census,* 146-47; *Checklist of Basic Municipal Documents,* 222, 223; *Heads of Families at the First Census, 1790,* 265; *Historical Statistics of the United States,* 145, 272; *Religious Bodies,* 354, 355; *Statistical Abstract of the United States,* 146, 272
U.S. Children's Bureau, *Infant Care,* 156, 157
U.S. Department of Commerce, *Bibliography of Technical Reports,* 310, 311; *National Associations of the United States,* 134
U.S. Congress, *Congressional Record,* 212, 213, 214; *Official Congressional Directory,* 211, 212; *Statutes at Large,* 213; *United States Code,* 212, 213
U.S. Copyright Office, *Catalog of Copyright Entries,* 336
U.S. Office of Education, *Biennial Survey of Education,* 287, 288; *Educational Directory,* 133, *134,* 288; *School Life,* 284; *Selected Radio Programs for School Listening,* 234
U.S. Federal Trade Commission, 62, 87
U.S. Bureau of Foreign and Domestic Commerce, *Commerce Yearbook,* 281
U.S. Board on Geographical Names, *Sixth Report,* 260
U.S. Government Printing Office, 209-10; *Style Manual,* 17
U.S. Office of International Trade, *Foreign Commerce Yearbook,* 280, 281
U.S. Library of Congress, 199, 204-05; *Catalog of Books Represented by . . . Printed Cards,* 204, 205; *Guide to United States Government Motion Pictures,* 232; *Monthly Checklist of State Publications,* 222, 223; *Quarterly Journal of Current Acquisitions,* 204
U.S. Bureau of Mines, *Minerals Yearbook,* 306, 307
U.S. National Archives, *Code of Federal Regulations,* 218, 219; *Federal Register,* 218
U.S. Nautical Almanac Office, *American Ephemeris and Nautical Almanac,* 89, 308
U.S. Post Office Department, *United States Official Postal Guide,* 116, 117
U.S. Superintendent of Documents, *Catalog of the Public Documents of the 53d to 76th Congresses,* 220, 221; *Checklist of United States Public Documents,* 220, 222; *Monthly Catalog,* 220, 221, 292, 319; *Price Lists,* 220, 222
U.S. Treasury Department, *Catalogue of Coins,* 334
U.S. Works Progress Administration, *American Imprints Inventory,* 202
United States Catalog, 199, 200
United States Code, 212, 213
United States Government Manual, 211, 217
United States Government Publications, 211
United States Government Publications Monthly Catalog, 220, 221, 292, 319
United States News, 168
United States Official Postal Guide, 116, 117
United States Quarterly Book Review, 21, 194, 195
Universal Etymological Dictionary, 25
Universal Jewish Encyclopedia, 353
Universal Pronouncing Dictionary of Biography and Mythology (Lippincott's), *101,* 102
Universities of the World Outside U.S.A., 288
University libraries, 3-4
Usage books, 47-48
Use of Reference Material, 20, 21

Van den Bark, *American Thesaurus of Slang,* 50, 51
Van Hoesen, Florence, 6, 8, 22, 56
Van Nostrand, *Subject Index to High School Fiction,* 348, 349
Van Nostrand's Scientific Encyclopedia, 299
Velázques, *Dictionary of the Spanish and English Languages,* 54
Ver Nooy, *Index to One-Act Plays,* 346, 347-48
Vertical File Service Catalog, 188, 189

Index

Virkus, *Compendium of American Genealogy*, 265
Visual arts, 327-32
Voltaire, *Philosophical Dictionary*, 59

Walker, *Rhyming Dictionary*, 52
Wall, *Dictionary of Photography*, 333
Wall Street Journal, 282
War in Maps, 258
Warner Library of the World's Best Literature, 345
Warren, *Dictionary of Psychology*, 286
Watt, *Bibliotheca Britannica*, 203
Watters-Courtis Illustrated Golden Dictionary for Young Readers, 46
"We, the People," 99
Weather Around the World, 306, 307
Weather Glossary, 306
Webb, *New Dictionary of Statistics*, 147
Weber-Costello Co., 123
Webster, Noah, 26
Webster's Biographical Dictionary, 101
Webster's Dictionary of Synonyms, 48, 49
Webster's Elementary Dictionary, 45, 46
Webster's Geographical Dictionary, 116
Webster's New Collegiate Dictionary, 42, 43-44
Webster's New International Dictionary, 31-35, 32
Webster's Students' Dictionary, 44, 45
Weedon's Encyclopedia, 83
Weld, *Glossary of Physics*, 305
Wentworth, *American Dialect Dictionary*, 50, 51
Westminster Historical Atlas of the Bible, 352, 353
Wheeler, *Dictionary of the Noted Names of Fiction*, 141; *Familiar Allusions*, 141; *Who Wrote It?*, 141
Whitaker's Almanack, 92, 94
Whitaker's Cumulative Booklist, 202, 203
Who Knows—and What, 108, 280
Who Was When, 101, 102
Who Wrote It?, 141
Who's Who, 106, 107, 265
Who's Who in America, 106, 107, 280
Who's Who in American Art, 331
Who's Who in Commerce and Industry, 279
Who's Who in Engineering, 299, 300
Who's Who in Labor, 279
Who's Who in Library Service, 247
Who's Who in Philosophy, 355
Who's Who in the Theatre, 346, 348
Wilcox, E., *Modern Farmers' Encyclopedia of Agriculture*, 320

Wilcox, J. K., *Manual on the Use of State Publications*, 223, 225; *Official War Publications*, 254
Wildflowers, 317
Williamson, C., *Who's Who in Library Service*, 247
Williamson, S., *American Craftsman*, 334
Wilson, H. W., 183
Wilson, H. W., Co., 161, 183-85
Wilson, M., *New Etiquette*, 157
Wilson Library Bulletin, 245, 246
Wilson periodical indexes, 183-87; *Agricultural Index*, 319; *Art Index*, 329; *Education Index*, 283, 284; *Index to Legal Periodicals*, 273, 274; *Industrial Arts Index*, 276, 295, 310; *International Index*, 184, 295, 354; *Library Literature*, 244, 245; *Nineteenth Century Readers' Guide*, 184, 187; *Readers' Guide to Periodical Literature*, 164, 184, 185-87
Winchell, *Guide to Reference Books*, 19, 20, 97
Winsor, Justin, 115
Winston, *Bibliographies and Footnotes*, 17
Winston Dictionary, 42, 44; *for Children*, 45, 46; *for Young People*, 44, 45
Woman's Home Companion Cookbook, 152; *Garden Book*, 154; *Household Book*, 153, 154
Wood, *Complete Book of Games*, 341; *Complete Rhyming Dictionary*, 52
Woods, *Naturalist's Lexicon*, 316
Words, 44
Work, *Bibliography of the Negro in Africa and America*, 271, 272
World Almanac, 89, 92, 93-94, 174, 177
World Bibliography of Bibliographies, 206, 296
World Biography, 106, 107
World Book Encyclopedia, 78, 81-83
World Book Encyclopedia Annual Supplement, 91, 92
World Council of Churches, 356
World List of Scientific Periodicals, 296, 297
World of Learning, 128, 130
World Topics Quarterly, 68, 84, 91, 92
World Weather Records, 308
World Words, 51, 52, 117
World's Living Religions, 355
Wright, G., *Westminster Historical Atlas of the Bible*, 352, 353
Wright, J., *Aids to Geographical Research*, 119, 260; *Bibliography of*

Index

Best References for the Study of Geography, 260
Writer's Guide and Index to English, 47, 48
Writing Documented Papers, 16
Writings on American History, 253, 254
Wyer, J. I., 2; Reference Work, 20, 21
Wyler, Book of Old Pottery, 334

Year in American Music, 336
Yearbook of Agriculture, 321
Yearbook of American Churches, 354, 355
Yearbook of International Organizations, 128
Yearbook of the United Nations, 96, 127
Yearbooks, 68, 88-89
Year's Work in English Studies, 343, 344
Year's Work in Librarianship, 247
Young, Dictionary of Social Welfare, 271, 272

Zigrosser, Book of Fine Prints, 332
Zimmerman, Scientific and Technical Abbreviations, 297, 298
Zoology, 314-18
Zurcher, New Dictionary of American Politics, 274, 275

Z
1035.1
S45
1972

OCT 22 1973